The Politics of Muslim Cultural Reform

Comparative Studies on Muslim Societies

General Editor, Barbara D. Metcalf

Abdurrauf Fitrat with two unidentified persons, ca. 1920.

The Politics
of Muslim
Cultural Reform

Jadidism in Central Asia

Adeeb Khalid

UNIVERSITY OF CALIFORNIA PRESS
Berkeley · *Los Angeles* · *London*

University of California Press
Berkeley and Los Angeles, California

University of California Press, Ltd.
London, England

© 1998 by
The Regents of the University of California

Library of Congress Cataloging-in-Publication Data

Khalid, Adeeb, 1964–
    The politics of Muslim cultural reform : jadidism in
Central Asia / Adeeb Khalid.
        p.   cm.—(Comparative studies on Muslim societies ; 27)
    Includes bibliographical references and index.
        ISBN 0-520-21355-6 (alk. paper). — ISBN 0-520-21356-4
(alk. paper)
        1. Islam—Asia, Central.   2. Islam and politics—Asia,
Central.   3. Islam and state—Asia Central.   4. Islam—Social
aspects—Asia, Central.   5. Asia, Central—Politics and
government.   I. Title.   II. Series.
    BP63.A34K54   1998
    958'.04—dc21   98-4189
                                                                  CIP

Printed in the United States of America
9   8   7   6   5   4   3   2   1

⊗ The paper used in this publication meets the
minimum requirements of American National
Standards for Information Sciences—Permanence
of Paper for Printed Library Materials,
ANSI Z39.48-1984.

for my parents

Contents

Tables

Preface

Whether it is in the obsession with multiculturalism in American academe or in facile visions of an impending, perhaps inevitable "clash of civilizations" in the mainstream public, it is culture that defines the essence of difference in the post–Cold War world. The Muslim world occupies a special place in this cultural geography, more closely identified with culture than any other part of the world. The cultural determinism implicit in such thinking can exist only by leaving unasked the question of the origins of culture. Although a substantial scholarly literature has argued at some length (but perhaps not very successfully, if one were to judge from how little its insights seem to illuminate mainstream debate), cultures are not immutable givens but themselves subject to change and flux. This applies to Muslim culture as much as to any other, although given the place Islam and Muslims occupy in the imagination of the "West," we are left constantly to reaffirm this basic fact. I have tried in this book to argue this basic point: that Islam, and Muslim culture, and the sense of being Muslim are far from immutable characteristics; rather, they change and evolve and do so through debate and the struggles of different groups in Muslim society.

The advent of new means of communication and new forms of sociability from the nineteenth century on introduced new ways in which debates over culture could take place, while the political and military imperatives represented by the rise of European power lent a special intensity to these debates. Modern historians have paid too little attention to what Muslims were debating in these new media. A few studies of major figures and their thought have provided us an overview of the trajectory of intellectual history of the period, but the emphasis in such studies remains either explicitly religious or explicitly political. The sea change that the Muslim intellectuals' view of the world, and of their place in it, underwent in the half-century before the Great War has never been evoked. Yet this change underlay the new directions in intellectual and political history that have appeared in the Muslim world in the twentieth century.

The foregoing applies with even greater force to Central Asia, an area largely forgotten by the outside world. When I began graduate work over a decade ago, I usually had to explain to inquisitive friends where Central Asia was. Then came perestroika, the demise of the Soviet Union, and the "emergence of Central Asia." These events have heightened interest in the region in a way that would have been inconceivable just a decade earlier. But while the amount of publishing on the region has increased manifold, the new literature is dominated by matters of geopolitics and prognostications about the future of the new countries, with remarkably little attention paid to topics of cultural or historical import, even as the literature of prognostication freely makes explanatory use of both culture and history.

This neglect stems from certain fundamental institutional factors: the passing of the old order in Russia in 1917 coincided, broadly, with a massive redefinition of the Muslim world in Western academe. The Muslim world came to be reconfigured in an Arab-centered manner, in which the Turks occupied only a marginal place. No fate was worse than that of Central Asia, which was consigned to oblivion by scholars of Muslim societies and left to the tender mercies of émigré scholars and experts on Soviet nationalities studies. (Mainstream Soviet studies, notoriously Moscow-centered in any case, saw little more than incomprehensible oriental exotica in Central Asia.) Much of the slim literature that was produced on Central Asia outside the Soviet Union during the Soviet period was marked by a heavy emphasis on politics and what might be called "national martyrology." A sensitivity to the Muslim cultural background of pre-Soviet Central Asia and the consequences of its transformation in the postrevolutionary period was seldom evident, for it was often beyond the competence of nationalities scholars and anathema to émigré nationalists. The result was a general absence of a comparative framework for thinking about Central Asian history.

This book has been a prolonged attempt at righting the balance. It proceeds from a recognition of the fact that the experience of Central Asians under colonialism was hardly unique in the Muslim world. The debates that this book examines were parallel to those capturing the attention of Muslim intellectuals the world over. Indeed, the Muslim elites of Central Asia in the tsarist period were part of a much broader, cosmopolitan community of the world's Muslims. One of my aims in writing this book is to reclaim Central Asia for the study of Muslim societies, for only by understanding this context may we understand the cultural politics in pre–Soviet Central Asia, and only by understanding pre–Soviet Central Asia may we understand Soviet Central Asia. And conversely, only by understanding how Central Asian Muslims debated issues common to their age may we acquire a comprehensive picture of the myriad forms modernity has taken in the Muslim world. This is more than an exercise in "academic" history, for it allows us challenge facile explanations of the contemporary world in terms of an inevitable "clash of civilizations" and to remember that the more intransigent visions of the utter incompatibility of Islam and modernity that capture the headlines today are but one of the many answers Muslim intellectuals have produced to the most crucial questions of the previous century.

Attention to debates within Central Asian society also permits a more nuanced view of Russian imperialism. The demise of the Soviet Union has created considerable interest in the imperial dimension of Russian history, which has already resulted in the publication of a number of works of commendable sensitivity. Yet, much of this work remains in the domain of Russian colonial history, i.e., the history of how imperial officials made sense (or tried to make sense) of the borderlands of empire. As long as scholars look solely (or largely) at imperial debates over policy in the borderlands, natives will remain natives, as mysterious to the historian of today as they were to the administrator of yore.

But for all the attention to these broader dimensions, I have tried throughout to keep Central Asia itself at the focus of my inquiry (a courtesy not usually extended to it), for ultimately this book is an attempt to comprehend the making of modern Central Asia. I have not mentioned Soviet historiography earlier. It had its achievements, but shedding light on the cultural transformations of the tsarist period was not one of them. As far as the Jadids were concerned, Soviet historiography obfuscated far more than it revealed. Many names (Behbudi, Cholpān, Fitrat) were simply written out of the history books, while others (Hamza, Awlāni, Qā-diri) were given highly tendentious biographies. Many of the most basic outlines of modern Central Asian history have to be delineated anew.

This has been a major goal in writing this book, as has been the sense that the tumultuous history of Soviet Central Asia may only be understood against the background of the tsarist period. For Central Asia might have been largely forgotten by the world of scholarship after 1917, but it experienced all the excesses of the twentieth century: revolution, "development," genocide, ecological disaster, social engineering, and virulent nationalism. There are many stories to be told here; this book is perhaps a first step.

I have been with this project longer than I care to remember and in the process have accumulated many debts of gratitude to people and institutions. An earlier version of this book was completed as a dissertation under Kemal Karpat at the University of Wisconsin–Madison. In Madison, Michael Chamberlain introduced me to the works of Pierre Bourdieu, while his own work on medieval Damascus provided an elegant example of how historians appropriate the work of social thinkers. David McDonald kept me honest about the Russian dimension of my work. Many thanks to Uli Schamiloglu for friendship, advice, and those microfilms.

Since then, I have benefited greatly from the advice and insights of a number of colleagues. Ed Lazzerini has for years been a font of searching questions; he has also generously shared copies of scarce materials with me. Hisao Komatsu also provided me copies of invaluable and impossible to find works fundamental to my work. Marianne Kamp shared her excellent judgment with me on several parts of the manuscript; she also gave permission to quote from her unpublished work. Dale Eickelman has given encouragement for several years and by inviting me to a National Endowment for the Humanities seminar on "Imagining Societies: The Middle East and Central Asia" at Dartmouth College, provided a captive audience for earlier versions of this book. John Perry invited me to a workshop on "Language, Literature, and Empire" at the University of Chicago in 1994, which produced valuable insights. Colleagues at the history department at Carleton College provided excellent comments on Chapter 2. Elyor Karimov allowed me to make copies of rare materials in his personal collection. Conversations with Vincent Fourniau, Garay Menicucci, Scott Seregny, and Gregg Starrett helped in various ways to clarify the argument. In Tashkent, Abdujabbar Abduvahitov, Akram Habibullaev, Saodat Kholmatova, and Saur Yaqupov provided inestimable friendship and support.

The research for the dissertation on which the book is based was funded by various agencies at the University of Wisconsin. Since then, the National Endowment for the Humanities has figured large in my professional life. A Summer Stipend in 1994 allowed me to return to Tashkent for archival research, and a Fellowship for College Teachers allowed me a precious break from teaching in 1996, during which I wrote the bulk of the manuscript for this book. My leave coincided with some of the darkest hours that the endowment has endured, which heightened my appreciation for the work that it does for the humanities in this country. This book would have taken a lot longer without its support.

I also gratefully acknowledge support from Carleton College. A faculty development endowment grant in 1994 contributed to the trip to the archives in 1994, and more recently the college provided generous support for the preparation of illustrations and maps for publication.

Little of the research for this study could have been accomplished without the assistance of library and archive personnel on three continents. The staff at Memorial Library of the University of Wisconsin–Madison, the (then) Lenin State Library in Moscow, its annex in Khimki, and the Central State Archives of the Republic of Uzbekistan in Tashkent deserve special gratitude. The Central State Archives of Cinematic, Audio, and Photographic Documents of the Republic of Uzbekistan provided the photograph reproduced here.

But my greatest debts are of a personal nature. Cheryl Duncan humored me throughout the many years it has taken me to finish this project. In the process, she has read more drafts of this work than seemed humanly possible. Her love and encouragement, as well as her editorial skills and historical insights, were my constant companions. Haroun arrived in this world unduly ahead of the manuscript and thereby delayed it considerably; the joy he brought with him, however, makes it all worthwhile.

Finally, my family has been my greatest source of inspiration. My brother Najeeb made it all possible in the beginning. My parents, Nazakat and Khalid Latif, always taught me to expect the utmost of myself. My father's library, especially his own book on the Muslims of the Soviet Union, first got me interested in Central Asia. When that interest led me in the unexpected direction of becoming a historian, my parents supported me in every way possible. It is to them that I dedicate this book.

Technical Note

TRANSLITERATION

There does not exist a universally accepted system for transliterating Central Asian Turkic into the Latin script. During this century, it has been written in five different alphabets in three scripts. I have resisted the temptation to transliterate all Uzbek according to modern Cyrillic-script spelling, given that even modern Uzbek publishers do not follow this practice. Instead, I have transliterated the names of individuals active before 1920 and the titles of their works directly from the Arabic script in which they wrote, using the six-vowel system (*a, ā, e, i, o,* and *u*) and disregarding vowel harmony. For modern Uzbek written in the Cyrillic script, I have used the system adopted in Uzbekistan in 1995, with the exception of rendering *o'* as *ŏ*, *k̄* as *kh,* and *g'* as *gh*. The two systems are thus rendered harmonious, except that the vowels transliterated from the Arabic script as *ā* and *o* appear as *o* and *ŏ*, respectively, when transliterated from the Cyrillic. I have followed the same logic in transliterating Tajik from the Cyrillic script, whereas "Tajik" in the Arabic script has been transliterated as Persian. Ottoman Turkish has been rendered in modern Turkish orthography on the basis of the 1968 Redhouse *Türkçe İngilizçe Sözlük,* and Tatar citations are vocalized using Tatar vowels and vowel harmony.

NAMES AND DATES

Personal names took many forms in Central Asia in the period discussed here. Some people used Russian-style surnames (e.g., Khojaev), whereas others adopted Tatar-style last names (e.g., Behbudi, Awlāni); yet others used pen names (*takhallus*, e.g., Ayni), although most were simply known by their first name (e.g., Hamza, Munawwar Qāri). I have used the form of name most commonly used by the person in question and have alphabetized the bibliography accordingly. When the name of the same person might be transliterated differently in works appearing in different languages, I have grouped all entries by the same author together in the bibliography.

All common-era dates are given according to the Julian calendar, which was twelve days behind the Gregorian calendar in the nineteenth century and thirteen days behind in the twentieth. The Julian calendar was in use in the Russian empire until February 1918; dates after February 1918 are in the Gregorian calendar, and the calendar is specified in cases where confusion might arise. Dates for periodicals published in the Ottoman empire are also given in the Julian calendar, which was the basis of the Ottoman fiscal calendar until 1917. I have used double dating only when the common-era year could not be determined with certainty for a publication dated in a *hijri* calendar.

Abbreviations

GARF	Gosudarstvennyi arkhiv Rossiiskoi Federatsii
IOLR	India Office Library and Records
ŎSE	*Ŏzbek sovet entsiklopediyasi*
SF	*Sadā-yi Farghāna*
ST	*Sadā-yi Turkistān*
TsGARUz	Tsentral'nyi Gosudarstvennyi arkhiv Respubliki Uzbekistan
TWG	*Turkistān wilāyatining gazeti*
UT	*Ulugh Turkistān*
ZhMNP	*Zhurnal Ministerstva Narodnogo Prosveshcheniia*

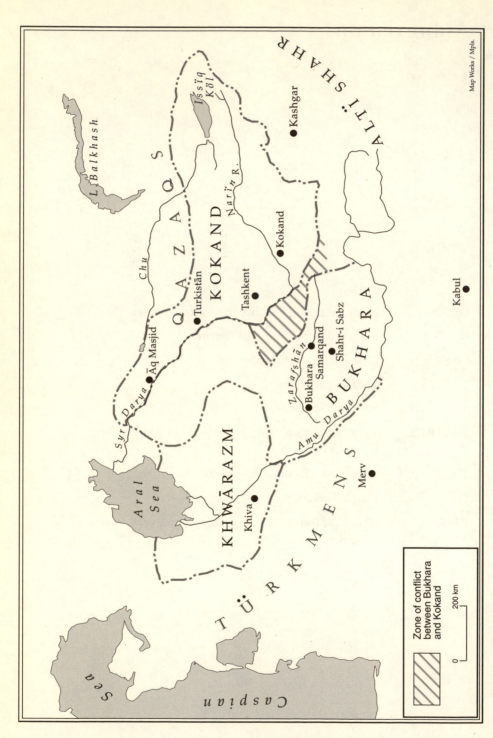

Map 1. Central Asia, mid-nineteenth century.

Zone of conflict
between Bukhara
and Kokand

0   200 km

L. Balkhash

Issïq Köl

ALTÏSHAHR

Kashgar

QAZAQS

KOKAND

Narïn R.

Chu

Kokand

Turkistān

Tashkent

Āq Masjid

Kabul

Syr Darya

Zarafshān

Samarqand

Bukhara

Shahr-i Sabz

BUKHARA

Amu Darya

KHWĀRAZM

Aral
Sea

Khiva

TÜRKMENS

Merv

Caspian

Sea

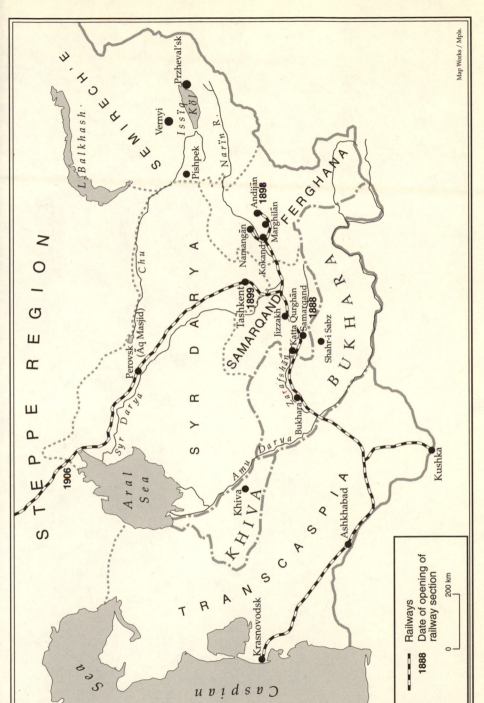

Map 2. Russian Central Asia.

Introduction

At present, we Turkestanis are not sufficiently acquainted
with religious and worldly knowledge. Our old maktabs and
madrasas are in ruins, reminiscent of the nesting places of
owls. Our madrasas, far from teaching worldly sciences,
don't even teach *tafsir* and *hadith,* [which are] the basis of all
religious knowledge. We do not have any teachers' training
colleges to train teachers, or any workshops to teach skills.
We do not have any merchants with modern business skills.
There are no organized schools for the elementary education
of our children. . . . If this . . . continues, soon even our present existence will be destroyed.

Hāji Muin b. Shukrullah, 1916

In combining intimations of mortal danger faced by Central Asian society with a profound faith in the power of education to provide the solution, this speech from one of the first pieces of modern Central Asian
theater neatly exemplifies the reformist project of the first generation of
modern Central Asian intellectuals, the "Jadids." The unease about the
present lay in a sense that traditions of the past were not only incapable
of meeting new needs but were also failing to transmit the values of the
past. A thoroughgoing reform of culture and society was needed if Central Asians were to survive the unprecedented challenges of the modern
world. Although the Jadids saw themselves as reformers of their society,
their enthusiastic embrace of modernity led them to radically new conceptions of society. Their attempts at rescuing tradition redefined it, and
their attempts to return to a "pure" Islam brought new understandings
of Islam and of what it meant to be a Muslim. The Jadids were successful in garnering considerable support for their project, but their call for
reform also evoked vigorous opposition from established elites (the *qadimchi*) in their society. It was through the debate over the meaning of
Central Asian culture that Central Asians came to imagine the modern
world and their place in it. This book tells the story of this debate.

I seek the roots of this debate in Central Asia's experience of modernity, a global condition that brings with it new forms of organization of self and society, new forms of intellectual production, and new ways of imagining the world (and one's place within it). Modernity is not reducible to the inculcation of culturally specific norms or traits; nor is it synonymous with economic development. Rather, as an enormous body of interdisciplinary literature has argued in recent years, the modern condition transforms tradition (indeed, it makes it possible to conceive of tradition as tradition); it takes—and produces—numerous cultural forms, and it inheres in (economic) underdevelopment as much as in development. This conception of modernity therefore differs substantially from that of classical modernization theory, which saw modernization as a unilinear process that dissolved all opposition to it in its conquest of traditional forms.

The Jadid formulation of the predicament of Central Asian society was as much a result of the profound transformation of Central Asia in the fifty years of imperial Russian rule as a response to it. When Russian forces abruptly conquered the khanates of Central Asia between the 1860s and the 1880s, there existed no theater, no printing press, and no benevolent societies. All of these means of cultural production arose in the half-century of Russian rule. Between the establishment of the governorate-general of Turkestan in 1867 and the Russian revolutions of 1917, Central Asia became increasingly intertwined with imperial (and hence global) economic networks; its social order was drastically reshaped, with the extinction of old elites and the emergence of new ones. Its political order was, of course, reconstituted. New groups, such as the Jadids, adopted and appropriated new forms of communication and sociability in their attempts to reform, creating, in the process, radically new understandings of tradition, religion, and the world.

The Jadids of Central Asia were far from alone in the Muslim world in this period in (re)evaluating their cultural heritage under the exigencies of modernity. Jadidism, as this movement for cultural reform is usually called, had much in common with similar modernist movements popular among intellectuals throughout the Muslim world. The aim of such movements was nothing less than to reconcile Islam with a modernity they very much admired. But whereas similar modernist movements in India, the Ottoman lands, Iran, Egypt, and Algeria have received extensive scholarly attention,[1] Jadidism, especially in its Central Asian

1. I have benefited from the following: Aziz Ahmad, *Islamic Modernism in India and Pakistan, 1857–1964* (London, 1967); David Lelyveld, *Aligarh's First Generation: Muslim*

form, remains virtually unknown. The volume of Western scholarship on tsarist Central Asia is slim, and work on Jadidism in Central Asia forms only a small part of it. Until very recently, specialist treatments of the subject were almost entirely lacking,[2] and one was left to retrieve Jadidism from brief passages widely scattered in broad-ranging synthetic works that subordinated Jadidism to much broader themes.[3] The very few longer pieces available on Jadidism suffered from the lack of access to primary sources that beset all study of Central Asia until the very last years of the Soviet regime.[4] Soviet scholars, while enjoying access to primary sources, were hampered by ideological constraints that often proved insurmountable. The situation has changed in recent years, but far less dramatically than many had hoped during the heady days of perestroika.[5] While the political context of scholarly production has been

Solidarity in British India (Princeton, 1978); Şerif Mardin, The Genesis of Young Ottoman Thought: A Study in the Modernization of Turkish Political Ideas (Princeton, 1962); Niyazi Berkes, The Development of Secularism in Turkey (Montreal, 1964); Albert Hourani, Arabic Thought in the Liberal Age, 1798–1939 (London, 1962); Hisham Sharabi, Arab Intellectuals and the West: The Formative Years, 1875–1914 (Baltimore, 1970); David D. Commins, Islamic Reform: Politics and Society in Late Ottoman Syria (New York, 1990); Hamid Algar, Mīrza Malkum Khān: A Study in the History of Iranian Modernism (Berkeley, 1973); Mangol Bayat, The First Iranian Revolution: Shiʿism and the Constitutional Revolution of 1905–1909 (New York, 1991); Nikkie R. Keddie, ed. and trans., An Islamic Response to Imperialism: Political and Religious Writings of Sayyid Jamāl ad-Dīn "al-Afghānī" (Berkeley, 1968); Keddie, Sayyid Jamāl al-Dīn "al-Afghānī": A Political Biography (Berkeley, 1972); Homa Pakdaman, Djemal-ed-Din Assad Abadi dit Afghani (Paris, 1969); Malcolm H. Kerr, Islamic Reform: The Political and Legal Theories of Muhammad ʿAbduh and Rashīd Ridā (Berkeley, 1966); Elie Kedouri, Afghani and ʿAbduh: An Essay on Religious Unbelief and Political Activism in Modern Islam (New York, 1966); Zaki Badawi, The Reformers of Egypt—A Critique of Al-Afghani, ʿAbduh and Ridha (London, 1976); Ali Merad, Le réformisme musulman en Algérie de 1925 à 1940: essai d'histoire religieuse et sociale (Paris, 1972).

2. The one exception was a monograph on Bukhara by Hélène Carrère d'Encausse: Réforme et révolution chez les musulmans de l'empire russe, 2nd ed. (Paris, 1981), now available in English as Islam and the Russian Empire, trans. Quentin Hoare (Berkeley, 1988).

3. Serge A. Zenkovsky, "Kulturkampf in Pre-Revolutionary Central Asia," American Slavic and East European Review 14 (1955): 15–42; Richard N. Pierce, Russian Central Asia, 1867–1917: A Study in Colonial Rule (Berkeley, 1960), 254–255 (one page on "Dzhadidism" in the context of "The Rise of Native National Consciousness"); Geoffrey Wheeler, The Modern History of Soviet Central Asia (London, 1964), 91 (one dismissive reference to prerevolutionary Jadidism as "merely a Muslim reformist movement with no separatist aims.")

4. Hélène Carrère d'Encausse, "The Stirring of National Feeling," and "Social and Political Reform," in Edward Allworth, ed., Central Asia: A Century of Russian Rule (New York, 1967), 172–206; Edward Allworth, The Modern Uzbeks: A Cultural History (Stanford, 1990); a brief account of Muslim reform, although based entirely on Russian sources, is found in Seymour Becker, Russia's Protectorates in Central Asia: Bukhara and Khiva, 1865–1924 (Cambridge, Mass., 1968), 193–209.

5. Central Asian scholars have brought back into print numerous works of Jadid authors, but larger synthetic studies of the period remain rare; see "Jadidchilik nima?" Sanʾat,

transformed in Central Asia in recent years, the severe economic dislocation of academic life (combined with new political demands from the
newly independent states) in the post-Soviet period has meant that little
new historiography has emerged on this important topic.[6] Outside the
former Soviet Union, interest in Central Asia has focused on the contemporary period, with Jadidism enjoying the attention of only a few
scholars. Thus, although detailed research on tsarist Central Asia has
begun to appear in recent years, much more remains to be done.[7] This
book is the first effort to comprehend Muslim cultural debates in Central Asia in a broad, comparative perspective.

REFORM, CULTURAL PRODUCTION, AND ELITE STRATEGIES

Much recent social thought has insisted that cultures, rather than being
timeless givens, are products of historical change, their meanings contested and constantly in flux. New understandings of the world emerge
through efforts by various groups in society to make sense of vastly new
conditions they confront. In the case of Central Asia, the Jadids, in diag-
nosing the ills of their society and prescribing the cure (to use the medical
metaphors they often favored), were usurping the moral and cultural authority of the established religious-cultural elites. Their prescription for
reform contained a radical re-visioning of society and the roles of various groups within it as well as a redefinition of Central Asian culture
and what was valuable within it. Not surprisingly, the Jadid project provoked considerable opposition.

1990, no. 12: 4–10; Begali Qosimov, "Jadidchilik," in *Milliy uyghonish wa ŏzbek filologiyasi masalalari* (Tashkent, 1993), 12–39; Qosimov, "Sources littéraires et principaux traits
distinctifs du djadidisme turkestanais (début du XXe siècle)," *Cahiers du monde russe* 37
(1996): 107–132.

6. On the politics of the rewriting of history in contemporary Central Asia, see the
very astute analysis by Stéphane A. Dudoignon, "Djadidisme, mirasisme, islamisme," *Cahiers du monde russe* 37 (1996): 33–36.

7. Two substantial works appeared while this book was being written: Stéphane A.
Dudoignon, "La question scolaire à Boukhara et au Turkestan russe, du «premier renouveau» à la soviétisation (fin du XVIIIe siècle–1937)," *Cahiers du monde russe* 37 (1996):
133–210; and Hisao Komatsu, *Kakumei no Chūō Ajia: aru Jadiido no shōzō* (Tokyo,
1996). Dudoignon's article covers much of the same ground as this study, but with a different emphasis and rather different conclusions. Komatsu's work, an extended biography
of Abdurrauf Fitrat in the context of revolutionary change in Central Asia, remains, unfortunately, beyond my ken. I am grateful to Katie Sparling for acquainting me with its
contents.

Western scholars have generally tended to ignore this opposition. As with modernist reform in the Muslim world in general, scholars of Jadidism have tended to focus on the Jadids as the sole voice of reason in their society while dismissing their opponents as unreasoning obscurantists opposed to all positive change. Thus, Edward Allworth sees the Jadids as "men . . . who dared reconsider the predicament of their people," who "for the indigenous population of the region . . . created or adapted six instruments for their purposes." Their opponents, however, are dismissed as "those internally governed by fixed habit and rigid tradition" who "failed to understand" the reforms suggested by the Jadids.[8] Soviet scholarship, on the other hand, acknowledged the contestation but reduced it to a Marxist metanarrative of class competition. The qadimchi were representatives of the feudal-colonial order, whereas the Jadids were mouthpieces of a rising nationalist bourgeoisie, both groups transparently expressing the ideology of their respective classes.[9] Both these views are misleading. The complete absence in Western scholarship of any analysis of the contested nature of Jadidism leaves us unable to explain the Jadids' modest success except through invoking such orientalist tropes as the obscurantist nature of traditional elites or the fanaticism of Muslim culture. The Soviet view, too, simplified matters even as it confused them. The debate in Central Asian society cannot be reduced to conflicting economic interests for the Jadids often shared common social origins with their opponents and economic issues seldom surfaced in the debate. Rather, much of the debate discussed in this book centered around the competing claims to cultural authority—the authority to create and interpret culture—in which new elites challenged the authority of the old, for in the attempt to reform society lay a claim for leadership that was profoundly subversive to the established order.

I argue that the struggle between the Jadids and their opponents was over the possession and redefinition of what Pierre Bourdieu has called "cultural capital."[10] The Jadids sought to redefine the culture their society should value, bringing to bear on the debate their access to new intellectual technologies and forms of sociability. Their opponents met the challenge by valorizing the cultural values that guaranteed their status

8. Allworth, *The Modern Uzbeks*, 120–121.

9. Lowell Tillett, *The Great Friendship Soviet Historians on the Non-Russian Nationalities* (Chapel Hill, N.C., 1969) remains the standard work on Soviet historiography of the nationalities.

10. Pierre Bourdieu, *The Logic of Practice* (Stanford, 1990 [orig. 1980]), 108–110.

and prestige. Neither group, however, entered the contest fully formed, and the lines between the two groups always remained porous. Many Jadids were members of the religious elite in their own right, and many others were only a generation removed. More significantly, however, the ideas of both groups were articulated and refined through this contest. I follow Pierre Bourdieu in contending that only by "apprehending the specific logic of the social world, that 'reality' which is the site of a permanent struggle to *define* 'reality,' "[11] may we begin to understand what was at stake.

Bourdieu's numerous works on the social reproduction of culture provide a valuable point of departure for this study. In his attempt to transcend the opposition between structures and representations, between the objectivist claims of twentieth-century social science (shared also by Soviet Marxism) and the phenomenological alternatives proposed to them, Bourdieu has defined a reflexive sociology that seeks to understand how social agents make sense of their world by plotting strategies of social action given the possibilities and constraints of the world. What is significant to Bourdieu are not the "rules" of society, but rather the strategies that social agents bring to bear on their social action. These strategies emerge from a "practical sense" represented by a logic of practice that is defined by the agents' experience of the world. This shift of attention from structures to practices, without denying the existence of structural constraints within which individuals and groups act, allows him to see the individual as an agent actively negotiating the social world rather than as a mere actor acting out a script dictated by structures; at the same time, it reminds us that social agents act on a terrain that contains limits as well as possibilities.[12] The social game is played with symbolic or cultural capital, markers of status and prestige, that signify the distinction of social agents. Wealth is certainly one such marker, but others, such as education, comportment, possession of culturally valued knowledge, and claims to august lineage, are also significant in their own right. The definition of what is culturally valuable, as well as the rules of the social game itself, are constantly being contested and negotiated by individuals and groups. Individuals and groups differ in terms of their symbolic capital, but Bourdieu sees them arranged not in

11. Pierre Bourdieu, *Language and Symbolic Power*, trans. Gino Raymond and Matthew Adamson (Cambridge, Mass., 1991), 224.

12. Bourdieu, *Logic*; Bourdieu, *In Other Words: Essays Towards a Reflexive Sociology* (Stanford, 1990 [orig. 1987]).

a rigid pyramidal hierarchy but in a social "field" in which groups have more properties and interests in common the closer they are to each other. The field becomes the arena for competition and contestation. In terms of cultural production, the competition of elites leads to the definition and elaboration of culture, as different groups seek to transmute "'egoistic,' private, particular interests . . . into 'disinterested,' collective, publicly avowable, legitimate interests."[13]

Such an approach has numerous advantages for this study. The notion of symbolic capital enables us to go beyond the vulgar-Marxist formulations of Soviet historiography without losing sight of the contested nature of reform. It also forces us to consider the competition within Central Asian society as a central feature of Jadid reform. The Russian conquest had transformed the nature of the social terrain in which social competition took place in Central Asia (indeed, the Jadids themselves were a result of that transformation); access to new means of communication and sociability allowed the Jadids to challenge the rules of the game, while at the same time contesting the value of the symbolic capital possessed by the older elites. The stakes for which the older elites put up such stubborn resistance to the ideas of the Jadids were nothing less than their social survival as an elite.

This approach also allows us to problematize the very notion of reform itself. As a trope for disinterested rectification of the social order, "reform" is a problematic enough notion when it is invoked by established states to reaffirm their authority (cases as disparate as those of the Ottoman empire during the Tanzimat era and the Soviet Union during perestroika illustrate this); it is far more so in cases where movement for reform comes from unofficial groups in society. In Central Asia, where the native state ceased to exist (as in Turkestan) or was not a participant in reform (as in Bukhara and Khiva), arguments for reform were nothing short of arguments for a reconstitution of society according to the vision of a new elite. Thus, only a focus on elite competition allows us to understand the politics of the 1917, when revolution redefined the rules of the game and brought competition into the open.

13. Bourdieu, *Logic,* 109; Bourdieu's works on the reproduction of culture include *Distinction: A Social Critique of the Judgement of Taste,* trans. Richard Nice (Cambridge, Mass., 1984 [orig. 1979]); Bourdieu, *The Field of Cultural Production* (New York, 1993); Bourdieu, *Homo Academicus,* trans. Peter Collier (Stanford, 1988 [orig. 1984]); and Pierre Bourdieu and Jean-Claude Passeron, *Reproduction in Education, Society and Culture,* trans. Richard Nice (London, 1977 [orig. 1970]).

By focusing on the social life of ideas and connecting it to the social fortunes of their carriers, we can also avoid reifying religious and national identities. This last is a task of considerable importance, for thinking about post-Soviet Central Asia is laden with misleading and facile assumptions about identity. Policy makers debate the potential of "Islamic fundamentalism" in Central Asia, a danger deemed to inhere in the fact of Central Asia being "Islamic." By showing how the meaning of Islam and of being a Muslim changed over time (and the period covered by this book was pivotal in this regard), I hope to bring some sophistication into the debate over the nature of Islam in Central Asia.[14] On the other hand, post-Soviet state elites in Central Asia have staked their legitimacy on fulfilling the historical destinies of nations that are deemed to have existed and to have developed together since time immemorial. This book also questions these claims by highlighting the historical process that underlay the construction of modern group identities in Central Asia.

The caveat against reification also applies to viewing Jadidism as a unified movement, as is often done in the existing literature, which tends to see Jadidism as a movement that spread out from its centers in the Crimea and the Tatar lands on the Volga and swept all before it throughout the Muslim borderlands of the Russian empire. Jadidism was a coherent movement to the extent that it was (or came to be) embedded in a set of self-reproducing institutions (e.g., new-method schools that recruited their own graduates to teach in them). Beyond that, it is difficult

14. Anthropologists in recent years have produced numerous excellent studies of "local knowledge" of Islam in diverse contexts: see the following: Clifford Geertz, *Islam Observed: Religious Development in Morocco and Indonesia* (New Haven, 1968); Dale F. Eickelman, *Moroccan Islam: Tradition and Society in a Pilgrimage Center* (Austin, 1976); Eickelman, "The Study of Islam in Local Contexts," *Contributions to Asian Studies* 17 (1982): 1–16; M. Nazif Shahrani, "Local Knowledge of Islam and Social Discourse in Afghanistan and Turkistan in the Modern Period," in Robert L. Canfield, ed., *Turko-Persia in Historical Perspective* (Cambridge, 1991); Michael Lambek, *Knowledge and Practice in Mayotte: Local Discourses of Islam, Sorcery and Spirit Possession* (Toronto, 1993); John R. Bowen, *Muslims through Discourse: Religion and Ritual in Gayo Society* (Princeton, 1993); Patricia Horvatich, "Ways of Knowing Islam," *American Ethnologist* 21 (1994): 811–826; Tone Bringa, *Being Muslim the Bosnian Way* (Princeton, 1995). In addition, although not directly related to this literature, but very pertinent to Central Asia, is Devin DeWeese, *Islamization and Native Religion in the Golden Horde: Baba Tükles and Conversion in Historical and Epic Tradition* (University Park, Penn., 1994).

This line of inquiry has helped dissolve the notion of a monolithic Islam. Indeed, Abdul Hamid el-Zein ("Beyond Ideology and Theology: The Search for the Anthropology of Islam," *Annual Review of Anthropology* 6 [1977]: 227–254) suggested that the notion of a single "Islam" be replaced by many "islams" to account for the multiplicity of Islamic expression. A similar argument has been made recently by Aziz al-Azmeh, *Islams and Modernities* (London, 1993).

to impute any unity to the "movement." To be sure, the Jadids of Central Asia used the same symbols, tropes, and metaphors as the Jadids of European Russia in their discourse, but there is no reason to assume that they necessarily imbued them with the same meaning intended by the original authors. As Roger Chartier forcefully argues, texts are open to multiple readings, since a work "acquires meaning only through the strategies of interpretation that construct its significances. The author's interpretation is one among several and it does not monopolize the supposedly unique and permanent 'truth' of the work."[15] Rather, social agents use, or "appropriate,"[16] texts for their own strategies and social struggles. In the case at hand, Central Asian Jadids used texts from elsewhere—from the Muslim centers of the Russian empire as well as the broader Muslim world—in struggles that were grounded in local realities. The Jadids were not moved by abstract ideas such as "reform" or "pan-Islam" or "nationalism," but rather used these abstractions to navigate the social struggles of Central Asia.

PRINT AND THE RE-IMAGINATION OF THE WORLD

Jadidism would have been inconceivable without print. The Jadids gloried in the powers of print (and printed books and newspapers) to spread knowledge and enlightenment, and publishing remained a significant field of endeavor for them. This marked a sharp contrast to the situation before the Russian conquest, when the production and transmission of knowledge in Central Asia existed in the scribal domain with a strong component of orality. Knowledge was transmitted in a ritualized setting through face-to-face interaction between individuals; the possession of knowledge provided moral and cultural authority in society, which translated into status and prestige, if not always directly into wealth, although that connection was common, too. The advent of the printing press, the railway, the telegraph, and the modern postal system transformed these patterns and allowed the Jadids to redefine the nature of cultural production in their society.

15. Roger Chartier, "Intellectual History and the History of *Mentalités*," in *Cultural History: Between Practices and Representations,* trans. Lydia G. Cochrane (Ithaca, 1988), 41.

16. Chartier again provides a splendid introduction to this notion; see his "Culture as Appropriation: Popular Cultural Uses in Early Modern France," in Stephen L. Kaplan, ed., *Understanding Popular Culture* (Berlin, 1984). Cf. Michel de Certeau's notion of "reading as poaching," in de Certeau, *The Practice of Everyday Life,* trans. Steven F. Rendall (Berkeley, 1984), 165–176.

New means of the production of knowledge were crucial to the Jadids in numerous ways. Most immediately, these means enabled an unprecedented flow of information, putting Central Asian intellectuals in contact with the broader world in ways that had hitherto been impossible. By the turn of the twentieth century, Central Asian readers could read books and (increasingly) periodicals published throughout the Russian empire as well as those imported from the Ottoman empire, Iran, and farther afield. This circulation of literature, accompanied by the circulation of people facilitated by modern transport, made Central Asia part of a broader world, or rather, a part of several overlapping translocal communities, in a far more immediate way than had ever been possible before.

Furthermore, modern means of communication were not transparent vessels for the communication of ideas; they helped shape new ways of imagining the world and thus transformed the parameters of debate in Central Asian society.[17] Print helped transform the social uses of literacy as it redefined the framework and, increasingly, the norms of public debate over culture. As a result, by the turn of the century, Central Asians not only debated new ideas, but they debated in a manner that was new. As I argue in Chapter 4, newspapers, magazines, books, and theater created a public space that became the central venue for discussing culture and society. Unlike the decades' worth of learning in the madrasa that provided entree to the cultural elite, access to the new public space required only basic literacy (and not even that for the theater). In the new public, the older cultural elite was increasingly marginalized.

This rapid flow of information combined with new means of communications wrought a fundamental transformation in the way in which Central Asian intellectuals had come to see the world. In different ways,

---

17. A considerable and rapidly growing literature has explored how print contributes to a desacralization of knowledge and its demystification. Some of the landmarks in this literature are Lucien Febvre and Henri-Jean Martin, *L'apparition du livre* (Paris, 1958); Elizabeth L. Eisenstein, *The Printing Press as an Agent of Change: Communications and Cultural Transformations in Early-Modern Europe,* 2 vols. (Cambridge, 1979); Roger Chartier, *The Cultural Uses of Print in Early Modern France,* trans. Lydia G. Cochrane (Princeton, 1987). Scholars of modern Muslim cultural history have recently paid considerable attention to the uses of print; see, Şerif Mardin, *Religion and Social Change in Turkey: The Case of Bediüzzaman Said Nursi* (Albany, 1989); Juan R. I. Cole, *Colonialism and Revolution in the Middle East: Social and Cultural Origins of Egypt's 'Urabi Movement* (Princeton, 1992); Beth Baron, *The Women's Awakening in Egypt: The Early Years of the Press* (New Haven, 1994); Francis Robinson, "Technology and Religious Change: Islam and the Impact of Print," *Modern Asian Studies* 27 (1993): 229–251; Adeeb Khalid, "Printing, Publishing, and Reform in Tsarist Central Asia," *International Journal of Middle East Studies* 26 (1994): 187–200.

the discovery of geological time and language families, the idea of Progress, and the modern map of the world all transformed how Central Asians could imagine their world. New conceptions of time and space were reflected in the Jadids' emphasis on history and geography, allowed a far-reaching historicization of the world that produced new, rationalist understandings of Islam and Muslimness. The growing consciousness that the grand narrative of history was not necessarily centered on Islam or the Muslim community, that they themselves were a product of history, and that they coexisted (often in disadvantageous situations) with other faiths and other communities were crucial to the elaboration of modern identities in Central Asia during this period. Their emergence, moreover, was a result of this basic reconfiguring of the world, not its cause.

Dale Eickelman has called this the "objectification" of Islam, the emerging perception of Islam as a coherent, systematic, and self-contained set of beliefs and practices, separate and separable from worldly knowledge, which came to displace previously held understandings of Islam as embedded in everyday social practice and as something irreducible to a textbook exposition.[18] Underlying the discourse of reforming tradition was a new kind of knowledge, produced and transmitted in a radically new context. Unlike the Jadids, their opponents often set forth an uncompromising traditionalism that valorized existing practices as the essence of "true" Islam. Yet, as I argue, this understanding of tradition was itself marked by modernity, since the very valorization of tradition made use of modern means and was an expression of its proponents' modern predicament.

Similarly, the community—its nature and its boundaries—also came to be reimagined, giving rise to the first articulations of modern Central Asian "national" identity. All nations are imagined,[19] but they may be imagined in many different ways. Jadid notions of identity were articulated in the context of new ethnographic knowledge produced by the colonial regime and the influx of romantic discourses of nationhood from the Tatars and the Ottomans; they were firmly rooted in the political realities on the ground in Turkestan. The objectification of Islam led to the emergence of a largely secular Muslim confessional nationalism in which Islam functioned as a marker of political and cultural identity

---

18. Dale F. Eickelman, "Mass Higher Education and the Religious Imagination in Contemporary Arab Societies," *American Ethnologist* 19 (1992): 643, 647–649.
19. Benedict Anderson, *Imagined Communities*, 2nd ed. (London, 1991).

for a community initially defined by its adherence to a religion. The relationship between ethnic and confessional definitions of the nation is fluid, rather than fixed;[20] in the Muslim world of the turn of the century, a certain tension between the two forms of community existed, but it could be elided more easily than the existing literature on the subject often realizes. It is well to remember this form of political Muslim identity today, when all "political Islam" has come to be synonymous with the most intransigent visions of the utter incompatibility of Islam and modernity.

DISCIPLINE AND ORGANIZE: NEW FORMS OF SOCIABILITY

Hāji Muin's call for organized schools reflected a central concern of the Jadids: the creation of a system of well-organized schools that would offer a standardized, disciplined education providing *both* religious and worldly education to future generations of the community. Indeed, the new-method (*usul-i jadid*) school gave the movement its name. Understanding the centrality of the faith both in knowledge and in organization provides crucial insights into the nature of Jadidism.

The Jadids' faith in the ability of the human intellect to solve the problems of the world was intertwined with the notion of progress that the desacralization and historicization of their outlook helped promote. I will explore the origins of this conception of the power of knowledge in Jadid thought at some length, for it represents an important aspect of their modernity. In the process, however, the concept of knowledge itself came to be subtly redefined, as it came to encompass new fields of knowledge and new ways of knowing. For the Jadids, of course, these transformations were transparent: They did not contravene tradition but helped bring it to its true fruition. There was no contradiction between the notion of progress and their faith in Islam. Indeed, only knowledge could enable Muslims to understood Islam properly, and Islam itself was the best guarantee of progress. As a closer inspection shows quite clearly, new notions of knowledge (and hence of religion, history, and politics) lay at the bottom of the Jadid critique of society.

But if knowledge was a panacea, it needed organized institutions to be properly produced and disseminated. The Jadids' critique of their society centered on the disorder that they saw prevailing in it. The maktab

---

20. M. Hakan Yavuz, "The Patterns of Political Islamic Identity: Dynamics and Transnational Loyalties and Identities," *Central Asian Survey* 14 (1995): 341–372.

was disorganized, unhygienic, and run by uncouth teachers with no training in pedagogy; there was no system for inspecting schools; there were no organizations for establishing schools; and the philanthropy of the rich, insufficient as it was, took no organized form. The Jadids' efforts to overcome this disorder are a central feature of their reformist project. Their faith in the efficacy of organization and order marks the Jadids as moderns. Their quest for new forms of organization—new-method schools, publishing houses, benevolent societies, and (eventually) political parties—was significant in itself in transforming the rules of the social game in Central Asia, as organized, impersonal (and to a certain extent, self-perpetuating) institutions increasingly became arenas for debate and the production and transmission of culture, replacing dialogic interaction in the informal settings where cultural practices had previously been located. The new-method school, for instance, was more than merely a reformed maktab: It was the site of a new cultural practice, that of schooling, which it marked off from everyday practice and objectified.

The Jadids' pioneering of incipient institutional forms in the Muslim society of Central Asia gave them a certain advantage over their opponents, who, for various reasons did not organize in similar fashion. A new public space was created for the interpretation of Central Asian culture, and of Islam itself, in which the traditional carriers of Islam were increasingly marginalized. The process of institutionalization was neither easy nor unilinear, since material difficulties combined with opposition from traditional elites and suspicion of the colonial state to ensure that a large gap remained between Jadid ambition and Jadid achievement. Nevertheless, by 1917, new-method schools were widespread, a print-based public space had taken hold, and the traditional elites' monopoly over the definition of culture had been shaken.

COLONIAL ENCOUNTERS
IN THE RUSSIAN BORDERLANDS

In pointing to the transformative role of Russian rule, it is by no means my intention to claim that imperial benevolence was the linchpin of cultural regeneration in Central Asia. Rather, I hope to distance the analysis from the hackneyed dichotomies of resistance and collusion, of native authenticity and "Westernization" (or, in our case, Russification), by suggesting that the social and institutional terrain on which struggles over culture take place in colonial settings is very much the product of colonial rule. To look for "responses" to colonialism in a domain located entirely outside of it is futile, since the very formulation of the response is inextricably intertwined in patterns of colonial knowledge.[21] Although this obviously applies to modernist re-visions of identity, even visions of the authenticity of native tradition are articulated through means of cultural production often introduced by the colonizer. For if culture is to be located in the struggles of elites, then the colonial presence was a major feature of the social terrain on which they took place. This presence may not have determined the nature of the competition, but it certainly provided a major resource even as it also defined the limits of the permissible.

The interconnections between empire and imperial knowledge have received considerable scholarly attention in recent years,[22] but the politics of native cultural production in the conditions of empire have been less popular. The Jadids, like many colonial intellectuals, occupied a liminal space between the colonial power and native society. From this position they could appropriate colonial ideas for their own uses, invoking the superiority of the colonizer to exhort their society to reform; at the same time, they talked back to the colonizer in the colonizer's own language. This involved them in bitter struggles over turf in their society with groups that had made their own compromises with the colonial regime.

In the Russian case, even the colonial nature of the regime remains a matter of dispute. Although the Russian empire was one of the largest empires in the world during the period under discussion here, sophisticated study of the Russian imperial experience is only now beginning. Scholars centrally concerned with one or more of the "nationalities" of the Russian empire have long been used to viewing the Russian state as a colonial entity (although often more as a matter of reflex than as an analytical preoccupation), but mainstream Russian history has seen imperialism only in Russian foreign policy, being content to study the borderlands as a problem of administration rather than imperialism.[23] And of all the borderlands, Central Asia remains the least known.

21. Frederick Cooper and Ann L. Stoler, "Tensions of Empire: Colonial Control and Visions of Rule," *American Ethnologist* 16 (1989): 609; Timothy Mitchell, *Colonising Egypt,* new ed. (Berkeley, 1991), xi.

22. The *locus classicus* of this debate is, of course, Edward Said, *Orientalism* (New York, 1978).

23. The major works on Russian imperialism are concerned almost entirely with imperial competition outside the boundaries of the Russian state, not with imperial interaction within it: Dietrich Geyer, *Russian Imperialism: The Interaction of Domestic and Foreign Policy, 1860–1914,* trans. Bruce Little (New Haven, 1987); John P. LeDonne, *The Russian Empire and the World, 1700–1917: The Geopolitics of Expansion and Containment* (New York, 1997). The recent work by Andreas Kappeler, *Rußland als*

To be sure, Russia's geographic contiguity to its empire made for several peculiarities of its colonial experience (the state usually did not recognize the borderlands as separate political entities), but the basic epistemological operations of empires were, nevertheless, present. Moreover, as I argue in Chapter 2, Central Asia, conquered between the 1860s and the 1880s, occupied a position that was in many ways unique in the empire. The distinctly colonial conception that informed Russian rule in the region contrasted markedly to earlier periods of annexation that had brought other Muslim and non-Muslim groups under Russian rule. If in previous periods of expansion, the Russian state had coopted local nobilities and absorbed conquered populations into its system of social classification, in Central Asia the rhetoric of conquest mirrored nineteenth-century notions of colonialism. Russian administrators constantly compared Turkestan to British India (the protectorates of Bukhara and Khiva were directly inspired by British treaties with various princely states in India) or French North Africa and sought to benefit from the experience of these powers in ruling "their" Muslims. The local population remained "natives," regardless of social standing.

Although such colonial policies and practices were very important to Central Asian cultural life, their appreciation is also crucial to understanding late imperial Russia as a whole. The fact that Russia was a multinational empire is often glossed over in mainstream Russian (as opposed to "nationalities") historiography, with a resultant loss of historical perspective. The imperial borderlands, perhaps Central Asia more so than any other, were not incidental to Russia. Their existence—and their subjugation—helped define Russia and Russianness in very tangible ways that are lost to analysis if Russia is seen as a unitary state.

The study of imperial interactions in the Russian borderlands also helps to deconstruct the notion of "the West." Scholarly discourse is so permeated with the dichotomy between Russia and "the West" (which events of the past decade have only entrenched more deeply) that it appears as a paradox that Russia should personify "the West" in its Asian borderlands. Yet, Russians saw themselves as resolutely European in Central Asia, sharing in the European civilizing mission to which all imperial powers pretended. If world history of the last two centuries is to be glossed as "Westernization," then we face the paradox that many of

---

Vielvolkerreich: Entstehung, Geschichte, Zerfall (Munich, 1992), is the first substantial treatment of Russia as a multiethnic empire.

TABLE I   RUSSIAN CENTRAL ASIA POPULATIONS

	Area (sq. mi.)	Populations	
		1897	1911
Syr Darya	189,150	1,478,398	1,816,550
Samarqand	33,850	860,021	960,200
Ferghana	55,210	1,572,214	2,041,900
Total three core oblasts	278,210	3,910,633	4,818,650
Transcaspia	231,238	382,487	472,500
Semirech'e	147,510	997,863	1,201,540
Total Turkestan	656,960	5,290,983	6,492,690
Bukhara	78,650	—	2,500,000
Khiva	26,070	—	550,000
Total Central Asia	761,680	—	ca. 9,550,000

SOURCES: V.I. Masal'skii, *Turkestanskii krai* (St. Petersburg, 1913), 348; *Aziatskaia Rossiia* (St. Petersburg, 1914), I: 91–92.

For Turkestan, population figures for 1897 are from the census of 1897; those for 1911 represent official estimates. Figures for the protectorates are estimates and pertain to 1909.

the agents of this process were not generally regarded as those of the West. Russia is scarcely the only exception; the burden of Europe was carried in other places by Spain or Portugal, countries that in the continental context were hardly epitomes of "the West." "Europe" and "the West" are but ideas that take various forms at various times and places.

But if "Westernization" is not a useful concept, "Russification"—the dominant paradigm for understanding cultural interaction in the Russian empire—is even less so. The latter concept has been popular with scholars of "the nationalities" of the Russian empire, who see in every Russian (or Soviet) policy an attempt to dominate and transform authentic national cultures. (It is a measure of the alterity of Russian history vis-à-vis Europe that "Russification," the local variant of "Westernization," carries a completely negative connotation.) By foregrounding themes of national struggle, while ignoring debates within society, such approaches render themselves incapable of exploring the politics of cultural production and identity formation on the Russian borderlands. Going beyond Russification is all the more crucial for the study of Central Asia, where in the tsarist period the state had neither the means nor the will to intervene directly in local cultural life. The impact of imperial power has to be sought in more subtle form than the paradigm of "Russification" allows.

CENTRAL ASIA

Russian Central Asia comprised the governorate-general of Turkestan as well as the protectorates of Bukhara and Khiva (see Table 1). For reasons of both space and clarity, I focus largely on Turkestan in this book, although since the writings of Bukharan Jadids (especially Abdurrauf Fitrat) were highly influential, Bukharan developments cannot be wholly excluded. Nor do I deal with the traditional lands of the Qazaqs incorporated in the Steppe province administered from Omsk. Its nomadic population had a conception of Islam very different from that of the inhabitants of the oasis cities of Transoxiana. Moreover, the Steppe province was under direct Russian rule far longer and subject to different administrative policies than Turkestan. During our period, the foci of Qazaq cultural life lay to the north, in Orenburg and even Kazan, rather than to the south in Tashkent or Samarqand. The administrative entity of Turkestan produced its own logic that was a salient feature of Central Asian life in the tsarist period.

CHAPTER I

Knowledge and Society in the Nineteenth Century

The three and a half centuries between the collapse of the Timurid order and the Russian conquest constitute the least understood period of Central Asian history. The literary production of the period still remains largely in manuscript form, and scholarly attention focuses on the more glamorous Timurids or the more accessible Russian period. In the absence of systematic research, we are left to struggle with V. V. Bartol'd's dictum that "in the nineteenth century, in contrast to the Middle Ages, Turkestan was among the most backward countries of the Muslim world." [1] Soviet scholarship tended to focus on the centralization of states in the nineteenth century as a positive sign (and to contrast it to the feudal dissension of the eighteenth); however, its judgment on the culture of this period was no more generous. Yet, if we are to understand the politics of cultural production that obtained on the eve of the Russian conquest, politics that the Jadids set out to reform, we need to rescue the topic from the domain of aesthetic judgment and place it firmly in the realm of social practice. This is a crucial task in its own right, but it is also of fundamental importance for understanding the politics of culture during the tsarist period.

1. V. V. Bartol'd, *Istoriia kul'turnoi zhizni Turkestana* (1927), in his *Sochineniia* (Moscow, 1963), II/1: 297.

KNOWLEDGE, LITERACY, AND CULTURE

A sharp critique of traditional Muslim education in nineteenth-century Central Asia is perhaps the only area of scholarship in which all observers, scholars and officials, tsarist and Soviet, agreed with Jadids and émigré nationalists. The maktabs and madrasas of Central Asia were the clearest sign of the stagnation, if not the degeneracy, of Central Asia. Judged by criteria these observers brought with them, the maktab and the madrasa not surprisingly appeared as inefficient, pointless, and even harmful. Yet, if we are to understand the logic of the practices surrounding the transmission of knowledge in pre-Russian Central Asia (many of which continued well into the twentieth century), we have to examine them in their own right, and not by the modernist criteria of observers standing outside the tradition.[2]

The tradition of learning replicated in the maktabs and madrasas of Central Asia was common to many premodern Muslim societies. It was characterized by two overriding concerns: the transmission of knowledge (*ilm*) and the cultivation of proper modes of behavior and comportment (*adab*). The primary impulse was conservational, the transmission to future generations of the finite, fixed truths revealed by God.[3] This tradition was marked by rigorous discipline, including severe corporal punishment, and often the insistence on memorization without explicit explanation. As Dale Eickelman has suggested, " 'Understanding' (*fahm*) in the context of such concepts of learning was not measured by any ability explicitly to 'explain' particular verses [of the Qur'an]. . . . Instead, the measure of understanding was implicit and consisted of the ability to use particular Quranic verses in appropriate contexts."[4] The finite and fixed nature of knowledge by no means precluded a dynamic tradition of interpretation, for it was only through an act of interpretation that divinely revealed knowledge could become meaningful for human beings. This interpretation required a carefully inculcated scholarly *habitus,* a set of predispositions and habits of mind that allow "practices and works to be immediately intelligible and foreseeable, and hence

---

2. The following discussion of the social uses of knowledge owes a great debt to Michael Chamberlain, *Knowledge and Social Practice in Medieval Damascus, 1190–1350* (Cambridge, 1994).

3. Dale F. Eickelman, "The Art of Memory: Islamic Knowledge and Its Social Reproduction," *Comparative Studies in Society and History* 20 (1978): 490.

4. Ibid., 494.

taken for granted."[5] The *habitus* reproduced in the maktabs, and especially the madrasas, of nineteenth-century Central Asia cultivated a certain relation to texts and to the world beyond them that provided the framework for life. The distinction between religious and secular knowledge in this world would have been impossible, for all knowledge emanated from God and was consequently imbued with a certain sacral value. Different crafts and sciences were similarly deemed to have been invented by various prophets. Noah, for instance, was the inventor of woodwork and David of metalwork.

If the transmission of knowledge (*ta'lim*) was one concern of the maktab, the other was the inculcation of proper modes of behavior and conduct (*tarbiya*). *Adab* as mimetic practice occupied a central place in Muslim societies. Originating in pre-Islamic Middle Eastern traditions of civility and refinement, *adab* was thoroughly Islamized after the eighth century through the works of such Muslim writers of Iranian origins as Ibn Muqaffa' (d. 756) and Firdawsi (d. 1020). In later centuries the term *"adab"* came to be understood in a more restricted fashion to denote knowledge necessary for a certain profession or station in life (and so it became possible to speak of *ādāb al-mufti,* the *adab* of one who holds the office of *mufti* [jurisconsult]).[6] In nineteenth-century Central Asia, proper *adab* marked the boundaries of civility and status and was a crucial element in cultural capital recognized in urban society. Manuals of civility existed,[7] but the primary arena for its transmission remained the maktab.

We have a number of descriptions of the Central Asian maktab, although most of them are the hostile views of outsiders.[8] Fortunately, in

5. Pierre Bourdieu, *The Logic of Practice,* trans. Richard Nice (Stanford, 1990), 58; see also Bourdieu, "Systems of Education and Systems of Thought," *International Social Science Journal* 19 (1967): 344.

6. F. Gabrieli, "Adab," *Encyclopedia of Islam,* new ed., vol. 1 (Leiden, 1960), 175; Dj. Khaleghi-Motlagh, "Adab," *Encyclopædia Iranica,* vol. 1 (New York, 1982), 431–439. On Iran's long tradition of ethico-didactic writing (*pand, andarz, nasihat,* etc.), which in Islamic times assimilated Muslim ethics as well, see *Encyclopædia Iranica,* II: 16–22, s.v. "Andarz." See also, Barbara Metcalf, "Introduction," in Metcalf, ed., *Moral Conduct and Authority: The Place of* Adab *in South Asian Islam* (Berkeley, 1984), 1–4.

7. For example, the *Ādāb us-sālihin* of Muhammad Sālih Kāshghari, translated from a lithographed edition by N. S. Lykoshin, "Kodeks prilichii na Vostoke," *Sbornik materialov po musul'manstvu,* vyp. 2 (Tashkent, 1900).

8. On the Central Asian maktab, the following are the most significant: V. P. Nalivkin, "Shkoly u tuzemtsev Srednei Azii," *Sbornik materialov dlia statistiki Samarkandskoi oblasti, 1887–1888 gg.* (Samarqand, 1889), 294–303; Nalivkin, "Chto daet sredne-aziatskaia musul'manskaia shkola v obrazovatel'nom i vospitatel'nom otnosheniiakh?" in *Turkestanskii literaturnyi sbornik v pol'zu prokazhennykh* (St. Petersburg, 1900), 215–278; N. P. Ostroumov, "Musul'manskie maktaby i russko-tuzemnye shkoly v Turkestan-

the writings of Sadriddin Ayni (1878–1954), we possess a unique source on the maktab and the madrasa as they existed in this period. Born in a small village outside Ghijduvān, Ayni was among the last generations of Central Asians to receive a traditional education. A prominent Jadid, he had an illustrious career after the revolution in education and publishing in which he helped found modern literatures in both Tajik and Uzbek. One of the few Jadids to survive the 1930s, he was greatly honored as a national hero of Soviet Tajikistan. This stature allowed him to publish in 1949, at the height of Stalinism, his reminiscences of old Bukhara, a text remarkable for its sensibility.[9] Although Ayni wrote of the period when Bukhara was a Russian protectorate, much of what he describes can safely be projected back to much of the nineteenth century, for the impact of the Russian presence on the internal life of Bukharan maktabs and madrasas was minimal in the 1880s and 1890s.

The education of a Central Asian boy began when his father took him to a teacher (*maktabdār, dāmlā*) and left him behind with the formula, "You can beat him as long as you don't kill him; the meat is yours, but the bones are ours." [10] As Ayni later recalled: "When my father left, the teacher sat me down close to him and ordered one of the older students to work with me. This pupil bade me look at my writing board as he said aloud, 'Alif, be, te, se.' I imitated him and repeated the names of these letters. Having taught me how to pronounce them, the student went over to other kids and started teaching them. The children called him *khalfa*." [11] The pupil was thus immediately thrust into a set of hierarchical social relationships. In addition to knowledge, the child acquired *adab* from direct contact with the teacher. The maktab had neither formal division into classes nor any examinations. The student progressed through school at his own pace, his status determined by the number of

skom krae," *ZhMNP*, n.s. 1 (1906): otd. nar. ob., 113–166; K. E. Bendrikov, *Ocherki po istorii narodnogo obrazovaniia v Turkestane (1865–1925 gody)* (Moscow, 1960), 36–48; Jiří Bečka, "Traditional Schools in the Works of Sadriddin Aini and Other Writers of Central Asia," *Archiv Orientální* 39 (1971): 284–321; 40 (1972): 130–163; R. R. Rakhimov, "Traditsionnoe nachal'noe shkol'noe obuchenie detei u narodov Srednei Azii (konets XIX–nachalo XX v.)," in *Pamiatniki traditsionno-bytovoi kul'tury narodov Srednei Azii, Kazakhstana i Kavkaza* (Leningrad, 1989).

9. Sadriddin Aynî, *Yoddoshtho*, 4 vols. (Stalinabad, 1948–1954). There exist numerous editions of this work, of which perhaps the most readily accessible is a 1984 Persian edition (*Yāddāshthā*, ed. Saʿīdī Sīrjānī [Tehran, 1984]), which I have used throughout.

10. Hāji Muin, *Eski maktab, yāngi maktab* (Samarqand, 1916), 17. This ritual phrase was common throughout the Islamic world; on its use in Morocco, see Eickelman, *Knowledge and Power in Morocco* (Princeton, 1985), 63.

11. Sadriddin Ayniy, "Eski maktab" (1935), in *Eski maktab* (Tashkent, 1988), 109.

books he finished. Although the students sat together in a "class," their relation to the teacher was individual and direct.

Having memorized the names of the letters of the alphabet, the student was introduced to vowels, which again he learned through memorization. "The lessons on 'zer-u zabar' were interesting. . . . I was taught to say, 'Alif zabar—a, zer—i, pesh—u.' . . . Thus I learned the letters from the beginning to the very end of the Arabic alphabet." [12] At the end of the year, Ayni started on the *abjad*.[13] He was told: " 'Say: "Alif bā be zabar—ab; jim bā dāl zabar—jad; abjad' . . . Once my father said, 'Now that you can read the *abjad*, I'll teach you how to count according to it,' and put in front of me a slate with the *abjad* written on it. Pointing to a letter, he asked, 'What [letter] is this? And this?' I could not answer a single question. I had absolutely no idea; nobody had ever shown me the letters." [14]

After the alphabet, the child started with the *Haftyak*, a compilation of selected verses from the Qur'an, beginning with the shortest *suras* usually located at the end. These too were memorized. The child was thus familiarized with the alphabet at the same time as he or she started the process of memorization of key texts. Of course, the Qur'an was taught in the Arabic, with no translation provided and no attempt made at explanation. The rules of the proper recitation of the Qur'an (*tajwid, tartil*) were taught from this stage, so that the child could recite the Word of God in an acceptable manner. Upon memorization of the *Haftyak*, the boy received the title *kitabkhwān* (reader of [a] book).[15] He then proceeded to the *Chār Kitāb*, an anthology providing basic information about Islamic ritual. As the name suggests, the anthology contained four works: *Nām-i Haqq*, a tract in verse by one Sharifuddin Bukhārī (fl. fourteenth century), dealing with rules for the fulfillment of ritual obligations of ritual purity, fasting, and prayer (*namāz*); *Chār Fasl*, by an anonymous author, providing a statement, in prose, of the bases of belief, the five pillars of Islam, and ritual purity; *Muhimmāt ul-Muslimin*, another anonymous work providing information on four things that are important to all Muslims (the unity of God [*tawhid*], fasting, prayers, and ritual purity); and selections from the *Pandnāma* of Fariduddin Attār, a

12. Ibid., 128–129.
13. The *abjad* was both a mnemonic device for learning the Arabic alphabet and a system for counting in which each letter of the alphabet was assigned a numerical value (allowing the use of the alphabet in cabals, etc.).
14. Ayniy, "Eski maktab," 129.
15. Rakhimov, "Traditsionnoe nachal'noe shkol'noe obuchenie," 122

major work in the *adab* tradition.[16] After finishing the *Chār Kitāb,* the student encountered poetry, both in Persian and Turkic, by Hāfiz, Sufi Allah Yār, Fuzuli, Bedil, Nawā'i, and Attār. The works of these poets constituted the canon of Central Asian literature, and acquaintance with them (and the ability to recite verses from memory at appropriate times) was *de rigueur* for an educated person.

The instruction up to this point was entirely oral. Students used written texts, but they were meant to be used as visual mnemonic aids. Having finished the *Haftyak,* the *Chār Kitāb,* and the Qur'an, Ayni "could still not read anything, except for what I had read with the [teacher]. For example, I could always read those verses of Hafiz which I had read at school, no matter whose hand they were in. But I could not read others that I had not [already] read—I was illiterate! Writing I did not know at all."[17] Although children were introduced to the alphabet, the acquisition of functional literacy was not the goal of their maktab experience. In a society organized around direct, face-to-face interaction between social agents, writing was of limited use and tended to become a specialized skill. The ability to read and write (and the two were different skills, separately acquired) was necessary for only a few spheres of endeavor, whereas vast spheres of life remained untouched by writing. Even in trade, large-scale transactions were carried out purely orally, with the personal guarantee of special intermediaries (*qāsid*s) taking the place of written documents as late as the 1870s.[18] At the same time, culture was transmitted largely orally. Central Asia, of course, boasted a vibrant tradition of oral poetry, but oral transmission also extended to texts that could be read aloud in various formal and informal settings. Itinerant reciters and storytellers (*maddāh*s, *qissakhwān*s) were a common phenomenon in Central Asia, as were evenings (*mashrab*) devoted to reading aloud from manuscript texts.[19] The ability to read was there-

16. For a description of a printed edition of the *Chār Kitāb,* see O. P. Shcheglova, *Katalog litografirovannykh knig na persidskom iazyke v sobranii LO IV AN SSSR,* 2 vols. (Moscow, 1975), nos. 600, 640, 650. A very similar anthology from Afghanistan is described by M. Nazif Shahrani, "Local Knowledge of Islam and Social Discourse in Afghanistan and Turkistan in the Modern Period," in Robert L. Canfield, ed., *Turko-Persia in Historical Perspective* (Cambridge, 1991), 170–175.

17. Ayniy, "Eski maktab," 132.

18. E.g., N. Stremukhov, "Poezdka v Bukharu," *Russkii vestnik* 117 (1875): 667.

19. A. L. Troitskaia, "Iz proshlogo kalandarov i maddakhov v Uzbekistane," in *Do-musul'manskie verovaniia i obriady v Srednei Azii* (Moscow, 1975), 191–223; Karl Reichl, *Turkic Oral Epic Poetry* (New York, 1992), 87–89; for contemporary descriptions, see F. H. Skrine and E. Denison Ross, *The Heart of Asia* (London, 1899), 400–401; O. Olufsen, *The Emir of Bukhara and His Country* (Copenhagen, 1911), 434.

fore not a necessary precondition for participation in the literary tradition of Central Asia, and indeed, the audience for written texts was always far greater than the number of competent readers. The high rates of illiteracy and the inability to write prevalent in Central Asia in the nineteenth century did not indicate a lack of education, let alone ignorance.[20] Rather, the emphasis on memorization and learning by rote emanated from a different concern: Knowledge was to be embodied by the learner so that his or her body could be marked by sacred knowledge.[21]

Writing was a separate skill altogether, not taught at all by many *maktahdārs*. When taught, it usually took the form of calligraphy. Just as students were left to learn their native language on their own while the maktab concentrated on Arabic and Persian texts, they were left to their own devices to learn the cursive hand, and only calligraphy was taught at the maktab. Calligraphy and the possession of a fine hand were thus analogous to rhetoric and the ability to quote verses as marks of a civilized individual. As with reading, calligraphy was acquired through imitation. Ayni recalled that he had acquired the rudiments of calligraphy before he could read fluently, having copied letters of the alphabet from a relative who had returned to the village for the summer from his Bukharan madrasa.[22] Many more people could read than could write.[23] At the same time, writing had significant ritual uses. Books were used not merely for reading the text but for divination and as charms and amulets.[24] Writing could be venerated in its own right as embodying the holiness of the message. The *Majmu'a-yi nurnāma,* an anthology of various prayers, promised, "Whoever reads this *Nurnāma* or carries it with him will be saved from the troubles of both the worlds."[25] Members of various craft guilds

20. Many scholars of Central Asian intellectual life of the period have seen the high rates of illiteracy in Central Asia as a grave indictment of the maktab and a sign of the stagnation of Central Asian life. See, for instance, Nalivkin, "Chto daet," 235. Criticism of the maktab on this account was, of course, a staple of Jadid discourse.

21. Frederick Mathewson Denny, "Qur'ān Recitation: A Tradition of Oral Performance and Transmission," *Oral Tradition* 4 (1989): 13.

22. Ayni, *Yāddāshthā,* 90–92.

23. Iuldash Abdullaev, *Ocherki po metodike obucheniia gramote v uzbekskoi shkole* (Tashkent, 1966), 79–86. Reading-only literacy was a common phenomenon throughout the world until the rise of universal schooling in the nineteenth century. In France, as late as 1866, 11.47 percent of the population (9.73 percent of men and 13.21 percent of women) could only read. (32.84 percent of the population could neither read nor write.) See François Furet and Jacques Ozouf, *Reading and Writing: Literacy in France from Calvin to Jules Ferry* (Cambridge, 1982), 17.

24. Divination through books (*fālbini*) was a common practice; see N. S. Lykoshin, "O gadanii u sredneaziatskikh tuzemtsev," *Spravochnaia knizhka Samarkandskoi oblasti* 9 (1907): 163–242.

25. *Majmu'a-yi nurnāma* (Tashkent, 1914), 12.

were similarly exhorted to know the *risāla* of their guild by heart, or else to carry it on their person; failure to do so could bring dire consequences. As the *risāla* of the guild of grooms stated, "If a groom does not know this *risāla* or has not heard it, all livestock is more forbidden than the flesh of the swine; he will be tortured in his grave by snakes and scorpions, and his face will be black on the day of judgment."[26] Writing had many ritual uses, but the ability to read fluently was a skill required only in a few, very specific niches in society.

The maktab was not a school at all in the sense of an institution set apart from other practices but a site for the acquisition by children of basic elements of culture and modes of behavior through interaction with an older, learned man. It existed wherever the teacher could teach, and any literate person with the proper credentials of *adab* and piety could teach. The maktab seldom had a building of its own: It could be housed in a mosque, the house of the teacher, or that of a wealthy resident of the neighborhood. A teacher seldom had more than a dozen or so pupils in his charge. He did not receive a regular salary but was supported by gifts from parents, which took the form of weekly donations of food, and occasionally money (*payshanbalik*), given every Thursday. In addition, the teacher received gifts of clothes on annual holidays or when a child finished a book.[27] The maktab was ubiquitous in the sedentary parts of Central Asia, especially the towns. As a relatively informal institution, without formal admissions or enrollments, the maktab was not reducible to the kind of census-taking that various tsarist statistical committees strove for. Numbers provided by nineteenth-century travelers should also be treated with the greatest caution, since they were invariably based on hearsay or on reports by local "informants," who usually provided mythical numbers. Nevertheless, O. A. Sukhareva's ethnographic data indicate that at the turn of the twentieth century almost every residential neighborhood in the city of Bukhara had its own maktab.[28] Maktabs were also common in rural areas of sedentary population; in 1903, nine of the fourteen villages of Chapkulluk volost in Khujand uezd had a maktab.[29] Among the nomads, the situation was rather different. Instruction for the children of nomads was generally provided by itinerant

26. "Risāla-yi chārwādārlik," in *ibid.*, 63.
27. Rakhimov, "Traditsionnoe nachal'noe shkol'noe obuchenie," 118–119, 122.
28. O. A. Sukhareva, *Kvartal'naia obshchina pozdnefeodal'nogo goroda Bukhary* (Moscow, 1976), 256–257.
29. N. Lykoshin, "Chapkullukskaia volost' Khodzhentskogo uezda," *Spravochnaia knizhka Samarkandskoi oblasti* 8 (1906): 157–158.

mullas from either the settled areas of Central Asia or from among the Volga Tatars. For a fixed salary (paid either in cash or kind), the mulla traveled with the family and taught the children; he was free to take on any other students from the aul.[30] Hiring a mulla from Bukhara or Kazan was a status symbol. Once a Türkmen fellow student offered to get Ayni's elder brother a summer job as teacher in a Türkmen village. Ayni's brother hesitated, because he knew no Turkic: "'That doesn't matter,' said the student to reassure my brother. 'The Turkmenian bais don't maintain teachers to teach their children to read and write. The main thing is that people should say: "Such and such a bai has had a teacher brought from Bukhara."'"[31] Concerns about civility and markers of respectability were differently defined among the nomads, and the maktab accordingly occupied a different place in nomadic society.

Of course, not every student stayed in the maktab for the duration; in an agrarian society with very low levels of surplus, few families could afford to remove their boys from productive labor for such long periods of time. Those who stayed to the end had only rudimentary literacy skills, but they had acquired basic norms of cultured behavior, of gesture and posture, and an ingrained attitude of deference to older men— in short, cultural capital that was a marker of social distinction in their society. They had also acquired an implicit knowledge of Islam as faith and practice, without which membership in the community was unimaginable. They had not acquired literacy, or skills such as arithmetic, or general knowledge such as history or geography, because these were transmitted elsewhere in society, in appropriate dialogic contexts.

Maktabs for girls existed and in many ways paralleled the boys' maktab. A very similar kind of instruction was provided by the *ātin*, who would teach young girls from the neighborhood in her house in return for presents from the parents or, possibly, help with housework. It was not unknown for some women to teach both boys and girls, since segregation by sex was not mandatory before puberty.[32] Ātins were often wives and daughters of imāms and other educated men, but they were respected members of the community in their own right. As Marianne Kamp has argued, "Women and girls formed their own chains of knowl-

30. T. T. Tazhibaev, *Prosveshchenie i shkoly Kazakhstana vo vtoroi polovine XIX veka* (Alma Ata, 1962), 57.

31. Sadriddin Aini, *Pages from My Own Story,* trans. George H. Hanna (Moscow, 1958), 34.

32. Ayni's father moved him to a girls' maktab (run by the imām's wife) when he realized that the teacher at the regular maktab was incompetent. "Eski maktab," 130.

edge transmission, without formal male instruction. In gatherings involving religious practice, . . . women's separation from men allowed the
creation of women's religious authority. Separate spaces and separate
knowledges reproduced gender-based networks."[33]

MADRASAS AND THE REPRODUCTION OF ISLAM

The transmission of knowledge beyond the maktab was diffused throughout society. Knowledge and skills were acquired in practical contexts of
work. Artisans received their training in craft guilds, whose structure,
admittedly very loose, incorporated a sacralized hierarchy: the apprentice was subordinate to a master (occasionally this relationship was mediated by a *khalifa*), who in turn was subordinate to an *āqsaqqāl*, the
leader of the craft organization in the whole city; the *āqsaqqāl* was ultimately subject to the symbolic authority of the patron of the guild, usually a pre-Islamic prophet. The master (*ustād*) would take the apprentice, usually at age twelve, into his house and over the next several years
teach him the required skills of the trade. The master was also responsible for teaching the child rules of proper behavior (*adab*) and, if he was
literate, knowledge about Muslim law (*ulum-i shariat*) and mysticism
(*ulum-i tariqat*). Initiation into a guild revolved around the memorization of the *risāla*, often in verse, that laid out the rules of initiation and
proper conduct to be followed by members. An apprentice was, for example, expected "to be well-bred and affect humility before the master,
not to be rude to him, not to walk in front of him, not to sit down without his permission, [and] not to address him by his name."[34] In order to
complete their education, apprentices were required to know the *risāla*
for the guild by heart. Beyond the world of artisans, even chancery practices were similarly endowed with sacred origins and intent, as is clear
from a late-eighteenth century manual of accountancy.[35] The connections
to the tradition of *adab* are quite obvious here.

33. Marianne R. Kamp, "The Otin and the Soviet School: The End of Traditional
Education for Uzbek Girls," paper presented to the annual convention of the American
Association for the Advancement of Slavic Studies, Boston, 1996, 3.

34. *Risāla-yi Chitgari*, ms., cited by R. G. Mukminova, "Remeslennye korporatsii i
uchinichestvo (po sredneaziatskim pis'mennym istochnikam XVI i XIX vv.)," in *Materialy
po istorii Uzbekistana* (Tashkent, 1973), 26; on *risāla*s in general, see M. Gavrilov, *Risolia sartovskikh remeslennikov: izsledovanie predanii musul'manskikh tsekhov* (Tashkent,
1912).

35. Mirzā Badiʿ Diwān. *Majmaʿ al-arqām*, ed. and trans. L. M. Epifanova (Moscow,
1976), 27–33.

It is in this context that the place of the madrasa in Central Asian society is best understood. Rather than being an institution of higher learning in the modern sense of the word, the madrasa was the site for the reproduction of one class of professionals, those concerned with various aspects of Islamic law. It was a place where, in dialogic interaction with a recognized scholar, the student acquired mastery over a number of authoritative texts of the Islamic tradition as understood locally. Although this knowledge existed in written form, it was transmitted orally. As numerous scholars have noted, the Islamic tradition of learning was marked with a profound distrust of the ability of the text to convey the author's intention. That could only be learned from the author himself, or through a chain of transmission going back to the author. Knowledge could be authoritative only if acquired through a recognized chain of transmission.[36] Further, the proof of mastery of knowledge lay not in a transcript of courses taken at an institution but in the *ijāza* (license) issued by the master in his own name, which signified a link in the chain of transmission.

A student entered a madrasa when a mudarris allowed him to listen to his lectures; there was no formal matriculation. A gift, usually but not necessarily of money, called the *iftitāhāna,* signified the beginning of a teacher-student relationship.[37] As in the maktab, progress through the madrasa was marked by successful completion of books; each student proceeded along the curriculum at his own pace. Attendance at lectures coincided with more informal peer learning in study circles organized by students. Members of a circle studied the same book, and those with a better command of the material helped others in return for food or clothing, since it was considered "a kind of vileness" to receive money in return for knowledge.[38] Some texts were studied only in such groups, and others were prepared thus before students listened to lectures on them from the mudarris. When a student had satisfied the professor of his command of a book (which often involved memorization), he could

---

36. Eickelman, "Art of Memory," 492; Timothy Mitchell, *Colonising Egypt,* new ed. (Berkeley, 1991), 148–154; Brinkley Messick, *The Calligraphic State: Textual Domination and History in a Muslim Society* (Berkeley, 1993), 25–26, 92–94.

37. Further gifts were given upon completion of each book. The more renowned teachers, who could have dozens of students, acquired a sizable fortune from their presents. (Aini states that in the 1890s, teachers' income only from their students could amount to 1,500 rubles, which could buy 2,500 puds [more than 40 tons] of grain; *Yāddāshthā,* 171.) In addition, a teacher received a portion of the endowed income from the waqf, as well as from any other posts (mufti, qāzi, etc.) he might hold.

38. Ayni, *Yāddāshthā,* 537–540; for a discussion of similar "peer learning" in Morocco, see Eickelman, *Knowledge and Power,* 98.

pass on to the next book by joining another study circle, possibly with another teacher.

Life in the madrasa began with the private study of several brief tracts: *Awwal-i ʿilm,* a short tract that covered the essential requirements (*zururiyāt*) of Islam in question-and-answer format; *Bidān,* an exposition of the basic rules of Arabic grammar in Persian; and *Ādāb-i mutaʿallimin,* which covered the *adab* of the student. After that, the student read *Sharh-i Mullā,* a commentary on Ibn Hājib's *Kāfiya* (which the student had already studied) by Abdurrahmān Jāmi, the Timurid poet; written in Arabic, this was the first book studied with a mudarris. At the same time, the student started studying formal logic with an assistant teacher, using the *Shamsiya* of Najmuddin Qazvīnī (d. 1276); when he was ready, he moved on to the *Hāshiya-yi Qutbi,* a commentary on *Shamsiya;* concurrently with the *Hāshiya,* the student was introduced to theology (*ʿilm-i kalām*) through the *ʿAqāʾid* of Abū Hafs Nasafī (d. 1142), which he read with an assistant teacher. Later, the student moved to various glosses on this book. These were followed by the *Tahzib ul-Mantiq waʾl kalām,* a tract on logic and dogma by Saʿduddīn Taftāzānī (d. 1381); *Hikmat ul-ʿayn* by Qazvīnī, a tract on natural science and metaphysics; *Mullā Jalāl,* a commentary by Jalāluddin Dawwāmi (d. 1502) on the *ʿAqāʾid ul-adūdiyat* of Abdurrahmān b. Ahmad al-Ījī (d. 1356), a tract on Muslim beliefs.[39] There was no formal termination of studies in the madrasa, and many students lingered on for decades. The core texts could, however, be mastered in nineteen years.

Formal lessons took place four days a week. The entire study group assembled; a designated reader (*qāri,* elected by the students) read out the passage to be discussed; the mudarris then translated the passage (if necessary) and proceeded to explain and comment on it; a disputation involving the students concluded the lesson.[40] There was no compulsion to take courses at the madrasa of residence; indeed, at many madrasas no lectures were held at all.[41] A student was free to learn from any pro-

39. The foregoing is based on Bečka, "Traditional Schools," 39: 296–299; 40: 135–136; Ayni, *Yāddāshthā,* 163–165; A. Mukhammadzhanov, *Shkola i pedagogicheskaia mysl' uzbekskogo naroda XIX—nachala XX v.* (Tashkent, 1978), 26–28.

40. The description of madrasa life in Ayni, *Yāddāshthā,* passim, is unique in both its substance and its sensibility; see also Eugene Schuyler, *Turkistan,* 2 vols. (New York, 1877), 1:162–165; V. Nalivkin and M. Nalivkina, *Ocherk byta zhenshchiny osedlogo tuzemnogo naseleniia Fergany* (Kazan, 1886), 61–65.

41. Sukhareva (*Bukhara,* 72–73n) counted eighty madrasas existing in Bukhara at the turn of the twentieth century; lectures were held at only those twenty-two whose waqfs provided for hiring a mudarris.

fessor in the city. This was especially the case in Bukhara. During the reign of the pious Shāh Murād (r. 1785–1800), many madrasas in the khanate were in such bad repair that the amir issued an edict giving property rights to whoever repaired or rebuilt *hujra*s in a madrasa.[42] As a result, the *hujra* became immovable private property and madrasas turned into hostels. Ownership of a *hujra* brought with it the right to receive a portion of the madrasa's endowed (*waqf*) income. The price of a cell therefore depended on the size of the madrasa's endowment. In the nineteenth century, many cells in the madrasas of Bukhara were occupied by men who had little connection with learning. Many individuals owned cells as a form of investment and leased or donated them to students in need.[43] Residents of madrasa cells were free from taxation and for much of the nineteenth century also received scholarships from the amir. During the reigns of Shāh Murād and Mir Haydar, large sums of money were set aside for the use of madrasa teachers and students.[44] This custom lapsed in mid-century as Nasrullah diverted funds toward defense, but at the end of the century, the amir still handed out pensions (*dehyak*) to students annually.[45] In this situation, a student's only connection with the mudarris of the madrasa where he lived was that they both derived income from the same *waqf*.

The madrasa was the site of the social reproduction of Islamic legal knowledge and its carriers, the ulama. The method of instruction was connected to this basic concern. It aimed to explicate the meaning of the text and to convey that meaning dialogically. At the same time, it inculcated in students a certain *habitus*, which allowed them to construct meaningful social action in the world. Students acquired the basic skills needed to practice their trade—literacy, a knowledge of canonical texts of Islamic law, and some command of Arabic. Successful completion of the madrasa opened up various possibilities of employment in the legal-administrative nexus of power. A madrasa education was necessary to

42. Ayni, *Yāddāshthā*, 161–162.

43. Ibid.; see also F. M. Kerenskii, "Medrese Turkestanskogo kraia," *ZhMNP* 284 (1892): 45–47.

44. Several travelers of the early nineteenth century state that large portions of government revenue from *zakāt* and customs were earmarked for support of madrasas and their students and teachers: Meer Izzut-oollah, *Travels in Central Asia in the Years 1812–13*, trans. P. D. Henderson (Calcutta, 1872), 58; Georges de Meyendorff, *Voyage d'Orenbourg à Boukhara fait en 1820* (Paris, 1826), 301; Alexander Burns, *Travels into Bukhara, together with a Narrative of a Voyage on the Indus*, vol. 1 (London, 1834), 306.

45. On the *dehyak* and its corruptions, see Ayni, *Yāddāshthā*, 774–779.

work as *mufti* (jurisconsult), *qāzi* (judge), or mudarris, and truly emi-
nent figures could hold several positions at the same time.

The madrasa was not concerned with other fields of knowledge, or,
indeed, with the nonlegal aspects of Islam. We know little about Sufism
in nineteenth-century Central Asia, but it is clear that most adult men
had a spiritual guide (*shaykh, ishān, pir*). However, the madrasas were
not involved in the initiation and learning of Sufi practices, which took
place in the *khānqāh*. This was true even when many mudarrises seem
to have been Sufi adepts and many ishāns possessed madrasa knowledge. A rough survey commissioned by a Russian administrator at the
end of the nineteenth century in Tashkent revealed that a number of ishāns
in Syr Darya oblast had attended madrasas in Bukhara.[46] Far from being
mutually exclusive, *shariat* and *tariqat* were often paired as sources of
proper conduct and understanding in Central Asian Islam; they remained
parallel phenomena entrenched in different social spaces. Similarly, while
many mudarrisses as well as students wrote poetry, as befitted any cultivated individual, poetry itself was not a subject of study in the madrasa.
Instead, poets gathered in literary circles to write and study poetry.
Princely courts patronized many such circles, but they also existed au-
tonomously.[47] The madrasas were not concerned with teaching literature or poetry.

Attendance at lectures was open, as Ayni remarked sourly, to "anyone who, having finished the maktab, was seized by the desire to 'become
a mulla' . . . whether he be literate, semiliterate, or completely illiterate."[48] But opportunities were not equal to all: The initial investment of
traveling to the madrasa, setting up house there, and providing the
iftitāhāna for the mudarris was considerable and thwarted many aspir-
ing students. Thereafter, the rate of attrition was high, as many students
struggled to make ends meet. Ayni tells of the various jobs he held in order to pay for his keep, from cooking for a circle of his brother's friends,
to working as a *mirzā* (clerk) for a merchant, to tutoring wealthy fellow
students. The school year, lasting from September to March, was short,
allowing students to work productively in the summer. Indeed, many stu-

46. I. Geier, "Ishany," *Sbornik materialov dlia statistiki Syr-Dar'inskoi oblasti,* 1
(1894): 70.
47. Ayni, in his *Yāddāshthā*, describes such literary activity at length. According to
A. Abibov, *Doirahoi adabii Bukhoroi sharqî* (Dushanbe, 1984), at the turn of the twentieth century, literary circles existed in such provincial towns as Hisār, Kulāb, Qarātegin,
and Darwāz.
48. Ayni, *Yāddāshthā*, 163.

dents left Bukhara for their villages in October to gather the harvest.[49] At the same time, sons of ulama began madrasa education with a distinct advantage in cultural capital, and wealthy students could always hire others to tutor them. Ayni came from a poor family but possessed cultural capital, for his father was literate and concerned with poetry and letters. Once in Bukhara, the patronage extended to him by Sharifjān Makhdum, scion of a notable Bukharan family, was crucial in ensuring that Ayni complete his education.

The madrasa did not only reproduce the learned elite, it also reproduced a certain understanding of Islam. The description above of the texts around which madrasa education centered in Bukhara is revealing. Students did not study the Qur'an and its exegesis, the traditions of the Prophet, or even jurisprudence, although they could do so if they could find a teacher willing to give them private lessons. Rather, instruction revolved around commentaries and supercommentaries, some of post-Timurid provenance. Moreover, students studied a given text (usually itself a commentary) individually or with a khalifa; the mudarris lectured on a commentary. Students aimed at expertise in the interpretation of the texts that connected them to the Islamic tradition as it was understood in Central Asia. "Islam" did not reside in certain scriptures that spoke for themselves; rather it was embedded in the social practices of transmission and interpretation, from which it could not be abstracted. Much the same process was evident even among the ulama, for whom access to the Islamic tradition lay through layers of authoritative interpretation and commentary carried out locally. This Islam was consequently not scripturally "pure." Motivated by a new vision of the world, latter-day critics such as the Jadids were to take the ulama to task on this account as they set about purifying Islam; but their critique arose from assumptions that were inconceivable in the nineteenth century.

The parallels between the madrasa, the craft guild, and the Sufi order point to the madrasa's place in society. The transmission of knowledge was embedded in everyday social practices and consequently diffused throughout society. The madrasa was one institution among many, transmitting one kind of knowledge among many. It was imbricated in the social reproduction of the learned elite and their social distinction, and it could not have been otherwise in the absence of the disciplinary apparatus of the modern state. The logic of cultural reproduction that

49. Ibid., 165–166.

underlay the madrasa accorded very well, however, with the vastly de-
centralized political and social order in which it existed.

STATE, SOCIETY, AND KNOWLEDGE

The political order of nineteenth-century Central Asia carried the legacy
of the decentralization of the preceding centuries. Shaybāni Khān's conquest of Transoxiana created a confederation of tribes that shared in the
sovereignty of the Chinggisid khan, to whom they paid nominal allegiance. This was formalized in the division of the realm into a number
of "appanages," usually centered on a town, which were the loci of real
political power. The authority of the khan, for all its aura of Chinggisid
descent, remained tenuous, since a number of potential Chinggisid rulers
existed at any given time. The resulting decentralization of effective political power meant that even revenue extraction and local administration
were the domain of appanage holders, in contrast to the unitary, hierarchical bureaucracies of the Mughal and (especially) the Ottoman empires of the same time.[50] The khan's authority included the customary
prerogatives to mint coinage, to have his name recited during the *khutba*
(sermon at the Friday prayer), and to receive tribute from the appanages.
Individual khans could attempt to assert their authority more fully, but
the tribes possessed enough power to thwart such attempts. This decentralization led to the secession of Khwārazm from the Shaybanid domains in the middle of the sixteenth century, but elsewhere, too, political
authority remained fragile and deeply contested. In the early eighteenth
century, decentralization reached such an extreme that the authority of
Abulfayz Khān, ruler of Bukhara, came to be limited to his fortified
palace. Some of the reasons were, to be sure, external; the expansion of
the Jungar empire in Inner Asia set in motion one last wave of nomadic
migration across the Eurasian plain, which resulted in the invasion of
Transoxiana by Qazaq tribes from the Qipchaq steppe, who united with
disaffected Ozbek tribes against the khan in Bukhara. The impact was
felt by the entire sedentary population of the area; an Indian Muslim
traveler to Central Asia in 1812 heard accounts of how Samarqand "had
fallen into such utter ruin and decay, that tigers and wolves had actually
taken up abode in the colleges . . . which are situated in the centre of the

50. R. D. McChesney, *Waqf in Central Asia: Four Hundred Years in the History of a
Muslim Shrine, 1480–1889* (Princeton, 1992), 59–60.

city."[51] Balkh and Ferghana seceded from even nominal allegiance to the Bukharan khan at this time. The unrelated invasion of Nādir Shāh Afshār, fresh from his sack of Delhi, sounded the death knell of the Ashtarkhanid dynasty in Bukhara itself, where a power struggle ensued for the right to nominate the ruler, in which the Manghit beat out the Keneges, even though the latter had better Chinggisid credentials.

It took members of the new dynasty much of the rest of the century to assert their authority over other tribes. Beginning with Shāh Murād, however, the rulers of Bukhara (who had taken the title *amir*) began a struggle against the power of the tribes that was to continue until the Russian conquest. Shāh Murād's reign was characterized by constant warfare with Ozbek tribes in Transoxiana as well as Türkmen tribes who inhabited the desert between his domains and Iran, but it was only under Nasrullah (r. 1826–1860), who gained notoriety in Britain for his execution of two British officers, but who also won from his subjects the epithet *amir-i qassāb* (the Butcher Amir), that the power of the tribal chiefs was broken.[52] Similar developments took place in Ferghana, where over the course of the eighteenth century the Ming khans consolidated their hold as independent rulers. By the turn of the nineteenth century they had captured Tashkent, where urban notables had managed to retain a considerable amount of degree of autonomy under nominal Qazaq rule for much of the eighteenth century. At the same time, the new dynasty made inroads against Qazaq tribes on the steppe in the north. The city of Kokand saw considerable public construction during this period, and the court of Umar Khan (r. 1800–1820) became the center of a minor cultural renascence.[53]

The reasons behind this trend toward the greater assertion of power by rulers remain to be explored fully. It may have been rooted in an attempt to control increasing trade with both India and Russia,[54] but it was also connected with the gradual sedenterization of large parts of the population over the course of the previous century. Nevertheless, centralization had its limits: The struggle against the tribes was not moti-

51. Izzut-oollah, *Travels*, 56. A later Bukharan chronicler recorded that only two quarters of the city remained inhabited during this period; cf. Yuri Bregel, "Bukhara: III," *Encyclopædia Iranica*, IV: 518.

52. Bregel, "Bukhara: III," 518.

53. Susanna S. Nettleton, "Ruler, Patron, Poet: ʿUmar Khan and the Blossoming of the Khanate of Qoqan, 1800–1820," *International Journal of Turkish Studies* 2:2 (1981–82): 127–140.

54. A. Z. V. Togan, *Bugünkü Türkili (Türkistan) ve Yakın Tarihi,* 2nd ed. (Istanbul, 1981), 212.

vated by any new notions of sovereignty, and it was not entrenched in new
forms of organization or control. In both Bukhara and Kokand, rulers
countered the influence of the tribal elites not by the creation of centralized institutions of government but by promoting to high positions persons (usually Iranian or Qalmuq slaves) personally beholden to them.
Shāh Murād had begun his career by having the *qushbegi* (the highest
state functionary, responsible for the treasury) and the chief *qāzi* of Bukhara murdered on accusations of corruption and oppression while his
father still ruled.[55] The only institutional development connected with
the attempted centralization was the establishment of standing armies
(*sarbāz*) in both Bukhara and Kokand, although their size remained
small.[56] Indeed, the political situation seemed anything but centralized
to our Indian traveler, who enumerated eight major rulers in the region.[57]
Shahr-i Sabz remained a Keneges stronghold in Bukhara down to the
Russian conquest, its rulers (*hākims*) inheriting their authority from
each other while maintaining the legal fiction of vassaldom to the amir
at Bukhara,[58] and the ascendance of urban power in Kokand proved
short-lived, as Qipchaq chiefs successfully reasserted their power in the
1840s and all but overthrew the Ming khan.[59]

Sovereignty was embedded in several levels of obedience and allegiance; it was exercised not through institutionalized means of domi-
nance but rather through a series of personal bonds. A centralized bureaucracy existed in only the most rudimentary form, and then it revolved
around the treasury (*diwān*). Soviet scholarship was fond of recon-
structing stable structures in the khanates of this period,[60] but it is cru-

---

55. Abdulkarīm Bukhārī, *Histoire de l'Asie centrale,* ed. and trans. Charles Schefer
(Paris, 1876 [ms. 1818]), 54–55 (text), 123–125 (trans.); Ahmad Makhdum Dānish,
Traktat Akhmada Donisha "Istoriia Mangytskoi dinastii," ed. and trans. I. A. Nadzhafova (Dushanbe, 1967 [ms. ca. 1890]) 29–30; *Istoriia Uzbekistana,* vol. 3 (Tashkent,
1993), 152.

56. N. Khanykov, *Bokhara: Its Amír and its People,* trans. Clement A. de Bode (London, 1845 [orig. 1842]), 87, reported "500 regular troops of Bokhara." A. Madzhlisov,
Agrarnye otnosheniia v vostochnoi Bukhare v XIX–nachale XX veka (Dushanbe, 1967),
38, puts the number at 800. The statement in the recent *Istoriia Uzbekistana,* III: 158, that
the *sarbāz* numbered 40,000, is without foundation.

57. Izzut-oollah, *Travels,* 60–61.

58. T. K. Beisembiev, "Unknown Dynasty: The Rulers of Shahrisabz in the 18th and
19th Centuries," *Journal of Central Asia* 15, no. 1 (1992): 20–22.

59. T. K. Beisembiev, *"Ta'rikh-i Shakhrukhi" kak istoricheskii istochnik* (Alma-Ata,
1987), 22, 76–77.

60. A. A. Semenov, *Ocherk ustroistva tsentral'nogo administrativnogo upravleniia
Bukharskogo khanstva pozdneishego vremeni* (Dushanbe, 1954); N. A. Kisliakov, *Patriarkhal'no-feodal'nye otnosheniia sredi osedlogo sel'skogo naseleniia Bukharskogo

cial to realize the informality of power in the nineteenth century. Ranks and titles were granted by rulers as markers of status and authority, but they did not correspond to stable offices, which did not exist. The conduct of the state could not be abstracted from the practice of social elites, which in turn did not have access to formal institutions. This pattern of personal, face-to-face relationships was replicated at all levels of society, including the realm of cultural reproduction.

Social bonds and the activities that depended on them (trade, irrigation, cultural reproduction) survived the political instability and nearly constant warfare precisely because the state was not a significant node of social solidarity. Social solidarities were enmeshed in a series of bonds that created numerous localized, often cross-cutting allegiances defined in sedentary society by residential, professional, and genealogical bonds. The urban neighborhood (*guzar, mahalla*), formed around a mosque and a holy site (*ziyārat,* usually a tomb [*mazār*]), was the locus of close ties of mutual assistance. The neighborhood community was territorial and brought together people of various standings; the more notable residents were expected to support and protect their neighbors.[61] The neighborhood community coexisted with craft guilds, each of which involved membership in a series of hierarchical relations headed by an elder.[62] These hierarchies replicated in society the multilayered pattern of political power outlined above and provided a means for the mediation of relations between rulers and the ruled.

These hierarchies rested on differentials of wealth and status and existed because they were widely recognized as "natural." The maintenance and reproduction of this notability was crucial to the social survival of the notables (and of the social order as constituted). Notability could reside in a number of sources, among which wealth was one.

khanstva v kontse XIX–nachale XX veka (Moscow, 1962), 42–63; Madzhlisov, *Agrarnye otnosheniia,* 20–70.

61. O. A. Sukhareva, *Kvartal'naia obshchina pozdnefeodal'nogo goroda Bukhary* (Moscow, 1976).

62. On the guilds of Central Asia, see M. Gavrilov, "O remeslennykh tsekhakh Srednei Azii i ikh statutakh—risolia," *Izvestiia sredne-aziatskogo Komiteta po delam muzeev i okhrany pamiatnikov stariny, iskusstva i prirody,* 3 (1928): 235–236, Tashkent; O. A. Sukhareva, *Pozdnefeodal'nyi gorod Bukhara kontsa XIX–nachala XX veka: remeslennaia promyshlennost'* (Tashkent, 1962) on Bukhara; R. G. Mukminova, "Remeslennye korporatsii i uchinichestvo," on Samarqand; I. Dzhabbarov, "Ob uchinichestve v remeslennykh tsekhakh Srednei Azii v kontse XIX i nachale XX v.," in *Materialy vtorogo soveshchaniia arkheologov i etnografov Srednei Azii* (Moscow, 1959), on Khorezm; E. M. Peshchereva, *Remeslennye organizatsii Srednei Azii v kontse XIX i nachale XX v.* (Moscow, 1960).

Substantial merchants (*sawdāga*r) could enjoy influence in society and
entrée at court. Equally important, though, were other less tangible at-
tributes, such as claims to august lineage, the possession of sacred knowledge, or a reputation for piety or civility. For the most part, the various
claims to notability were compatible and mutually reinforcing: merchants could acquire a reputation for piety through patronage of the
learned or construction of pious sites, and the learned and the pious
could (and did) accumulate considerable wealth. More broadly, knowledge and commonly decipherable codes of civilized behavior served as
significant markers of status, whose cultivation in succeeding generations was crucial to the social reproduction of distinction that underlay
the social order of nineteenth-century Central Asia. The maktab and (especially) the madrasa were significant channels for the production and
reproduction of such social distinction.

The mediated nature of political power meant that the domain of law
existed in the interpretive practice of legal experts at some remove from
the power of the state. While appointments to the various offices of law
were often made by the ruler, the prestige and authority of judges and
jurisconsults was largely defined by peer groups. The decision of a qāzi
carried authority not because he was a functionary of the state but because of his reputation for piety and the knowledge he possessed. This
was symbolized by the seals used by qāzis, which carried the name of the
qāzi and a ritual phrase in Arabic and nothing else. Madrasa education
was an instrument for the reproduction of the social distinction and social position of the ulama as a group.

Social distinction did not automatically translate into political power,
however. The relationship between the rulers and the ulama was dynamic. In times of weakness for the state, the ulama could exercise power
in their own right. In fifteenth-century Samarqand, Khoja Ahrār played
a very significant role in the social and political life of the city,[63] and the
Juybāri khojas in Bukhara accumulated vast wealth and political influence in Bukhara in the Shaybānid period.[64] In Tashkent, the ulama ruled
in their own right for much of the eighteenth century.[65] At other times,
rulers honored the ulama and placed them in places of high influence,

63. Jürgen Paul, "Forming a Faction: The *Himāyat* System of Khwaja Ahrar," *Inter-national Journal of Middle East Studies* 23 (1991): 533–548.

64. P. P. Ivanov, *Khoziaistvo dzhuibarskikh sheikhov: k istorii feodal'nogo zemle-vladeniia v Srednei Azii v XVI–XVII vv.* (Moscow, 1954).

65. O. D. Chekhovich, "Gorodskoe samoupravlenie v Tashkente XVIII v.," in *Istoriia i kul'tura narodov Srednei Azii (drevnost' i srednie veka)* (Moscow, 1976), 149–160.

granting them tax exemptions as well as control of substantial endowed (*waqf*) property and patronizing madrasas and *khānqāh*s.[66] The Manghit amirs Shāh Murād and Mir Haydar seem to have formed especially strong alliances with them. Several ranks among the ulama came to be reserved for Sayyid Atā'i and Juybari Khojas. Shāh Murād had apparently been under the influence of a shaykh before ascending the throne, and his murders of the *qushbegi* and the qāzi of Bukhara were prompted, it was claimed, by his dismay as much at their moral turpitude in smoking water pipes, then a new habit in Bukhara, as at their propensity for oppression. Mir Haydar, described by a contemporary as having the temperament of a scholar (*mullā tabī'at*), spent a great deal of his time in learned discussions with the ulama (although that did not prevent him from also being enamored of women [*zan dost*] and contracting a great many marriages).[67] Both were generous in their support of the ulama, and as a result both acquired excellent reputations with chroniclers. In both Bukhara and Kokand, intermarriage between the ruling dynasties and leading Sufi families was widespread during the first half of the nineteenth century.[68]

But such deference or alliance did not come automatically. We are told that Alim Qul, khan of Kokand (r. 1800–1810) "did not believe in Sufis and shaykhs." Abdulkarim Bukhāri relates the unpleasant experience at his hands of a shaykh who claimed to possess miracles:

One day, seated by a pond, Alim Qul ordered a rope to be flung across it, and then asked for the said shaykh to be presented to him. The shaykh appeared along with a few disciples. Alim Qul said, "O Shaykh! Tomorrow, on the day of resurrection, you will lead your disciples across the bridge of Sirāt over the fires of hell. Today, why don't you cross this rope, so that I may witness one of your miracles." The shaykh began to preach admonitions and to recite hadith and the Qur'an, but the khan was inflexible and ordered him to walk the rope at once. No sooner did the shaykh step on the rope than he slipped and fell into the pond. Blows rained down on him from all sides until he died.

66. A. L. Troitskaia, *Katalog arkhiva kokandskikh khanov XIX veka* (Moscow, 1968); M. A. Abduraimov, *Ocherki agrarnykh otnoshenii v Bukharskom khanstve*, 2 vols. (Tashkent, 1970), II: 28–52.

67. Bukhāri, *Histoire*, 76 (text), 169–170 (trans.); Mir Haydar's reputation for piety was also noted by all contemporary travelers.

68. Beisembiev, "Dukhovenstvo v politicheskoi zhizni Kokandskogo khanstva v XVIII–XIX vekakh," in *Dukhovenstvo i politicheskaia zhizn' na Blizhnem i Srednem Vostoke v period feodalizma* (Moscow, 1985), 37–46; Khanykov, *Bokhara*, 246; M. Abduraimov, *Voprosy feodal'nogo zemlevladeniia i feodal'noi renty v pis'makh Emira Khaidara* (Tashkent, 1961), 7–8; *Istoriia Uzbekistana*, III: 338–343.

[After that,] wherever [Alim Qul] saw a dervish or a man attired in Sufi robes [*khirqa-pūsh*], he had him arrested and turned into a camel driver.[69]

In such cases, kingship was its own justification. As Devin DeWeese has recently shown us, popular understandings of Islam in post-Mongol Central Asia fully assimilated myths of conversion to Islam with the very origin of the community itself, which was often defined in terms of rulership.[70] Dynasts also claimed august lineages that tied them, through an Islamizing figure, to both the Prophet (through ʿAlī) and Chinggis Khan, and these claims were constantly renewed through intermarriage with saintly families.

Thus the prestige of scholars of Muslim law did not mean that the states of Central Asia were theocratic or governed by an immutable Islamic law. The ideal was considerably different. Ruing the demise of the old order, Ahmad Makhdum Dānish, a disaffected Bukharan courtier writing in the 1890s, recalled the days when the world was right side up. During the reign of Shāh Murād, the son of an *ākhund* killed a shopkeeper who was rude to him. The victim's father petitioned the amir for justice, but the amir was so outraged by the temerity of the victim that he imposed a fine on the father instead, exclaiming that if the victim had not been killed, he would have had him thrown from the Minār-i Kalān. "It is clear from the aforesaid," Dānish concluded, "how knowledge and its servants were in ascendance at that time, and how strong were the opinions of the ulama and the rulers."[71] Shariat was honored because its carriers were honored.

As long as the old order continued to exist on its own terms, the madrasa made perfect sense and served crucial purposes in reproducing knowledge and the social order. The demise of the old order, however, cast everything in doubt.

THE LUXURY OF ISOLATION

Madrasas continued to be built and endowed and manuscripts continued to be written in the nineteenth century. If anything, the first half of the nineteenth century was a period of cultural florescence: A majority of

69. Bukhāri, *Histoire*, 94–95 (text), 211–212 (trans.).
70. Devin DeWeese, *Islamization and Native Religion in the Golden Horde: Baba Tükles and Conversion to Islam in Historical and Epic Tradition* (University Park, Penn., 1994).
71. Dānish, *Traktat*, 30–32.

the madrasas in existence in Tashkent and Kokand in the first years of
Russian rule had been built in the nineteenth century.[72] The khans of both
Kokand and Khiva cultivated vast literary circles that produced numerous works of poetry and history.[73] Yet, this florescence was highly traditionalist, the central preoccupation being with writing poetry on the
models of Timurid or earlier poets and writing commentaries on existing works. Central Asia's isolation contributed to this conservatism of
local cultural practices and tastes. The shift of world trade routes from
land to sea after the fifteenth century marginalized the economy of Central Asia; the political dislocation of the eighteenth century added to
it.[74] As a result, Central Asia was little affected by the globalization of the
world economy taking place in those centuries, which greatly affected
other Muslim lands. The low levels of technicalization that obtained in
Central Asia until the Russian conquest provide a measure of this isolation from the world economy.

The picture of Central Asian isolation can be overdrawn, to be sure.
In the nineteenth century, Central Asian merchants conducted a vigorous
trade with Russia, Afghanistan, India, and China. The reach of Indian
trade was considerable. As Stephen Dale has recently demonstrated, an
Indian world economy encompassed much of Eurasia in the early modern period.[75] Although its heyday was over by the nineteenth century,
trade was still sizable. In July 1826, an Indian merchant arrived in Orenburg with a cargo of gold and silver coin, muslin, and silk brocades.[76]
Khanykov reported in 1842 that the volume of trade with Afghanistan
and India averaged 3,000–5,000 camel loads annually.[77] A substantial
population of Indian merchants resided in the principal cities of Central
Asia, where they enjoyed a near monopoly over moneylending.[78] Cen-

---

72. N. P. Ostroumov, "Madrasy v Turkestanskom krae," *ZhMNP*, n.s., 7, (1907): otd.
nar. obr., 7–12; A. B. Vil'danova, "O sostoianii nauki v sredneaziatskikh gorodakh XVI–
pervoi poloviny XIX veka," *Obshchestvennye nauki v Uzbekistane*, 1989, no. 7: 32–36.

73. Umar Khan of Kokand and Rahim Khan of Khiva (r. 1864–1910) were both celebrated patrons and poets in their own right. For notices on the works of members of their
court circles, see H. F. Hofman, *Turkish Literature: A Bio-Bibliographical Survey*, 6 vols.
(Utrecht, 1969), II: 87–90, IV: 144; see also Nettleton, "Ruler, Patron, Poet."

74. This latter point is made by Morris Rossabi, "The 'Decline' of the Central Asian
Caravan Trade," in James D. Tracy, ed., *The Rise of the Merchant Empires: Long-Distance
Trade in the Early Modern Period, 1350–1750* (Cambridge, 1990).

75. Stephen Frederic Dale, *Indian Merchants and Eurasian Trade, 1600–1750* (Cambridge, 1994).

76. G. A. Mikhaleva, *Uzbekistan v XVIII–pervoi polovine XIX veka: remeslo, torgovlia i poshliny* (Tashkent, 1991), 74.

77. Khanykov, *Bokhara*, 221–228.

78. Meyendorff, *Voyage*, 176.

tral Asia still served as an entrepôt for trade between Russia and China, and merchants from Ferghana had acquired a dominant commercial position in Eastern Turkestan, where in 1826 Madali Khan obtained the right to levy taxes in Altï Shahr.[79] But the most extensive trade was with Russia, whose goods had come to dominate the Central Asian market well before the Russian conquest. Arminius Vámbéry, who traveled in Central Asia in 1863, wrote, "It is by no means any exaggeration to assert that there is no house, and even no tent, in all Central Asia, where there is not some article of Russian manufacture."[80] This trade was carried on through annual caravans that braved nomad territory on the way to Orenburg and beyond. Orenburg, founded in 1742, had a Bukharan colony, and Bukharan merchants had been allowed to trade at the Makariev fair (which later moved to Nizhnii Novgorod) since 1807.[81] The return trade was in the hands of Tatars, however, and few Russians set foot in Central Asia.

There was also considerable circulation of people. The ulama retained contacts with India. In 1842, Kokand's embassy to St. Petersburg was headed by one Sāhibzāda Miān Fazl Khalil, a Sirhindi Sufi from Peshawar. His cousin headed the Naqshbandi order in Kokand from his arrival there in 1826 until his death in 1869.[82] Those who could also traveled to Arabia for the hajj, although a Kokand notable found that it took him seven years to make the trip in the 1820s.[83] Similarly, the incipient modernization of the armies in the khanates was made possible largely by imported soldiers. Iranian soldiers, many of them slaves captured in war or by Türkmen tribes, provided most of the manpower for

79. Tōru Saguchi, "The Eastern Trade of the Khoqand Khanate," *Memoirs of the Research Department of the Toyo Bunko*, no. 24 (1965): 82–89; Joseph Fletcher, "The Heydey of the Ch'ing Order in Mongolia, Sinkiang and Tibet," in John K. Fairbank, ed., *Cambridge History of China*, vol. 10 (Cambridge, 1978), 360–395.

80. Arminius Vámbéry, *Travels in Central Asia* (London, 1864), 475–476; for an earlier expression of the same phenomenon, see Mohan Lal, *Travels in the Panjab, Afghanistan, and Turkistan* (London, 1846), 142. There is a considerable literature on trade relations between Russia and Central Asia; see M. K. Rozhkova, *Ekonomicheskie sviazi Rossii so Srednei Aziei (40–60 gody XIX veka)* (Moscow, 1963); G. A. Mikhaleva, *Torgovye i diplomaticheskie sviazi Rossii so sredneaziatskimi khanstvami cherez Orenburg* (Tashkent, 1982); Kh. Z. Ziiaev, *Ekonomicheskie sviazi Srednei Azii s Sibir'iu v XVI–XIX vv.* (Tashkent, 1983).

81. Mikhaleva, *Torgovye i posol'skie sviazi*, 22–27.

82. T. K. Beisembiev, "Farghana's Contacts with India in the 18th and 19th Centuries," *Journal of Asian History* 23 (1994): 126–128.

83. W. H. Wathen, "Note of a Pilgrimage Undertaken by an Úsbek and His Two Sons from Khokend or Kokan, in Tartary, through Russia, &c. to Mecca," *Journal of the Asiatic Society of Bengal* 3 (1834): 379–382.

the newly organized standing armies.[84] Similarly, several Indian Muslims with experience in the armies of the East India Company served in Kokand, one of them rising to be governor of Tashkent for several years.[85] The maverick British traveler John Wolff was "most agreeably surprised" when a band of soldiers in Bukhara played "God Save the Queen" for him one evening in Bukhara in 1844.[86] Three decades later, the American diplomat Eugene Schuyler, visiting Kokand on the eve of its final annexation, found local troops being drilled with a mixture of English and Russian commands, many of them seemingly fully nativized into local Turkic.[87]

Nevertheless, this reorganization of armies was directed primarily at regional struggles. The khanates of Central Asia were surrounded by deserts inhabited by nomadic tribes, and the concerns of rulers continued to focus on the shifting calculus of power involving neighboring khanates and the nomads; relations with outside powers, always sporadic because of the distances involved, were seen through the prism of local rivalries. The khans of Kokand had paid tribute to the Qing dynasty since the 1750s, but this relationship remained largely nominal. To the extent that the khans dealt largely with *amban*s in Kashgar (over the years, only eight Kokand missions were allowed to visit Beijing), this relationship too remained a regional one.[88] Russia was the only external power to have any significant presence in this regional theater of diplomacy, although as long as the steppe remained beyond Russian control, its power to act was limited. Successive embassies traveled to St. Petersburg over the course of the eighteenth and nineteenth centuries, and a smaller number of Russian missions paid visits to Central Asia capitals.

The Ottomans maintained sporadic diplomatic contact, although again the vast distances separating the two realms made it impossible for either side to give these relations any substance. The Ottomans initiated relations with Bukhara in the aftermath of the treaty of Küçük Kaynarca, in the hope of opening a second front against Russia. The pious Shāh Murād was distinctly unenthusiastic about the cause, informing the Otto-

84. Khanykov, *Bokhara*, 87; Vámbéry, *Travels*, 225–227; Semenov, *Ocherk ustroistva*, 59.

85. Beisembiev, "Farghana's Contacts with India," 126.

86. Joseph Wolff, *Narrative of a Mission to Bokhara, in the Years 1843–1845, to Ascertain the Fate of Colonel Stoddart and Captain Conolly*, vol. 1 (London, 1845), 351–352.

87. Schuyler, *Turkistan*, II: 15–16.

88. Saguchi, "Eastern Trade," 49–52. According to Abdulkarim Bukhāri, the Chinese emperor had granted Alim Qul a pension (*'alūfa*) in return for making sure that the sons of Sarimsaq Khoja, the last ruler of Kashgar, did not cross Kokand territory to attack their father's lost domains; see Bukhāri, *Histoire*, 96 (text), 217–218 (trans.).

man envoy Alemdar Mehmed Said Ağa that it was "impossible to wage war on a power such as Moscow without cannon and armor," but asking instead for help against "our real enemy . . . Iran and the Rāfizis [Shi'is]."[89] In the ensuing decades, rulers of the three khanates sent a steady succession of envoys to Istanbul, seeking help in religious as well as military matters. Yet it was clear to the Porte that even when Central Asian rulers offered to swear allegiance (bi'at) to the sultan as caliph (as the rulers of both Bukhara and Khiva did in the 1810s), it was in the hope of gaining symbolic supremacy in local struggles rather than with the intent of subordinating their sovereignty to that of the sultan.[90]

The same distances that isolated Central Asia also provided its rulers with a certain comfort and safety from colonial intrusion. Unlike the Muslim states of the Mediterranean, the khanates of Central Asia did not feel directly the military threat of modern powers until the middle of the nineteenth century. Central Asia's neighbors had similar levels of technology and did not therefore mount a significant challenge to its external security. No direct challenge arose from foreign powers until the 1830s, when expanding spheres of British and Russian influence threatened Central Asia. Even when this isolation was broken, the low level of institutionalization in the Central Asian khanates meant that the intensive reform from the top experienced by the Ottoman empire or Egypt could not take place in Central Asia. The result was a measure of freedom in isolation that was available to few other Muslim states in this period. The relative security of obscurity allowed the Islamic tradition unquestioned domination in Central Asian intellectual life. The Russian conquest, so rude in its abruptness, ended this isolation and put Central Asia and its civilization in a completely different situation.

89. Mehmet Saray, *Rus İşgali Devrinde Osmanlı Devleti ile Türkistan Hanlıkları arasındaki Siyasi Münasebetler (1775–1875)* (Istanbul, 1990), 21.
90. Ibid., 28–53.

CHAPTER 2

The Making
of a Colonial Society

THE RUSSIAN CONQUEST

The gradual subjugation of the Bashkir and Qazaq steppe by the Russian state over the preceding century and a half had brought Russia into geographical contiguity with the khanates of Central Asia by the middle of the nineteenth century. In the confrontation that followed, the technological and organizational superiority of Russian forces proved to be its own justification for conquest, which was accomplished with great ease and rapidity. Although the motivation behind the Russian expansion has been a matter of much debate, it seems quite clear that the initiatives of willful and ambitious generals played significant and irreversible roles in the conquest of Central Asia.[1]

---

1. Soviet historiography long focused on the economic impulse behind Russian expansion, asserting, not entirely convincingly, the necessity of a nascent bourgeoisie in Russia to find new markets. See the classic statement in N. A. Khalfin, *Prisoedinenie Srednei Azii k Rossii (60–90-e gody XIX v.)* (Moscow, 1965). Much of Western historiography of Russian expansion into Central Asia, in positing a calculated Russian advance against India, is still hostage to the nineteenth-century British understanding of it; for a recent vulgarization of this theme, see Peter Hopkirk, *The Great Game* (London, 1990). The assumption of a grand strategy behind Russian expansion has been questioned, quite convincingly in my opinion, by David MacKenzie, "Expansion in Central Asia: St. Petersburg vs. the Turkestan Generals (1863–1866)," *Canadian Slavic Studies* 3 (1969): 286–311; and Peter Morris, "The Russians in Central Asia, 1870–1887," *Slavonic and East European Review* 53 (1975): 521–538.

Russia's first territorial acquisition at the expense of a khanate came in 1853, when Russian forces under the command of General V. A. Perovskii took the Kokand fortress of Āq Masjid to complete the Orenburg line of frontier fortifications. Further action was stalled for a decade, when the decision was made to connect the Orenburg and Siberian lines. The resulting advance led to the conquest of the towns, nominally under Kokand rule, of Turkestan (Yasi) and Awliya Ata, and it finally enclosed the Qazaq steppe behind Russian lines. This was, however, only the beginning of bigger things. The following spring, M. G. Cherniaev, promoted to the rank of major general for his recent exploits, marched on Tashkent and conquered it against the express wishes of his superiors in St. Petersburg. Cherniaev's actions in Tashkent set the pattern for Russia's military activity in Central Asia over the next two decades, as military men repeatedly presented *faits accomplis* to imperial authorities. Military action took place in remote, barely known areas, which left imperial authorities with no ability to monitor the actions of men on the spot, for whom the militarily weak khanates represented an easy source of military glory.[2]

Cherniaev was decorated and the territories conquered by him retained. War thus came to Bukhara. Amir Muzaffar showed little enthusiasm for taking on the Russians, preferring to continue his campaign against Kokand, but he was surprised by his own population. In early 1866, with the Russians at Jizzakh, the ulama of Bukhara led a vast throng to the amir's palace demanding the declaration of war.[3] A similar uprising took place in Samarqand. The amir was forced to fight, but the hastily assembled army, including many volunteers with no experience of war, suffered a massive defeat. The next years were a period of uncertainty. The amir sought help from outside: an embassy led by one Muhammad Pārsā traveled to India and the Ottoman empire, but to no avail.[4] Meanwhile, his troops suffered a number of defeats, which cost him the

---

2. On the Russian conquest of Central Asia, see Khalfin, *Prisoedinenie Srednei Azii;* good summaries in English are Richard N. Pierce, *Russian Central Asia, 1867–1917: A Study in Colonial Rule* (Berkeley, 1960), ch. 2; Seymour Becker, *Russia's Protectorates in Central Asia: Bukhara and Khiva, 1865–1924* (Cambridge, 1968), chs. 2–7; and Hélène Carrère d'Encausse, "Systematic Conquest, 1865–1884," in Edward Allworth, ed., *Central Asia: A Century of Russian Rule* (New York, 1967), 131–150.

3. 'Abdul 'Azīm Sāmī, *Tuhfa-yi shāhī* (ms., ca. 1899–1900), quoted by L. M. Epifanova, *Rukopis'nye istochniki Instituta Vostokovedeniia Akademii Nauk UzSSR po istorii Srednei Azii perioda prisoedineniia k Rossii* (Tashkent, 1965), 34; Ahmad Makhdum Dānish, *Traktat Akhmada Donisha "Istoriia Mangitskoi dinastii,"* ed. and trans. I. A. Nadzhafova (Dushanbe, 1967), 45ff.

4. For a description of the letter to the sultan, see Epifanova, *Rukopis'nye istochniki,* 69–70; for some Ottoman documents concerning the embassy, see *Osmanlı Devleti ile Kafkasya, Türkistan ve Kırım Hanlıkları Arasındaki Münasebetlere dâir Arşiv Belgeleri* (An-

provinces of Khujand and Samarqand. In 1868, Bukhara was forced to pay reparations and to sign a treaty formalizing the loss of territory and granting Russian merchants equal rights in the country. Similar terms were imposed by treaty on the rump khanate of Kokand.

The khanates were allowed to exist for several interconnected reasons. Authorities in St. Petersburg, especially the Ministry of Finance, showed a marked reluctance to take on the expenditure of administering new regions. There was also the need to minimize British concerns about Russian expansion, as well as an uncertainty about the ability to control a large population little known or understood by the Russians. Only the initial conquests were to be incorporated directly into the Russian empire. Yet, the very logic of military success undermined this hope. Each round of warfare resulted in the acquisition of extra territory as reparations. In 1873, a major campaign that reduced Khiva to vassal status gained considerable territory for Russia. In Kokand, Khudāyār Khān found it difficult to assert his authority over his diminished realm and in 1875 lost his throne in an uprising that rapidly turned into a movement against the Russian presence. Russian troops invaded and occupied Kokand; the protectorate was abolished and the khanate incorporated into the Russian empire. Finally, in the 1880s, the Türkmen steppe, where no khanate had managed to assert control, was conquered, often with the use of exemplary brutality (the most notable being Skobelev's massacre at Gök Tepe in 1881). Thus, at the end of the period of conquest, for all its reluctance to take on additional expense, the Russian state found itself in the possession of a vast new densely populated territory.

The 1868 treaty with Bukhara was eventually replaced in 1873 by a new, more far-reaching version that defined Bukhara's status until 1917. It made the amir "acknowledge himself to be the obedient servant of the Emperor of All the Russias." The amir also "renounce[d] the right to maintain direct and friendly relations with neighboring rulers and khans and to conclude with them any commercial or other treaties [or to] . . . undertake any military actions against them without the knowledge and permission of the supreme Russian authority in Central Asia."[5] Once he

---

kara, 1992), 133–134, 136–138; see also Muhammad Anwar Khan, *England, Russia and Central Asia (A Study in Diplomacy)* (Peshawar, 1963), 107–112; Mehmed Saray, *Rus İşgali Devrinde Osmanlı Devleti ile Türkistan Hanlıkları Arasındaki Siyasi Münasebetler* (Istanbul, 1990), 81–88.

5. For an English translation of the treaty, see Becker, *Russia's Protectorates*, 316–318 (quote on 316).

had accepted Russian suzerainty, Amir Muzaffar set about making the best of it. Through a series of adroit political maneuvers, Muzaffar and his successors carved out for themselves a position of authority that their ancestors had only dreamed of. Now, despite his military defeat, Muzaffar was installed as a ruler by the Russians, who henceforth had an interest in the security of his throne. (Nor was the defeat complete. In 1873, the Russians made the khan of Khiva cede territory on the right bank of the Amu Darya to the amir of Bukhara, whom the Russians trusted more. The amir also gained territory, with Russian blessings, in Qarātegin and Darwāz and in the Pamirs.)[6] On more than one occasion, Russian troops were deployed in Bukhara to quell disorders. Muzaffar and his successors kept on good terms with Russian elites, both in Tashkent and St. Petersburg, and backed these contacts with frequent personal gifts and public donations.[7] Domestically, Muzaffar presented himself as the most powerful surviving Muslim monarch in Central Asia. He even turned defeat into victory by claiming credit for having prevented a complete takeover by Russia.[8] He appealed to religious piety and grounded his legitimacy in his support for the "traditional" Islamic order in Bukhara. He and his successors jealously guarded against the introduction of any new institutions that might compromise their absolute power by casting all change as a *bid'at* (innovation). The nature of Bukhara's political order was transformed as a result of the protectorate, Russia's professions of nonintervention notwithstanding. With the delineation of its boundaries in the treaty, Bukhara also became, for the first time, a strictly territorial entity.

Bukhara's autonomy was further reduced in 1885, when it was included in the Russian customs boundary and a Russian "political agency" was created to conduct relations with Bukhara (which until then had been carried on through irregular emissaries). The Transcaspian Railway, built in the 1880s to connect Samarqand and Tashkent with the Caspian Sea, also cut through Bukhara. A new treaty made the railway itself and all stations along it sovereign Russian territory. The po-

6. Ibid., 90–92, 157.

7. Thus, while Amir Abdulahad stoutly refused permission for Jadid schools in his domain, he donated 52,000 rubles in the 1890s for the establishment of a Realschule (*real'noe uchilishche*) for Russian students in Tashkent. The tradition was maintained by Ālimjān (r. 1910–1920) as well. See A. Dobromyslov, *Tashkent v proshlom i nastoiashchem* (Tashkent, 1912), 227; B. Kh. Ergashev, "Iz istorii obshchestvenno-politicheskoi zhizni Bukhary nachala XX veka," *Obshchestvennye nauki v Uzbekistane*, 1992, no. 2, 49–53.

8. Hélène Carrère d'Encausse, *Réforme et révolution chez les musulmans de l'empire russe*, 2nd ed. (Paris, 1981), 86–89.

litical agency, directly inspired by the British experience of dealing with princely states in India, was located nine miles from Bukhara, in Kāgān, which in time became an important outpost of Russian Turkestan. The political agent was appointed by the governor-general of Turkestan, who could thus keep a closer eye on the amir and project Russian influence into Bukhara more easily. The Russian government periodically contemplated outright annexation of Bukhara, but for the same reasons that had militated against annexation in 1868, the amir escaped unscathed, his autocratic powers intact, until the revolution of 1920.[9]

The khan of Khiva was less successful. His realm was smaller and poorer, and the peace treaty accordingly more punitive. Over the decades, Muhammad Rahim Khān (1864–1910) and his successor were far less prominent in Russian public life, but since they could not make claims to authority like those of the amirs of Bukhara, they proved more open to reform. Their authority over their realm was less certain, however, and an uprising by nomadic tribes in 1916 led to massive Russian intervention that all but abolished the protectorate.

Yet, only the military could be wholeheartedly enthusiastic about the progress of Russian arms in the region. The Ministries of Finance and Foreign Affairs took a different view of the matter, the former worrying about the expense of administering vast new territories in a period of fiscal restraint, and the latter fearing "complications" in its relations with Britain, which saw any Russian advance as a direct threat to its occupation of India. The fears of these two ministries were reflected in the final outcome, but the military succeeded in setting the pace of conquest. Russian expansion ended when the southern boundaries of the empire were defined in a series of treaties with Britain, which thus made Russian actions subject to European international law. By that time, however, the Russian empire had acquired numerous new subjects and huge tracts of land that it ruled directly. This rule proved quite stable, at least partly because strategic considerations remained paramount in the eyes of local administrators.[10] It was also backed by large numbers of troops, usually numbering around 50,000, who were frequently deployed.[11] There

9. Becker, *Russia's Protectorates*, ch. 12.

10. David MacKenzie, "Turkestan's Significance to Russia (1850–1917)," *Russian Review* 33 (1974): 167–188, provides a nuanced view of the changing significance of Turkestan to Russia. As the discussion below of irrigation policy shows, however, strategic considerations never completely disappeared.

11. David MacKenzie, "Kaufman of Turkestan: An Assessment of His Administration," *Slavic Review* 26 (1967): 272.

were few overt challenges to Russian rule until the uprising of 1916, although a certain unease about the thinness of their authority never left the minds of the new rulers.

IMAGINING TURKESTAN

The Turkestan *krai* (region) was created in 1867 and put in the charge of a governor-general.[12] In view of the unsettled and largely unknown conditions in the area, civilian and military rule down to the uezd (district) level were placed in the same hands (although uezd administrators were relieved of military command in 1884), and the Ministry of War, rather than Internal Affairs, enjoying ultimate jurisdiction over it. The region was to be ruled by a governor-general, appointed by the tsar himself and answerable only to him. K. P. Kaufman, the first governor-general, enjoyed immense plenipotentiary powers over administration and the conduct of Russian relations with neighboring states. Given its peculiar position, Turkestan was to be governed under its own statute. The tsar promulgated a Provisional Statute in 1867, but the drafting of a permanent statute was delayed by differences between the various ministries involved, and a final version was not published until 1886. For the first two decades of Russian rule, therefore, Turkestan was governed provisionally, with everyday policy being set by Kaufman. The earliest Russian policies and practices bore the stamp of his preferences.

Central Asia's otherness was palpable to nineteenth-century Russians. As Monika Greenleaf has ably argued, since the early nineteenth century, Russian elites had sought to buttress their Europeanness through participation in the discourse of orientalism.[13] The same could be said of the discourse of imperialism. In his 1864 memorandum to Russian missions in Europe, Foreign Minister A. M. Gorchakov argued in terms of mid-century imperialism common to all Europeans: "The position of Russia in Central Asia is that of all civilized States which are brought

12. *Polnoe sobranie zakonov Rossiiskoi Imperii*, 2nd ser., vol. 42, no. 44831 (St. Petersburg, 1868). The krai initially consisted of two oblasts, viz. Syr Darya and Semirech'e; later the Samarqand and Ferghana oblasts, comprising lands annexed from Bukhara and Kokand, respectively, were added. In 1882, Semirech'e was transferred to the Steppe krai, ruled from Omsk, but returned to Turkestan in 1892, when the Transcaspian oblast, representing the last fruits of Russian expansion, was also transferred to Turkestan from the viceroyalty of Transcaucasia. Both, however, continued to be ruled under their own statutes.

13. Monika Greenleaf, *Pushkin and Romantic Fashion: Fragment, Elegy, Orient, Irony* (Stanford, 1994), 145.

into contact with half-savage, nomad populations, possessing no fixed social organization. . . . In such cases it always happens that the more civilized State is forced . . . to exercise a certain ascendancy over those whom their turbulent and unsettled character make most undesirable neighbours. . . . It is a peculiarity of Asiatics to respect nothing but visible and palpable force; the moral force of reason and of the interests of civilization has as yet no hold upon them."[14] Nor was this memorandum simply eyewash for the benefit of foreign governments. Educated Russians saw their presence in Central Asia as part of the greater European imperial expansion of the nineteenth century. The Russian intelligentsia might debate its relation to Europe, but no one doubted that Russia represented Europe in Central Asia.[15] Most Russians in Central Asia saw their goals in terms of the usual nineteenth-century imperial notions of replacing the arbitrary, "Asiatic" despotism of local rulers by good government, the pacification of the countryside, and the increase in trade and prosperity. The earliest administrators took pride in the lower levels of taxation Russian rule had brought (even, for some, at the expense of rendering Turkestan "unprofitable"). Kaufman saw the growth of trade as the key to the future prosperity of the region and spent a considerable amount of energy in organizing a biannual trade fair at Tashkent. (The experiment was less than successful and was soon abandoned.)[16]

Russia as progress stood in contrast to Central Asia as fanaticism and barbarity, much of which was seen to reside in Islam. "Fanaticism" came to be the defining characteristic of Central Asia, although precisely what it entailed could vary a great deal; its semantic range included everything from armed struggle against the Russians, through the refusal to send

14. Great Britain, Parliament, *Central Asia, No. 2 (1873): Correspondence Respecting Central Asia,* C. 704 (London, 1873), 70–75.

15. This bears emphasis for two reasons: first, current discussions of post-Soviet Russia take for granted its otherness from "Europe"; and second, the considerable literature that exists on Russian views of Asia tends to privilege those Russian authors who had more ambivalent feelings toward Europe (and consequently, toward Asia), thus overstating the prevalence of such views. See, for example, Milan Hauner, *What Is Asia to Us?* (London, 1990). In any case, as Mark Bassin ("Russia between Europe and Asia," *Slavic Review* 50 [1991]: 13) has shown, even those Russian writers who asserted Russia's difference from Europe tended nevertheless to see "the gulf separating Russia from the Occident as considerably less deep than that separating it from the Orient"; Central Asia remained a "purely Asiatic land," a colony of Russia, no matter how un-European Russia might be.

16. *TWG* was full of reports and proclamations about the trade fair in the early 1870s. The fair distinctly failed to amuse Eugene Schuyler, the American minister in St. Petersburg, who visited Central Asia in 1873; see his scathing critique in Schuyler, *Turkistan: Notes of a Journey in Russian Turkistan, Khokand, Bukhara, and Kuldja,* vol. 1 (New York, 1877), 207–212.

children to Russian schools, to abstention from alcohol. As David Edwards has pointed out, establishing the other as fanatical denies him or her moral status, since he or she exists beyond the realm of rationality, and gives those whose moral superiority is thus affirmed a free hand in defending their interests.[17] In locating the fanaticism in Islam, Kaufman and his contemporaries were part of a much broader phenomenon of nineteenth-century European thought. As European armies of conquest encountered armed resistance, often in the name of Islam and many times organized around Sufi brotherhoods, the "fanaticism" of Muslims became a commonplace in the literature of imperialism. The view of Islam as a conspiratorial religion (Sufi brotherhoods, dimly understood, were particularly suitable grist for this mill), implacably hostile to Christianity (or Europe or the West), provided a common framework for colonial administrators in Asia and Africa.[18] Russian administrators in Turkestan (some of whom were prominent orientalists) looked to the experience of the British and the French in ruling "their" Muslims, and they avidly read the works of Western European orientalists. The Russians had encountered the same phenomenon in their prolonged conquest of Daghestan, where resistance, led by Shamil, had been organized in Sufi brotherhoods. Similarly, the role of the ulama in forcing the amir of Bukhara to fight was proof to many of the implacable fanaticism aroused by Islam. This fear of Islam remained a constant component of policies toward Muslim peoples through the colonial world, although its intensity varied with the political situation. By the end of the century, the fear of traditional Islam organized in Sufi brotherhoods began to give way to a fear of Islam, fanatical as ever, but now mixed up with nationalism and modern education. Bureaucrats in Turkestan could never make up their minds as to which kind of Islam was more dangerous. Nevertheless, the fear of the conspiratorial nature of Islam rendered certain religious practices, such as the hajj, the locus of suspicion, and hence targets of control.

At the same time, in common with other Europeans, educated Russians had boundless confidence in the inherent superiority of their civilization, a belief repeated often by administrators in Turkestan. Writing

17. David B. Edwards, "Mad Mullahs and Englishmen: Discourse in the Colonial Encounter," *Comparative Studies in Society and History* 31 (1989): 31, 655.
18. Christopher Harrison, *France and Islam in West Africa, 1860–1960* (Cambridge, 1988), esp. ch. 1; R. S. O'Fahey and Brend Radtke, "Neo-Sufism Reconsidered," *Der Islam* 70 (1993): 61–64.

in the aftermath of the Andijan uprising of 1898, a group of orientalists could blandly state: "Of course, at the present time, no one doubts that Islam has had its day and that each day it nears its final collapse and decomposition. No evidence is needed to show that a renascence of the world of Islam is not possible: left to itself, it must either meet its final destruction or it will have to adopt a different culture."[19] Russian policies in Turkestan were therefore the product of a curious combination of hubris and paranoia. The superiority and ultimate victory of the civilization they represented was assured, but the natives were nevertheless prone to a fanatical hatred of it. Yet, astute exercise of power (and the utilization of expert knowledge) could ensure the perpetuation of Russian rule and even the diminution of native fanaticism. For Kaufman, policy choices were obvious: Russian authorities were to tread cautiously and leave all aspects of local life that were not of a political nature untouched, so as not to arouse the fanaticism of the natives, while setting before them the example of the superior civilization of their new rulers. The natural corollary to nonintervention was "ignoring" (*ignorirovanie*) Muslim institutions. Kaufman was critical of the treatment of religious functionaries by the earliest Russian rulers in Central Asia, who had attempted to organize them into a hierarchy that had, in his opinion, only strengthened their position.[20] His own approach was to be different: "Finding that Islam was accustomed to living in the closest association with the state and to using its power for its own purposes, the local administration realized that the best way to fight it [Islam] would be to ignore it completely. In such a situation, the state, by not allowing Islam to unite under its wing, would condemn it to a process of decay."[21] While the decay took its course, the state was to avoid at all costs inflaming the fanaticism of the local population. This approach laid the foundations for an often paradoxical administrative policy that in its broad outlines was pursued down to the end of the old regime. The policy, with its intended and unintended consequences, was of fundamental importance in the evolution of Central Asian culture during the half-century of tsarist rule.

19. V. P. Nalivkin et al., "Kratkii obzor sovremennogo sostoianiia i deiatel'nosti musul'manskogo dukhovenstva, raznogo roda dukhovnykh uchrezhdenii i uchebnykh zavedenii tuzemnogo naseleniia Samarkandskoi oblasti s nekotorymi ukazaniiami na ikh istoricheskoe proshloe," in *Materialy po musul'manstvu*, vyp. 1 (Tashkent, 1898), 21.

20. Cherniaev had reappointed the *qāzi kalān* and the *shaykh ul-Islām* of the city to their offices: N. P. Ostroumov, "Poslednie po vremeni Sheikhul'-Islam i Kazy-Kalian goroda Tashkenta, brat'ia Ai-Khodzha i Khakim-Khodzha," *Protokoly zasedanii i soobshcheniia chlenov Turkestanskogo kruzhka liubitelei arkheologii*, 20 (1914–1915): 20, 13.

21. Quoted in Beliavskii, *Materialy po Turkestanu* (St. Petersburg, 1884), 59.

No religious dignitaries were to be appointed to positions of authority, as Cherniaev had done in the aftermath of the conquest of Tashkent. Thus the positions of *qāzi kalān* and *shaykh ul-Islām* in Tashkent were abolished. On his travels around Turkestan, Kaufman often pointedly rebuffed religious dignitaries. He also kept Turkestan out of the jurisdiction of the Muslim Spiritual Administration based in Orenburg (a creation of Catherine II, who had sought to provide a bureaucratic structure for Islam to parallel the Holy Synod), since it would have meant providing an organizational structure to local Islam. Isolating Islam in Turkestan was a natural corollary to the policy of disregarding it. Even before Kaufman left St. Petersburg to take up his new appointment, he had written to the Ministry of the Interior asking for an amendment to existing passport regulations that would make it impossible for Turkestanis to obtain foreign passports for hajj without his permission.[22] Over the next three years, his chancellery worked out detailed regulations for the granting of passports to his subjects; finding that "while it is not possible to prevent this movement altogether, there is also no need to make it easy and affordable," it sought to make the practice as difficult as possible by setting high fees for applications for hajj passports.[23] In 1876, Kaufman was writing to the Minister of Education D. A. Tolstoi raising his concern about the active trade in printed Qur'ans and other religious books between Kazan and Turkestan. "Finding the dissemination of Muslim teachings by as powerful a weapon as the printed word harmful for Russian interests in Central Asia," Kaufman asked Tolstoi to take measures to limit the entry and distribution of Muslim books in Central Asia.[24] The request was impossible to implement, but it showed that even the principles of free trade so dear to Kaufman could readily be sacrificed at the altar of stability.

More significant was Kaufman's decision to make a clear distinction between the sedentary and nomadic populations of the area. The distinction had a long tradition in Russian thinking about Islam, although the relative values assigned to nomad and sedentary differed over time. As late as 1864, Gorchakov had presented the nomads as the problem ("half-savage . . . populations, possessing no fixed social organization") and foreseen stable neighborly relations with the "more civilized" seden-

22. Kaufman to A. A. Lobanov-Rostovskii, 22 July 1867, TsGARUz, f. 1, op. 11, d. 1, ll. 1–2.

23. "O poriadke vydachi zagranichnykh pasportov" (February 1870), TsGARUz, f. 1, op. 11, d. 1, ll. 46ob–47; the regulations were published in *TWG*, 15 March 1871.

24. Kaufman to Tolstoi, 6 February 1876, TsGARUz, f. 47, d. 11, ll. 2–3.

tary khanates. Kaufman reversed the valences. For him, sedentary populations were repositories of the fanaticism so harmful to Russian interests; the nomads, whose "way of life [was] . . . based on natural and still primitive principles," might "officially adhere to Islam [but] in reality shun it and have no specific religious faith."[25] The aim of Russian policy ought to be to protect these noble savages from the influence of the fanatical Islam produced in the cities. Kaufman established distinct patterns of administration for each type of population and even hoped to redraw administrative boundaries to perpetuate the "natural demarcation" of the settled from the nomad.[26] Although this territorial demarcation never came about, sedentary populations were placed under the jurisdiction of Muslim religious law (shariat), while personal law among the nomads was to be based on custom (adat); in both cases, judges (called qāzis among the sedentary population and biy among the nomads) were to be elected. The distinction between the two, never as clear as Kaufman had assumed, blurred considerably during this period, largely as a direct result of Russian rule over nomadic territory, which rendered it safe for both Tatar and Uzbek ulama to operate on the steppe. By 1917, a new group of Muslim scholars had appeared among the nomadic population as well. Nevertheless, the dichotomy underlay Russian administrative policies until 1917, leading to distinct patterns of political development among the sedentary and nomadic populations in Central Asia.

These initiatives were combined with a number of other precautionary measures. Kaufman forbade all missionary activity by the Orthodox church in his realm, and the ban lasted until 1917. As a result, Turkestan never experienced the politics of conversion and resistance to it that marked the cultural life of the Volga basin and gave Tatar Jadidism its flavor. Kaufman also prohibited Russian settlement outside of towns and postal stations and did not allow Russians to purchase land.[27] This prohibition was short-lived, as the Statute of 1886 allowed Christians and local Muslims the right to buy property in Turkestan, and in time large-

---

25. Quoted in Daniel R. Brower, "Islam and Ethnicity: Russian Colonial Policy in Turkestan," in Daniel R. Brower and Edward J. Lazzerini, eds., *The Russian Orient: Imperial Borderlands and Peoples, 1700–1917* (Bloomington, 1997), 122.

26. K. P. fon-Kaufman, *Proekt vsepoddanneishogo otcheta General-ad"iutanta K. P. fon-Kaufmana po grazhdanskomu upravleniiu i ustroistvu v oblastiakh Turkestanskogo general-gubernatorstva 7 noiabria 1867–25 marta 1881 g.* (St. Petersburg, 1885), 82. The concern with protecting the nomads from the influence of their sedentary neighbors, both Tatars and "Sarts," is a constant theme in this report (see esp. ibid., 141–149, 440–441).

27. Ibid., 246.

scale resettlement of Russian peasants appeared on the government's agenda, but the caution behind it persisted and served to place limits on the scale of Russian immigration.

Yet, Islam did not "decay." Kaufman was wrong, of course, in asserting that "Islam was accustomed to living in the closest association with the state." Kaufman's hope that "Islam" would decay if bereft of state support therefore proved to be unfounded. There were other reasons, too, why the disregard of Islam did not produce the expected results. Noninterference in native life was not incompatible with fundamental change. Over the half century of tsarist rule, Central Asia was framed with new kinds of knowledge, bureaucratic practices, and forms of economic and political power that profoundly reshaped local understandings of Islam and ensured that it did not simply decay the way Kaufman and his successors had hoped.

The confidence that knowledge could subjugate difference led to the production of colonial knowledge that began immediately after the conquest. Alongside the new administration came statistical committees and their publications, which set about bringing order to the land. Numerous expeditions, Russian as well as foreign, visited Central Asia in the 1870s and 1880s to gather geographical and ethnographic information. Central Asia was surveyed and mapped, its natural features and social institutions described, and its inhabitants, their fanaticism notwithstanding, photographed, counted, measured, and classified.[28] Soon this attention extended to archeology and history as well. This research was formalized in a number of learned societies that appeared in Tashkent to further the study of the region's history and archeology, all of which enjoyed official support.[29] The aim was to make the region more comprehensible by rendering it an object of familiar modes of description and classification, thus facilitating the new rulers' ability to rule.

This impulse toward rigorous ("scientific") description coexisted with a will to exoticize Central Asia, however. When Kaufman first arrived in Tashkent, he was accompanied by Vasilii Vereshchagin, one of Russia's most prominent painters, who specialized in orientalist themes (he was

28. Physical anthropology and craniological research came to Turkestan at this time. See the numerous photographs of nude specimens of the various ethnographic types of the local population in Ch. E. de Ujfalvy de Mező-Kovesd, *Expédition scientifique française en Russie, en Sibérie et dans le Turkestan,* vol. 4 (Paris, 1879), passim.

29. B. V. Lunin, *Nauchnye obshchestva Turkestana i ikh progressivnaia deiatel'nost': konets XIX—nachalo XX v.* (Tashkent, 1962); Brower, "Ethnicity and Imperial Rule."

a disciple of Jean-Léon Gérôme). During two stays in Turkestan, Vereshchagin painted and sketched numerous scenes of local life that illustrated the fanaticism and barbarity of the newly conquered territory: dervishes with irrationally dilated eyes, battle scenes with pyramids of (Russian) skulls, and slave auctions all served to fix the otherness of Central Asia in the mind of a wide audience that extended well beyond Russia.[30] Arjun Appadurai has suggested that enumeration and exoticization were intertwined strands of a single colonial project in nineteenth-century India.[31] Russian rule over Central Asia was based on similar epistemological processes.

The knowledge created by the new regime was a force in its own right. Statistical committees even counted what was not really amenable to counting; the maktab, as I have argued, was an unstructured site for the interaction of older men and children; the new regime saw them as "native schools" and insisted on collecting statistical data on them. These data are, to be sure, highly unreliable, but the process of counting itself imparted a new meaning to the phenomenon of the maktab. The regime was even more interested in the ethnic classification of the population and over time reified ethnic categories by using them to classify the population. These classifications were to play an important role in native discourses of identity.

But no amount of knowledge could assuage the fear of the natives' fanaticism, which tended to subvert intentions of introducing citizenship to the area. This was reflected in the new administrative structure created in Turkestan. In order to minimize the chance of provoking the "fanaticism" of the local population, the internal administration of the native population was left in the hands of local functionaries. In its broad outlines, the administrative structure that emerged in Turkestan was similar to that of European Russia in the aftermath of Emancipation, where the peasantry was also left to administer itself, but the implementation of this structure in Turkestan owed as much to the fear of fanaticism as to a principled stance on the part of officialdom to establish

---

30. Vereshchagin's sketches illustrated the two-volume travelogue of Eugene Schuyler (*Turkistan* [New York, 1876]), perhaps the most substantial work on Central Asia to appear in English in the 1870s. Vereshchagin's vision thus became the standard view of Central Asia in Britain and the United States as well. Many of his paintings have been reprinted in E. V. Zavadskaia, *Vasilii Vasilevich Vereshchagin* (Moscow, 1986).

31. Arjun Appadurai, "Number in the Colonial Imagination," in Carol Breckenridge and Peter van der Veer, eds., *Orientalism and the Postcolonial Predicament* (Philadelphia, 1993), 315.

empire-wide structures in the newly acquired territory.[32] Existing systems of land tenure and revenue collection often continued unaltered during the period of conquest, often for several years, before the new administration could mobilize resources to reorganize them. Once that was done, lower-level administration was organized at the village and volost levels. In areas of settled population, property owners met to elect electors (*piatidesiatniki, ellikbāshi*), who in turn elected village elders (*āqsaqqāl*), officials in charge of overseeing irrigation channels (*ariq āqsaqqāl*), and volost chiefs. In the cities, different wards elected their own āsaqqāls. A parallel system of administration was created among the nomadic population, with electors choosing leaders at the aul and volost levels. These officials performed basic functions and assisted the Russian administration in tax assessment. These functionaries were responsible for all matters not having a "political" character, such as revenue collection and the administration of justice.[33] For the same reasons, the local population was not put under the obligation to serve in the military. Although this measure was no doubt popular with the newly conquered population, it also meant that the bifurcation between the two tiers of administration was complete. A few Tatars and Qazaqs served in the military administration, but Turkestani functionaries remained confined to the "native" tier. The Russian administration, which existed only at the uezd and higher levels, had control over the election and functioning of these officials. Oblast governors retained the right to annul the results of any election (the right was frequently exercised). The 1886 Statute retained these elective officials, and they continued to function until 1917. Larger towns were granted organs of elective public economic administration (*khoziaistvennoe obshchestvennoe upravlenie*), with the task of overseeing local fiscal affairs and determining taxes, but Kaufman, citing widespread corruption and misuse of power, aborted the experiment in 1877

32. Motivated both by a spirit of paternalist protectionism and the fear of rural radicalism, the state sought to retain the peasant commune in the aftermath of the emancipation of the serfs in 1861. Volost-level administration was in the hands of elected peasants and volost courts adjudicated according to customary, rather than case, law. The argument can easily be made that the Russian state's relationship to its peasantry was colonial. But many Russian intellectuals sought to overcome their alienation from the peasantry, and the middle of the nineteenth century was the high point of the romanticization of the peasant as representative of pure Russianness. In Turkestan, on the other hand, the distance from the local population was self-evident to most Russians and tended to affirm their sense of Russianness. In time, many officials came to see in the settlement of the region by Russian peasants the solution to the problem of Turkestan's otherness. Empire could reconcile the state to its peasantry in a way not possible in European Russia itself.

33. Kaufman, *Proekt*, 43.

and transferred these functions to the uezd administration.[34] The one exception was Tashkent, where municipal self-government was organized from early on.

Although this policy of "ignoring" Islam was questioned as early as 1882, it remained in force until 1917. Immediately upon Kaufman's death, with an impasse still continuing in the debate over the permanent statute, the imperial government instituted an inspection (*reviziia*) of the region to assess the needs of imperial policy there. The inspector F. K. Girs argued for radical change in the region's administration. Arguing that the population was peaceful and well inclined to Russian rule, he recommended the abolition of the special features of the Provisional Statute and its replacement by empire-wide structures.[35] These recommendations were not taken into account, and when the permanent statute was enacted in 1886, the two-tier administrative structure remained in place. A second inspection in 1908 recommended replacing the 1886 statute with one granting far greater rights to the local population, including the gradual introduction of *zemstvo* self-government.[36] The proposals provoked considerable debate, which continued until the outbreak of the Great War pushed such matters to the background.

Similarly, Kaufman's policy of "disregarding" Islam was also debated but not changed in any fundamental way until after the revolution. The strongest attack on it came in the aftermath of the Andijān uprising of 1898, when about 2,000 followers of Madali (Dukchi) Ishan, a minor Sufi shaykh, attacked the Russian barracks in Andijān and killed 22 soldiers while they slept and injured some 16 to 20. The insurgents, who were armed only with knives and cudgels, soon dispersed and were eventually hunted down. Russian retribution was swift: 18 of the insurgents were hanged, 360 were exiled to Siberia, and Mingtepe, Madali's village, was razed to the ground and replaced with a Russian settlement.[37] The attack did not produce any other incidents, but it sent shock waves through Russian society and officialdom since it reaffirmed official fears

---

34. Ibid., 60–66.

35. F. K. Girs, *Otchet revizuiushchego, po Vysochaishemu poveleniiu, Turkestanskii krai, Tainogo Sovetnika Girsa* (St. Petersburg, 1883), 453–463.

36. K. K. Palen, *Otchet po revizii Turkestanskogo kraia, proizvedennoi po Vysochaishemu poveleniiu Senatorom Gofmeistorom Grafom K. K. Palenom*, 19 vols. (St. Petersburg, 1910–1911); see also Pierce, *Russian Central Asia*, 87–91.

37. The literature on this episode is considerable; for a variety of viewpoints, see, V. P. Sal'kov, *Andizhanskoe vozstanie v 1898 g.: sbornik statei* (Kazan, 1901); Fozilbek Otabek oghli, *Dukchi Eshon woqeasi* (Tashkent, 1992 [orig. 1927]); Beatrice Forbes Manz, "Central Asian Uprisings in the Nineteenth Century: Ferghana under the Russians," *Russian Review* 46 (1987): 261–281.

about the thinness of Russian rule in Turkestan. In a memorandum to the tsar, the governor-general, S. M. Dukhovskoi, saw in the uprising the failure of all policies of the Russian state toward its Muslim subjects. He attacked the policies not just of Kaufman but of Catherine II, who had created the Spiritual Administration for Muslim Affairs in Ufa and encouraged the Islamization of the Qazaq steppe. Rather, "Islam, . . . a teaching extremely inert and undoubtedly inimical to Christian culture, excludes all possibility of a complete moral assimilation of our present Muslim subjects with us. A pure Muslim, strongly believing in the letter of the Qur'an and the shariat, cannot be a sincere and trusted friend of a Christian."[38] With this much Kaufman could have agreed; Dukhovskoi, however, drew other conclusions. A rapprochement between Muslims and the "Russian people" was possible only once the Muslim faith weakened, and that did not appear likely to Dukhovskoi. "Islam is so strong in the imaginations of the dark and passionate Asiatics that it would be useless to expect a rapid decline [in its influence]."[39] It was therefore no longer possible to continue disregarding Islam; rather active measures were necessary to control it, such as the abolition of the Spiritual Administration at Ufa, close supervision over all Muslim institutions, and the creation of a special censor for Muslim publications. In addition, Dukhovskoi suggested using modern medicine as a vanguard for breaking down the fanaticism of the Muslim, especially of women, as well as encouraging mixed marriages between Russians and Muslims (or, since the Church would not recognize such marriages, simplifying procedures for the adoption of children born of such cohabitation).[40] If the dark and passionate Asiatic fanaticism of the local population could be thinned by Russian blood, then it was to be coopted into the service of the state.

On the whole, Dukhovskoi's dark warnings met only a lukewarm reception in St. Petersburg and did not result in any significant change in policy. In the end, "nonintervention" proved durable because it was rooted not so much in the whims of a governor-general but in a very real shortage of resources, both human and financial, which placed strict limits on the Russians' ability to effect substantial change. Turkestan was vastly undergoverned even by Russian standards. Central Asia was

38. S. M. Dukhovskoi, *Vsepoddanneishii doklad Turkestanskogo General-Gubernatora Generala ot Infantarii Dukhovskogo: Islam v Turkestane* (Tashkent, 1899), 13.

39. Ibid., 14.

40. Ibid., 18.

conquered at a time when the Russian government was deep in debt after the Crimean War and the Great Reforms and every expenditure was closely scrutinized. Once the conquest had been accomplished, the central government continued to be extremely tight-fisted with funds for the new region. Thus, at the time of its creation in 1867, the Syr Darya oblast was staffed with only nineteen career (*shtatnye*) officials with a budget of only 48,500 rubles.[41] At that time, the Ministry of State Control refused to release funds to provide housing for the new administrators, and even the premises for the governor-general's chancellery were built from local taxes.[42] Simultaneously, down to the end of the old regime, there was a remarkable shortage of capable men to administer the region. As a governor-general pointed out in his report to the tsar in 1897, Turkestan suffered in comparison even with other borderlands administered by the Ministry of War. Samarqand oblast, for example, with a population a little smaller than that of Terek province in the Caucasus, had only half as many permanent staff and no chancellery. The uezd administration lagged behind even more; Samarqand's was run by a mere seventeen officials, compared with fifty-two in Tiflis and forty-four in Erevan, both of which had far smaller populations.[43] The 1908 senatorial inspection voiced the same complaints. Ferghana oblast, with a population of two million, was administered by only forty-three career bureaucrats, including two translators. Of these, only nine had a higher education, all in technical fields.[44] And with the exception of the few capable orientalists among them, Russian administrators had no acquaintance with local languages. The question of providing courses for administrators in local languages was raised at the official level after the turn of the century, but nothing tangible came of it.[45]

THE END OF ISOLATION

Administrative policies might profess to minimize interference, but they could not keep at bay the profound economic transformation of the region as a result of its incorporation into the Russian empire.[46] Central

41. Beliavskii, *Materialy*, 37.
42. Kaufman, *Proekt*, 92.
43. "Vsepoddaneishii doklad Turkestanskogo General-Gubernatora za 1895–97 gg.," TsGARUz, f. 1, op. 31, d. 53a, ll. 100b–11.
44. Palen, *Otchet*, XIV: 47.
45. Lunin, *Nauchnye obshchestva*, 22.
46. What little economic history of Central Asia has been written in the West deals with the Soviet period. Much, of course, has been published on the imperial period in

Asia's isolation was quickly breached. The telegraph arrived in Tashkent in June 1873, and the first bank opened in May 1875.[47] After a slow beginning, the region was also linked to Russia by railway. Purely strategic reasons (the conquest of the Türkmen steppe) motivated the construction of the Transcaspian Railway, the first railway project in the area. It reached Samarqand from the Caspian only in 1888, and Tashkent and the Ferghana valley were connected only a decade later. The Orenburg–Tashkent line, providing a much more direct link with European Russia, was built between 1900 and 1906. Until then, travel to European Russia from Tashkent entailed a journey through the Türkmen desert to Krasnovodsk on the Caspian, a steamer ride to Baku or Astrakhan, and further train or steamer connections onward. Even so, the new technology represented an immense saving of time and money over previous forms of transport. Not only did it effectively tie Turkestan to Russia, it also altered patterns of overland trade with neighboring countries. The conquest had already subjected the trade with India to Russian tariffs (and the customs boundary was extended to include Bukhara as well in 1885); the introduction of railways and steamships proved to be the last nail in the coffin of the caravan trade, for it became much cheaper and faster to send goods to India via Odessa and Bombay than overland across Afghanistan.

The conquest also led to the triumph of a cash economy in Central Asia. The Statute of 1886 recognized the right to possession of land by those who cultivated it. In sedentary areas, this effectively created private ownership of land in the hands of a class of smallholders. In nomadic areas, the state claimed ownership of the land since it was not cultivated. Long-distance trade was replaced by far more intensive exchange with Russia, which eventually led to the demise of local crafts production and its replacement by industrial goods from European Russia. The key role in this transformation was played by cotton. Cash crop production brought the cash economy to the countryside, created a greater economic surplus than ever before, and caused the emergence of a pros-

---

Russian, however, with the exception of a few monographs published in the 1920s, this literature suffers from the necessity to reconcile the Central Asian experience with official interpretations of Marxism. An example of the earlier work is P. G. Galuzo, *Turkestan—koloniia* (Moscow, 1929). Many of the orthodoxies of the last three decades of the Soviet period may be found in A. M. Aminov, *Ekonomicheskoe razvitie Srednei Azii (kolonial'nyi period)* (Tashkent, 1959).

47. *TWG,* 28 June 1873; 3 June 1875.

TABLE 2   YIELDS OF AREAS SOWN WITH COTTON,
BY OBLAST (IN DESIATINAS)

Year	Ferghana	Syr Darya	Samarkand	Total
1888	34,669	25,841	7,980	68,490
1893	85,300	31,500	21,488	138,288
1898	106,230	14,716	17,132	138,078
1903	149,056	11,019	9,812	169,887
1908	190,884	28,007	21,683	240,574
1913	274,897	76,726	31,758	383,373
1916	348,459	64,535	60,305	473,299

SOURCE: A. P. Demidov, *Ekonomicheskii ocherk khlopkovodstva, khlopkotorgovli i khlopkovoi promyshlennosti Turkestana* (Moscow, 1922), 36.

perous city-based class of merchants and middlemen that did more to alter the social terrain in Central Asia than any conscious government policy. Cotton had long been grown in Central Asia and exported to Russia, but its production took a quantum leap in the 1880s with the introduction of long-fiber American cotton into the region. A rapidly developing textile industry in Russia and Poland provided an almost insatiable market that had hitherto been completely dependent on imported cotton. Kaufman early on encouraged the adoption of long-fiber cotton by local cultivators. An experimental farm was established on the outskirts of Tashkent in 1878; three years later, it was providing seed and information gratis to interested peasants.[48] In 1884, a certain A. Wilkins planted 300 desiatinas (800 acres) with Sea Island and Upland cotton in the Tashkent area on an experimental basis. The Upland variety succeeded beyond all expectation.[49] Table 2 shows the growth of cotton production in Turkestan in the ensuing three decades. It was accompanied by shifts in patterns of land use, especially in Ferghana oblast, where cotton accounted for 44 percent of cultivated land.[50] The foundations for Soviet Central Asia's economic catastrophe were already in place.

48. *TWG*, 18 June 1881, 3–4.
49. A. P. Demidov, *Ekonomicheskii ocherk khlopkovodstva, khlopkotorgovli i khlopkovoi promyshlennosti Turkestana* (Moscow, 1922), 35–36.
50. *Sotsial'no-ekonomicheskoe polozhenie Uzbekistana nakanune oktiabria* (Tashkent, 1973), 30. The table refers only to the three core oblasts of Turkestan. An additional 60,362 desiatinas were sown with cotton in 1916 in Semirech'e and Transcaspia. Cotton cultivation was also widespread in the protectorates, where in 1915, the area under cotton amounted to 146,000 desiatinas (ibid., 29).

By the turn of the century, Turkestan had acquired a new significance to the Russian economy. The tsarist government supported cotton production in Turkestan, which it saw as a way of achieving freedom for the textile industry of European Russia from cotton imports from the United States and India. In the oft-quoted words of the minister of agriculture in 1912, "Every extra *pud* of Turkestani wheat [provides] competition for Russian and Siberian wheat; every extra *pud* of Turkestani cotton [presents] competition to American cotton. Therefore, it is better to give the region imported, even though expensive, bread, [and thus] to free irrigated land in the region for cotton." [51] But since the government's interests lay primarily in encouraging the textile industry of European Russia, and not the economic development of Turkestan, it limited its encouragement to imposing high tariffs on imported cotton (by 1900, the import duty on cotton was four rubles per *pud*). Little was done to improve matters locally by funding improvements in irrigation and transportation or credit to small farmers. [52] Yet, cotton reconfigured the social order in Central Asia. It required intensive amounts of labor (which altered work patterns in the countryside) as well as cash (to buy seed, pay for transport, and buy food during the growing season), which was available to few peasants. Cotton-buying firms were only too willing to advance large sums of money against the harvest, often at exorbitant rates, thus tying the peasantry into a never-ending cycle of debt. [53] This dislocation was cause for some concern among local administrators, since it threatened to provide fertile grounds for disaffection that could lead to an explosion of "fanaticism." The state's interest in maintaining the region's stability could act as a damper on Russia's economic exploitation of the region. From the beginning, governors-general had enacted paternalistic legislation to protect Central Asians from outsiders. They had waged a constant struggle with usurers (mostly Indian), placing limits on what they could claim in return for defaulted loans. [54] Similarly, a 1902 decree forbade the seizure of plots of under one desiatina for debt. [55] In the 1910s, an ambitious project for financing a large-scale irrigation works at the Moscow Stock Exchange came to naught in part because of concerns among

51. A. V. Krivoshein, *Zapiska glavnoupravliaiushchego zemledeliem i zemleustroistvom o poezdke v Turkestanskii krai v 1912 godu* (St. Petersburg, 1912), 7.
52. Demidov, *Ekonomicheskii ocherk*, 86.
53. Ibid., 123ff.
54. *TWG*, 19 December 1877.
55. A. Iuldashev, *Agrarnye otnosheniia v Turkestane (konets XIX–nachalo XX vv.)* (Tashkent, 1969), 175–176.

the Turkestan authorities about the political consequences of concessions sought by the Moscow financiers.[56]

At the same time, with the imperial government beginning to sponsor resettlement of Russian peasants in the borderlands in the 1890s, Turkestan was cautiously opened to peasant settlement, directed mainly to the nomadic areas of Semirech'e and Syr Darya oblasts, where the state claimed ownership of land not cultivated by the nomads. Settlement was seen by many as an instrument of control and economic exploitation of the new territory; perhaps the most vocal proponent of this view was Minister of Agriculture A. V. Krivoshein, who in 1909 offered the simple formula of "cotton + settlement + irrigation = a new Turkestan" as a means of knitting the region more tightly to the empire. His view was not overwhelmingly popular in the bureaucracy, however, as many worried that unbridled resettlement would lead to mounting disaffection and the emergence of a political issue, as was happening in the neighboring Steppe region, where the "land question" had become a major spur to Qazaq nationalism.[57] The volume of rural settlement remained small, and as of 1 January 1910, there were 382,688 Russians living in Turkestan, comprising 5.9 percent of the population. (The figure was only 153,651 [3.2 percent] for the three core oblasts.)[58]

Almost all of the cotton produced in Central Asia was exported to the textile centers of inner Russia and Poland. Since production was dispersed among numerous smallholders, the task of procuring the harvest, and of advancing loans for the next one, fell to local middlemen, who made hefty profits. This group, which came to be known as the *chistach* (a corruption of the Russian word *chistit'*, to clean, since most of them were agents for cotton-cleaning firms), arose from among the local merchantry or usurers but in time diversified their operations.[59] From its ranks emerged a fledgling modern merchant class in Turkestan. Also, land alienated from smallholders tended to concentrate in the hands of wealthier landholders, many of whom belonged to the urban merchantry. Central Asia experienced an unprecedented expansion of its economy, especially in the cities, whose populations swelled. The largest growth

56. Muriel Joffe, "Autocracy, Capitalism and Empire: The Politics of Irrigation," *Russian Review* 54 (1995): 387.

57. In 1909, for instance, the governor-general, P. I. Mishchenko, in a memorandum to the minister of war, warned of the potential of any "artificial growth" of resettlement to lead to antigovernment sentiments; TsGARUz, f. 2, op. 2, d. 369, ll. 110b–12.

58. The figures are from V. I. Masal'skii, *Turkestanskii krai* (St. Petersburg, 1913), 362.

59. Iuldashev, *Agrarnye otnosheniia,* 104.

was in Tashkent, which grew from around 76,000 in 1870 to 234,289 in 1911. In the same year, Kokand, at the center of the cotton boom, had a population of 113,636 and Samarqand 89,693.[60]

A NEW SOCIAL MAP

Local society underwent a major realignment in the first decade of Russian rule. In Bukhara and Khiva, Russian support strengthened the rulers against chiefs and governors, allowing a greater degree of centralization than the rulers had been able to achieve themselves. Yet, since this centralization was not entrenched in any new formal institutions of administration, the protectorates did not see the emergence of functionaries in the manner of Turkestan. The ulama, too, enjoyed less autonomy in their affairs, even though their jurisdiction was wider in the protectorates than in Russian territory. The amir also managed to turn the ulama, who had proved so troublesome in 1866 and 1868, into a state-supported estate, providing numerous sinecures and establishing a hierarchy that had never existed before.[61] But the new wealth also affected the protectorates, which were fully absorbed into the Russian economy after 1885. The amir of Bukhara, one of the world's largest traders in astrakhan, acquired a vast personal fortune; others too, native Bukharans as well as Russian subjects from Turkestan and many Tatars, amassed great wealth from this trade.

Change took a rather different direction in Turkestan. In the sedentary areas, the most profound upheaval was the almost total disappearance of the warrior elites. The colonial nature of the conquest of Turkestan, as well as its suddenness, left little room (or need) for the cooptation of native elites, as had been the case in other Muslim areas of the empire, such as the Crimea and the Qazaq steppe. A few scions of ruling families received titles and admission into the Russian armed forces, but their numbers remained small.[62] Warlords who fought against the Russians met varying fates. Many were pensioned off, others were exiled to provincial towns in European Russia, while some escaped to Afghanistan to live out their days. The Statute of 1886, which granted de facto property rights in land to those who cultivated it, struck a direct blow at the eco-

60. *Aziatskaia Rossiia*, vol. 2 (St. Petersburg, 1914), 352–353.

61. Sadriddin Aini, *Istoriia Mangytskikh emirov* (1921–23), in *Sobranie sochinenii*, 6 vols. (Moscow, 1971–75), VI: 293–294.

62. A. Z. V. Togan, *Bugünkü Türkili (Türkistan) ve Yakın Tarihi*, 3rd ed. (Istanbul, 1981), 272.

nomic power of the tribal chiefs, and the introduction of elections for administrative positions undermined their political power.

The disappearance of the tribal chiefs was accompanied by a realignment of existing groups and the emergence of new ones. Proximity to the Russians and a knowledge of their language came to be a new source of notability. Anxious to create a group in local society loyal to them, the Russians created a new group of "honorable" (*pochetnye*) citizens from among those who had welcomed the conquest. Many of the wealthiest merchants of Tashkent, for instance, had favored annexation by the Russians as early as the 1850s, and had even maintained contact with the Russians in Orenburg. When Tashkent was finally taken in 1865, these merchants provided the conquerors with their initial footing in an unknown and hostile environment. On 17 July 1865, Cherniaev decorated thirty-one men for "assiduous service and attachment to the Russian government . . . [and] for services rendered during the conquest of Tashkent."[63] This laid the foundations for a new elite of notables who served as intermediaries between the colonial regime and local society. Immediately after Tashkent was taken, the conquerors were lionized by two of the wealthiest merchants in the city, Said Azim-bāy and Sharafi-bāy Zaynulabidin, the latter a Tatar who had lived in Tashkent for a long time.[64] Between them, they owned the two largest caravansaries in the city and maintained extensive trading interests in Russia.[65] Both were well rewarded: Said Azim-bāy received the rank of "hereditary honorable citizen" from the emperor himself in St. Petersburg, and Sharafi-bāy was appointed chair of the first Public Economic Administration of the old city.[66] Other such appointments followed in Tashkent and in every other city conquered by Russian forces. Said Azim-bāy's family remained prominent in local affairs until 1917: Two of his sons, Said Karim-bāy and Said Ghani-bāy, were elected to the Tashkent City Duma, and a son-in-law won election to the Second Duma in 1906 (although he refused to serve). The family's house acquired a permanent place on official itineraries in the old city, and as late as 1906 the newly appointed governor-general stopped by the house for tea as part of his initial tour of Tashkent.[67] Said Ghani's millions ensured his appointment in 1908 as the

63. F. Azadaev, *Tashkent vo vtoroi polovine XIX v.* (Tashkent, 1959), 72–75.
64. P. I. Pashino, *Turkestanskii krai v 1866 godu. Putevye zametki* (St. Petersburg, 1868), 96, 104, 106, 119.
65. Ibid., 154n.
66. N. P. Ostroumov, *Sarty* (Tashkent, 1908), 98–99; Azadaev, *Tashkent*, 2–4, 104.
67. *Taraqqi—Orta Azyaning umr guzārlighi*, 3 February 1906.

official guide in charge of supervising the arrangements for the hajj for Muslims of all Russia.[68] With time, the ranks of these honorable citizens swelled to include local merchants as well as some ulama and other functionaries. Honorable citizens received medals and ceremonial robes, were invited to official functions, and acquired numerous formal and informal privileges. The new economy also produced its own heroes. By the turn of the century, a number of wealthy merchants (*bāys, aghniyā*) had emerged as prominent social figures. Some of them were decorated by the authorities, while others enjoyed the fruits of the stability provided by Russian rule, the monetized economy, and freedom from competition with military or khanly elites, as had been the case before the conquest.

Kaufman's policies also ensured that the ulama survived the conquest well. The impulse to nonintervention left the madrasas largely intact. The Provisional Statute of 1867 did not alter the status of waqf property, and although the 1886 statute sought to regulate such property more closely, the concept as such was never abolished. Similarly, the state retained Muslim courts, which, although placed under bureaucratic supervision, continued to function as before and to be staffed by the ulama themselves. Kaufman's hope that the removal of state support would lead to a sharp decline in the authority of the ulama proved misguided, partly because the qāzis were more closely tied to the state now than before. Indeed, given the decline in the fortunes of the old warrior elites, the relative position of the ulama increased in Turkestan. Similarly, judicial affairs remained largely in Muslim hands. Among the settled population, every volost and city ward elected, indirectly through *ellikbāshi*s, a qāzi. Anyone over the age of twenty-five without a criminal record could aspire to this office. The jurisdiction of the qāzis was strictly defined by law, although Russian administrators had few means of ensuring strict compliance. Qāzis could sentence people to arrest for up to eighteen months or a fine of up to 300 rubles.[69] They were not competent to hear cases involving documents written in Russian or cases involving non-Muslims. Their decisions were subject to review by Russian circuit courts. Qāzis did not receive a fixed salary but were allowed to charge fees for each case heard or each document signed.[70] Apart from avoiding active interference in the religious life of the local population, these

---

68. *Odesskii listok* (Odessa), 19 July 1908.
69. *Polozhenie ob upravlenii Turkestanskogo kraia* (St. Petersburg, 1886), § 217.
70. On Muslim courts, see F. Bakirov, *Chor Turkistonda sud, shariat wa odat* (Tashkent, 1967); N. Lykoshin, *Pol zhizni v Turkestane* (Petrograd, 1916), 52–96.

institutions were a means of cutting costs. By making the seeker of justice responsible for its cost, the Russian authorities removed a substantial source of expenditure from the colonial budget. Moreover, these institutions were meant to destroy the authority of traditional Islamic
elites among the settled population and of tribal and clan structures
among the nomads, a task deemed necessary for turning natives into citizens of the empire.[71]

The application of the electoral principle to qāzis had been aimed at
diminishing the moral authority of the office in the eyes of the population. (The 1886 Statute further eroded the moral authority inherent in
the office by turning qāzis into "popular justices.") This was only partly
successful, for although the qāzi's became an elected office, the population in the settled areas of Turkestan continued to recognize the cultural
capital of the ulama. Many men who had been qāzis in the last years of
Muslim rule returned to office through election. Muhiddin Hakimkhoja-
oghli, for instance, the son of the last qāzi kalan of Tashkent, was elected
qāzi of the Sibzār part of Tashkent and continued to be reelected until
1902.[72] Of the 253 qāzis serving in the three core oblasts of Turkestan
on 1 June 1883, 225 had the usual madrasa credentials.[73] There was also
a marked reluctance on the part of the population, especially in the early
years of Russian rule, to have recourse to Russian justice. In the three
years 1880–1882, there were only three instances of natives turning to
a Russian court when such recourse was not obligatory.[74] After 1886,
when qāzis became "popular justices" overnight, a struggle ensued about
the meaning of their office. The state tried to coopt them as its agents and
provided them with new seals, made of steel, and inscribed in Russian
with the name of the office. Qāzis had traditionally been appointed because of their personal merits, and the silver seals they had used indicated only the name of the individual. Many qāzis resisted the new reg-

71. Among the nomads, volost boundaries were drawn on a strictly territorial basis,
without regard to tribal and clan affiliations of the population. This was intended to loosen
tribal affiliations, but some observers saw it as only fueling further intrigue, as members
of various tribes sought to elect their tribesmen to office: Iu. Iuzhakov, "Itogi 27-letnego
upravleniia nashego Turkestanskim kraem," Russkii vestnik, 1891, no. 7, 70–73; A. A.
Divaev, "Atkamnary (stranitsa iz zhizni Kirgiz)," Sbornik materialov dlia statistiki Syr-
Dar'inskoi oblasti, 3 (1894): 3–17.
72. V. V. Bartol'd, Istoriia kul'turnoi zhizni Turkestana (1927), in his Sochineniia,
9 vols. in 10 (Moscow, 1963–1977), II/1: 359–360. Reelection of incumbents seems to
have been routine; in 1880, five of the eight functionaries (fours qāzis and four āqsaqqāls)
up for election retained their offices; TWG, 29 August 1880.
73. Girs, Otchet, 326.
74. Ibid., 327.

ulation under various pretexts, and some used both seals for a period. According to the reminiscences of a zealous functionary, this practice ended only when he personally broke the old seals with a hatchet.[75]

The story reveals much more than native obstreperousness or Russian bureaucratic zeal: The meaning of the institution was in flux. The struggle was over whether the qāzis were to operate as agents of the colonial state or as members of a traditional Islamic elite. The Russians also sought to bring order to what seemed to them the chaos of traditional Islamic law. As I argued in Chapter 1, shariat is best understood as interpretive practice in which the possession of knowledge of appropriate texts gave the jurist license to issue his opinions. Abstracted from this discursive context, the manuals of fiqh were rendered incomprehensible and chaotic. The Russians brought a different understanding of law, as a code, accessible to all and universally applicable. The shariat itself was often (mis)taken as such a code; Dukhovskoi, for instance, could state simply that the "shariat . . . a multivolume commentary on the Qur'an [is] considered by Muslims to be a universal codex, in which believers find answers to all questions, without any exceptions, of religious, state, public, and personal life."[76] Dissatisfied therefore with the practice of qāzis, who cited no precedents and followed no particular procedure, officialdom set out to refashion the shariat as a civil code. The British invention of "Anglo-Mohammedan" law in India, a formalized code of personal law based on shariat precepts and Anglo-Saxon procedure, provided the inspiration. Already in 1893, B. D. Grodekov had translated the *Hidāya* (an eleventh-century manual of fiqh by ʿAlī b. Abī Bakr al-Marghinānī used as the basic code for "Anglo-Mohammedan" jurisprudence) from the English, and other attempts at the creation of what Brinkley Messick has aptly called "colonial shariat" continued down to the end of the old regime.[77] Yet, characteristically, little came of the effort, and the tension between the various conceptions of the status of Muslim law and qāzis was never fully resolved. The ulama, however, came to be seen as keepers of the Muslim tradition, the last bastions of Islam. With political power gone and compromises required in navigating the new

75. Lykoshin, *Pol zhizni*, 70–71.
76. Dukhovskoi, *Vsepoddanneishei doklad*, 5.
77. Brinkley Messick, *The Calligraphic State: Textual Domination and History in a Muslim Society* (Berkeley, 1993), 58–66; on attempts to create "colonial shariat" in Turkestan, see Bartol'd, *Istoriia kul'turnoi zhizni*, 386–388; N. A. Smirnov, *Ocherki istorii izucheniia Islama v SSSR* (Moscow, 1954), 76.

social and economic order, traditional practices came to be valorized as the sources of Muslim identity.

Local notables operated inside a precarious matrix of loyalty and suspicion. Kaufman was fond of majestic displays of his power, for he believed in behaving like an "oriental" monarch in the Orient. On his travels around the region, and especially on his return from military campaigns, he preferred to be welcomed by local notables with suitable imperial pomp. When Kaufman returned from a trip to St. Petersburg in 1873,

> officials, as well as Russian and Muslim merchants of Tashkent met Kaufman three chaqirim outside the city. They welcomed him with a laden table. . . . The Governor General stopped and gave those present the Emperor's greetings to the inhabitants of the region. Later, he mounted his carriage and entered the city, where he reviewed the soldiers who stood, row upon row, from the head of the street to his mansion. At his mansion also, he conveyed the greetings of the Emperor to the officials who had gathered there [to greet him]. Upon hearing this, the men were very pleased and returned home with joy. . . . Later, after nightfall, all streets and houses were illuminated in order to celebrate the return of the esteemed Governor General.[78]

The notables played their part, as they did in presenting addresses and petitions to the new rulers. During the Russo-Ottoman War of 1877, notables from Aq Masjid presented Kaufman with assurances of loyalty and 10,000 rubles for wounded soldiers collected from the nomadic population of the uezd.[79] Others sent their sons to Russian schools and built European-style houses in the Russian parts of town. Yet, nothing could dislodge suspicion of even the most loyal notables from the minds of Russian officialdom. For all the prominence Said Azim-bāy acquired, Kaufman felt it "necessary to deal with Said Azim-bāy very cautiously, because he wants to boss everyone and everything."[80] We have seen that the fear that local notables and functionaries would place their interests before those of the state ("corruption," "misuse of power") led to the demise of organs of municipal self-government in the 1870s. In 1906, the veteran administrator V. P. Nalivkin rued the fact that the Russians had from the beginning enclosed themselves in a "living wall" of op-

78. *TWG*, 28 February 1873; see also Schuyler, *Turkistan*, I: 81–82.
79. *TWG*, 29 April 1878.
80. Quoted in N. P. Ostroumov, *Konstantin Petrovich fon-Kaufman, ustroitel' Turkestanskogo kraia. Lichnye vospominaniia N. Ostroumova* (Tashkent, 1899), 321.

portunists and ill-wishers.[81] Other administrators, realizing their dependence on these intermediaries, but helpless to do anything, fretted over their evil designs. Many in Tashkent suspected that Russian policy in Bukhara was hostage to the machinations of a small group of translators who had "taken over" the political agency in Kāgān.[82] As fears of pan-Islam gathered strength after the turn of the century, honorable status proved no protection against arbitrary searches. Said Karim's house was searched in 1914 because of numerous suspicions harbored against him by the police (ranging from conspiracy to take over the publishing trade in Tashkent to collecting money on behalf of the Ottoman war effort).[83] Yet, such searches, while a reminder of the precariousness of their position, did not undermine the notables' prominence in Muslim society.

The Russian presence, for all its professions of noninterference, had created new sources of notability and thus redefined the politics of status and prestige in local society. The new rulers' dependence on the decorated notables and the translators gave them a degree of informal influence in local society. Muslim functionaries in the new apparatus similarly appeared as intermediaries between the local population and the Russian state, as well as figures of authority. The ulama retained their source of moral and cultural authority and became the sole bulwarks of moral authority; indeed, the elimination of tribal chiefs, who had often competed with the ulama, gave the latter a stature in society that was in many ways unprecedented. These new elites reached their compromises with the new order, which in turn defined the positions they came to occupy in the new politics of culture in Turkestan.

RUSSIANS AND NATIVES

But Muslim society was no longer autonomous; it was set against a new settler society that took root as a direct result of the Russian conquest. The earliest Russians to arrive were members of the conquering armies. They were followed by civilian functionaries and, in time, by traders, workers, and divers adventurers, so that quite soon a settler Russian society, complete with its own schools, churches, newspapers, and markets, appeared in Turkestan. Given the cautious approach to peasant re-

81. V. P. Nalivkin, *Tuzemtsy ran'she i teper'* (Tashkent, 1913), 72–75, passim; see also Togan, *Türkili*, 274.

82. See, for instance, the report of a police agent sent from Tashkent to Bukhara on a secret mission in April 1910, in GARF, f. 102, op. 240 (1910), d. 277, l. 23.

83. "Spravka" (21 May 1915), TsGARUz, f. 461, op. 1, d. 2263, l. 160b.

settlement in Turkestan, the majority of its Russian population was connected with administration and trade. The emergence of Russian society also transformed the urban landscape. The Russians built their own quarters, which were self-consciously designed as advertisements for the superiority of the conquering civilization, adjacent to native cities. In common with urban development in other European colonies, these quarters were laid out according to a regular plan, their straight, wide streets contrasting to the labyrinthine neighborhoods of the traditional cities. Imperial architecture and the presence of churches further defined these quarters as different, and disproportionate expenditure and allocations ensured the maintenance of this order. Such "new cities" arose next to all major cities in Turkestan (in Bukhara, they developed along the Transcaspian Railway), while in nomadic territory, urban life emerged for the first time during this period. Vernyi (present-day Almaty), Pishpek (Bishkek), and Askhabad (Ashgabat) were all established as Russian settlements in this period and remained predominantly Russian. Although common in the colonial world, this pattern of urbanism was unique in the Russian empire. Similarly, in common with other settler societies, there were marked differences in wages between settler and native populations. As an American traveler observed in 1910, "Wages of Europeans are very high. A Russian labourer or servant expects twice or three times as much as he gets at home, but the wages of natives are low, 25 and 30 cents a day being the maximum." [84] This combination of cheap native labor and high salaries for settlers meant that even the poorest sections of the Russian population enjoyed a standard of living considerably higher than the majority of the native population.

All this served to underscore Turkestan's uniqueness in the empire. Unlike other Muslim areas of the Russian empire, Turkestan was a relatively densely populated region with practically no Russian settlement in the beginning. It differed dramatically in that respect from the Volga region and the Crimea, which were also inhabited by Muslims but where the demographic balance was quite different and Russian rule much better entrenched. It also meant that the relationship between the rulers and the ruled was different—and more distant—than elsewhere in the Russian empire. The nomenclature adopted for classifying the local population gives some indication of this difference. Most non-Russian groups inhabiting the Russian empire were designated *inorodtsy* (a term best translated by the French *allogènes*). Although the term had a consider-

---

84. William Eleroy Curtis, *Turkestan: "The Heart of Asia"* (London, 1911), 289.

able semantic range, it connoted inhabitants of the Russian state who were somehow alien.[85] For legal purposes, the population of Central Asia was classified as *inorodtsy*, but the term was never used in Central Asia itself, where the term *tuzemtsy*, directly translatable as "native," with all its connotations, held currency. Unlike *inorodtsy*, the term *tuzemtsy* asserted the connection of the given population to the land; conversely, the term also affirmed the foreignness of the Russians in the region in a manner that was inconceivable in other parts of the empire.[86] Moreover, in Turkestan, the otherness of the local population acquired a social as well as a political or ethnic connotation, for the native population fit the state's system of classifications only awkwardly. Table 3, which classifies the local population by social categories, shows the ambivalence inherent in the state's classifications of its newest subjects. While entry into various estates was open to the native population of Turkestan, natives remained simply natives unless marked by some form of social mobility. As the figures for Tatars show, this was not the fate of all *inorodtsy* in the empire.[87]

Yet the lines between European and native were not entirely rigid. The new Russian cities were never segregated. The vast majority of the European population lived in those quarters, but a substantial proportion of their population was invariably of local origin. "Russian" Tashkent grew rapidly after its establishment in 1866. It had a population of 2,073 in 1870, 4,926 in 1877, 33,276 in 1901, and well over 56,000 in 1911.[88]

---

85. The concept behind this term has attracted little attention. Its legal and popular meanings differed considerably, and even the former did not remain constant over the last century of the old regime; see the succinct overview in Henning Bauer et al., *Die Nationalitäten des Russischen Reiches in der Volkszählung von 1897*, 2 vols. (Stuttgart, 1991), I: 416–419; see also L. Shternberg, "Inorodtsy: obshchii obzor," in A. I. Kastelianskii, ed., *Formy natsional'nogo dvizheniia v sovremennykh gosudarstvakh* (St Petersburg, 1910), 531–534.

86. In actual bureaucratic practice, *tuzemtsy* and *inorodtsy* could be used as mutually exclusive categories. In 1906, the special regulations governing the election of candidates from Turkestan to the State Duma divided the electorate into "native" (*tuzemnoe*) and "non-native" (*netuzemnoe*) groups, thus classifying the nonnative *inorodtsy* with the Russians; see "Polozhenie o vyborakh v Gosudarstvennuiu Dumu," *Polnoe sobranie zakonov Rossiiskoi Imperii*, 3rd ser., vol. 25 (St. Petersburg, 1907), no. 26662, § 1, *prilozhenie*. The confusion resulting from attempts to implement this distinction is recorded in TsGARUz, f. 1, op. 17, d. 616, l. 134.

87. As a recent statistical analysis of the 1897 census has shown, Kalmyks and the "small peoples" of Siberia were the only other groups in the empire among whom large parts of the population remained simply *inorodtsy*; see Bauer et al., *Die Nationalitäten des Russischen Reiches*, II: 197.

88. N. A. Maev, "Topograficheskii ocherk Turkestanskogo kraia," *Materialy dlia statistiki Turkestanskogo kraia*, 1 (1872): 10–11; Azadaev, *Tashkent*, 134; A. I. Dmitriev-Mamonov, ed., *Putevoditel' po Turkestanu i sredne-aziatskoi zheleznoi doroge* (St. Petersburg, 1903), 352; *Istoriia Tashkenta* (Tashkent, 1988), 145.

TABLE 3   SOCIAL CLASSIFICATION BY NATIVE LANGUAGE
(THREE CORE OBLASTS, 1897)

	Tajik	Sart	Ozbek	Turk	Kirgiz	Tatar
Gentry	5	1	1	32	14	85
Personal nobles	10	1	5	15	44	22
Honorary citizens	1	3	0	38	5	13
[Christian] clergy	1	0	0	0	5	0
Merchants	85	18	18	36	6	103
Townsfolk	2,801	378	84	1,055	1,190	2,019
Peasants	397	200	338	179	203	1,009
Inorodtsy	345,828	949,155	724,597	438,446	1,216,021	1,805
Miscellaneous	4	5	2	4	19	115
Foreign subjects	890	1,662	469	160	273	455

SOURCE: *Pervaia vseobshchaia perepis' naseleniia Rossiiskoi Imperii, 1897 g.,* vols. 83, 86, 89 (St. Petersburg, 1905), table 24.

The figures for Tatar speakers pertain only to Samarqand and Syr Darya oblasts; in Ferghana, Tatar was counted as one of the "Turko-Tatar" (*tiurko-tatarskie*) languages, thus rendering both "Tatar" and "Turk" incomparable across oblasts. On the classifications used by the census, see Chapter 6.

It presented a marked contrast to the old city, and already in 1873 a foreign visitor felt that "one can live for years in Russian Tashkent without even suspecting the existence of the Sart part of town."[89] As early as 1870, members of the local population owned sixty-nine shops in the new city, and they comprised more than one-fifth of its population. By 1901, Muslims (including Tatars) accounted for one-third of the civilian population of the new city,[90] which had sixteen mosques in 1913 (compared with fifteen churches and two synagogues).[91]

Nor could officialdom turn unequivocally to the settler population for support, for it was not immune from the suspicion directed at local notables. Russian autocracy jealously guarded its monopoly over matters of state policy from the interference of any public groups, Russian or not. In colonial borderlands such as Turkestan, this monopoly often

89. Ujfalvy, *Expédition scientifique,* II: 14.
90. Dmitriev-Mamonov, *Putevoditel',* 352.
91. *Aziatskaia Rossiia,* I: 320.

came up against the need to find broader support for Russian rule. Dukhovskoi's suggestion for the genetic Russification of the region was only
the most blunt (because desperate) expression of the hope, frequently
expressed in bureaucratic correspondence, that the answer to the lack of
personnel resources in Turkestan was to entrust the supervision of various aspects of local life to members of the Russian population. Yet, seeking such support from society implied a partnership with society that the
autocracy found unacceptable even after the revolution of 1905. In Turkestan, administrators hoped that Russian society would recognize its
duty to empire and act in the interests of state, and they expressed aston-
ished dismay when it failed to do so. The political agent in Bukhara wrote
in 1906 of the deleterious effects of the revolution on "Russian prestige"
in Bukhara, and in 1910, Governor-General Mishchenko turned literary
critic in order to remind the editor of the Tashkent journal *Sredniaia
Aziia* of his duties to Russian power in the region. Presented with a com-
plimentary copy of the new publication, he found "extremely weak in
literary terms" a sketch that presented in a poor light the behavior of
army officers. "This story belongs to phenomena," he wrote, "that are
altogether undesirable, especially in Central Asia."[92] Russian society did
not always agree with officialdom. It was the only segment of Turkestan's population to be involved in the revolution of 1905; in the ensuing elections to the State Duma, local Russians largely voted for radical
parties of the left.[93] The files of the political police indicate that the state
found itself governing settler society almost as sternly as native society.

Along with the Russians came members of other groups that further
complicated the dichotomy between Russian and native. Some, such as
Ukrainians, Belorussians, and even Poles and Germans, tended to be
lumped together with the Russians both in terms of perception and legal
privileges. Others, such as Jews, Armenians, and Tatars, occupied separately delineated spaces in the new colonial society. A sizable Jewish
community had existed in Bukhara since at least pre-Mongol times and
played a significant role in the area's economic life. In 1833, Bukharan
Jews were granted the same rights to trade in Russia as Muslim merchants
from Bukhara and Khiva, and this pattern of equal legal treatment for
all subjects of the amirs of Bukhara was maintained after the conquest.

---

92. TsGARUz, f. 1, op. 28, d. 1119, l. 112.
93. On the considerable revolutionary activity among the Russian population of
Turkestan, see A. V. Piaskovskii, *Revoliutsiia 1905–1907 godov v Turkestane* (Moscow,
1958).

Kaufman saw Bukharan Jews are a good influence in Turkestan as well as a channel for Russian influence in Bukhara. Under the terms of the 1873 treaty with Bukhara, Bukharan Jews had the right to own property and to settle anywhere in Turkestan, a right denied Russian Jews. As a result, large communities of Bukharan Jews appeared in Tashkent, Samarqand, and the cities of the Ferghana valley, where they were very successful in business. This success, as well as general anti-Jewish sentiment of the reign of Alexander III (r. 1881–1894), led to a gradual curtailment of their favored status, culminating in a 1910 law that made it illegal for Bukharan Jews to reside in all but a few towns of Turkestan unless they could prove that their ancestors had lived in the area before the Russian conquest. The needed documents were duly produced, and many Jews remained in Turkestan.[94] Some of them had acquired sizable fortunes, especially three families in Ferghana that had concentrated a great part of the raw cotton export to Russia in their hands. According to one estimate, the Vodiaevs alone managed 60 percent of this trade.[95] In 1914, there was a large enough Jewish community in Kokand to support a newspaper, *Rahamin*. The wealth of the community, as well as its contacts abroad (extremely sketchy notices in contemporary travelers' accounts refer to the fact that many local Jews had contacts in Western Europe and that many spoke French fluently), allowed it to negotiate increasing legal disabilities.

An Armenian community similarly developed in the major urban centers of Turkestan, performing similar entrepreneurial functions in the economy, its arrival facilitated by the Transcaspian Railway. But for our purposes, the most important community was the Volga Tatars. Under Russian rule since the middle of the sixteenth century, the Tatars enjoyed affinities of language as well as of religion with Central Asia and had played a central role in Russia's trade with Central Asia during this period. Bukharan madrasas were also a common destination for Tatar ulama. A number of Tatars moved to Turkestan after the Russian conquest, partly because their familiarity with both Central Asia and Russia gave them a considerable competitive advantage in the area. True to form, the administration attempted to stem this unauthorized movement of people, although the repeated prohibitions are evidence of a distinct lack

---

94. On Bukharan Jews, see Michael Zand, "Bukhara VII: Bukharan Jews," *Encyclopædia Iranica*, IV: 530–545, with an exhaustive bibliography.

95. Catherine Poujol, "Approaches to the History of Bukharan Jews' Settlement in the Fergana Valley, 1867–1917," *Central Asian Survey* 12 (1993): 553–554.

of success.[96] Some Tatar and Bashkir officers served in the Russian army
and therefore appeared in administrative roles; many more served as interpreters and guides; but the vast majority of Tatars living in Central
Asia were connected with trade and private business. As *inorodtsy*, they
suffered from a number of legal disabilities—they could not legally own
immovable property—and were often the objects of suspicion, but they
nevertheless occupied a space quite distinct from the local population.
They were not *tuzemtsy*, and as Table 3 again shows, were much better
integrated into Russian social classifications. Their position with regard
to local society was, however, always ambivalent; their religious and linguistic affinities with it had made them the natural intermediaries in the
Russian trade before the conquest, but they nevertheless remained outsiders. "A number of Noghays [the Turkestani term for Tatar] have arrived in these parts lately," a newspaper reader stated in 1876. "Some
want to buy property here and marry locally because life is good here and
the climate is better. But local Sarts and Qazaqs don't want to give them
their daughters."[97] The disdain was mutual, however, as the Tatars in
Turkestan soon formed a close-knit community, which self-consciously
delineated itself from the local population and looked to phenomena in
the Tatar lands of European Russia for inspiration. Numerous markers
separated them from the local population: Most chose to live in Russian
quarters, far more Tatars sent their children to Russian schools, and
Tatar women followed different codes of dress and comportment than
Turkestani women. The Tatar community in Tashkent organized a benevolent society with its own school in 1902, which further served to demarcate it from the rest of Muslim society.[98]

Yet for all the intermediary groups and the differences within Russian
society, the Russian-native dichotomy came to provide the parameters
within which difference and hierarchy were imagined in Turkestan. The
settler population's oppositional proclivities did not render it sympathetic to the native population. The otherness of the native population
was too widely shared in Russian discourse for that, and the emergence
of a colonial economy tended to reinforce the differences. Even though
the entire spectrum of Russian political life appeared in Turkestan, all
sections of it were united in taking for granted the exclusion (or disre-

96. *TWG*, 29 March 1874, 19 December 1874.
97. *TWG*, 28 July 1876.
98. *Tāshkand shahrining orus chāstida istiqāmat etub masjid-i jāmi'imizga qawm bulub turghuwchi hamma ahl-i mahalla noghāy khalqiga ruski tātāriski ishkolāning pāpichitilstvāsining predsidātilidan dāklād* (Tashkent, 1902).

gard) of the natives from mainstream politics. This fact was to be of fundamental importance in 1917. But the dichotomy was also shared by non-Russian groups in Turkestan, who appropriated it for their own uses. The vocabulary of progress and backwardness inherent in the dichotomy was also to figure prominently in the politics of cultural reform in Muslim society itself, which was made necessary by changes in society noted above and the need to make new choices in new circumstances unleashed by the Russian conquest.

CHAPTER 3

The Origins of Jadidism

In 1899, a young man of twenty-five boarded the Transcaspian Railway in Samarqand and headed off to Transcaucasia on his way to Istanbul, Cairo, and Mecca. The journey was to be a turning point in the life of Mahmud Khoja ibn Behbud Khoja, who later took the surname, in the Tatar fashion then becoming popular, of Behbudi. In his travels Behbudi saw current developments in public education in the Ottoman empire and Egypt and met leading figures concerned with cultural reform. Upon his return to Samarqand eight months later, he took out a subscription to the newspaper *Terjüman,* published by the Crimean Tatar reformer Ismail Bey Gasprinskii (1851–1914) in Bahchesaray. Behbudi's public career began with the appearance of his first essays in the official *Turkistān wilāyatining gazeti* (*TWG*) in 1902 and proved to be the most illustrious of his generation. He also supported a school that taught literacy according to the new method championed by Gasprinskii. Over the years, he wrote a number of general information books as well as primers for new-method schools; he edited and published a newspaper and then a magazine of his own. His publishing activities expanded considerably and in 1913 he opened a bookstore that stocked books from all over the Muslim world. That same year he became Central Asia's first playwright when his *Padarkush* (The Patricide) opened in Samarqand. Down to the premature end of his life in 1919 he continued to exhort his compatriots to "awake from their sleep of ignorance" and acquire the knowledge that the new age demanded.

Yet for all his enthusiasm for reform, Behbudi (1874–1919) came from the old cultural elite of Turkestan. His father was qāzi in the village of Bakhshi Tepe on the outskirts of Samarqand, and Behbudi was taught the standard madrasa texts of the time at home by his father and uncles. But his father died when Behbudi was twenty, and he was forced to find work. He worked as *mirzā* (scribe) to an uncle who served as qāzi, before becoming a qāzi himself.[1] The family was prosperous enough for Behbudi to travel abroad, and he was astute enough not to squander his wealth. In 1913, he owned houses in both the Russian and native parts of Samarqand (he himself lived in the Russian part) as well as ten desiatinas of agricultural land. He also traded in grain in addition to keeping his position as a *mufti* in Samarqand.[2]

Behbudi's experience was exceptional only in that he was the most prominent figure in the Jadid movement that arose in Central Asia around the turn of the twentieth century. He was very much a figure of his time, experiencing the world in a manner that would have been impossible for his compatriots a generation earlier and making use of forms of communication and organization that had not existed before. Behbudi's career embodied all the seeming paradoxes of Muslim cultural reform in Central Asia: Its most vocal proponent was rooted in the tradition of Muslim learning, yet advocated the adoption of new cultural forms; although Jadidism generally raised the hackles of Russian officialdom, its earliest expressions emerged in the organ of officialdom; and although it was a response to Russian rule, its most constant feature was a ruthless critique of Muslim society. These are paradoxes, however, only if we insist on seeing Jadidism merely as a "response" to colonization or "the challenge of the West," an expression of nationalism, directed solely at the colonizer. The "challenge" was not inherently obvious to all. Rather, Jadidism is to be located at the intersection of Russian cultural policies and processes of social and economic change set in motion by the Russian conquest which put older patterns of cultural production under

1. Typically also for the Jadids, details of Behbudi's biography are not well known. Apart from Behbudi's own copious writings, our best source for biographical information is an article by his disciple, Haji Muin [Shukrullah], "Mahmud Khoja Behbudi (1874–1919)," *Zarafshan* (Samarqand), 25 March 1923; see also Sherali Turdiev, "Mahmudkhŏja Behbudiy," *Muloqot*, 1994, no. 3–4, 44–48; and Ahmad Aliev, *Mahmudkhŏja Behbudiy* (Tashkent, 1994).

2. TsGARUz, f. 461, op. 1, d. 1312, l. 665; see also the reminiscences of Behbudi's daughter in Solih Qosimov, "Behbudiy wa jadidchilik," *Özbekiston adabiyoti wa san"ati*, 19 January 1990.

strain and allowed new voices to emerge. Jadidism was both a social and a cultural phenomenon.

THE FIRST GENERATION

The advocacy of comprehensive modernizing cultural reform was not the "natural" outcome of Russian conquest. Indeed, the dichotomy of Russian and native served to reinforce existing cultural practices as essential markers of difference. The authority of the decorated notables rested on their status as intermediaries between Russians and natives; the clear demarcation of boundaries between the two as separate entities came to be of crucial importance to them. Cultural practices—texts, dress, food, posture, gesture—and the manner of their reproduction became the bedrock of a traditional way of life that differentiated natives from Russians, Muslims from Christians. The ultimate authority for this newly objectified tradition rested in "Islam," which was inextricable, as I have argued, from the practices surrounding its transmission. The Russians had seen in Islam the essence of Central Asia's otherness. For rather different reasons, an appeal to Islam became the source of the new elites' authority.

The notables, as intermediaries between society and the colonial regime, kept a foot in both worlds. Wealthy merchants such as Said Azimbāy built houses in the new Russian cities; many ulama accepted decorations from the state, learned Russian and sometimes sent their sons to Russian educational institutions. Sattār Khān Abdulghaffār oghli (1843–1901), a qāzi in Chimkent at the time of the Russian conquest of the city, exemplifies the trajectory of many such individuals. In the dislocation following the Russian conquest of the town, Sattār Khān lost his position. He made the acquaintance, however, of a Muslim officer in the Russian army, a certain Yenikeev, from whom he learned Russian. Sattār Khān became convinced of the need for Central Asians to learn Russian; for three years, between 1871 and 1874, he taught Russian in a school that he established in Chimkent. Later, in 1881, he moved to Tashkent, where he worked as a translator for various government departments, including the offices of the *TWG*. In Tashkent, he lived in the Russian part of town in a house furnished in the European manner and sent his sons to the *gimnaziia*.[3] Muhiddin Khoja, son of the last *qāzi kalān* of Tashkent, was decorated with the orders of St. Stanislav and St. Anna. He

---

3. N. P. Ostroumov, *Sarty: etnograficheskie materialy (obshchii ocherk)*, 3rd ed. (Tashkent, 1908), 190–215.

remained a qāzi all his life, but he learned Russian and consorted with Russian officials. Although initially opposed to it, he taught Russian to his sons, one of whom attended the *gimnaziia*. But Muhiddin also taught that son the usual madrasa texts at home and married him off at the age of sixteen.[4]

The colonial regime had left the practice of Muslim law intact; it also allowed for the survival of the maktab and the madrasa. Kaufman's cultural policies stemmed from his general outlook on Islam. Properly ignored and deprived of state support, maktabs and madrasas would automatically lose their attraction for the population. The state was to be concerned with attracting the local population to Russian schools, where they would study together with Russian students. Kaufman saw as the aim of the educational system the creation of "useful citizens of Russia" regardless of religion.[5] Since the basic aim of public education in the region "must be its development in the direction of Russian interests . . . the religious convictions of the natives must remain without any encroachment and schools for natives must not have a confessional character."[6] The state was to support only Russian schools, where Russians and natives would study together, for only such education could produce the useful citizens Kaufman foresaw. Kaufman concentrated his efforts on the Qazaqs, where education would allow "[us] to fulfill the humanitarian responsibility of drawing them into the family of civilized peoples . . . [as well as] to distance them from Muslim influence that have already begun to appear among the nomads."[7]

The local population in its turn steadfastly ignored the new institutions (see Table 4). The numbers of Muslims in Russian institutions remained minuscule, and most of this small number belonged to Tatar or Qazaq families, or were sons of the decorated notables. On the other hand, the maktab and the practices associated with it continued. Traditional Muslim education retained its prestige and its value after the conquest. To be sure, the period of conquest did prove disastrous for many madrasas, as in the confusion many waqfs were embezzled and turned into private property.[8] Upon the conquest of Samarqand, waqfs benefit-

4. Ibid., 121–131.

5. Ostroumov, *Konstantin Petrovich fon-Kaufman, ustroitel' Turkestanskogo kraia* (Tashkent, 1899), 49.

6. S. M. Gramenitskii, *Ocherk razvitiia narodnogo obrazovaniia v Turkestanskom krae* (Tashkent, 1896), 4–5.

7. Quoted by K. E. Bendrikov, *Ocherki po istorii narodnogo obrazovaniia v Turkestane (1865–1925 gody)* (Moscow, 1960), 64.

8. N. S. Lykoshin, *Pol zhizni v Turkestane* (Petrograd, 1916), 68.

TABLE 4   MUSLIMS IN RUSSIAN EDUCATIONAL
INSTITUTIONS (SELECTED YEARS)

Institution	1885	1897	1909	1916
Gimnaziia and *progimnaziia*	14	14	106	170
Realschule	—	7	4	26
Higher primary schools	145	160	341	272
Teachers' seminary	10	7	13	18

SOURCES: 1885: D. Aitmambetov, *Dorevoliutsionnye shkoly v Kirgizii* (Frunze, 1961), 49; 1897: S. Gramenitskii, *25-letie uchebnogo dela v Turkestanskom krae* (Tashkent, 1901), 3; 1909: Palen, *Otchet po revizii Turkestanskogo kraia, proizvedennoi po Vysochaishemu poveleniiu Senatorom Gofmeistorom grafom K. K. Palenom,* VI, 150–177; 1916: N. A. Bobrovnikov, "Sovremennoe polozhenie uchebnogo dela u inorodtsev vostochnoi Rossii," *ZhMNP,* n.s., 69 (1917): 72.

ing properties located in Bukhara were confiscated while the amir of Bukhara refused to allow *mutawalli*s ("trustees") from madrasas in the conquered territories to collect revenues in his domains.[9] According to the 1886 legislation, endowed populated lands passed into the possession of those who worked them, while the status of other kinds of waqf property had to be verified and confirmed by the local uezd administration.[10] New waqfs could be established only with the permission of the governor-general himself, and waqf property was subject to local taxes.[11] This process proceeded with the usual glacial speed, and many claims were rejected on technicalities.[12] Despite such difficulties, though, the cultural authority of madrasas and the knowledge to be acquired in them remained intact and young men continued to consider spending several years in residence a worthwhile experience. According to some reports, the numbers of madrasas actually increased after the conquest, especially when the introduction of cotton through the 1890s increased the income of their waqfs manifold.[13] During this period, the madrasas of

9. N. A. Maev, "Dzhizak i Samarkand," *Materialy dlia statistiki Turkestanskogo kraia,* 2 (1874): 271; Beliavskii, *Materialy po Turkestanu* (n.p., n.d. [St. Petersburg, 1884]), 60.
10. *Polozhenie ob upravlenii Turkestanskogo kraia* (St. Petersburg, 1886), §§ 265, 267.
11. Ibid., § 266.
12. V. P. Nalivkin, "Polozhenie vakufnogo dela v Turkestanskom krae do i posle ego zavoevaniia," *Ezhegodnik Ferganskoi oblasti,* 3 (1904): 1–56.
13. This prosperity was, however, relative. According to Ostroumov, the combined waqf income of the thirty-seven madrasas in the city of Kokand was "not more than 50,000 rubles" on the eve of the First World War (N. P. Ostroumov, *Vvedenie v kurs islamovedeniia* [Tashkent, 1914], 183). Similarly, the waqf income of madrasas in Andijan city totaled 34,955 rubles in 1908 (A. Sharafiddinov, "XIX asr okhiri–XX asr boshlarida Farghona oblastida madaniy hayot tarikhidan," *Obshchestvennye nauki v Uzbekistane,* 1978, no. 2, 27). In contrast, in 1908, the Tashkent men's *gimnaziia* alone had an annual

Kokand were especially densely populated and attracted students even from Bukhara. New madrasas were founded after the conquest: Of the fifty-eight madrasas in existence in Samarqand oblast in the years 1892–1893, no fewer than ten had been founded since the conquest, and thirty-six in the nineteenth century.[14]

The earliest commentaries on the changed fortunes of Central Asia came in traditional genres. The feeling of a world turned upside down expressed in these lines by Zākirjān Furqat (1858–1909), the popular Kokand poet, was widely shared in the literary milieu of the first generation after the conquest:

> Ah! The commonfolk are honored, the learned wretched
> The unwise hold their heads high, and the wise are trampled underfoot
> And the exalted have become lowly, and the lowly exalted.[15]

Chronicles by disaffected court officials such as Ahmad Makhdum Dānish and Abdulaziz Sāmi in Bukhara continued to cast the narrative of the decline of Muslim fortunes in Central Asia in the same framework well after the turn of the century.[16] Many poets, however, went beyond such laments and used verse to describe, with praise or satire, many of the new phenomena they witnessed. Much of this poetry appeared in the *TWG,* which, along with its longtime editor N. P. Ostroumov, played a central (if seemingly paradoxical) role in the articulation of new voices.

Historians have tended to dismiss the *TWG* all too hastily. In the influential opinion of Alexandre Bennigsen and Chantal Lemercier-Quelquejay, "Despite the considerably important role of Muslims in its publication, it [*TWG*] was conservative, [and] very hostile to all manifestations of Jadidism. . . . Edited by Russians, [it] cannot be considered a true 'Muslim' newspaper."[17] A closer look shows that the newspaper's

---

budget of 73,913 rubles (although tuition fees accounted for 21,512 rubles): K. K. Palen, *Otchet po revizii Turkestanskogo kraia, proizvedennoi po Vysochaishemu poveleniiu Senatorom Gofmeistorom grafom K. K. Palenom,* 19 vols. (St. Petersburg, 1910), VI: 153.

14. V. P. Nalivkin, "Svedeniia o sostoianii medrese Samarkandskoi oblasti v 1892/93 uchebnom godu" (ms., ca. 1894), TsGARUz, f. 455, d. 1, l. 20b.

15. Quoted in A. Abdughafurov, *Zokirjon Furqat: hayoti wa ijodi* (Tashkent, 1977), 20.

16. Ahmad Makhdum Dānish, *Traktat Akhmada Donisha "Istoriia Mangytskoi dinastii,"* ed. and trans. I. A. Nadzhafova (Dushanbe, 1967 [ms. ca. 1890]); Sāmī, *Tarikh-i salatin-i manghitiyya* (1906), discussed in Jo-Ann Gross, "Historical Imagination, Cultural Identity and Change: 'Abd al-'Aziz Sami's Representation of Nineteenth-Century Bukhara," in Daniel R. Brower and Edward J. Lazzerini, eds., *The Russian Orient: Imperial Borderlands and Peoples, 1700–1917* (Bloomington, 1997), 203–226.

17. Alexandre Bennigsen and Chantal Lemercier-Quelquejay, *La presse et le mouvement national chez les musulmans de Russie avant 1920* (Paris, 1964), 25–27. Similarly, writers such as Baymirza Hayit (*Türkistan Rusya ile Çin Arasında,* trans. Abdülkadir

role was far more ambivalent. It began life in 1870 as a weekly supplement (with "Sart" and Qazaq editions alternating every week) to the *Turkestanskie vedomosti* printed at the newly established printing press at the military headquarters in Tashkent. In 1883, the Qazaq edition was abandoned altogether and the Sart version turned into a weekly newspaper in its own right; it became biweekly in 1908. The *TWG* was one of the first Turkic-language periodicals in the Russian empire, and except for two brief periods in 1906–1908 and 1913–1915, when a vernacular commercial press existed in Turkestan, it remained the only local newspaper in Central Asia in the tsarist period.

The newspaper was established by Kaufman's decree in order to "inform the populace of all manner of decrees issued by the governor-general." The first issue of the newspaper promised that "it will also include all kinds of news about trade and happenings in Tashkent and other cities." [18] Its first editor was Shahimardan Ibrahimov, a Tatar from Orenburg who worked as translator in the governor-general's chancellery. In its first years, the newspaper was aimed at native functionaries, whom it sought to keep abreast of the latest regulations and decrees; it also served to provide a record of Kaufman's comings and goings, and his conquests. The effect of these dreary reports (often written in convoluted prose that gave every indication of its origins in Russian bureaucratese) was lightened by the publication of tales from the *Thousand and One Nights* and random news bits from the Russian press. By the mid-1870s, however, the newspaper began publishing pieces by its readers, as well as "useful information" about the modern world. Useful information ranged from an account of the world's geography and the names of important states, through descriptions of hot-air balloons, railways, and telephones (as early as 1881), to instructions about the cultivation of cotton and silkworms. In 1879, when Ibrahimov went to Europe on vacation, he sent back descriptions of his travels for readers of the newspaper, thus providing the first description of Berlin in Central Asian Turkic. Readers' contributions usually recounted local affairs and scandals, but they also began to air opinions about the shortcomings of Central Asian society.

Sadak [Ankara, 1975], 168–170) and H. B. Paksoy (*Alpamysh: Central Asian Identity under Russian Rule* [Hartford, 1989], 19) see the newspaper only in the context of Ostroumov's efforts to create a Sart language, and hence dismiss it as pernicious. For a recent defense of its place in Central Asian cultural history, see A. Jalolov and H. Özganboev, *Özbek ma"rifatparwarlik adabiyotining taraqqiyotida waqtli matbuotining örni* (Tashkent, 1993), 17–59.

18. *TWG*, 28 April 1870.

The arrival at its helm of Nikolai Petrovich Ostroumov in 1883 changed the newspaper. A student of Nikolai Il'minskii at the Kazan Spiritual Seminary, where he specialized in Arabic, Turkic languages, and Islam, Ostroumov (1846–1930) arrived in Tashkent in 1877 in the capacity of inspector of schools for Turkestan.[19] Over time, he was to serve as director of the newly founded Turkestan Teachers' College, and then the director of the Tashkent men's *gimnaziia*. His education was solidly missionary, but in Turkestan, where Kaufman had prohibited proselytization by the Church, Ostroumov saw himself as an upholder of "Orthodox monarchism," using his orientalist learning to ensure the state's best interests in the region. His orientalist credentials attracted the attention of the authorities, and he soon had easy access to Kaufman and Cherniaev, who, during his brief tenure as governor-general between 1882 and 1884, appointed him editor of *TWG*, in which position he served until 1917. Over the years, Ostroumov became the resident expert on everything connected with local life, and the authorities routinely solicited his opinions on subjects ranging from Islamic dogma to policy concerning new-method schools; he also served as censor for books published locally. In addition, he maintained a copious correspondence with missionaries and orientalists, in Russia as well as abroad, and produced an astonishing amount of writing in a number of registers. His missionary interests are reflected in his translation of the Bible into "Chaghatay," as well as in the publication of a series of textbooks of Islamic studies. But such work was pushed to the background by his copious output on the archeology, ethnography, and history of Central Asia, which appeared in a steady succession of articles and monographs. As the epigraph to one of his books asserted, "It is necessary to study the moral constitution, the beliefs and the way of life of the Sarts in order to beneficially influence their lives."[20]

Once understood, however, Sarts had to be enlightened, and that task Ostroumov made his own. Ostroumov's appointment as editor was part of a broader shift away from Kaufman's policies, as his successors became concerned with the local population's continued disinclination to learn Russian. The *TWG* was to be an instrument of the new policy of cautious enlightenment, and it was to be used much more effectively than

19. Ostroumov's life and work have largely escaped scholarly notice; the most detailed treatment is in B. V. Lunin, *Istoriografiia obshchestvennykh nauk v Uzbekistane: bio-bibliograficheskie ocherki* (Tashkent, 1974), 259–271.

20. Ostroumov, *Sarty,* epigraph.

had been the case in Ibrahimov's tenure as editor. Orientalism could en-
lighten orientals and do so in such a way that their interests coincided
with those of autocracy. The *TWG* published useful information, en-
lightening but politically harmless, in its columns with redoubled effort.
In 1891, Ostroumov made the acquaintance of the poet Furqat. At Ostroumov's invitation, Furqat visited the *gimnaziia* and the theater in the
Russian part of Tashkent and wrote poems describing them that Ostroumov published in *TWG*. Ostroumov ensured that Furqat received a modest honor for his efforts.[21] In 1891, when Furqat left Tashkent to travel
through Istanbul, Greece, Bulgaria, Egypt, Arabia, and India (he eventually settled in Yarkand in Chinese Turkestan), he maintained his correspondence with Ostroumov, who continued to publish his poetry and
correspondence in *TWG*.[22] At the same time, Ostroumov encouraged
contributions from the local population, and the *TWG* often hosted lively
debate among its contributors. For Ostroumov, it was much better to
have the natives debate matters under his watchful eye than on their
own. Hence his suspicion of those—Tatars, Jadids, even other Russian
officials—who encroached on his turf. Many poets and writers developed lasting personal friendships with Ostroumov, for apart from any
personal charms, Ostroumov offered patronage and protection from the
caprices of the bureaucracy. Others, such as the numerous Jadid writers
who wrote for the *TWG*, although not personally beholden to him, maintained proper relations with him, for the paper he edited offered them a
unique forum. The bitterest criticism of Ostroumov invariably came
from Tatar writers, who were more likely to focus on his missionary
background and his official position. When *TWG* ran a polemic against
an article in the very first issue of *Taraqqi* in 1906, Ismail Abidi (Gabitov), its Tatar editor, bitterly denounced "this newspaper whose publisher and editor is the famous missionary Nikolai Ostroumov, while
Mullā Ālim [its "native" subeditor and contributor] is a writer who for
several years has been selling his honor for thirty or thirty-five rubles a
month."[23] For Ostroumov, the reason for this attitude was simple: "Not
having great success among the natives, progressive Tatars do not hide
their dislike of the Editor of the native newspaper [*TWG*], calling him a
missionary in the civil sense, i.e., a Russifier, since he defended and de-

21. A. Abdughafurov, "Zokirjon Furqat haqida yangi ma"lumotlar," in *Furqat ijodiyoti* (Tashkent, 1990), 34–40.
22. Abdughafurov, *Zokirjon Furqat,* 44–101.
23. *Taraqqi,* 5 July 1906.

fends the autonomy of the nationality and language of the natives of Turkestan from Tatar attempts to involve the Sarts in the progressive Tatar movement. The native newspaper more than once expressed distrust of such attempts and printed direct indications that the constitutions of Turkey and especially Iran will bring no good. Recent events justify this conviction of the Editor."[24] Yet, for all this, Ostroumov maintained a long, if sporadic correspondence with Gasprinskii, who started publishing his *Terjüman* in the same year that Ostroumov became editor of *TWG*. The two editors exchanged subscriptions and invariably maintained a high level of civility both in print and in correspondence.[25]

JADIDISMS

Although it is impossible to date the beginning of Jadidism in Central Asia with any precision, by the end of the century poetry in praise of the theater and gimnaziia gave way to expressions of profound dissatisfaction with the current state of Central Asian society and passionate appeals for change. In its broad outline and its emphasis on elementary education, this new critique was inspired by similar currents of opinion among emergent cultural elites in other Muslim regions of the Russian empire. The term "Jadidism" came from the new (i.e., phonetic) method (*usul-i jadid*) of teaching the Arabic alphabet pioneered by Gasprinskii in the Crimea in the 1880s. Gasprinskii traveled widely among the Muslim communities of European Russia (he visited Central Asia twice) spreading his message. In addition to the reform of the maktab, he advocated the acquisition of modern knowledge, the creation of new civic institutions, and the improvement in the position of women in Muslim society.[26] From 1883 on, he single-handedly published the newspaper *Terjü-*

24. "Raport Redaktora Turkestanskoi tuzemnoi gazety N. Ostroumova," 12 March 1910, TsGARUz, f. 1009, d. 150, l. 63.

25. A small portion of this correspondence is conserved in Ostroumov's personal archive (TsGARUz, f. 1009). When Gasprinskii died in 1914, *TWG* joined the Muslim press in mourning him; the obituary (*TWG*, 25 September 1914) was written by Mir Muhsin Shermuhammadov, and Ostroumov added an appreciation of his own.

26. With work in the relevant archives not possible until very recently, the basic source on Gasprinskii's life remains the biography written by a disciple: Cafer Seydahmet, *Gaspıralı İsmail Bey* (Istanbul, 1934); for a study of Gasprinskii's reform program, see Edward J. Lazzerini, "Ismail Bey Gasprinskii and Muslim Modernism in Russia, 1878–1914" (Ph.D. diss., University of Washington, 1973); and Lazzerini, "Ismail Bey Gasprinskii (Gaspıralı): The Discourse of Modernism and the Russians," in Edward Allworth, ed., *Tatars of the Crimea: Their Struggle for Survival* (Durham, N.C., 1988).

man to propagate his ideas.[27] After an indifferent beginning, the new method became widespread among the Tatar populations of the Crimea and the Volga-Urals region. This success was linked to the emergence, after the middle of the nineteenth century, of an urban mercantile middle class among the Volga Tatars, who, living in the heartland of the empire, were directly affected by the escalating economic change in European Russia. The last half-century of the old regime saw an explosion of publishing activity among the Volga Tatars; modern schooling also become widespread and new genres of literary production emerged. Similar phenomena also developed in Muslim Transcaucasia.[28]

The Russian conquest put Central Asia at the margins of the debates that accompanied the rise of Jadidism among those groups. As early as 1885, *Terjüman* had 200 readers in Turkestan,[29] and it figures prominently in the intellectual biographies of every prominent Central Asian Jadid. Gasprinskii himself was held in the highest esteem by Central Asian Jadids, many of whom were acquainted with him personally. Similarly, Jadid schools used Tatar textbooks until (and sometimes even after) local editions became available, and after 1905, the Tatar press served as the model for its Central Asian counterpart. In addition, some Muslims from other parts of the Russian empire came to Central Asia to teach in new-method schools. However, to assert that Jadidism in Central Asia arose simply as a result of Tatar influence or that it remained a pale reflection of a better organized movement in European Russia is inaccurate.

The view of Tatars as the prime movers of Jadid reform in Central Asia comes from two mutually antagonistic sources. On the one hand, it is rooted in the fears and suspicions of Russian officialdom of the period. Russian officials in Turkestan were always suspicious of Tatar influence,

27. On *Terjüman*, see Bennigsen and Lemercier-Quelquejay, *La presse*, 37–42; Edward J. Lazzerini, "Ismail Bey Gasprinskii's *Perevodchik/Tercüman*: A Clarion of Modernism," in H. B. Paksoy, ed., *Central Asian Monuments* (Istanbul, 1992).

28. Dzh. Validov, *Ocherk istorii obrazovannosti i literatury tatar* (Moscow, 1923; reprint ed., Oxford, 1986); Abdullah Battal Taymas, *Kazan Türkleri*, 3rd ed. (Ankara, 1988), chs. 11–14; Azade-Ayşe Rorlich, *The Volga Tatars: A Profile in National Resilience* (Stanford, 1986), chs. 6–9; S. Hakan Kırımlı, *National Movements and National Identity among the Crimean Tatars (1905–1916)* (Leiden, 1996); Alan W. Fisher, *The Crimean Tatars* (Stanford, 1978), ch. 10; Hüseyin Baykara, *Azerbaycanda Yenileşme Hareketi: XIX. Yüzyıl* (Ankara, 1966); Tadeusz Swietochowski, *Russian Azerbaijan, 1905–1920: The Shaping of National Identity in a Muslim Community* (Cambridge, 1985); Audrey L. Altstadt, *The Azerbaijani Turks: Power and Identity under Russian Rule* (Stanford, 1992), esp. ch. 4.

29. Z. Radzhabov, *Iz istorii obshchestvenno-politicheskoi mysli tadzhikskogo naroda vo vtoroi polovine XIX i v nachale XX vv.* (Stalinabad, 1957), 387.

pernicious by definition, over their new wards. Kaufman had early attempted to minimize such influence by attempting to ban Tatar printed books from his domain; lack of success in such attempts only strengthened the suspicions. Ostroumov complained to Gasprinskii in 1900: "I cannot, of course, determine the course of history, but I always regret that in three and a half centuries Tatars have remained aloof from the Russians and . . . pass along their aloofness to other *inorodtsy* of the Muslim faith."[30] Similar sentiments are legion in official correspondence from the period. Scholars, both Soviet and Western, have tended to accept this official view as an accurate reflection of a reality that was far more complex.[31] This picture of Tatar influence also fit well with the self-image of many Tatars, who saw themselves as the natural leaders of the Muslim community in the Russian empire. It was their mission to awaken Central Asia to the cause of reform, and many took for granted that they would be able to dictate the terms of this awakening. Ultimately, however, Tatars wrote for a Tatar audience, in which Central Asians occupied a marginal place, and as their responses indicate, Central Asian Jadids were fully aware of this fact.[32]

Professions by later émigré historians of a common bond against the Russians need not hide from view the ambivalence of Tatar opinion about Central Asia. On the one hand, the region exercised a fascination for many Tatar intellectuals, who saw it as the cradle of Turkic civilization, and in the years before the revolution, Nurshirvan Yavushev and Zeki Velidi (Togan) traveled to Central Asia for scholarly purposes.[33]

30. Ostroumov to Gasprinskii, n.d. [1900], TsGARUz, f. 1009, d. 90, l. 540b.

31. Hélène Carrère d'Encausse ("The Stirring of National Feeling," in Edward Allworth, ed., *Central Asia: A Century of Russian Rule* [New York, 1967], 178), for example, in speaking of the leading role of the Tatars in Turkestan, cites A. V. Piaskovskii (*Revoliutsiia 1905–1907 godov v Turkestane* [Moscow, 1958], 102), who in turn cites a memorandum from the military governor of Syr Darya oblast to the Department of Police expressing disapproval of the spread of pan-Turkic ideas in Turkestan through *Terjüman*.

32. Perhaps the most striking evidence of this is the long essay, "Türkistanda bugünke häyat" (Contemporary Life in Turkestan), serialized in the Orenburg magazine *Shura* in 1916 and 1917. It was written by Abdürrauf Müzaffer, a Tatar functionary who served for many years in Turkestan. During his stay in Tashkent, he was involved in local cultural life, primarily as a regular contributor to *ST* (1914–1915). The tone of the essay is purely ethnographic, explaining an exotic land and its people to a home audience; the concern with the Turkestani lack of progress is firmly pushed to the background.

33. Yavushev, who spent several years in Turkestan and Chinese Turkestan, wrote copiously in both the Tatar and the Central Asian Jadid press about his travels as well as the history of the areas he visited. He died in 1917; his obituary is in *Hurriyat*, 17 November 1917. Ahmed Zeki Velidi (1890–1970) went on to become the leader of the Bashkir national movement during the revolution and civil war, and later, in emigration, under the surname Togan, found renown as one of the foremost Turkologists of the century.

Containing half the empire's Muslim population, Central Asia also became important to Tatar politicians who founded the All-Russian Muslim movement in 1904. For others, the desire to spread the message neatly coincided with the necessity of getting a job. Tatars (and Transcaucasian Muslims) held a competitive advantage in the field of new-method education in Central Asia. Nevertheless, Tatars formed distinct communities in Central Asia cities, with their own schools and organizations, and those visiting from European Russia found Central Asia quite alien. Traveling in 1893, Mehmed Zahir Bigiev found himself surrounded by backwardness. The students in the famed madrasas of Bukhara and Samarqand surprised him by "their complete ignorance of the world"; his guides could not answer his questions; numerous customary practices, "holdovers from paganism," contravened explicit commands of the shariat; and the position of women was "extremely pitiable." All of this Bigiev contrasted to the situation in "our Russia [*bizim Rusya*]."[34] According to a Tatar employee of the police department who traveled incognito in Ferghana in 1909 to gauge the "mood of the population" (a common exercise), Tatars had stopped interacting with the local population, which they referred to as *ülek khalïq* (dead people) for reasons of their political inertia.[35] This impatience with Central Asia also led to constant criticism in the Tatar press. The Muslim press in Transcaucasia was no kinder to Central Asia. The illustrated satirical magazine *Mulla Nasreddin* of course spared nobody, but the Baku newspaper *Iqbal* also ran numerous articles harshly critical of Central Asia. A certain Muhammad Said from Transcaucasia visited new-method schools in Turkestan in 1913 and 1914 and was not impressed by what he saw. First he lectured the schoolteachers of Turkestan in the local press on the shortcomings of their schools and their methods of teaching, and then he went home and declared in *Iqbal* that "there is not a single genuine and selfless teacher in Turkestan."[36] All through 1914 and 1915, *Iqbal* kept up a barrage of criticism of Central Asia that was harsh even by prevailing standards. If the Jadids could come in for such treatment, the rest of society could expect little mercy.

In the end, different elite strategies defined the various styles of Jadidism in the Russian empire. These various Jadidisms shared several fea-

34. Muhammed Zahir Bigiev, *Maveraünnährdä siyahät* (Kazan, 1908).
35. TsGARUz, f. 1, op. 31, d. 540, l. 1780b.
36. Muhammad Said, "Adab wa tarbiya," *Āyina*, 10 May 1914, 557–559; 17 May 1914, 567–568; "Imtihān masalasi," *ST*, 11 May 1914. The article in *Iqbal* prompted a response from Abdulhakim Sārimsāqov, "Izhār-i haqiqat yā bayān-i hāl," *ST*, 8 July 1914.

tures (the new-method school, an emphasis on education, readership of common newspapers), but their proponents faced markedly different struggles in society. Volga Tatar Jadidism was defined by the concerns of a nascent mercantile middle class facing the consequences of economic change in the center of the empire along with intense pressure from the Church, which threatened to obliterate the very existence of the Tatar community, which had already been turned into a demographic minority. Among the Crimean Tatars and the Qazaqs, reform was first championed by aristocratic elites who had been coopted into the Russian social hierarchy, many of whom had Russian educations. In Transcaucasia, Jadidism arose in a situation of conflict with neighboring non-Muslim communities that threatened to marginalize the Muslim population in an oil-based industrial economy. In Central Asia, in the new social terrain that emerged in the first generation of Russian rule, reform was articulated by a group occupying a different position in society. Although Central Asian reformers appropriated the rhetoric and methods of the Jadids of European Russia, their use of them was defined by imperatives, constraints, and possibilities peculiar to Central Asia.

Once it is located in society, Jadidism does not appear as an undifferentiated intellectual movement emanating from a well-defined center to the periphery. Instead, there were many Jadidisms in the Russian empire, each with its own concerns rooted in local social struggles. This accounts for the fruitlessness of repeated attempts at cooperation at the all-Russian level, as illustrated by the lack of success of attempts to create a common Turkic literary language (a favorite project of Gasprinskii's) or to create a fully representative political movement.

THE JADIDS OF CENTRAL ASIA

In calling for society to reform itself, the Jadids of Turkestan set themselves up against the social order that had emerged in the generation after the Russian conquest. The Jadids most commonly called themselves *ziyālilar* (intellectuals) or *taraqqiparwarlar* (progressives). The term most often used by others in society was *yāshlar* (the youth). The label *usul-i jadidchilar* or *jadidchilar* (proponents of the new method) was actually less frequently used, although it has acquired standard usage in scholarship. The emergence of the Jadids also created, largely as a residual category, their opponents, who came to be called *usul-i qadimchilar*, or *qadimchilar* (the proponents of the old method). The debate over reform had turned quotidian cultural practices into objectified traditions. But the emphasis on the conflict of ideas implicit in these labels does not help us in locating the Jadids on the new social map, even though their place in society was to be of fundamental importance to their project.

The task of locating the Jadids in their society is not easy. Although the lives of the Jadids are chronologically not very distant, they can be extremely difficult to reconstruct. They were born in a society in which written documents did not mark a person's progress through life (although some of them developed a mania for documenting their lives), and few accumulated private papers. Even the concrete remains of their lives perished against the twin assaults of Stalinist repression and urban development. No plaques mark places where the Jadids lived and worked, for most have not survived; the few "house-museums" that exist have undergone so many changes that they fail to evoke the lives of their former occupants. Often the most basic details of their biographies are difficult to establish with any certainty. Nevertheless, as the following survey shows, it is possible to trace the basic outlines of a collective biography.

Behbudi remained the most respected Jadid in Central Asia down to the revolution. In Samarqand he found support from a number of active colleagues and disciples. His circles included Abdulqādir Shakuri, Ajzi, and Hāji Muin. Shakuri's (1875–1943) father was an imām, and his mother ran a maktab for girls.[37] He studied at the Ārifjan-bāy madrasa in Samarqand and taught children according to the old method in his village of Rajabamin on the outskirts of the city. Then he came in contact with Gasprinskii's *Terjüman* at a Tatar friend's shop and became a devotee of the new method.[38] He opened one of the first new-method schools in his village and in time published three textbooks for use in such schools. He traveled to Kazan in 1909 and to Istanbul in 1912 to observe at first hand the workings of modern Muslim educational institutions.[39] Sayyid Ahmad Siddiqi (1864–1927), who wrote under the pen name "Ajzi," was born in a family of modest means. Orphaned early, he was apprenticed to a watchmaker and worked for several years in this craft before going to Bukhara to attend a madrasa.[40] He dropped out after two or three years and worked at various jobs, including a stint as a

37. Wadud Mahmudî, "Muallim Abduqodir Shakurî," *Sadoi Sharq*, 1990, no. 8, 5.
38. M. Fattaev, *Vidnye pedagogi Samarkanda* (Samarqand, 1961), 5–6; Mahmudî, "Muallim Abduqodir Shakurî," 7.
39. Mahmudî, "Muallim Abduqodir Shakurî," 22.
40. Muhammadjon Shukurov, "Zindaginomai Ajzî," *Sadoi Sharq*, 1992, no. 2, 123–124.

scribe for the qāzi of Khātirchi.[41] Like all Jadids from Samarqand, Ajzi was perfectly bilingual in Persian and Turkic, and at about this time, he learned Russian from personal friends (two Russians and a Qazaq). Ajzi had inherited a parcel of land from his father, which he sold in 1901 to go on the hajj. He traveled in Turkey, Egypt, and Arabia (where he worked as a translator at the Russian consulate in Jeddah) for two years. On the way back, he visited Moscow and St. Petersburg before returning to Turkestan through the Caucasus. In Baku, he made the personal acquaintance of leading Transcaucasian Jadids. As for Behbudi, this trip acquainted Ajzi with contemporary intellectual life in other Muslim countries, and upon his return he opened a new-method school in his village.[42] Ajzi was also active in publishing and started the Zarafshān Bookstore in Samarqand in 1914. He was an accomplished poet who contributed frequently to *TWG* as well as Behbudi's *Āyina,* but his biggest contribution to Jadid reform was two long poems in Persian (both later translated into Turkic), *Anjuman-i arwāh* (The Gathering of Souls) and *Mir'at-i ibrat* (The Mirror of Admonition), which came to be the standard Jadid indictment of Turkestani society. Hāji Muin ibn Shukrullah (1883–1942) was born in the family of a shopkeeper but orphaned at the age of twelve and brought up by his grandfather, whom he accompanied on hajj in his youth. He established a maktab in Samarqand, which he switched to the new method in 1903. Over the next decade, he published a primer and poetry, in addition to being a regular contributor to both the Central Asian and Tatar press and translating between Turkic and Persian. After the success of Behbudi's first play in 1914, Hāji Muin diverted his energies to writing plays for the stage and produced several pieces, of which three were published.[43]

Tashkent was the largest center of Jadid activities. Its publishing trade was the largest, and its new-method schools most numerous in Turkestan. Munawwar Qāri Abdurrashid Khān oghli (1878–1931) was in many ways Behbudi's counterpart there. Also born in a family of cultural accomplishment (his father and two elder brothers were mudarrises), Munawwar Qāri attended the Yunus Khān madrasa in Tashkent before spending some time at a madrasa in Bukhara. He returned to

41. Ibid., 124.

42. Ibid., 125–126; Fattaev, *Vidnye pedagogi,* 20–21; see also Begali Qosimov, "Shoir khotirasini izlab," *Sharq yulduzi,* 1989, no. 10, 178–184; Shuhrat Rizaev, "Khalqdin yorliq istarman . . . ," *Guliston,* 1990, no. 8, 9–10.

43. R. Muqimov, "Hoji Muin kim edi?" *Muloqot,* 1994, no. 5–6, 27.

Tashkent in 1901 and opened a new-method school. We know little about his personal motivation, although one author has recently hinted at the significance of his friendship with a Crimean Tatar.[44] This school eventually became the largest and the most organized new-method school in all of Turkestan. Munawwar Qāri also wrote numerous textbooks, ran a bookselling and publishing business, was instrumental in publishing at least two newspapers, and also became involved with theater after 1914. He was at the center of a *gap,* or a discussion circle, in Tashkent that provided the focus for Jadid activity in the city.[45] Munawwar Qāri's friends, disciples, and acquaintances included practically everybody involved in reform in Central Asia.

One of his closest comrades was Abdullah Awlāni (1878–1934), whose father was allegedly a weaver[46] but whose family was prosperous enough for Awlāni to own a house in Tashkent, which he converted into a new-method school. In his youth, Awlāni had attended both the maktab and madrasa. In his own words, around the age of fourteen, "I began reading *Terjümän* and became aware of the world."[47] In 1908, he published the short-lived newspapers *Shuhrat* and *Azya,* subsequently authored several textbooks and collections of poetry (often for classroom use), and organized a reading room in Tashkent. He, too, was involved in publishing and was partner, along with ten other Tashkent Jadids, in the Maktab publishing company floated in 1914. After 1914, Awlāni also wrote a number of plays for the theater, with which he was involved also as actor, director, and manager, founding Turkestan's first regular theater troupe in 1916.[48]

In Ferghana, with its cotton-boom economy and many small towns, Jadid circles were more numerous and dispersed. One of the first advo-

44. Sirojiddin Ahmad, "Munawwar qori," *Sharq yulduzi,* 1992, no. 5, 107.

45. GARF, f. 102, op. 244 (1914), d. 74, ch. 84B, l. 71.

46. This information comes from Awlāni's own account of his life, written in 1933, when the need to find such proletarian origins was quite pressing; see Abdulla Awloniy, "Tarjimai holim," in *Toshkent tongi,* ed. B. Qosimov (Tashkent, 1979), 373–374. Despite Awlāni's prominent position in the official pantheon, details of his life are sketchy, as existing biographies tend to focus on the period after 1917. See A. Bobokhonov and M. Mahsumov, *Abdulla Awloniyning pedagogik faoliyati wa ta"lim-tarbiya tŏghrisidagi fikrlari* (Tashkent, 1966); Abdulla Abdurazzakov, "Pedagogicheskoe nasledie uzbekskogo prosvetitelia Abdully Avloni" (Candidate's diss., Tashkent, 1979); U. Dolimov, "Abdulla Awloniy—atoqli metodist olim," in *Milliy uyghonish wa ŏzbek filologiyasi masalalari* (Tashkent, 1993), 40–50; and *ŎSE,* I, 14–15, s.v. "Abdulla Awloniy."

47. Quoted by Bobokhonov and Mahsumov, *Abdulla Awloniyning pedagogik faoliyati,* 32–33.

48. T. T. Tursunov, *Oktiabr'skaia revoliutsiia i uzbekskii teatr* (Tashkent, 1983), 10–12.

cates of reform in the region was Ishāq Khān Tora Junaydullah oghli (1862–1937), who began writing in *TWG* in the 1890s. Like Behbudi, he came from a well-to-do family and likewise possessed madrasa knowledge (he had attended madrasa in Kokand and was qāzi in his native village of Tora Qurghān). He had traveled in Arabia, Iran, Afghanistan, India, and Chinese Turkestan for five years between 1887 and 1892. Upon his return home, he went into the publishing trade, which he used to publish his own work, including such useful books as a six-language lexicon and a compendium of scripts used all over the world. In 1908, he purchased a printing press, which he devoted largely to propagating the message of reform.[49] By that time, new-method schools were widespread in Ferghana, and their teachers provided a substantial core for Jadidism. Again, many came from the older cultural elite. Āshurali Zāhiri (1885–1942?), a prominent contributor to the press and author of the first guide to the orthography of Central Asian Turkic, had attended madrasas in Kokand and Bukhara.[50] But perhaps the most active proponent of reform in Ferghana was Hamza Hakimzāda Niyāzi (1889–1929), whose background and activities encapsulated many characteristics of Central Asian Jadidism.

Hamza's father had studied in Bukhara and was one of the most renowned apothecaries of Kokand. He also wrote poetry and mingled with the literary elite of Kokand. He had traveled extensively in Chinese Turkestan and India, which is evidence of a certain prosperity.[51] Hamza's education was traditional: After the maktab, he spent seven years in a madrasa in Kokand. Hamza wrote poetry in Persian and corresponded with his father only in Arabic. But by 1907, he began reading *Vaqït* and *Terjüman,* and, as he later recalled, "I began to think about old superstitions, about [reform] of the madrasas, changes in the people's life, civilization, and society."[52] He had started working as a scribe in the office of Ābidjān Mahmudov,[53] but in 1910 he went to Bukhara to perfect his Arabic. He arrived, however, just as riots broke out in the city, and in-

49. O. Usmon, *Özbekistonda rus tilining ilk targhibotchilari* (Tashkent, 1962), 40; Aziz Bobokhonov, *Özbek matbaasi tarikhidan* (Tashkent, 1979), 112–113; Ulughbek Dolimov, *Ishoqkhon Ibrat* (Tashkent, 1994).

50. Iuldash Abdullaev, *Ocherki po metodike obucheniia gramote v uzbekskoi shkole* (Tashkent, 1966), 147.

51. Siddiq Rajabov, "Özbek pedagogik fikrining asoschisi," *Özbek tili wa adabiyoti,* 1989, no. 5, 15.

52. Hamza, "Tarjimai hol," in Hamza Hakimzoda Niyoziy, *Tŏla asarlar tŏplami,* ed. N. Karimov et al., 5 vols. (Tashkent, 1988–1989), IV: 293.

53. Personal document in Hamza, *Tŏla asarlar tŏplami,* V: 185.

stead he worked in a printing press in Kāgān and returned by way of Tashkent.[54] It was during this visit that he first saw a new-method school. He also made the acquaintance of a number of Jadids in that city. Upon his return to Kokand, Hamza opened his own school and began teaching. At some point during this period, Hamza had learned Russian (perhaps at a Russo-native school).[55] In 1912, he married a Russian woman who converted to Islam. Almost immediately afterward, Hamza left, via Afghanistan and India, for hajj. He also visited Syria and Istanbul before returning through Odessa and Transcaspia to Kokand.[56] Over the next five years, Hamza opened a number of schools in various cities of Ferghana, although some of them do not seem to have lasted very long. He also wrote a number of textbooks and primers for his use, although none was published. Other works did get published: articles in the Jadid press, several volumes of "national" poetry, a piece of fiction that may be considered the first attempt to write a novel in Central Asia, and several plays. Hamza was also involved in publishing and bookselling, a benevolent society (it does not seem to have had a very successful career), and a theater troupe. We have practically no information about Hamza's private life and only the sketchiest knowledge of his financial situation. Teaching seems to have been an economic necessity as much as a passion for Hamza, but he could also look for support from wealthy friends. He had worked for Ābidjān Mahmudov in 1908, and when Mahmudov brought out the newspaper *Sadā-yi Farghāna* in 1914, Hamza wrote for it. His friends also included merchants such as Mir Zāhid Mir Āqil oghli of Kokand and Said Nāsir Mir Jalilov of Turkestan, both of whom helped him out with loans in times of need.[57]

Hamza's roots were firmly in the tradition of Muslim knowledge reproduced in the madrasa, and he could utilize all the resources available to a well-connected man in cultivated society.[58] Indeed, the number of Jadids who emerged from the cultural elite of the pre-Russian period is striking. A number of the most prominent Jadids were ulama in their own

---

54. Hamza, "Tarjimai hol," 293–294.
55. Rajabov, "Özbek pedagogik," 15.
56. *Hamza Hakimzoda Niyoziyning arkhivining katalogi,* 2 vols. (Tashkent, 1990–91), I, 305. The fact that Hamza was a *hāji* was never brought up in his Soviet biographies.
57. Cf. several unpublished private documents in Hamza, *Tŏla asarlar tŏplami,* V: 189–192; see also Ghaffor Mŏminov, "Hamza biografiyasining bir sahifasi," *Hamza ijodi haqida* (Tashkent, 1981), 140–141.
58. This needs to be reiterated given the misrepresentation of Hamza's life in Soviet biographies. See, e.g., Laziz Qayumov, *Hamza: esse* (Tashkent, 1989), 17–18.

right. Behbudi and Munawwar Qāri both possessed the cultural capital that came from the possession of madrasa knowledge and maintained personal relationships with noted ulama. It is important to remember, too, that the ulama were not as benighted a group as they are often portrayed. Edward Allworth, for instance, in describing the *qadimchilar* as "internally governed by fixed habit and rigid tradition. . . . ultraconservative officials and clerics [who] could not imagine that they might benefit from the notions of these cultural-social thinkers [the Jadids],"[59] unreflexively adopts the rhetoric of the Jadids. In practice, the lines separating the Jadids from their opponents were considerably more porous. Others active in the Jadid cause were even more closely tied to the madrasa milieu. Sayyid Ahmad Wasli (1870–1920) of Samarqand wrote copious poetry in praise of the new method but accepted an appointment as mudarris at the Hazrat-i Shāh madrasa in 1915.[60] His support for reform was more circumscribed, stopping short, as we shall see, of the embrace of theater and changes in the place of women in society. The Beglarbegi and Kokaldāsh madrasas in Tashkent were the center of considerable literary activity; such poets as Tawallā, Kami, Khislat, and Sidqi (all of whom appeared as champions of reform in the Jadid press) lived and wrote there.[61] Abdullah Qādiri's early biography also reminds us of the impossibility of drawing strict boundaries between the ulama and the Jadids. Qādiri (1894–1938), who was to become the first Uzbek novelist after the revolution, came from a learned family. His maternal grandfather was a *muezzin,* and the poet Miskin (1880–1937) was a maternal cousin.[62] His father was in his seventies when Abdullah was born, and the family was in dire financial straits. After the maktab, Abdullah held a number of menial jobs in succession before being hired by a merchant as a scribe. His employer put him in a Russo-native school so he could learn Russian.[63] He spent four years in this school, after which he went to work for another merchant. He became interested in writing and published his first play in 1915. Yet, after all this involvement in Jadid reform, he went back to a madrasa in the years 1916–1917.[64]

59. Edward Allworth, *The Modern Uzbeks: A Cultural History* (Stanford, 1990), 120.
60. *Āyina,* 1 June 1915, 430.
61. Begali Qosimov, "Tawallo (1882–1939)," preface to Tawallo, *Rawnaq ul-Islom,* ed. Begali Qosimov (Tashkent, 1993), 4.
62. Habibulla Qodiriy, *Otam haqida* (Tashkent, 1983), 5–24.
63. Abdulla Qodiriy, "Tarjimai hol" (1926), in *Kichik asarlar* (Tashkent, 1969), 205.
64. Ibid., 206.

Other ulama, in Tashkent as well as elsewhere, were involved with different versions of reform. Abdulqādir Sayyāh, for instance, fits the profile of many Jadids: He traveled extensively, he was a copious author and was involved in publishing, and in 1915 he began publishing the magazine *al-Islāh* (Reform). But he was no enthusiast of the new method of education. The reform he advocated in his magazine concerned questions of religious purity and exactitude. Although it too sought to rectify what it saw as the current perversion of Islam, it derived its authority not from the discourse of progress and knowledge but from a strengthening of the tradition itself. We know rather little about such intellectual currents in Central Asia, but it seems likely that the contributors to *al-Islāh* formed a revivalist movement akin to that of the modernized madrasa at Deoband in India. Contacts with ulama in India had survived the Russian conquest, and by the turn of the century older patterns of travel had been reversed and many ulama now went to India to study. The modernized madrasa at Deoband received students from as far away in the Russian empire as Kazan. In 1914, there were enough students at Deoband from Bukhara and Kazan to form an association.[65] Although *al-Islāh* remained inimical to the main thrust of Jadidism, its pages did see some discussion of proposals to reform madrasas. One set of proposals, submitted by a mudarris from Bukhara, suggested a fifteen-year curriculum, with two subjects being taught every year. These proposals would have gone some way in turning madrasas into colleges, with the introduction of a fixed curriculum, grades, and examinations.[66]

The distinction between such revivalist ulama and the Jadids is a crucial one, for it points to a significant characteristic of Jadidism; as such, it is well worth a short digression. A number of scholars in the West have sought to ground Jadidism in an indigenous Muslim tradition of re-

65. "'Dār ul-ulum Deoband'dagi Rusyali Islām talabalaridan tashakkur," *Āyina*, 16 October 1914, 1225. During the first century of its existence (1867–1967), Deoband graduated 70 students from "Russia (including Siberia)" (Barbara D. Metcalf, *Islamic Revival in British India: Deoband, 1860–1900* [Princeton, 1982], 110–111). Although the figure of 70 students is an aggregate for the entire century, the great majority, if not all, of these students must have matriculated before 1917. To put the number of Russian Muslim students in context, it must be remembered that the total for all students from outside South Asia was only 431 for this period. The college at Deoband was founded by reformist ulama in the late 1860s; it offered instruction only in religious subjects, but it was organized along modern lines, with annual examinations, grades, and division into classes (ibid., ch. 3).

66. Mudarris Sayyid Ahmad Wasli, "Himmat ur-rijāl taqlaʿ ul-jibāl," *al-Islāh*, 15 July 1915, 392–394; Wasli, "Islāh-i tadris haqinda," *al-Islāh*, 15 September 1915, 514–516; Qāri Ziyāʾuddin Makhzum b. Dāmlā Fayzurrahmān Mudarris, "Insānning birinchi wazifasi wa ham māya-i saʿādat," *al-Islāh*, 15 September 1915, 516–519.

form.[67] Jadidism was the outcome, according to this view, of a long struggle in Bukharan madrasas to break the bonds of *taqlid* (obedience to canonical opinion) and for a return to the scriptural sources of Islam. This view was a corrective to Soviet-era conceptualizations of intellectual history as a battle between "enlighteners," secular, antireligious, and progressive by definitions, and upholders of various reactionary ideologies, of which Jadidism was one.[68] By pointing to the origins in Islamic theology of the reformism of such Tatar figures as Abdunnasir Kursavi (1776–1812) and Shihabiddin Märjani (1818–1889), scholars situated Tatar intellectual history in its Muslim context.

But such a view is much more difficult to maintain with respect to Central Asian Jadidism. To be sure, much of the reformism of Kursavi and Märjani owed a great deal to their educations in the madrasas of Bukhara, but we have very little evidence to date of debates about *taqlid* among Bukharan ulama, and Jadidism's connection to such debates is even more problematic. The problem is usually solved by seeing the Bukharan savant Ahmad Makhdum Dānish (1826–1897) as the "theoretical precursor" of the Jadids, indeed a figure so important that "few men have shaken . . . traditional attitudes as deeply as he."[69] Unfortunately, Dānish's own work scarcely bears this heavy burden. Much of his work is marked by a sensibility that belongs very much to the world whose passing he mourns, rather than the brave new world that the Jadids celebrated, and his literary style aims to reproduce the golden age of Persian prose of yore. Furthermore, Dānish wrote while in disgrace, and his work remained in manuscript until well after his death. Dānish's influence was no doubt substantial in the literary circles of Bukhara, but his name never once appeared in a Jadid publication before the revolution. His reputation as the first of the moderns was created almost single-

67. This is the theme of several articles by French, Uzbek, and German scholars published in "Le réformisme musulman en Asie centrale: du «premier renouveau» à la soviétisation, 1788–1937," ed. Stéphane Dudoignon and François Georgeon, in *Cahiers du monde russe* 37 (1996): 7–240; for comment pertaining specifically to Central Asia, see Dudoignon, "La question scolaire à Boukhara et au Turkestan russe, du «premier renouveau» à la soviétisation (fin du XVIIIe siècle–1937)," 140–146.

68. Edward J. Lazzerini, "The Revival of Islamic Culture in Pre-Revolutionary Russia: Or, Why a Prosopography of the Tatar *Ulema*?" in Ch. Lemercier Quelquejay et al., eds., *Passé turco-tatar, présent soviétique: études offertes à Alexandre Bennigsen* (Paris, 1986), 367–372.

69. Carrère d'Encausse, "The Stirring of National Feeling," 172; Carrère d'Encausse has made the same claim elsewhere as well (*Réforme et révolution chez les musulmans de l'empire russe,* 2nd ed. [Paris, 1981], 105–109), and the view has recently been repeated by Stéphane Dudoignon, "La question scolaire," 142.

handedly in the 1920s by Sadriddin Ayni, whose view has been accepted much too readily by scholars.

But there is a further, more fundamental problem with a continuity between debates over *taqlid* and Jadidism, for it places Jadidism in the realm of "religion" (or, to be more precise, theology) rather than in that of cultural transformation. As I will argue, theological argumentation was conspicuous by its absence in Jadid writing, even though the Jadids made use of modernist theology being produced elsewhere. The trajectory of Jadidism that I have outlined in this chapter places it in the transformations of Central Asian society wrought by the Russian conquest, as a modern "response" to modernity, which sought to reconfigure the entire world, including Islam. If there was widespread debate in Bukhara in the nineteenth century on the questions of *taqlid* and a return to scripturalist Islam, its inheritors were not the Jadids but the revivalist ulama who published *al-Islāh*.

The relationship between the Jadids and the moneyed elite of Turkestan was also ambivalent. Said Karim-bāy, Said Azim's son, published the newspaper *Tojjār* in 1907 and occasionally wrote for it, too. He was a founding member in 1909 of the first Muslim benevolent society in Tashkent, in which the prime movers were Munawwar Qāri and Awlāni. Said Ahmad, Said Karim-bāy's son, was a partner in the Maktab Publishing Company, launched in 1914. Mirzā Hakim Sārimsāqov, a textile merchant, was a collaborator of Munawwar Qāri and Ubaydullah Khojaev in publishing *Sadā-yi Turkistān* (to which he contributed) and a partner in the Turkestan Bookstore.[70] But the most prominent merchant in Jadid ranks was Ābidjān Mahmudov of Kokand, merchant of the second guild, who, in addition to his substantial business, was active in the publishing trade. In 1914, he established his own printing press and published the newspaper *Sadā-yi Farghāna*.[71] The Jadids and the new moneyed elite were part of the same phenomenon, i.e., the transformation of the Central Asian economy under Russian rule, but the two elites had different stakes in the future. As a new cultural elite, the Jadids proceeded from the assumption that it was necessary to transform the cultural tradition they inherited in order to cope with the new conditions. The moneyed elite, on the other hand, had fared well under the new regime, and most, content to make money from the new opportunities without changing the old ways, saw no pressing need for reform.

70. TsGARUz, f. 461, op. 1, d. 1311, l. 2420b, 255.
71. TsGARUz, f. 19, d. 19074, ll. 14, 30–300b.

They flaunted their newly acquired status in ostentatious displays of wealth at various feasts (*toys*). For the Jadids, the wealth possessed by the merchantry represented a great resource that could free the Jadids from economic constraints if used according to their priorities. But the merchants (*bāys*) only occasionally spent their wealth in the service of reform, especially since that reform was articulated by a marginal group of youth. As we shall see, in their literature and drama, the Jadids presented their ideal of the *bāy* as a philanthropist patron of reform. In pressing the wealthy of their own community for help, Turkestani Jadids pointed to the example of the Tatar and Transcaucasian Muslim middle classes, who provided considerable financial assistance to their compatriots. The results were indifferent; Turkestan saw nothing comparable to the large-scale philanthropy of the Taghievs of Baku or the Hüseyinovs of Orenburg.

The Jadids came from various backgrounds. What they had in common was a commitment to change and a possession of cultural capital. This disposed them to conceive of reform in cultural terms, and the modicum of comfort that most enjoyed in their lives allowed them to devote their energies to it. In the end, the Jadids were constituted as a group by their own critical discourse. Their sense of cohesion came from their shared vision of the future as well as their participation in common activities and enterprises. The basic institution of Jadid reform was the new-method school itself. These schools were the site of the struggle for the hearts and minds of the next generation. Through them the Jadids disseminated a cognitive style quite different from that of the maktab and thus created a group in society that was receptive to their ideas. These schools were also crucial to the social reproduction of the movement. If the first new-method schools were founded single-handedly by a few dedicated individuals, by 1917 new-method schools were often staffed by their own graduates.[72] The Jadids also enthusiastically adopted such new forms of sociability as benevolent societies. Ultimately, though, the structure of the movement was quite diffuse, with a correspondingly wide range of sensibilities and attitudes toward other groups in society as well as the state.

Munawwar Qāri represented perhaps the conservative end of the Jadid spectrum. Police documents indicate that many of his closest associates

---

72. See, for example, A. F. Ardashirov, "K voprosu o roli novometodnykh maktabov (po materialam Andizhanskoi oblasti)," *Uchenye zapiski Andizhanskogo gospedinstituta*, no. 6 (1957): 132–172.

were ulama not otherwise associated with the Jadid cause, and his writings remained, in terms of genre and content, the most traditionalist.
Other Jadids were far more outspoken in their criticism of the old order
and the role of the ulama in it. Indeed, it is possible to discern a second
"generation" of Jadids in Turkestan by 1910. Younger, and with a less
thorough grounding in the madrasa tradition, they were more impatient
with the current state of their society and harsher in their tone. Abdulhamid Sulaymān oghli, who wrote under the name Cholpān, began
publishing in the last years before 1917. He was the scion of a wealthy
family and had attended a Russo-native school after the maktab.[73] Mirmuhsin Shermuhammadov (1895–1929) attended a new-method school
in Tashkent and started writing in *TWG* in 1914. A prolific writer (he also
contributed to other periodicals), he fearlessly took on every topic and
every person, including Behbudi himself.[74] Even Hamza, whose madrasa
credentials were impeccable, was fond of harsh criticism, as in this *āshula*
(poem set to a folk tune):

> Cry, cry o Turkestan
> May soulless bodies swing, cry o Turkestan
> Is there a nation like ours, sunk in infamy?
> Deceived into foolishness, devoid of chastity?[75]

This powerful language contrasted to the more cautious tone of Behbudi
or Munawwar Qāri. When Hamza sent Munawwar Qāri a manuscript
for publication, he was told to tone down the language and to avoid using impolite (*adabdan khārij*) words.[76]

The first Jadids in Central Asia were, by and large, men of the old order whose personal experiences had convinced them of the need to
change. Yet, they were also products of their time. Many of them had traveled extensively. They possessed the cultural capital of the past, but almost none had experienced a purely Russian education. Many of them
knew Russian, but it was usually self-taught in adult life; they had not
been through the formative experience of Russian education. This con-

73. A. Z. V. Togan, *Hâtıralar: Türkistan ve Diğer Müslüman Doğu Türklerinin Millî
Varlık ve Kültür Mücadeleleri* (Istanbul, 1969), 118–119; Ibrohim Haqqulov, editor's introduction to Chölpon, *Bahorni soghindim* (Tashkent, 1988), 4; for a full biography of
Cholpān, see Naim Karimov, *Abdulhamid Sulaymon ŏghli Chölpon* (Tashkent, 1991).
74. Begali Qosimov, "Mirmuhsin Shermuhamedov (Fikri) wa uning adabiy muhiti"
(Candidate's diss., Tashkent, 1967); ÖSE, VII: 274, s.v. "Shermuhamedov, Mirmuhsin."
75. Hamza Hakimzāda Niyāzi, *Milli āshulalar uchun milli she'rlar majmuasi* (Eski
Marghilān, 1916), 1.
76. Munawwar Qāri to Hamza Hakimzāda, 4 November 1915, in *Hamza arkhivining
katalogi*, II: 283–284.

trasts markedly with the Jadids of European Russia and Transcaucasia, many of whom had a Russian (and, in some cases, even a European) education. Gasprinskii, who had attended a military academy in Moscow and worked for two years in Paris as Turgenev's secretary,[77] is hardly unusual in that respect. Central Asian Jadids, on the other hand, remained much closer to the Islamic cultural tradition than Jadids in other parts of the Russian empire.

Yet, for all this, their youth was a striking characteristic. Ishāq Khān and Ajzi, born in the 1860s, were by far the oldest members of the cohort. Behbudi was twenty-eight when he launched his public career and Munawwar Qāri only twenty-three; Awlāni began writing poetry at the age of sixteen. Those who became active in the last few years before the revolution were even younger. Hamza was twenty-one when he opened his first school in 1910, the same age at which Abdullah Qādiri wrote his first play. When Cholpān sent in his first poem to the newspaper *Shuhrat* in 1908, he signed the accompanying letter "a maktab pupil." He was probably only ten years old then.[78] The youth of the Jadids was testimony to their prodigious talent and a source of their seemingly inexhaustible energy but, in a society where age was cultural capital in itself, also their greatest handicap.

They also differed from the small number of Central Asians with a modern, secular Russian education. Ubaydullah Khojaev, the Tashkent lawyer and publisher, and the Samarqand doctor Abdurrahmān Farhādi, who was appointed Russian consul in Najaf in 1914,[79] were perhaps the only representatives of this group prominent in public life before 1917. (Several others, such as Tāshpolāt Nārbutabekov and Nazir Toraqul oghli, became active in that year.) The vast majority of Muslims in Central Asia with a Russian secular education were Qazaq or Tatar. Whereas the Jadids originated in the old cultural elite of the region, these intellectuals often came from aristocratic elites. The Tatars came from among the ranks of the more prosperous sections of the community that had arrived in Turkestan after the Russian conquest. The Qazaqs, on the other hand, often came from aristocratic families and were southern analogues to a secular Qazaq elite that had formed in the Steppe province by the middle of the nineteenth century. The Qazaq elites of the steppe

77. Seydahmet, *Gaspıralı İsmail Bey*, 12–19.

78. The newspaper was closed down by the authorities and its papers seized before it could be published. The poem is to be found in TsGARUz, f. 1, op. 31, d. 489a, l. 31.

79. *Äyina*, 7 December 1913, 167; see also Mahmudî, "Muallim Abduqodir Shakurî," 26.

had been sending their children to Russian schools since the first quarter of the nineteenth century.[80] The absence among the Qazaqs of a tradition of book learning entrenched in madrasas made the transition to secular education easy, since the survival of a cultural elite was not at stake, and by the middle of the nineteenth century, this interaction had produced the genius of Choqan Valikhanov, equally at home in Qazaq and Russian society.[81] A number of these secular intellectuals received a university education in Russia. Mustafā Choqāy (1890–1941), who was descended from the Khivan royal family, attended the Tashkent *gimnaziia* on a substantial scholarship and went on to study law at St. Petersburg University.[82] While in Petersburg, he worked at the offices of the Muslim Faction in the State Duma, drafting speeches for Muslim deputies.[83] In choosing to wage his struggles in the sphere of politics rather than cultural reform, Choqāy was typical of the secular intellectuals, whose activities went on in parallel with that of the Jadids. We find little evidence of interaction between the two groups before 1917. The Jadids represented the modernization of the Muslim cultural tradition of Central Asia; the secular intellectuals were fluent in the idiom of European thought. The Jadids spoke to Muslim society in order to achieve cultural change; the secular intellectuals spoke to the Russian state and Russian society in order to achieve political change. With Islam Shahiahmedov, a Tatar born in Tashkent and Choqāy's contemporary in St. Petersburg who was arrested in 1907 for spreading revolutionary agitation in the Tashkent garrison,[84] we have come a long way from Wasli and Munawwar Qāri. Although a police report described him as "belonging to the

---

80. An "Asiatic school" to teach Russian to Qazaq children with the aim of producing translators was opened at Omsk as early as 1786. A school directed at the children of the Qazaq aristocracy started at Khanskaia Stavka in 1841, followed by another one at Orenburg in 1850 (T. T. Tazhibaev, *Prosveshchenie i shkoly Kazakhstana vo vtoroi polovine XIX veka* [Alma Ata, 1962], 17, 22–23). Many Qazaqs also attended Russian civilian and military schools at Omsk and Orenburg.

81. The Russian conquest of Turkestan brought the Qazaq steppe under greater influence of the Islam reproduced in madrasas, as madrasa students found it safer to travel to the steppe in the summer. Writing in 1910, Ahmet Bukeykhanov saw two competing new elites emerging in the Qazaq lands, one formed like him in Russian institutions, the other increasingly Muslim and formed in the madrasas of Central Asia and the Volga; see A. Bukeikhanov, "Kirgizy," in A. I. Kastelianskii, ed., *Formy natsional'nogo dvizheniia v sovremennykh gosudarstvakh* (St. Petersburg, 1910), 597–598.

82. TsGARUz, f. 47, d. 787, l. 192.

83. Dzhumabaev, "Nash vozhd'," in *Iash Turkestan: pamiati Mustafy Chokai-beia* (Paris, 1949), 5–6; see also Ozod Sharafiddinov, "Mustafo Chŏqaev," *Sharq yulduzi,* 1992, no. 4, 85–93.

84. "Spravka" (12 May 1916), TsGARUz, f. 1, op. 31, d. 1113, l. 28–280b.

so-called Bolshevist-Leninist current of the RSDWP," [85] Shahiahmedov contributed to both liberal and radical periodicals in St. Petersburg, and upon his return to Turkestan in 1915, he edited the "progressive, non-party" newspaper, *Turkestanskii krai*.[86] In the heady days of 1917, when organized politics became a possibility, Jadids and Russian-educated intellectuals coalesced in a single political movement in which the latter tended to assume positions of leadership. The leading role of the modern educated intellectuals in 1917 was out of all proportion to their numerical strength or to their influence in local society before the revolution. Active politics required a command of the Russian language and of the Russian political idiom, and in this regard the Russian-educated intellectuals held a clear advantage over the Jadids.

COLONIAL SENSIBILITIES IN THE AGE OF EMPIRE

The Jadid project was predicated on a new sense of the world and of Central Asia's position within it. The cornerstone of this worldview was an assimilation of the idea of progress. The Jadids explicitly understood that their age was different from any other: "[In the past], one science or craft [used to] develop [at a time]," a Jadid textbook read. "In this century, [however,] all sciences and crafts develop [together]. . . . This is the century of science and progress. The sciences seen in this century have never been seen before." [87] Science developed its own authority, as new discourses of hygiene and public health brought more and more aspects of life into the realm of human agency. The term used for "progress" was *taraqqi,* with a semantic range that covered "development," "growth," and "rise" (those who had achieved progress were *mutaraqqi*).[88] The centrality of progress to the Jadid project was underscored by the fact that perhaps the most common term used to describe them as a group, both by themselves and by others (albeit with more derision than pride), was

85. Ibid., l. 280b.

86. *Turkestanskii krai,* 5 April 1916. Bennigsen and Lemercier-Quelquejay (*La presse et le mouvement national,* 168) count *Turkestanskii krai* as a "Muslim" newspaper. This assertion is not borne out by the evidence of the newspaper itself. The newspaper spoke in the idiom of Russian liberalism; its readership was overwhelmingly Russian, and it had no choice but to cater to their interests. As such, it scarcely differed from any other liberal Russian-language newspaper published in Turkestan.

87. Ghulāmuddin Akbarzāda, *Ta'līm-i sāni* (Tashkent, 1913), 27–28.

88. See O. Usmonov and Sh. Hamidov, *Özbek tili leksikasi tarikhidan materiallar (XIX asrning okhiri–XX asrning boshlari)* (Tashkent, 1981), 153, 231, for examples of usage.

taraqqiparwar, "proponents of progress." This progress was a universal phenomenon accessible to all who cultivated knowledge. Europe and Russia had achieved a higher level of progress because of superior knowledge; they were models to be followed. This attitude was subversive of the dichotomy of Russian and native (colonizer and colonized) on which the colonial order was based, but it served a crucial rhetorical purpose for the Jadids.

The idea of progress was predicated upon the growth of a historical conception of time among the Jadids. The Islamic tradition, it is probably fair to say, had never seen history as a road to progress; rather, the past was a sacralized record of divine intervention in the affairs of men. Just how new the idea of constant progress and change over historical time was becomes clear from the pains Abdurrauf Fitrat took to explain the notion from first principles in an article devoted to outlining the goals of life. Humanity was weak and bereft of knowledge and skills at the beginning of Creation, but slowly it conquered the elements:

> It is impossible to deny the changes wrought by humans in the world. Are these changes . . . progress or decline? That is, have humans [*insānhā*] been moving forward or backward from Creation to the present day? Of course forward, i.e., they have been progressing, and they have not stopped at a point to our day. For example, a few years ago, we considered the railway the ultimate means of transport. [But] after a while, the power of human knowledge invented the aeroplane and proved us wrong. Thus, it becomes obvious that humanity [*bani Ādam*] has progressed from Creation to our days, and after our time too, it will progress, that is, move forward." [89]

Fitrat then relates his theme to that of religion, but even there the notion of progress is prominent. God has provided guidance to humanity through the ages, but earlier prophets conveyed God's message to specific groups. Only after humanity had progressed to a certain level was it ready for God's final message. Fitrat thus grafts Islam on to an evolutionary vision of history. From our point of view, however, the article is important in that it unequivocally treats history as a record of human progress.

Geography similarly provided the Jadids a completely different conception of their place in the universe. Modern geography brought with it new conceptions of space, as something that could be envisioned in the form of a map or a globe but that also was finite. It provided a sense

---

89. Abdurrauf Fitrat, "Hayāt wa ghāya-yi hayāt," *Āyina,* 14 December 1913, 196–197, and 21 December 1913, 220–222; quote from 220.

of the interconnectedness of peoples and countries.[90] The study of geography occupied a very important place in Jadid thinking because it provided a graphic appreciation of the modern world. The Europeans had conquered the world by knowing it, Behbudi had implied; conquered nations likewise had to know the world. Munawwar Qāri's geography textbook, for instance, provides detailed factual information (population, type of government, and capital city) about every country in the world; Munawwar Qāri paid special attention to Muslim populations in each country.[91] The Jadids' fascination with maps, globes, and atlases went beyond the classroom. Behbudi published a four-color wall map of Central Asia inscribed in Turkic,[92] and his bookstore carried numerous atlases and maps, mostly of Ottoman provenance.[93]

The significance of the new writing then appearing in Tatar, Ottoman, and Arabic in shaping the worldviews of educated Central Asians was central. The new bookstores operated by the Jadids in the major cities of Central Asia stocked books published in India, Iran, Istanbul, Cairo, and Beirut, as well as the various Muslim publishing centers of the Russian empire. In Samarqand, at Mahmud Khoja Behbudi's bookstore opened in 1914, the interested reader could find a large number of books in Tatar, Ottoman, Arabic, and Persian on topics such as history, geography, general science, medicine, and religion, in addition to dictionaries, atlases, charts, maps, and globes.[94] Among these imported books were many translations or adaptations of European works. In the absence of any significant local translations, these Ottoman and Tatar translations became Central Asia's window on Europe, a fact quite obvious to Behbudi: "Ottoman, Caucasian, and Kazan Turks daily increase the number of translations of works of contemporary scholars, which means that the person who knows Turkic knows the world."[95] But it is easy to overlook the continuing importance of Persian and Arabic. Persian printed books continued to be imported from India (and some booksellers even had their books printed in India),[96] and Persian-language

90. Thongchai Winichakul, *Siam Mapped: A History of the Geo-body of a Nation* (Honolulu, 1994).

91. Munawwar Qāri, *Yer yuzi* (Tashkent, 1913).

92. *Āyina*, 1 March 1914.

93. Cf. price list in *Āyina*, 6 September 1914, 1095.

94. Much of the information in the following section is derived from a number of detailed price lists of books published by Behbudi in *Āyina* in 1914.

95. Behbudi, "Ikki emas, tort til lāzim," *Āyina*, 26 October 1913, 13.

96. G. L. Dmitriev, "Rasprostranenie indiiskikh izdanii v Srednei Azii v kontse XIX–nachale XX vekov," *Kniga: materialy i issledovaniia*, no. 6 (1962): 239–254.

newspapers such as *Chihra-numā* (Cairo), *Habl ul-matin* (Calcutta), and the *Sirāj ul-akhbār* (Kabul) were widely read in Jadid circles. The Jadids' madrasa educations also gave them access to Arabic. Hamza corresponded in it; Shakuri worked as a translator in the Russian consulate in Jeddah; and Abdullah Qādiri read the works of the modernist Arab historian Jurjī Zaydān in the original.[97]

Jurjī Zaydān was only one example of modern scholarship influencing Jadid thinking. It intruded in other ways as well. Fitrat, in his *Tales of an Indian Traveler,* quotes a long passage from "the great French professor" Charles Seignobos about the glories of medieval Islamic civilization.[98] European scholarship on history, linguistics, and anthropology was often held up as validating arguments made by the Jadids. References to Gustav Le Bon, John William Draper, and Reinhart Dozy show up frequently in Jadid writings. Such writing also influenced the style of Jadid argumentation. Fitrat imported Seignobos's anticlericalism whole cloth into his argument against the influence of the ulama in contemporary Bukhara, which he compares to the influence of the Church in the Dark Ages.[99] Almost all Jadids knew Russian, but it was not a significant channel for the transmission of modern knowledge to Central Asia.

In addition to the printed word, travel provided important links with Muslim movements and intellectuals overseas. When Jadids traveled, they invariably went to other Muslim countries. One of the transformative moments of Behbudi's life was his 1900 visit to Egypt, where he visited al-Azhar and, most likely, met with reformers such as Muhammad ʿAbduh.[100] Behbudi visited Istanbul and Cairo again in 1914. In the meantime, he maintained his contacts in those places, so that when, a decade after his first trip abroad, a disciple of his left Samarqand to attend al-Azhar, Behbudi was able to provide him with letters of introduction to a benevolent society in Istanbul.[101] The Ottoman empire occupied a special place in the imagination of the Central Asian Jadids, who followed closely the debates of the Second Constitutional Period inaugurated by the Young Turk revolution of 1908, finding them much livelier than anything possible in the Russian empire at the time. They sympa-

---

97. Qodiriy, *Otam haqida,* 59.
98. Fitrat, "Bayonoti sayyohi hindî," ed. Kholiq Mirzozoda, *Sadoi Sharq,* 1988, no. 6, 28.
99. Ibid., 27–28.
100. Hāji Muin, "Mahmud Khoja Behbudi."
101. Äbdusälam Azimi, "Behbudi haqqida khatira wa tääsuratim," *Zarafshan,* 25 March 1923. Abdussalam Azimi also carried a letter of introduction to Gasprinskii, with whom Behbudi was on close terms.

thized primarily with the Islamists rather than the Turkists, but they also picked and chose among other ideas.[102] There existed a considerable community of Central Asian students in Istanbul in the years preceding the outbreak of World War I. Muhammad Sharif Sufizāda (1869–1937), who was born in Chust in Ferghana, spent his life traveling. He went to Istanbul in 1902 and after three years of serving as imām in various Sufi lodges, he entered the Imperial Teachers' College (Darülmüallimin-i Şahane) in 1905. He did not finish the course but returned to Turkestan in 1906, in order, he claimed, "to serve his own coreligionists and compatriots."[103] Over the next eight years, he taught according to the new method in various cities of Turkestan as well as in Qonghirāt in Khiva. In 1913, he opened a new-method school in Chust, but opposition from neighbors forced him to close it and leave town.[104] He went to Afghanistan where he contributed to the Sirāj ul-akhbār. In 1919, when the government of Soviet Turkestan sent a diplomatic mission to Afghanistan (Awlāni was one of its members), Sufizāda served as its translator and returned home with it.[105]

The most famous Central Asian to study in Istanbul, however, was Fitrat (1886–1938), who spent the tumultuous period between 1909 and the summer of 1914 in Istanbul.[106] The son of a merchant who had traveled extensively in the Ottoman empire, Iran, and Chinese Turkestan, Fitrat attended the Mir-i Arab madrasa in Bukhara, but in 1909 the Tarbiya-yi Atfāl (Education of Children) society gave him a scholarship to study in Istanbul. Fitrat's years in Istanbul were formative, although the precise details of his activities remain frustratingly elusive. During this time, he published his first three books, at least two of which (*Debate between a Bukharan Mudarris and a European* and *Tales of an Indian Traveler*) achieved great popularity back in Central Asia. He first

---

102. The Ottoman Islamists were modernists very critical of traditional practices of Islam; few of them came from traditional *Ilmiye* backgrounds. Rather, they shared the theological views of the Egyptian modernist Muhammad 'Abduh (whose writing appeared frequently in the leading Islamist journal, *Sırat-ı Müstakim* [later *Sebilürreşad*]). Their rhetoric of awakening and strength through knowledge was very similar to that of the Jadids of Central Asia, but their most fundamental problem was to ensure the survival of the Ottoman empire on the basis of Muslim solidarity. See Tarik Zafer Tunaya, *İslâmcılık Cereyanı* (Istanbul, 1962); İsmail Kara, *Türkiyede İslâmcılık Düşüncesi: Metinler, Kişiler*, 2 vols. (Istanbul, 1986–1987), I: xv–lxvii.

103. *Khurshid*, 19 October 1906.

104. On this incident, see *TWG*, 3 February 1914.

105. *ÖSE*, X: 478–479, s.v. "Sŏfizoda."

106. The only full-length biography of Fitrat is in Japanese: Hisao Komatsu, *Kakumei no Chūō Ajia: aru Jadiido no shōzō* (Tokyo, 1996); otherwise, see Begali Qosimov, "Fitrat (chizgilar)," *Sharq yulduzi*, 1992, no. 10, 170–180.

appeared in print the Islamist newspaper *Hikmet,* published by Şehben-
derzade Filibeli Ali Hilmi, a prominent Islamist whose difficulties with the
C.U.P. government led to the closure of the newspaper on several occasions; Fitrat also contributed to *Sırat-ı Müstakim,* the flagship Islamist
journal edited by Mehmet Âkif (Ersoy).[107] But in 1914 Fitrat was enrolled
in the Medreset ül-Vâizin,[108] a reformed madrasa created earlier that
year to prepare a new kind of religious functionary. Its wide-ranging
curriculum included Turkic history, taught by Yusuf Akçura, the chief
ideologue of pan-Turkism.[109] Behbudi's intellectual range was similarly
broad. The reading room he organized in Samarqand received *Sırat-ı Müstakim,* and Behbudi sent its editors copies of his publications (along with
a recent copy of *TWG*) as a gift.[110] But he also maintained commercial relations with the main Turkist organ *Türk Yurdu* (whose offices in Istanbul stocked Behbudi's map of Turkestan inscribed in Turkic),[111] and in his
own *Āyina,* he reprinted articles from the entire spectrum of the Ottoman
press until the war cut relations.

Istanbul at the time was probably the most cosmopolitan city in the
world, and a cauldron of Muslim opinion, as émigrés and exiles from all
over the Muslim world gravitated to it. The role of Muslim émigrés from
the Russian empire, such as Yusuf Akçura and Ahmed Ağaoğlu (Agaev),
in laying the foundations of pan-Turkism is generally recognized, but the
substantial presence of Iranian exiles in the city has provoked less interest.[112] Fitrat, who at that time wrote exclusively in Persian, was clearly
influenced by the *Travels of Ibrahim Bek* by the Iranian exile Zayn ul-
'Ābidīn Marāgha'ī, published in Istanbul, for the parallels between the
novel and Fitrat's own *Tales of an Indian Traveler* are striking.[113] Simi-

107. Abdurrauf, "Hasbihāl bahamwatanān-i bukhārāyī," *Hikmet,* 18 November
1910; Buharalı Abdürraüf, "Buhara Veziri Nasrullah-bi Pervaneçi Efendi Hazretlerine Açık
Mektub," *Tearüf-i Müslimin,* 25 November 1910, 10 (only the title and the byline are in
Ottoman; the text is in Persian). On *Hikmet* and its publisher, see Kara, *Türkiyede İslâm-
cılık,* I: 3–4.
    108. *Āyina,* 17 May 1914, 588.
    109. Hüseyin Atay, *Osmanlılarda Yüksek Din Eğitimi* (Istanbul, 1983), 308–311.
    110. "Samarkand'dan," *Sırat-ı Müstakim,* 16 September 1910, 66–67.
    111. "Turkistān Bukhārā Khiwa kharitasi," *Āyina,* 1 March 1914, 356.
    112. Jamshīd Bihnām, "Manzilgāhī dar rāh-i tajaddud-i Īrān: Islāmbūl," *Īrānnāma,*
11 (1993): 271–282; Thierry Zarcone and Fariba Zarinebaf-Shahr, eds., *Les iraniens
d'Istanbul* (Paris, 1994).
    113. The novel was published in several instalments between 1903 and 1910, in
Cairo, Istanbul, and Calcutta, and has enjoyed considerable popularity ever since. See
H. Kamshad, *Modern Persian Prose Literature* (Cambridge, 1966), 17–21; M.R.
Ghanoonparvar, *In a Persian Mirror: Images of the West and Westerners in Iranian Fiction*
(Austin, 1993), 39–43.

larly, in using the dialogue format in his *Debate,* Fitrat followed a practice common in Iranian modernism.

The Jadids were part of a cosmopolitan community of Muslims knit together by readership of common texts and by travel. They lived in the last generation when Muslim intellectuals in different countries could communicate with each other without the use of European languages. Central Asian Jadidism was located squarely in the realm of Muslim modernism. It was Muslim because its rhetorical structures were rooted in the Muslim tradition of Central Asia and because the Jadids derived ultimate authority for their arguments in Islam. The Jadids never disowned Islam in the way that many Young Turks had done well before the end of the nineteenth century.[114] Rather, modernity was fully congruent with the "true" essence of Islam, and only an Islam purified of all accretions of the ages could ensure the well-being of Muslims. Informed by a new vision of the world, the Jadids arrived at a new understanding of Islam and what it meant to be a Muslim.

114. For an excellent exposition, see M. Şükrü Hanioğlu, *The Young Turks in Opposition* (New York, 1995), ch. 2.

CHAPTER 4

The Politics of Admonition

PUBLICS AND PUBLIC SPHERES

Jürgen Habermas's notion of the public sphere has attracted much attention in recent years. Since Habermas very consciously defines his public sphere as a specific moment in the history of bourgeois Europe, its utility as a model for comparative research is limited (although it has been attempted). We are unlikely to find private individuals (each both "owner of goods and persons and one human being among others, i.e., *bourgeois* and *homme*") "com[ing] together as a public [and] soon claim[ing] the public sphere regulated from above against the public authorities themselves" in settings other than the ones Habermas investigates, and least of all in the colonial world.[1] Indeed, as a number of scholars have argued, Habermas's description of the public sphere remains highly idealized even for eighteenth-century Europe.[2] Nevertheless, the emergence of the press, a substantial publishing trade, intensive sociability in discussion groups and benevolent societies all reconfigured the nature of cultural production in Central Asia. There may not have been any bour-

1. Jürgen Habermas, *The Structural Transformation of the Public Sphere: An Inquiry into a Category of Bourgeois Society*, trans. Thomas Burger with Frederick Lawrence (Cambridge, 1989 [orig. 1962]), 27, 55.
2. Robert Darnton, "An Enlightened Revolution?" *New York Review of Books*, 24 October 1991, 34. See also the essays in Craig Calhoun, ed., *Habermas and the Public Sphere* (Cambridge, 1992).

geois, but the transformation of the context in which culture was produced and reproduced was significant. In our disappointment at not finding an exact match with Habermas's description, it is easy to overlook the similarities. Jadidism as a critical discourse arose in a realm of public debate that had come into existence as a result of the transformations wrought by the Russian conquest. The advent of print had begun to redefine the parameters of debate in Muslim society, in which the authority of older elites could be challenged in public. The Jadids' enthusiastic advocacy of print and new forms of sociability was not incidental, for Jadidism's strength as a cultural or political force was directly related to the strength and extent of the new public sphere constituted by these new forms. This proved to be a formidable problem, for neither the economic nor the political situation was particularly salubrious for the public sphere, and Jadidism had constantly to maneuver between the twin perils of a weak market and a hostile colonial state in order to propagate its reform.

The colonial context marked the new public sphere in two fundamental ways. First, the state had a significant presence in it, both as protagonist and antagonist. From the earliest period, the authorities attempted to inculcate "useful knowledge" among the local population to counter what they considered its inherent fanaticism and to render it more amenable to Russian rule. They also kept a stern watch on the public, using their wide-ranging powers of censorship and oversight with abandon. Second, the "native" public sphere existed alongside, and alterior to, a local Russian public sphere. The existence of a public sphere in Russia, where autocracy jealously retained control over all matters of state import, is problematic in itself, although recent scholarship has seen plentiful evidence of it in the flourishing of a popular press and voluntary organizations in the postreform period.[3] This form of public life also appeared in Turkestan, where a nonofficial Russian-language press emerged early.[4] Although its relationship with officialdom remained tense, it could engage the state in political dialogue, especially after 1905. By contrast, the native public sphere was subject to different rules and the object of much greater official suspicion. Permission to publish newspapers was

3. Jeffrey Brooks, *When Russia Learned to Read* (Princeton, 1985); Louise McReynolds, *The News Under the Old Regime* (Princeton, 1992); Edith Clowes, Samuel Kassow, and James West, eds., *Between Tsar and People: Educated Society and the Quest for Public Identity in Late Imperial Russia* (Princeton, 1991).

4. M.P. Avsharova, *Russkaia periodicheskaia pechat' v Turkestane (1870–1917)* (Tashkent, 1960).

granted by the governor-general himself. Once in business, editors had constantly to worry about the censors, for the slightest misstep could result in the closure of a newspaper. The administration could go to extremes of bureaucratic obscurantism to deny permission or to revoke it once it was granted. Writing in emigration, Mustafā Choqāy recalled how an application he submitted was rejected because it was "too simply worded."[5] With few qualified personnel to monitor vernacular newspapers, local authorities erred on the side of caution and suspended publication of newspapers at the slightest excuse.[6] As Munawwar Qāri wrote of the forced closure of *Taraqqi* in 1906: "When a Russian newspaper is arraigned before a court or prohibited from publication for some reason, it is allowed to publish under a new title so that subscribers keep receiving something. But this system apparently does not apply to Muslims."[7] Officialdom also attempted surveillance over native society through a network of police agents whose presence, judging by the volume of the reports they filed, must have been quite pervasive. Given this suspicion, and Turkestan's disenfranchisement from imperial politics after 1907, the native public sphere became largely depoliticized. Eschewing a discourse of political rights aimed at the state, it focused largely on debates about culture and society. This accounts for the fact that the reformist project was articulated in terms of a harsh critique of Central Asian society itself, in which all problems were the result of shortcomings of Central Asians themselves, and where the solution lay in self-improvement.

The difference between the Russian and native spheres was, however, primarily a matter of language, for there were no legal restrictions on the entry of "natives" into the Russian press. Rather, the exclusion was primarily based on cultural capital—the knowledge of Russian and professional or academic accomplishment in "Russian" domains, although attempts by natives to enter the sphere never failed to provoke official suspicion. Until 1917 the spheres remained distinct. The Russian-language

5. Mustafa Chokaev, "Dzhadidizm" (ms., 1931), L'Archive de Moustafa Tchokai Bey, carton 7.

6. Immediately after *Sadā-yi Turkistān* began publication in April 1914, the governor of Syr Darya oblast asked the governor-general to delegate the task of monitoring it to a competent orientalist such as Ostroumov or Semenov because no person higher in rank than a translator could be found in the Syr Darya chancellery with the necessary linguistic skills. The chancellery of the governor-general, however, could not spare the services of the men requested and the task remained with the translator. The correspondence is in TsGARUz, f. 1, op. 31, d. 957, ll. 1–5.

7. "Afsus," *Khurshid,* 6 September 1906.

press in Turkestan had little in common in theme, tone, or content, with its vernacular counterpart. Few people were active in both spheres. Ubaydullah Khojaev, a trained lawyer who also published the newspaper *Sadā-yi Turkistān,* was perhaps the only such figure. The Jadids were not hostile to the Russian sphere, however, for as I shall argue, the central goal of Jadid reform was to enter this sphere while retaining the bifurcation between Russian and native.

Beyond this dichotomy of Russian and native publics, as we have seen, Central Asia was also located on the fringes of two other publics: one composed of the Muslims of the Russian empire and centered around *Terjüman* and other Tatar newspapers; and the other an international, cosmopolitan public of readers of newspapers from all over the Muslim world. Debates in these other publics influenced the tenor of Central Asian Jadidism, but the fortunes of the Jadids were determined on the ground.

PRINT AND THE PUBLIC

Printing arrived in Central Asia with the Russian armies. The new authorities' faith in the power of the printed word equaled that of the Jadids a generation later. One of Kaufman's first acts was the establishment of a printing press, complete with Arabic characters, which were used also to print *TWG* from 1870. The state also published a small number of booklets and brochures (some of them reprints from the *TWG*) containing useful information (such as books about the history of Russia and the Romanov dynasty, a history of Egypt, a life of Columbus, but also pieces from Pushkin and Tolstoy in translation) or official reports and proclamations in Turkic. Commercial publishing took off only after the appearance of lithography in 1883, but then developed rapidly. In 1898, two British orientalists visiting the book market in Bukhara found "the counters of its shops . . . piled high with standard works in lithograph editions, and here and there a manuscript. Great finds may sometimes be obtained by connoisseurs, though there are still enough native bibliophils in Bokhārā to render good finds by Europeans exceptional."[8] Manuscripts might have become a rarity, but it is impossible to speak of a printing revolution in Central Asia in the manner that many scholars

---

8. F.H. Skrine and E. Denison Ross, *The Heart of Asia* (London, 1899), 371.

claim for early modern Europe.[9] The new trade was coopted by the existing network of manuscript trade, and dealers in manuscripts (*sahhāf, warrāq*) were the first Turkestani publishers. The local publishing trade remained in the hands of the *nāshir* (publisher), the individual who bore the cost and the risk of putting a new book on the market. The role of the publisher could range from that of a sponsor, responsible only for the financial outlay, to that of calligrapher, printer, and bookseller as well. The output of the printing trade was dominated by traditional genres. Lithographed books did not look any different from manuscripts, although they were far more ubiquitous. New genres appeared in local publishing only after the turn of the century and were largely the work of the Jadids.[10]

Print was central to the strategies of the Jadids, many of whom were deeply involved in publishing. The bulk of publishing remained in the hands of individuals and hence subject to limited resources and the frailties of individual initiative. The Jadids sought to put the business on sounder footing and pioneered bookstores (*kutubkhāna*), larger corporate entities that served also as publishing houses. In 1910, seven men, including such well-known Jadids as Munawwar Qāri, Abdussami Qāri, and Abdullah Awlāni, applied for permission to open a bookstore called Umid (Hope). The request was categorically denied,[11] no doubt because Munawwar Qāri and Awlāni had earlier incurred the ire of the authorities with their involvement with independent newspapers between 1906 and 1908. Awlāni was more successful in 1914, when he opened the Zamān (Time) Bookstore in the Russian part of Tashkent.[12] In 1916, he joined with a number of Tashkent professional booksellers and philanthropists to form the Maktab Nashr-i Maārif Shirkati (Maktab Education Company).[13] Behbudi's diverse activities included operating a bookstore, located in his house in Samarqand,[14] where Abdulqādir Shakuri also started the Zarafshān Bookstore in 1915.[15] The largest growth of bookstores, however, took place in the towns of the Ferghana valley,

9. The strongest statement is made by Elizabeth Eisenstein, *The Printing Press as an Agent for Change: Communications and Cultural Transformations in Early-Modern Europe*, 2 vols. (Cambridge, 1979).

10. For more attention to this point, see Adeeb Khalid, "Printing, Publishing, and Reform in Tsarist Central Asia," *International Journal of Middle East Studies* 26 (1994): 187–200.

11. GARF, f. 102, op. 244 (1914), d. 74, ch. 74B, l. 442.

12. TsGARUz, f. 17, d. 17273, ll. 94, 95.

13. "'Maktab' nashr-i maārif shirkatining qānuni," *Turān* (Tashkent), 5 May 1917.

14. "Behbudiya kutubkhanasi," *Āyina*, 27 April 1914, 522.

15. Wadud Mahmudî, "Muallim Abduqodir Shakurî," *Sadoi Sharq*, 1990, no. 8, 30.

where several such companies were launched between 1913 and 1915. Such bookstores had larger financial resources and, as corporate entities, were less vulnerable to the fickleness of individual fortunes. Nevertheless, it would be a mistake to assume that these bookstores were able to function like modern publishing concerns. Maktab, which began operation with a capital of 5,500 rubles, paled in comparison with such Tatar publishers as the Karimov Brothers of Orenburg, not to mention established Russian publishers.[16] Ghayrat (Energy) was a larger operation. It had hoped to raise 50,000 rubles through the sale of shares, although success was limited. Primarily concerned with supplying textbooks and stationery to new-method schools and selling books and newspapers when it first received permission to operate on 27 February 1915, its executives were, by late 1916, aiming to acquire a printing press with the eventual goal of publishing a newspaper.[17]

For all the moral urgency with which the Jadids invested it, publishing was a commercial enterprise in which the decision to put a certain text in print was largely, but not solely, determined by the need to sell. This was a fact of crucial importance for the fate of Jadid reform, since the Jadids constantly came up against the stark realities of a market in which they occupied only a small niche. Benedict Anderson has argued that "print capitalism" went a long way toward creating standardized languages and fostering a new sense of community in many parts of the world.[18] For the Jadids, however, the market proved to be the most formidable obstacle. The market imposed harsh limits on what the Jadids could accomplish. They sought, instead, to bypass the market through recourse to philanthropy, patronage, and charity, but they were not entirely successful in institutionalizing philanthropy in Turkestan, and Jadid reform remained subject to significant economic pressures. (Indeed, it was only after the revolution, when the market was abolished, that print produced the kind of change that Anderson ascribes to "print capitalism" in early modern times.) Although books and newspapers were the stock in trade of Jadid reform, Jadid publications occupied only a

16. The Karimov brothers received permission to start a company to publish and sell books in 1898. They began with an operating capital of 20,000 rubles; Abrar Karimullin, *Tatarskaia kniga nachala XX veka* (Kazan, 1974), 22; The Moscow firm of I. D. Sytin & Co. began with a capital of 75,000 rubles in 1884; by 1914, when it was the largest publishing concern in Russia, the company was worth 3.4 million rubles; Charles A. Ruud, *Russian Entrepreneur: Publisher Ivan Sytin of Moscow, 1851–1934* (Montreal, 1990), 27, 141.

17. TsGARUz, f. 1, op. 31, d. 1144, ll. 340b–36.

18. Benedict Anderson, *Imagined Communities*, 2nd ed. (London, 1991).

small part of local production. According to the only accurate and reliable bibliographical information we possess, of the seventy printed editions of sixty-nine different works that appeared in Central Asia between October 1910 and August 1911, only eleven could be classified as Jadid publications. The balance of the publishing output comprised new editions of classical works or new works of poetry in the traditional idiom.[19]

Publishing remained a precarious business, and many Jadid publications continued to be financed by their authors. The publishing career of Hamza Hakimzāda's *Milli āshulalar* (National Songs), a collection of poetry for use in new-method schools, provides an example of publishing practices from the period. Hamza apparently completed the manuscript in February 1913, when he wrote to the printing press of the newspaper *Vaqït* in Orenburg for quotes on the price of printing the collection of verse. The Vaqït press was well known for the quality of its work, but apparently the quality work came at a price. The press asked 80 rubles for printing 1,000 copies, although an order of 1,500 copies would have cost only 105 rubles. This was apparently beyond Hamza's means (he had just returned from a long trip abroad), and he dropped the matter. In 1915, he approached Munawwar Qāri at Turkistān Bookstore in Tashkent for publishing the work piecemeal. He was offered royalties of 100 copies for each printing if Turkistān were to publish the book of its own accord. Hamza chose a different option, whereby Turkistān supplied the paper and covered other expenses, but Hamza still had to pay the cost of printing, which, for 1,000 copies, came to 28 rubles. For its services, Turkistān retained 285 copies (another 15 went for "censor, etc."), leaving Hamza 700 copies to sell for himself. For publishing later parts of the series, however, Hamza turned to two friends, Iskandar Baratbāev and Said Nāsir Mirjalil oghli, who published seven parts during 1916 and 1917, receipts from the sale of one part apparently financing the publication of the next.[20] Hamza could, moreover, count on the support of friends in his search for ready cash needed to publish his work.

19. L. Zimin, "Bibliografiia," *Sredniaia Aziia*, 1911, nos. 2, 3, 4, 6, 8. It should be noted that as low as these figures might be, they are significantly higher than those generally quoted in the literature. Soviet sources usually cited a figure of thirty-three titles in "Uzbek" for the year 1913 (*Istoriia knigi v SSSR 1917–1921* [Moscow, 1986], III: 168); these figures were also used by Edward Allworth, *Central Asian Publishing and the Rise of Nationalism* (New York, 1965), 36.

20. This correspondence can be followed in *Hamza Hakimzoda Niyoziy arkhivining katalogi*, 2 vols. (Tashkent, 1990–1991), II: 9, 28, 283–284, 286–290, 293–294, 305; see also Tŏkhtamurod Zufarov, "«Milliy She"rlar Majmualari»ga doir yangi hujjatlar," *Ŏzbek tili wa adabiyoti*, 1989, no. 1, 42–52.

In July 1914, for instance, sixteen friends raised a total of 139.50 rubles among them for printing and publishing *Yāngi Saādat*.[21] But the onus for mustering resources remained on the authors themselves in the publishing world of Turkestan before 1917.

THE PRESS

Economic constraints similarly haunted attempts to establish an independent vernacular press in Turkestan, although officialdom was responsible for the demise of many newspapers. The newspaper held a particular fascination for the Jadids, who celebrated the mere existence of newspapers as a sign of progress and a source of enlightenment. A writer in one of the earliest Turkic-language newspapers in Tashkent likened newspapers to true sages and skilled physicians (*hukamā-yi sādiq wa atibbā-yi hāziq*) who cure the ills of the community, and several years later, Behbudi saw newspapers as leaders of society through their constant criticism of its shortcomings.[22] Newspapers also provided information about the rest of the world, making their readers aware of world affairs and of progress achieved by other peoples. Articles extolling the virtues of newspapers became a staple in the Jadid press, and protagonists in Jadid literature spent a lot of time reading newspapers.[23]

We do not know whether the *TWG* owed its monopoly solely to officialdom, which denied permission for publication of other vernacular periodicals, but we do know that Turkic and Persian newspapers published in the Ottoman empire, Iran, and Europe, as well as *Terjüman*, were widely read in Central Asia. The postal system, which reached Central Asia with the conquest, made this possible, and although officialdom saw censorship as an immutable right, it did not extend to a complete ban on imported publications. The political liberalization in the wake of the revolution of 1905, along with the political enthusiasm it aroused, led to the appearance of the unofficial press in March 1906. The first independent vernacular newspaper was also the most unusual. It was published by I. I. Geier, a local Russian of moderate socialist persuasion, with the aim of acquainting the local population with the new political ideas. Much of the copy was translated from Russian newspapers by Mu-

---

21. *Hamza arkhivi katalogi*, I: 306.

22. Behrāmbek Dawlatbāev, untitled article, *Taraqqi*, 23 July 1906; Mahmud Khoja [Behbudi], "Gazīt chīst?" *Samarqand*, 3 May 1913.

23. E.g., Behbudi, "Gazet ne dur?" *Tojjār*, 11 November 1907; "Ba'zī fawā'id-i rūznāma," *Bukhārā-yi sharīf*, 11 March 1912.

hammadjan Aydarov, an interpreter retired from official service. This made for ponderous prose, which showed up even in the title of the newspaper, *Taraqqi—Orta Aziyaning umr guzārlighi* (Progress—Central Asian Life). There were already several new-method schools in Tashkent, and the Jadids, then still a small group, took the opportunity to appear in print. Munawwar Qāri, who never contributed to *TWG* because of personal and political differences with Ostroumov, published his first articles here. Nevertheless, the brief career of this newspaper (it folded for financial reasons after seventeen issues spread over three months) is important mostly because it represented one of the very few attempts by local Russians to include the native population in political dialogue.

The newspaper's failure did not deter Ismail Abidi (Gabitov), a Tatar Social Revolutionary, from trying again. Abidi brought out *Taraqqi* (Progress), which managed to appear nineteen times before being shut down by the Tashkent high court. *Taraqqi* had much in common with its predecessor, except that its political views were more radical and it avoided the infelicities of language that had plagued *Taraqqi—Orta Azyaning umr guzarlighi*. Again, local reformers flocked to the newspaper to take advantage of the forum and to air their criticisms of society. Such criticisms created their own scandals, but the undoing of the newspaper was its radical tone, directed in the fashion of those days against bureaucracy as the enemy of the newfound liberties of the land, which proved too much for local officialdom to bear. Problems began early as police raided its offices after the publication of its third issue and confiscated several hundred unsold copies because inaccurate translations of two editorial articles had led them to believe that the newspaper favored killing members of educated nationalities. Abidi was called to the police station and released only on bail.[24] The newspaper was shut down after nineteen issues by court order for publishing an editorial containing unacceptable material.[25]

Within three weeks of *Taraqqi*'s closure, Munawwar Qāri brought out his own newspaper, *Khurshid* (The Sun). It had *Taraqqi*'s feisty tone and did not shun explicitly political topics (it published several articles about Russia's still volatile political situation, as well as covering political events in Iran, Egypt, and India with overt anticolonial sympathies).

24. See his account of the incident in "Bāylar, buyraqarātiya wa ghazita," *Taraqqi*, 27 July 1906.

25. TsGARUz, f. 1, op. 4, d. 1003, ll. 117, 119, 188.

All of this invited official wrath, and after only ten issues the newspaper was ordered closed for its "extremely harmful direction."[26] The same fate befell *Shuhrat* (Fame), published in December 1907 by Abdullah Awlāni with the cooperation of Ahmetjan Bektimirov and Munawwar Qāri, which also lasted ten issues, as well as its successor *Aziya* (Asia), which could manage only five issues. The much more moderate *Tojjār* (Merchants), published by Said Karim-bāy, the decorated notable, shunned politics ("Our purpose is not opposition to the government [unlike *Taraqqi* and *Khurshid*] but rather to be the friends and supporters of the Russian state in a way that does not harm religion"),[27] but could not attract enough readers to pay its way, and Said Karim-bāy apparently being unwilling to foot the bill himself, folded after thirty-seven issues. By March 1908, the independent vernacular press had ceased to exist in Central Asia.

The first attempt to revive it came in Bukhara in 1912 and took a more institutionalized form. In 1912, a group of Bukharan Jadids managed to secure permission for the publication of a Persian-language newspaper called *Bukhārā-yi sharīf* (Bukhara the Noble) in Kāgān. The newspaper was financed by a joint-stock company for which 9,000 rubles were raised almost immediately.[28] Mir Jalil Mirbadalov, the chief translator at the Russian Political Agency, was apparently instrumental in securing permission, although the agency reserved the right to censor the newspaper. Edited by an Azerbaijani, *Bukhārā-yi sharīf* published daily (although in July, when it launched a biweekly Turkic supplement titled *Turān,* its frequency declined). The two newspapers survived on their own for several months but were closed down in January 1913 by Russian authorities at the request of the amir.[29] In April of that year, Behbudi, who by this time was deeply involved in writing and publishing, launched *Samarqand* as a biweekly newspaper. The venture was not successful financially, and in September he abandoned the newspaper and channeled its finances into Central Asia's first magazine, *Āyina* (The Mirror), which he managed to put out almost weekly for the next twenty months. Again, sales were poor and the onset of war did not help matters. At the end of the first year, the number of paid subscribers was 234, and

26. TsGARUz, f. 1, op. 31, d. 536, l. 16.
27. "Matbuāt ālami," *Tojjār,* 21 August 1907.
28. A. Samoilovich, "Pechat' russkikh musul'man," *Mir Islama* 1 (1912): 478n.
29. Sadriddin Ayni, *Bukhara inqilabi tarikhi uchun materiyallar* (Moscow, 1922), 94–101.

the situation does not seems to have improved.[30] When Behbudi was told by his doctors in the summer of 1915 to take the waters, he closed the magazine down.[31] It was never published again.

But 1914 had been the banner year for journalism in Central Asia. In March, Munawwar Qāri, Abdullah Awlāni, Ubaydullah Khojaev, and four others launched *Sadā-yi Turkistān* (Voice of Turkestan) as a joint-stock venture in Tashkent.[32] Almost simultaneously, Ābidjān Mahmudov, Jadid activist and merchant of the second guild in Kokand, began *Sadā-yi Farghāna* (Voice of Ferghana). The two newspapers, alike in many ways, shunned politics and focused on educational and cultural goals, ceaselessly exhorting their compatriots to wake up (a favorite metaphor) to the necessity of reform. In early 1915, when reformist ulama in Tashkent launched their own magazine, *al-Islāh* (Reform), five periodicals (including *TWG*) were being published in Turkestan. But this situation did not last; although political caution saved them from the censor's axe, all but *al-Islāh* fell victim to the market, the small readership being unable to sustain them. *Sadā-yi Turkistān* folded in May 1915 for financial reasons, *Sadā-yi Farghāna* followed soon afterward, and *Āyina*'s last issue came out in June 1915. There were two attempts to publish news sheets containing only agency reports in translation and an unsuccessful bid to revive *Sadā-yi Turkistān* in Andijān in 1916.[33] When the old order was cast asunder by revolution in March 1917, the only unofficial vernacular periodical being published in Central Asia was *al-Islāh*.[34]

The Jadid press had a marked didactic flavor. For the Jadids, the newspaper was a platform from which to broadcast their exhortations to reform. The model for the Central Asian press was provided, of course, by Gasprinskii's *Terjüman,* which for a generation had stood as the only unofficial Muslim newspaper in the Russian empire of any consequence, but Turkestan newspapers shared the general attitudes and style common to much Muslim journalism of the turn of the century, in both the

30. "Muhtaram khwānandalargha!" *Āyina,* 16 November 1914, 40–41.

31. "Idāradan," *Āyina,* 15 June 1915, 442.

32. GARF, f. 102, op. 244 (1914), d. 74, ch. 84B, l. 125.

33. Ziyo Said, *Özbek waqtli matbuoti tarikhiga materiallar* (1927), in his *Tanlangan asarlar* (Tashkent, 1974), 101.

34. On the press in Central Asia, see Said, *Özbek waqtli matbuoti;* the sections on Central Asia in Alexandre Bennigsen and Chantal Lemercier-Quelquejay, *La presse et le mouvement national chez les musulmans de Russie avant 1920* (Paris, 1964), otherwise the standard work on the subject, are often incorrect and should be used with caution.

Russian and Ottoman empires, as well as in the Ottoman and Iranian diasporas. Newspapers ran to four pages and appeared usually twice a week (the exception being *Bukhārā-yi sharīf*, which appeared daily). They carried news, mostly from other newspapers or from telegraph agencies, since none could afford to post correspondents, but the bulk of the space was occupied by essays, editorial and opinion pieces dealing with the usual themes of education, progress, and admonition. Poetry, usually critical or exhortatory, was a prominent feature. Readers from all over Central Asia wrote to comment on shortcomings or problems in their localities or in Central Asia in general. The central feature of all newspapers remained the *filyatun* (*feuilleton* via the Russian), a long essay which often took up as much as a quarter of each newspaper. The *filyatun* was either critical or informative, usually both, as authors managed to inform readers about the achievements of other societies while using the invidious comparison to Turkestan to exhort their readers to reform, to act as the "society's physicians." Sometimes the *filyatun* was written as fiction; Cholpān's *Doctor Muhammadyār*, perhaps the first modern short story in Central Asian Turkic, appeared as a series of *filyatun*s in *Sadā-yi Turkistān* in the summer of 1914. Behbudi's *Āyina* had a similar tenor of exhortation and admonition, although he also published a great deal of informational material, such as a series of articles on the antiquities of Samarqand, a long essay on "Why Did the Turkish State Decline?" reprinted from *Terjüman*, and Behbudi's own observations on a two-month trip to the Ottoman empire in 1914.

It was this content that distinguished the Jadid press from the *TWG* on one side and *al-Islāh* on the other. The earliest voices of reform appeared in *TWG*, which also featured the *filyatun*. The tone, however, was never so single-mindedly exhortatory as it was in the Jadid press. *Filyatun*s in *TWG* were generally "informational," such as numerous articles on the tercentenary of the Romanov dynasty in 1913, the centenary of the Napoleonic invasion, or the history of the conquest of Turkestan. Indeed, the appearance of an independent Muslim press after 1905 brought about a change in the character of the newspaper, which seems to have become more circumspect in giving voice to reform. Much of the copy in the last decade of its existence was written by its native editor, one Mullā Ālim, a protégé of Ostroumov, who frequently sparred with editors of other periodicals, both Central Asian and Tatar. *Al-Islāh*, on the other hand, did not write about seeking admonition from Europeans; the reform to which it was committed emanated from different sources. Its prose, heavily larded with Arabic and Persian expressions, was also broken up with lengthy quotations in Arabic (without translation) which served, among other things, to demarcate its readership.

With the exception of *al-Islāh,* the ulama did not attempt to join the fray by launching their own publications. Because they did not leave a published record, it is difficult to surmise their reasons. Significant no doubt was the traditionalist ulama's distaste for engaging in debate with those outside their own circles, those who had not dedicated themselves for years to the acquisition of knowledge and *adab.* However, a second, more fundamental reason for the ulama's absence from the world of journalism was that the bulk of their constituency continued to exist in a largely oral world in which literacy remained a sacralized skill. For the traditionalist ulama, written knowledge was still transmitted through face-to-face interaction, and the impersonal use of the written word inherent in the newspaper was not widely accepted by them. Reading, even for those who were literate, was primarily a devotional activity. Attention to such different uses of the written word and different (culturally valued) reading habits might also help explain the lack of financial success the Jadids met in their publishing efforts. The obvious reasons for the low demand for newspapers and magazines, and for the printed word in general, were the low purchasing power of consumers in a poor agrarian economy and the low levels of literacy among the population. But as I argued in Chapter 1, low levels of literacy did not in themselves mean a lack of education or of interest in the literate tradition. Texts could always be read aloud and shared by those who could not read themselves. Therefore, we have to look further than low levels of literacy for possible explanations of low demand for the printed word.

Historians of Europe have remarked on the transition from "intensive" to "extensive" reading practices in the eighteenth century. "Intensive" reading involved the communal reading and rereading, often aloud (and accompanied by memorization) of a small number of texts belonging to only a few genres; such reading was embedded in reverential attitudes toward both the act of reading itself and the book being read. "Extensive" reading, which developed in the age of print, is marked by the reading, silently and individually, of a large number of texts devoid of any reverential or sacral meaning.[35] Such a line of inquiry yields fruit-

---

35. For an excellent introduction to this literature, Roger Chartier, "Du lire au livre," in Chartier, ed., *Pratiques de la lecture* (Marseilles, 1985), 69ff.

ful insights into the Jadid experience with disseminating reform through the printed word.

In the tradition reproduced by the maktab, texts were sacralized objects accessible only through the mediation of a recognized master. The newspaper represented a completely new use of the written word. Its impersonal text, usually in quotidian language rather than rhymed prose or verse, was a desacralized commodity that did not fit existing patterns of usage for the written word. And while the newspaper itself was the best source for the dissemination of new reading habits, the continued existence of older reading habits proved to be the major obstacle in its growth. The new-method schools inculcated different reading practices, and a new generation of their graduates might have formed a reading public to support Jadid publishing efforts, but in the period under review, such was not the case. Newspapers published by the Jadids therefore failed to attract a wide readership and consequently faced severe financial hardships. *Shuhrat* had a print run of only 300 when it was closed down by the administration,[36] and as noted above, the number of paid subscriptions to Behbudi's *Āyina* hovered around 200 for most of its existence.

A NEW LITERATURE

The Jadids' first attempts to write prose fiction also date from this period. Ostroumov had published pieces by Tolstoy in the *TWG*, and prose fiction in Tatar and Ottoman had made its appearance in Central Asia. A translation from Azerbaijani of *Robinson Crusoe* published in 1912 by Fāzilbek Ātābek oghli introduced the term *romān* to Central Asia. Hamza Hakimzāda Niyāzi called his 1915 story of the happiness brought by knowledge a "national novel" (*milli romān*). The Jadids hoped for nothing less than to create a new canon more in keeping with the needs of the moment than the existing literature, which they harshly criticized for its obsolescence and decadence. Hamza wrote his *New Happiness* for the following reasons: "This book is not for use in the maktab; rather it was written with the aim of providing a book for reading [*qirāat risālasi*] for use in place of the books currently read by the common people, such as *Jamshed, Zarqum, Aldarkushā,* [various] *bayāz*es, *Dalla Mukhtār, Gul andām, Afandi,* etc., which are all full of superstition and

36. TsGARUz, f. 461, op. 1, d. 57, l. 6070b.

nonsense, injurious to morals, and [entirely] baseless."[37] Much like the press, Jadid literature remained firmly subordinated to an overriding didactic concern. This was especially true of the plays which usually culminated in lengthy speeches in which a mouthpiece of the Jadids would rouse the audience by pointing to the moral of the story. There is no character or plot development and no concern with the internal struggles of human beings. The interiorized self of bourgeois modernity is nowhere to be found in the Jadid literature of this period. For all their denigration of the oral romance tradition, the Jadids could not escape its conventions. Many characters did not even have individual names but rather represented social types. The plot served to highlight social ills and to present Jadid remedies for them, but assertion took the place of demonstration through plot development. The effect was rather lugubrious, and most theater evenings were leavened with the inclusion of light comedy (although the didactic intent was never far beneath the surface even in comedy: a skit called *The Fool* puts the difficulties encountered by a country bumpkin in the city to generic ignorance, whereas in *Is It Easy to Be a Lawyer?*, the lawyer frequently rises above the antics of his bumbling clients to lecture the audience about the need to reform).[38] Nevertheless, many of the writers who began writing in the last years before 1917 went on to become accomplished men of letters in the following decade, and the history of modern Central Asian literature can scarcely be imagined without the names of Fitrat, Cholpān, Qādiri, and Hamza (although generations of Soviet scholarship attempted to do precisely that).

Poetry, however, retained its central place in Central Asian literary life, and much of the Jadid exhortation took this form. Sadriddin Ayni's characterization of "Tajik" literature of this period as "old in form but with new topics" applies also to literary output in Turkic.[39] The Jadid press regularly published poetry (odes to the press were a standard feature), and poetry had an important place in the curriculum of new-method schools. Sayyid Ahmad Ajzi wrote two long poems in the *masnawi* tradition ruing the fallen state of the Muslim community and exhorting it to reform. But there were new uses for poetry, too. The advent of the gramophone had made folk tunes respectable, and both Aw-

37. Hamza Hakimzada Niyazi, *Yāngi saādat: milli romān* (Kokand, 1915), 2.
38. Abdullah Badri, *Ahmaq* (Samarqand, 1915); Abdullah Awlāni, *Ādvokatlik āsān mi?* (1916), in Abdulla Awloniy, *Toshkent tongi*, ed. B. Qosimov (Tashkent, 1978), 300–319.
39. Sadriddīn Aynī, *Namūna-yi adabiyāt-i Tājīk* (Moscow, 1926), 529.

lāni and Hamza wrote lyrics with "national" (i.e., reformist) themes for folk melodies.

MODERN THEATER

Theater exercised a deep fascination for Jadids throughout the Russian empire. Looking back on a quarter century of reform, Ismail Bey Gasprinskii could write in 1901 on the emergence of theater as a major achievement.[40] As with newspapers, the mere existence of theater was deemed a sign of progress and civilization. Modern theater came to Central Asia with the Russian conquest, but until the turn of the century, theatrical activity was confined to the Russian community in the larger cities. A dramatic literature and professional troupes had developed among the Muslims of Transcaucasia and the Tatar lands by the end of the nineteenth century. Transcaucasian and Tatar troupes toured Turkestan in 1911, after which such tours became common.[41] In addition, dramatic activity was sustained locally by expatriate Tatars who began staging plays for their community at least as early as 1905, and by 1913, this activity was strong enough to support a standing Tatar theater group in Tashkent led by Zeki Bayazidskii.[42]

The repertoire of these troupes came whole cloth from European Russia or Transcaucasia, and it was performed in the languages of those areas. Local Jadids realized the advantages of the medium and sought to use it for their own goals. Mahmud Khoja Behbudi wrote *The Patricide*, the first play to be set in Central Asia, as early as 1911, but difficulties with the censor delayed its publication until 1913 and its performance until 1914. When it did first play, in Samarqand on 15 January 1914, it was an instant success.[43] The group that performed it, composed of seven Central Asians, a Tatar, and an Azerbaijani, traveled to Kokand,

40. Ismail Bey Gasprinskii, "First Steps toward Civilizing the Russian Muslims," trans. Edward J. Lazzerini, in Lazzerini, "*Ğadidism* at the Turn of the Century: A View from Within," *Cahiers du monde russe et soviétique,* 16 (1975): 257.
41. Gulam Mämmädli, "Azärbayjan teatrï Orta Asiyada," in *Iskusstvo Azerbaidzhana,* vol. 3 (Baku, 1950), 228–229; M. Buzruk Salihov, *Ozbek teatr tarixi ucun materiallar* (Tashkent, 1935), 58.
42. Salihov, *Ozbek teatr,* 57, 61.
43. According to the report in *Āyina,* admittedly written by Behbudi himself, the audience numbered 370 (the theater seated 320, so another 50 seats had to be installed temporarily) and many others had to be turned back; Behbudi, "Turkistānda birinchi milli tiyātir," *Āyina,* 25 January 1914, 227. The play again attracted a sellout crowd when it came to Tashkent on 6 March 1914; see *TWG,* 6 March 1914.

Tashkent, and Katta Qurghān in the next few weeks.[44] By early September, *The Patricide* had been performed fifteen times by different groups in Turkestan, often without the permission of the author.[45] The next three years saw intense activity in local theater.[46] Central Asian Jadids favored plays that dealt specifically with local issues over those translated from Tatar or Azerbaijani, and therefore many of them turned playwright and produced a number of plays addressing questions of purely Central Asian interest.[47] Samarqand was the greatest center of this activity where Behbudi's disciples Hāji Muin b. Shukrullah and Nusratullah b. Qudratullah produced a number of scripts. In addition, Hamza in Kokand, Awlāni in Tashkent, and Abdullah Badri in Bukhara wrote numerous plays in this period, several of which were never published.[48] Theatrical performances, often in the form of artistic soirées, became commonplace even in smaller towns like Osh, Namangān, and Katta Qurghān. This activity was paralleled by visits from Azerbaijani and Tatar troupes, who also began to perform local plays. Moreover, a number of Tatar and Transcaucasian plays were translated into local Turkic and sometimes adapted to a Central Asian setting.[49] Local amateur theater groups began to form immediately after the first performance of *The Patricide*. The original cast of the play, which rehearsed at Behbudi's house in Samarqand, coalesced into a troupe and began touring Turkestan. Behbudi had apparently directed the troupe in the beginning, but later the position passed to the Azerbaijani director Ali Asghar Askarov.[50] Other amateur groups formed in Tashkent and Kokand as well as in smaller towns. Hamza was at the center of one such group in Kokand, which performed plays written or translated by Hamza himself. The first

44. Mamadzhan Rakhmanov, *Uzbekskii teatr s drevneishikh vremen do 1917 goda* (Tashkent, 1968), 280.

45. Mahmud Khoja [Behbudi], "Padarkush wajhidan," *Āyina*, 13 September 1914, 1130.

46. For an overview, see A. Samoilovich, "Dramaticheskaia literatura sartov," *Vestnik Imperatorskogo Obshchestva Vostokovedeniia*, 1916, no. 5, 72–84; Edward Allworth, "The Beginnings of the Modern Turkestanian Theater," *Slavic Review* 23 (1964): 676–687; Allworth., *The Modern Uzbeks* (Stanford, 1990), 147–152.

47. See, for instance, Khālmuhammad Ākhundi, "Namangāndan maktub," *Āyina*, 16 May 1915, 399. Local reviews and reports of theatrical performances in *Āyina* also expressed disapproval of Tatar actors for various reasons: "Samarqanda tiyātir," *Āyina*, 1 February 1914, 263; "Katta Qorghānda tiyātir," *Āyina*, 29 March 1914, 349.

48. Buzruk Salihov (*Ozbek teatr*, 82–84) lists seventeen locally written plays that were staged before February 1917. In addition, another twenty-four plays of Tatar, Transcaucasian, and Ottoman origin had been staged by that time.

49. Samoilovich, "Dramaticheskaia literatura," 73.

50. Rakhmanov, *Uzbekskii teatr*, 280.

engagement of the group was Hamza's *Zaharli hayāt* (A Poisoned Life), performed in October 1915.[51] In Tashkent, a group formed around Aw-lāni, who had been involved in local Tatar theater since at least 1909. In 1916, the group was formalized as the Turan Amateur Dramatic Society, with the mission to "develop the love of serious drama among the population . . . [and] to stage spectacles for the people, [in order to] provide healthy diversions to them."[52] In Bukhara, dramatic activity remained in the hands of local Tatars, who were, however, allowed to stage their plays in old Bukhara.

In founding a modern theater in Central Asia, the Jadids sought to distance it from the long tradition of folk theater known as *maskhara-bāzlik*. Satire was the stock in trade of this theater, and maskharas could poke brutal fun at various aspects of society, including the khans and Islam itself.[53] Yet, in preconquest Central Asia, the whole enterprise was located beyond the pale of *adab* (*adabdan khārij*) and hence denied any moral authority. Moreover, the maskharas' use of music was always susceptible to attack by the ulama on Islamic grounds, and their bodily movements contravened the rules of proper deportment conveyed by the maktab. To be a maskhara was the opposite of being a cultured individual; for cultured individuals to take on the activities of the maskharas was scandalous. The Jadids sought to make theater respectable through an appeal to the nation and the needs of the age. For Behbudi, for instance, "theater is a place for preaching and exhortation [*majlis-i waʿz-u nasihat*]" for society and in its lofty purpose had nothing in common with the crude craft of the maskharas.[54] The Jadids drew inspiration from the modern, print-based theater of Europe, which had also been adopted by other Muslim communities of the Russian empire. Indeed, the print antecedents of Jadid theater need to be emphasized. Unlike the maskharas, the Jadids transmitted their theatrical work in print. The Jadids published the transcripts of many of their plays, partly in the hope that all productions of the same play would convey a uniform message. In conveying its message orally, Jadid theater still aspired to the uniformity made possible by print.

Theater was immediately put to philanthropic use. The play itself spread the message while the performance was used to raise money for

51. Ibid., 290.
52. Quoted in T. T. Tursunov, *Oktiabr'skaia revoliutsiia i uzbekskii teatr* (Tashkent, 1983), 10.
53. See Rakhmanov, *Uzbekskii teatr*, 195–198, for examples.
54. Behbudi, "Tiyātir, musiqi, sheʿr," *Āyina*, 18 December 1914, 111–114.

other Jadid causes. Since all the actors were amateurs, usually Jadid activists, there were no performance fees and a large percentage of the revenue could be used for other purposes. In the three years of its existence,
Jadid theater was staged to benefit reading rooms, new-method schools,
a Muslim field hospital on the war front, and wounded Muslim soldiers.
Thus, the first ever performance of *The Patricide* in Samarqand raised
329.69 rubles for the city's Muslim Reading Room. This figure represented the entire net income from the evening after expenses of 170 rubles
had been paid.[55] A performance of the same play in Khujand raised 590
rubles for the Red Crescent in January 1915,[56] and a performance of
The Feast in Samarqand the previous December raised 245 rubles, a quarter of which was donated to the war wounded and the rest to new-
method schools in the area.[57] The popularity of theater led to the emergence of cultural soirées that combined cultural, economic, and political
functions in one event. A soirée typically included at least one play in addition to music and a program of songs. The Tatar singer and Jadid activist Kamil ul-Mutigi Tuhfatullin toured Central Asia at least twice between 1913 and 1915, giving concerts of Tatar music, including poems
by such prominent Tatar Jadids as Abdullah Tuqay set to music.

NEW FORMS OF SOCIABILITY

The activity surrounding the theater was crucial in forming a public that
came together under new rules to discuss issues concerning society. It es-
chewed overtly political matters, but it redrew the boundaries of debate
about cultural and social issues. Similarly, informal discussion circles remained the primary institutional form of Jadidism in Turkestan. (The situation was different in Bukhara, where official hostility drove the Jadids
into secret societies.) The Central Asian tradition of *gap*, circles that
brought together men of various crafts or neighborhoods for weekly or
monthly gatherings of mutual hospitality, was appropriated for new aims
by the Jadids. Munawwar Qāri was reported by the tsarist police to be
leader of one of the largest *gap*s in Tashkent.[58] But for many Jadids such
"modern" *gap*s were merely the beginning. For the Jadids, the key to
progress and development lay in organized effort. Hamza saw all asso-

55. *Āyina*, 25 January 1914, 237.
56. *Āyina*, 30 January 1915, 206.
57. *Āyina*, 30 December 1914, 135–137.
58. GARF, f. 102, op. 244 (1914), d. 74, ch. 84B, l. 71.

ciational endeavors, even commercial ones, as an expression of unity. When he wrote to prospective investors in 1914, he expressed this hope: "Maybe in this way our unity will develop, and the rule of joint organization [*shirkat qānuni*] will take root among the Muslims of Ferghana and Turkestan, and soon all our affairs, currently decaying, will again turn to progress and development."[59] The bookstores and publishing ventures described above were the most successful in this regard, and they do show a process of greater institutionalization throughout the decade preceding 1917. These ventures were commercial, to be sure, but by their nature they also served as an institutional basis for cultural reform. The Jadids, though, invested their highest hopes in benevolent societies, such as those which had flourished among the Tatars since the 1890s. As forms of institutionalized philanthropy geared to social (rather than individual) goals, such societies neatly tied together the various strands of Jadid reform in an institutional framework. The issue of establishing a benevolent society in Turkestan was raised in 1906 in the general atmosphere of enthusiasm,[60] but nothing came of it until 1909, when the Imdādiya (Aid) society was formally established with Munawwar Qāri and Abdullah Awlāni, who had collaborated on the newspaper *Shuhrat* the previous year, among its founders. The society defined its aim as "the improvement of the moral and material position of needy persons of the Mohammedan faith in the Syr Darya oblast," through opening shelters for the poor, supporting hospitals, and helping students.[61] The educational goals were broadened in 1913 to include the opening of schools and reading rooms and the establishment of scholarships.[62] The society secured the financial help of Said Karim-bāy (who also served as chair for a year), and it lasted until the revolution. It acquired a niche for itself in the public life of Muslim Tashkent without ever making the kind of difference its founders had hoped for. Membership dues (a modest six rubles) were the main source of revenue, although the advent of theater provided another. Still, the total expenditure for 1914 stood at only 1,975.20 rubles, roughly one-third of which went to students in various kinds of schools.[63]

59. *Hamza arkhivi katalogi*, I: 38.
60. *Taraqqi*, 27 July 1906; 3 August 1906; 12 August 1906; "Tāshkand Jamiyat-i khayriya," *Khurshid*, 21 September 1906.
61. *Ustav musul'manskogo obshchestva "Pomoshch'" v Tashkente* (Tashkent, 1909).
62. TsGARUz, f. 17, d. 17416, l. 29.
63. *ST*, 21 January 1915.

Imdādiya remained the only benevolent society to operate among the native population of Turkestan, although numerous such societies existed among the European and Tatar communities in various cities. Other attempts at organized philanthropy also had limited success. Thirteen activists led by Behbudi founded a "Muslim reading room" (*qiraatkhāna wa mutāliakhāna islāmiyasi* [sic]) in Samarqand in 1908. It began with 125 subscriptions, but by 1912, only seven members remained and daily attendance averaged barely ten persons a day.[64] In 1912, Abdullah Awlāni opened the Turān reading room in Tashkent, which received periodicals from all over the Muslim world, most of them obtained gratis from their publishers. Nevertheless, financial worries never left it, and it seems to have folded in early 1917.[65]

A PUBLIC SPHERE

Numerous stalled initiatives to publish newspapers and a small share of the publishing market do not seem to indicate huge success for Jadid reform. However, two points should be kept in mind. The Jadid presence in the publishing field increased rapidly in the years after 1912, both in terms of titles published and publishing ventures launched, and modern theater, perhaps the most successful medium of Jadid reform, began in 1914 and was hugely successful in the following years. This in spite of an economic slump that hit Turkestan about that time and worsened at the onset of the world war, with its inflation and often crippling paper shortages. The collapse of the periodicals launched in 1913 and 1914 was at least partly due to this slump, since even the officially bankrolled *TWG* was feeling the pinch; its frequency had been reduced in 1916, and there was talk in early 1917 of cutting it back even further.[66] Second, the lack of success of local publishing (especially of the periodical press) was to some extent compensated for by the appearance of Turkic-language newspapers from other parts of the Russian empire. *Terjüman* had always been popular; after 1905, it was joined by the very vibrant periodical press that emerged among the Volga Tatars. Indeed, the success

64. Behbudi, "Hisābi-ātchut," *TWG*, 4 March 1910; Behbudi, "Qiraatkhāna wa mutaliakhāna islāmiyasi bābinda mukhtasir bayānnāma," *Samarqand*, 11 June 1913; *Āyina*, 7 December 1913, 144.
65. A. Abdurazzakov, "Pedagogicheskoe nasledie uzbekskogo prosvetitelia Abdully Avloni" (Candidate's diss., Tashkent, 1979), 56–58; A. G. Kasymova, *Istoriia bibliotechnogo dela v Uzbekistane* (Tashkent, 1981), 32–33.
66. TsGARUz, f. 1, op. 8, d. 528, l. 5.

of Tatar newspapers, much better produced and often cheaper than their local counterparts, worked to the disadvantage of Central Asian press by encroaching upon an already small market.[67]

Yet, for all these difficulties, print had subtly transformed the manner in which culture was produced and reproduced in Central Asia. As in early modern Europe, print helped sever the link between intellectual production and courtly patronage.[68] It also redefined the boundaries of debate. Beginning with the informational pieces in the *TWG*, it had led to the creation of a public in which entree was gained by the ability to read (or hear) the printed word. Moreover, the new ubiquity of the written word carried in it seeds of a profound change in cultural attitudes toward knowledge and its place in society. The scarcity of the written word in the scribal age endowed it with a sacral aura. Writing itself was the object of reverence and the mnemonic, ritual, and devotional uses of the written word overshadowed its more mundane documentary functions. Further, in the tradition of Islamic learning entrenched in the madrasas of Central Asia, access to the written word was mediated by authoritative, face-to-face interaction with a recognized master. The ubiquity of print undermined these relations by making the written word more accessible and tended to render the mediation of the learned unnecessary, thereby producing two interrelated results.

On the one hand, print allowed the Jadids to challenge the monopoly of the traditionally learned over authoritative discourse. In their writings, the Jadids tended to address a public composed of all those who could read. The use of print allowed the Jadids to go beyond the concerns of intellectual pedigree and patronage that provided the framework for literary production in the manuscript age. The Jadid project involved nothing less than the redefinition of the social order, for when Behbudi claimed that newspapers were spiritual leaders of society, or that the theater was a "house of admonition" (*ibratkhāna*) where society could take stock of its ills,[69] he was directly challenging the authority of the traditional cultural elite. The knowledge of the ulama was now neither necessary, nor sufficient to cure society's ills. Similarly, the new prose literature, with its critical posture, independent of the constraints of *adab*, was crucial to the Jadids' attempt to carve out a discursive space

67. Siddiqi, "Turkistān jaridalari," *Āyina*, 27 September 1914, 1181; Abdurrauf Müzaffer, "Türkistanda bugünke häyat," *Shura*, 15 February 1917, 83.

68. E.g., Alvin Kernan, *Samuel Johnson and the Impact of Print* (Princeton, 1987).

69. Mahmud Khoja [Behbudi], "Tiyātir nedur?" *Āyina*, 10 May 1914, 550–553.

for themselves in their society. The printed word redefined the boundaries of the public space within which debate was carried out. The creation of a print-based public space led to a new cultural politics in Central Asia.

The ubiquity of print also contributed to a certain desacralization of writing itself. Combined with the spread of functional literacy, the ubiquity of print tended to shift the focus of learning from the master to the text, the secrets of which were now available to all who could read. Newspapers and printed forms further tended to encourage quotidian uses of writing. The Jadids' denigration of the medieval commentaries and glosses used in the madrasa, and their call for a "return" to the textual sources of Islam were rooted in this new attitude toward writing. The market-oriented print trade also led to the commodification of the written word: unlike manuscripts, printed books had to be sold, much like any other commodity. Publishers were not patrons, and although sometimes putting a godly book in print was seen as a pious act, few publishers could afford to do so regularly. This commodification further contributed to the desacralization of writing in the age of print. Both these phenomena were highly subversive of the authority of the ulama. Access to printing allowed the Jadids to reconfigure cultural debate in their society and to lay the foundations for a broad-based movement of cultural reform beyond the control of the older cultural elite.

THE MIRROR OF ADMONITION

The following assessment by Munawwar Qāri, published in *Khurshid,* perhaps the most outspoken of the newspapers of 1906–1908, is fairly typical of Jadid thought:

> [A]ll our acts and actions, our ways, our words, our maktabs and madrasas and methods of teaching, and our morals are in decay. . . . If we continue in this way for another five or ten years, we are in danger of being dispersed and effaced under the oppression of developed nations [*mutaraqqi millatlar*]. . . . O coreligionists, o compatriots! Let's be just and compare our situation with that of other, advanced nations; . . . let's secure the future of our coming generations [*awlādimiz uchun ham fā'idalik yollar āchib*] and save them from becoming slaves and servants of others. The Europeans, taking advantage of our negligence and ignorance, took our government from our hands and are gradually taking over our crafts and trades. If we do not quickly make an effort to reform our affairs in order to safeguard ourselves, our nation, and our children, our future will be extremely difficult.
>
> Reform begins with a rapid start in cultivating sciences conforming to our times [*zamānagha muwāfiq ulum-u funun*]. Becoming acquainted with the

sciences of the [present] time depends upon the reform of our schools and our methods of teaching.[70]

Much about Central Asia and its culture had to be reformed and recast if the challenge were to be met properly; continuation in the old ways could lead to the extinction of the community. The Jadids saw as their mission the awakening of their nation (*millat*) from the sleep of ignorance through combining exhortation and self-criticism with warnings of dire consequences if the call were not heard. Faith in the power of knowledge (and education) to ameliorate the situation was central to the Jadid project, and I will examine it in greater detail in the Chapter 5. Suffice it to note here the connection between the decay in morals and ignorance as well as the intimation of mortal danger if society does not change its ways. The reverse of progress was decay. The Jadids espied not just stagnation but decline in their society. If knowledge needed proper social organization in order to flourish, the Jadids saw only disorder and chaos around them. Earlier Muslims had cultivated knowledge, but succeeding generations, through their heedlessness, had forgotten even the names of their forebears. Jadid writers often evoked the names of Ibn Sinā (Avicenna), al-Fārābi, al-Bukhāri, and Ulugh Bek as exemplars of a previous age of learning that had been forgotten. The Bukharan writer Mirzā Sirāj, surveying the decline around him, asked, "If the Minār-i Kalān [the thirteenth-century tower that is Bukhara's most imposing structure] were to fall down today, would we be able to rebuild it?"[71]

Knowledge for the Jadids was universal, not culturally specific. Comparisons with "developed" nations were therefore not just permissible but mandatory, and the Jadids constantly made them. The central rhetorical tool for the Jadids was *ibrat*, seeking admonition or heeding laudable example. The Jadids saw themselves as showing their society the mirror of admonition so that society could reform itself. Much of what the Jadids wrote about other societies (or their own) stemmed from this rhetorical purpose. Their accounts of "developed" countries were entirely positive. Behbudi in particular was fond of publishing statistics showing numbers of newspapers, theaters, schools, or expenditures

70. "Islāh ne demakdadur," *Khurshid,* 28 September 1906. This message, in its broad outline as well as in its details, was repeated time and time again in the following decade; see, e.g., Jalāl, "Che bāyad kard?" *Bukhārā-yi sharīf,* 14 March 1912; Behbudi, "Ihtiyāj-i millat," *Samarqand,* 12 July 1913; Hāji Muin b. Shukrullah, *Eski maktab, yangi maktab* (Samarqand, 1916), 27–28.

71. M.S. Mirzā Khurdāf, "Qadari fa'āliyat lāzim ast," *Bukhārā-yi sharīf,* 22 March 1912.

on education in various countries of the world. Newspapers wrote of technological progress, philanthropy, and collective effort in other countries, all the while exhorting their readers to heed the call and follow the example. Even when dealing with questions of morality, Europe presented a positive image. This is worth noting, since all too often scholarly literature on Muslim perceptions of Europe focuses on criticism of the loose morality of Europeans. There is virtually no condemnation of European morals in the writings of the Jadids of Central Asia. An article on "Alcoholism among the French," for instance, described not the moral decrepitude of Christian (or capitalist) society but efforts at countering alcoholism that the Muslims of Central Asia might emulate.[72] And when they described travels abroad, they painted a uniformly positive picture.

In 1902, Mīrzā Sirāj Rahīm, the son of a wealthy Bukharan merchant, embarked on a six-month visit that took him through Russia to Istanbul and then to all the major capitals of Europe. Almost immediately upon his return, he left again for India, Afghanistan, and Iran, where he ended up staying for many years. Returning to Bukhara in 1909, he became prominent in local reform circles, editing Bukhara's first Turkic newspaper in 1912, and contributing to periodicals in Turkestan, Iran, and Istanbul until his premature death in 1914.[73] In 1911, he published an account of his travels of the previous decade that provided the first extensive Central Asian portrayal of the outside world to the local audience.

Mīrzā Sirāj takes great pleasure in describing the wonders of Europe to his readers, with the focus squarely on progress, order, and material achievement. He traveled first class across Europe. There is no mention of any difficulties he experienced or any sense of alienation in being in a foreign land. In his bourgeois cosmopolitanism there is not a trace of the native fanaticism that frightened Russian administrators. Upon arriving in a city, he would hire a cab to be driven around the sites before settling down to a round of visits that included museums, schools, universities, and theaters. (Only in London did he visit a factory.) In Vienna, he provides a detailed description of the etiquette involved in a visit to the theater. In Berlin we get copious detail about his hotel, which was "as good as, or rather, better than the palaces of the monarchs of Asia." He was especially fond of Paris ("Whoever comes into this world and does not

---

72. Bāsit Khān Zāhid Khān oghli, "Firānsuzlarda ichkulik," *Khurshid*, 12 November 1906.

73. See his obituary in *Āyina*, 11 January 1914, 291–292.

see Paris might as well not be born"), with whose boulevards and cafés he fell in love.[74] The descriptions are repetitive and perhaps superficial, but they always serve to remind the reader of the achievements of developed states. The source of this progress was not far to seek. "The instruments of progress and improvement [*taraqqi wa tarbiyat*] that I saw in the cities of Germany are also present in villages and towns in proportion to their size. Every village has a complete elementary school, an organized secondary school, a hospital, a theater, a hotel, and a recreational park. . . . The expenses of these are the responsibility of the constitutional state of Germany."[75] In Vienna, "every person, big or small, man or woman, reads the newspaper. Every day, several newspapers are printed in the presses of this city. An idle, illiterate person is never to be found."[76] The comparison, invariably invidious, with Central Asia, is always implicit, and occasionally bursts out in impassioned prose.

> I did not see in Europe a single person whose clothes were old or torn, not one building in ruins, nor a street that was unpaved. . . . But in our country, our poor merchants and shopkeepers, in their cells and shops dark with dust and [surrounded by] crowds of beggars, cannot find a minute to breathe properly. . . . Pity on us, pity on us. All the time I toured Paris, [my] beloved homeland was constantly in my mind, and all the time tears flowed from my eyes.[77]

Leaving Paris for the last time, he felt very sad until he reminded himself, "No matter what, I am going to my country and the lands of Islam."

> Even if it is bad, it is our homeland. . . . One should not despair of one's homeland, and one should not exile its love from the heart. The fault is not with our country, it is with its children for they are ignoble and do not know the rights of their mother. Whatever there is comes from the homeland, and its love has been decreed by the Pride of the Universe to be a pillar of the faith: "*hubb ul-watan min al-imān*" [love of the homeland is part of faith]. We do not know the worth of our land, and do not attempt to work for its prosperity and improvement. The fault does not lie in our country, but in ourselves.[78]

For Behbudi, who provides us the other Jadid view of the world beyond, this didactic purpose is firmly foregrounded. Behbudi traveled in the Ottoman empire in 1914 and described his impressions in detail in *Āyina*. Again we get detailed descriptions of the order and cleanliness of

---

74. Mirzā Sirājiddin Hāji Mirzā ʿAbdurrauf, *Safarnāma-yi tuhaf-i Bukhārā*, ed. M. Asadiyān (Tehran, 1992), 107–109, 113, 121. This book was originally published as *Tuhaf-i ahl-i Bukārā* (Kāgān, 1911), but I have been unable to locate a copy of the original.
75. Ibid., 115.
76. Ibid., 106–107.
77. Ibid., 133–135.
78. Ibid., 149.

Russian cities (in Transcaucasia) and the industry and effort of Europeans, but every such description is turned around to a criticism of the
present state of the Muslim world. The reader is constantly reminded of
the backwardness and ignorance of Muslims and of the price they are pay-
ing for it. In Rostov, the 5,000 Muslims do not have their own school.
In Edirne, all the trade is in the hands of non-Muslims while the Turks
only govern; he finds the same situation in Palestine, where all the shops
were owned by Jews. All grocery stores sell wine, which is gladly im-
bibed by the local Arabs who do not go to the *rüşdiye* schools opened by
the state because they consider them *harām* (forbidden).[79] Similarly, he
is appalled to find a brothel overlooking a cemetery in Jaffa but disagrees
with his interlocutors, who place the blame on foreign consuls and their
Jewish or Christian protégés; the blame must rest squarely with the
Muslims and their ignorance.[80] Pilgrims and tourists come from afar to
visit the Holy Land, all equipped with guide books describing the sights
in detail. Muslim pilgrims are the exception. No guide books exist in
any Muslim language, and Behbudi notes that he was one of only three
Muslims visiting the sights. Even when Behbudi is delighted at the number of wealthy Muslims in Baku, he rues the fact that they do not support the city's newspapers sufficiently. Behbudi rhapsodizes over the glory
of the Selimiye mosque in Edirne and the Umayyad mosque in Damascus
as examples of the effort and zeal of early Muslims and their support for
Islam. The contrast with his contemporaries could not be more starkly
drawn. Standing amidst the ruins of the recent war in Edirne, he declares
them to be "part of the ruins of ignorance and disorder [*ilmsizlik wa
idārasizlik*]."[81]

Travelogues and foreign Muslims had other rhetorical uses, too. Fitrat used a fictional Indian Muslim traveler to present his desiderata of
reform in Bukhara. The *Tales of an Indian Traveler* was published in
Persian in Istanbul but was freely available in Turkestan (although the
amir of Bukhara attempted to ban it from his domain). While some of
the criticism in it pertains specifically to Bukhara, the tract became a favorite of the Jadids of all Central Asia and Behbudi published a Russian
translation in Turkestan.[82]

79. Mahmud Khoja [Behbudi], "Sayāhat khātiralari—XVIII," *Āyina*, 25 October
1914, 1238.
80. Behbudi, "Sayāhat khātiralari—XXIII," *Āyina*, 8 December 1914, 104–105.
81. Mahmud Khoja [Behbudi], "Sayāhat khātiralari—VIII," *Āyina*, 10 August 1914,
1003.
82. Abdurrauf Fitrat, *Bayānāt-i sayyāh-i hindi* (Istanbul, 1911); I have used a modern
Tajik edition of this text: Abduraufi Fitrati Bukhoroi, "Bayonoti sayyohi hindî," ed.

The Traveler arrives at the city gates to find them closed for the night. While he is arguing with the gatekeeper, carriages containing Armenians and Jews are allowed into the city without any questions being asked. Then the doors open again, an Armenian emerges and calls out to someone. His dog, accidentally left behind, appears and is admitted to the city while Muslim travelers wait outside for dawn. The next morning, the Traveler finally enters the city and takes a carriage to an inn in the city but immediately runs into a traffic jam in the narrow streets, as oncoming carriages refuse to yield out of honor ('*ār*). As fighting erupts, the Traveler asks his driver, "Brother, aren't there the ruler's men around to settle this?"

"What do the ruler's men have to do with this?" comes the reply.

The affair is settled only after a physical confrontation, but the theme of chaos and disorder is firmly established in the narrative, as is its connection with the state's incompetence and dereliction of duty. Both are repeated continuously throughout the narrative. Later, when the Traveler visits the town of Qarshi, he has the following exchange with a master weaver:

> "Really, the people of Qarshi are very skilled in weaving *alacha* [the Traveler said]. Thanks to this noble skill they reap a great deal of profit these days. But what is your opinion of the future of this craft?"
>
> The owner of the workshop did not understand my question and looked at me in surprise. I explained my question further. "Will the affairs of the craftsmen of Qarshi be in the same healthy state ten or twelve years from now or not?"
>
> The master understood me this time, but since such a question had not even occurred to him until now, was surprised again, and said nothing. I added, "Esteemed master, Europeans, when they set their hands on something, keep their eyes on how it will develop over ten, twenty, even a hundred or two hundred years. You people of Qarshi are highly skilled, but do you not think of the future of this trade?"
>
> Master: "Our trade was good a few years ago. Now too it's not bad. But only God knows its future."
>
> I: "True, but have you done anything [to ensure] the development of your trade over the next ten years?"

Kholiq Mirzozoda, *Sadoi sharq*, 1988, no. 6, 12–57. The book was widely read in Central Asia at the time of its publication, and Behbudi published a Russian translation in 1914: Abd-ur-Rauf, *Razskazy indiiskogo puteshestvennika: Bukhara kak ona est'*, tr. A. N. Kondrat'ev (Samarqand, 1913); a Turkic edition, however, did not appear until 1991, when it was published in modern Uzbek: Abdurauf Fitrat, "Hind sayyohining qissasi," trans. Hasan Qudratullaev, *Sharq yulduzi*, 1991, no. 8, 7–39.

Master: "Our affairs are good now; who knows who'll be dead and who alive in ten years?" [83]

Planning and foresight were essential to progress and modernity, and they were lacking in Central Asia. For Fitrat, they constituted an essential duty of the state, for the Traveler then proceeds to outline an economic policy that Bukhara should follow in order to secure its prosperity.

The theme of sanitation and public health also figures prominently in the Indian Traveler's account. He finds Bukhara unhygienic and employs the discourse of public health to criticize it. In the middle of the trip, he falls ill and finding that none of the practitioners of Bukharan medicine can explain his illness to him, refuses to be treated by them and insists of calling a Russian doctor. Modern medicine cures him, of course, and he recounts in detail his conversation with the Russian doctor on sanitation, public health, and medical education.

The superiority of modern medicine over its traditional Central Asian counterpart, demonstrated by experience, had become an arena of contestation early on. We will remember Governor-General Dukhovskoi's suggestion of harnessing medical science to the task of overcoming native fanaticism. But while individual patients cured by modern medicine were doubtless impressed, public health, a major concern of officialdom, encountered many difficulties as the local population resented the extension of state power into newer domains that such initiatives represented. The most extreme case were the so-called cholera riots in Tashkent in 1892, when attempts by the authorities to regulate burials during an epidemic led to the most serious outbreak of violence in Tashkent of the tsarist period.[84] The Jadids also embraced this discourse of public health, while criticizing traditional medicine. As a contributor to *Āyina* wrote, "Our *tabib*s are ignorant of the science of medicine and have no skills other than that of worsening the disease and sending off the patient to the other world speedily." [85]

Ignorance led to corruption of Islam itself. The Indian Traveler also visits the tomb of Bahāʾuddin Naqshband on the outskirts of Bukhara and is dismayed at what he sees there. Pilgrims kissed sacred relics such as rams' horns and a flagpole bearing the *mazār*'s banner and prayed to

---

83. Fitrat, "Bayonoti sayyohi hindî," 40.
84. This episode remains little studied. The last full-length treatment of the subject was V. Zykin, *Vosstanie v Tashkente v 1892 g.* (Tashkent, 1934).
85. H. M., "Tib wa hifz us-sihhatda riʿayatsizlikimiz," *Āyina*, 7 June 1914, 778–779.

the buried saint. The Traveler considers this idolatry, and asks, "Is it possible that you consider others 'infidels' for idolatry and worshipping the cross, and but worship flagpoles in mazars, ask Bahā'uddin about your needs, and yet consider yourself Muslims?"[86] Criticism of customary practices for being not "truly Islamic" and hence connected to ignorance was a common feature of Jadid discourse.

MATTERS OF SURVIVAL

The sense of impending doom evoked by Munawwar Qāri was widely shared by the Jadids, who had to do no more than read their newspapers, which they all did diligently, to be reminded of this Darwinian fact. The middle of the first decade of this century, when the first Jadid newspapers appeared, was a time of great optimism in the wake of revolution in Russia (as well as in Iran), and the hope of a liberal constitutional regime in Russia was very much alive. But the situation changed rapidly. Political life in Russia chilled after 1907, while the news from the Muslim world was uniformly bad. Morocco's rapid subjugation to France and Spain coincided with the virtual disintegration of Iran, but it was the numerous wars faced by the Ottoman empire in the period after the Young Turk revolution of 1908 that shaped a sense of crisis among the Jadids of Central Asia (as indeed among Muslim intellectuals the world over). The wars were covered extensively in the Muslim press of Russia, including the *TWG*, and brought to the Jadids a certain sense of urgency. Hāji Muin cited the example of recent territorial losses suffered by the Ottoman empire and Morocco to bring home the same point: "With the help of the development of science and technology [*ilm-u fan*], Europeans can keep an eye on the affairs of all kinds of people in the world. The world has become a struggle for life in which every powerful thing destroys the powerless."[87] To stay in the game, every nation had to acquire the means necessary for survival, of which knowledge was the most basic. "No nation can survive in the battleground of life without knowledge," wrote a contributor to *Āyina*. "Any such nation, whether master [*hākim*] or subject [*mahkum*], will succumb to other nations who possess industry and skills. . . . If subject nations wish to survive without losing their religion and nationhood [*din wa milliyat*], they must

---

86. Fitrat, "Bayonoti sayyohi hindî," 19–20.
87. Hāji Muin b. Shukrullah, "Istiqbāl qāyghusi," *Āyina*, 2 November 1913, 11.

acquire wealth."[88] Fitrat once wrote that a nation lacking resolve and determination had no right to exist.[89] The responsibility for survival therefore lay with the nation itself.

Progress and enlightenment were sources of both power and danger. Jadid authors constantly pointed to Jews and Armenians as both sources of danger and models for emulation. On the steamer from Odessa to Istanbul, Behbudi had a long conversation with a Jew bound for Palestine. " 'How are the new cities around Jerusalem?' I asked. 'Praise the Lord, they progress by the day,' he said. 'Doctor Herzl founded these cities with money collected from people with great effort. . . . Now there is a Jewish bank there, teachers' colleges, gimnaziias, etc. Now at the invitation of the Doctor we are learning the old Jewish tongue (Hebrew). I did not know anything other than Russian. But I studied Hebrew two hours a week for a year and now I can speak, read, and write it.' . . . And we study Arabic for twenty years and still cannot speak or write it!"[90] Jews and Armenians, small stateless communities, even more than the powerful imperial nations of Europe, proved to the Jadids the truth of their general assertion that knowledge was the key to progress.[91] At the same time, they were the perfect example of a Darwinian world in which survival was assured only by disciplined effort.

Ignorance could be fatal. Death constantly stalks Jadid literature. In Behbudi's *The Patricide,* a rich merchant refuses to send his son to school; the latter, unable to tell right from wrong, falls in with bad company. One night, in need of money to pay for a prostitute, the group attempts to break into the merchant's house and ends up killing the merchant.[92] In Abdullah Qādiri's *The Unfortunate Groom,* an impecunious young man forced to conform to custom and celebrate his wedding with an expensive feast (*toy*), goes bankrupt and commits suicide along with his wife.[93] In Hamza's *A Poisoned Life,* a young woman married off by

88. Niyāzi Rajabzada, "Ibtidāi maktablarimizning tartibsizligi, yākhud taraqqining yoli," *Āyina,* 12 July 1914, 908–909.

89. Abdurrauf Fitrat, "Himmat-u sabāti bolmagān millatning haqq-i hayāti yoqdur," *Āyina,* 14 January 1915, 162.

90. Behbudi, "Sayāhat khātiralari—V," *Āyina,* 17 July 1914, 929–930.

91. This is worth noting, for the Jadids' views on this question have usually been cited in the Soviet literature (and occasionally in non-Soviet works as well) as examples of their national chauvinism and even anti-Semitism; see, e.g., Büzrük Salīhof, *Özbek ädäbijatïda millätcilik körünişläri* (Tashkent, 1935), 11–12; Z. Radzhabov, *Iz istorii obshchestvenno-politicheskoi mysli Tadzhikskogo naroda vo vtoroi polovine XIX i v nachale XX vv.* (Stalinabad, 1957), 401–402.

92. Behbudi, *Padarkush* (Samarqand, 1913).

93. Abdullah Qādiri, *Bakhtsiz kiyāw* (Tashkent, 1915).

her ignorant parents to a wicked old *ishān,* takes her life and is followed
to the other world by her erstwhile suitor, a young man of modern learning and good intentions.[94] In Chŏlpon's *Doctor Muhammadyār,* murder
takes place almost at random, the result of the ignorance that reigns in
Central Asian society.[95] (Occasionally the wages of ignorance are other
than death. In Qādiri's *The Pederast,* the protagonist murders several rivals and is sent off to Siberia as a result.[96]) And Ajzi painted a portrait
of his city in the future, when splendid prosperity reigns over it but all
its madrasas have been turned into restaurants and its mosques replaced
by churches; there are no Muslims left.[97]

PUBLIC MORALITY

The road to death and destruction passed through immorality, and the
Jadids saw plenty of evidence of that in their society. Russian rule had
brought with it legal prostitution and the sale of alcohol, both of which
were quite popular in Turkestan. We read of a brothel in Samarqand
with "nearly 400 Turkestani, Bukharan, Tatar, and Russian prostitutes,"
without any indication that it was in at all unusual.[98] Even more trou-
bling to the Jadids, however, was the widespread practice of dancing boys
(*bachcha, jawān, besaqqāl*) who, dressed as women, figured in evenings
of entertainment (*bazm, maʿraka*) and who were often also prostituted.
This form of pederasty was a widespread practice (and perhaps had become more widespread under Russian rule).

For the Jadids, the practice was a sign of the worst depths of degradation to which Central Asia had sunk. Fitrat's Indian traveler is appalled
when he witnesses pederasty at the tomb of Bahā'uddin Naqshband:

> Woe to me! Next to this noble paradise were open the doors to hell. Next to
> these sacred tombs had arisen the vileness of the tribe of Lot! Among the tea
> stalls people sat in circles of five or ten; in the center of each circle was a young
> boy who with innocence and modesty read several verses from memory. All
> those around him pressed up against him, staring at the poor child with eyes
> full of lust, just like the devil!!! This terrible and impious spectacle made my
> whole being shiver. . . . I said to myself, "O Muhammad! . . . Rise! O edu-

94. Hamza Hakimzāda, *Zaharli hayot* (1916), in *Tŏla asarlar tŏplami,* ed. N. Karimov et al., 5 vols. (Tashkent, 1988–1989), III: 15–41.
95. The story was serialized in *ST* in 1914; cf. Chŏlpon, "Dŏkhtur Muhammadyor,"
Sharq yulduzi, 1992, no. 1, 132–138.
96. Qādiri, *Jawānbāz* (Tashkent, 1915).
97. Sayyid Ahmad Siddiqi [Ajzi], *Tarjima-yi mirʾat-i ibrat* (Samarqand, 1914), 25–26.
98. *Āyina,* 8 February 1914, 281.

cator, take a look at the actions of these savages! O reformer of people! Either find a way of reforming them, or else show them a place under the earth, like the people of Lot! Don't let the filthy existence of these shameless people harm the glory of the Qur'an.[99]

For Munawwar Qāri, "Forbidden acts such as drinking, gambling, pederasty, feasting, turning men into women and women into men [*erkekni khātun qilmāq wa khātunni erek qilmāq*], adultery, backbiting" were the reason why "our lands were captured and we were reviled and demeaned [*khwār-u zalil bolduk*]."[100]

Many of these practices came together in the often extravagant feasts (*toys*) celebrating circumcisions, weddings, and deaths that were an integral part of Central Asian life. They were defended, even by ulama, as worthy ancestral traditions. By the turn of the century, they had become a means for the newly rich to celebrate their wealth and to assert their social status. The more extravagant feasts lasted several days, with guests (often numbering in the hundreds) arriving from all over Central Asia; the central feature was a party featuring alcohol and dancing boys. The Andijān millionaire Mir Kāmil-bāy hosted a *toy* in 1911 that lasted twenty-five days; guests came from all over Turkestan, and charity and food were provided for "widows and travelers" throughout this period. The awestruck report in *TWG* ("a royal feast neither heard, nor seen, nor known to people of previous generations") estimated the total expenditure to have been 25,000 rubles.[101] The Jadids took a dim view of such practices, which they saw as a waste (*isrāf*) of resources that should better be spent for the public good, and especially after a wave of bankruptcies during the economic slump of 1913, as a sign of ignorance leading to destruction. Jadid authors expressed opposition to *toys* in newspapers and school textbooks, much of which was encapsulated in the 1914 play *The Feast* by Behbudi's disciples Hāji Muin and Nusratullah b. Qudratullah.

The play depicts the dire consequences of ignorance and wastefulness. A rich merchant plans to celebrate his son's circumcision with a *toy*, brushing aside exhortations against wastefulness and other acts "forbidden by the shariat." Vanity and selfishness govern his actions ("If you give a huge feast, your wealth will be known and you will be fa-

99. Fitrat, "Bayonoti sayyohi hindî," 21.

100. Munawwar Qāri ibn Abdurrashid Khan, untitled article, *Taraqqi—Orta Azyaning umr guzārlighi*, 7 March 1906.

101. *TWG*, 28 April 1911.

mous"); only the rich are invited, while the poor are insulted ("I didn't have this feast for beggars and the poor; get lost!"). The feast, complete with alcohol and *bachcha*s, is duly celebrated, but goes 4,000 rubles over the already extravagant budget of 15,000 rubles, leaving the merchant with a bank balance of precisely 130.23 rubles. He has to default on a payment of 5,000 rubles to the Moscow Bank, which had conveniently (for the plot) fallen due at that time, and as a result his store is sealed. The stage is set for the protagonist to deliver his speech:

> When will we Muslims of Turkestan [save ourselves] from this ignorance? Ignorance has turned us into drunkards, pederasts, fools, and wastrels. And now it has dishonored us and laid waste our homes. Other nations spend their money in the path of knowledge and learning, on religious and national causes, and therefore progress by the day. We, because of our ignorance, waste our money, and even sell [lose] our houses and orchards on feasts parties, and *kobkāri,* and soon will be begging for a piece of bread. If we Muslims don't take advantage of this time [remaining] and do not change our wasteful customs, soon we'll be deprived of what we have [left] and be cast into the streets. May God grant all Muslims the eyes of admonition.[102]

The cause of moral corruption was ignorance, and knowledge was the only true guarantee of good morals and piety. "Schools are blessed places built for our good," a textbook informed pupils. "Mosques are also extremely sacred places built for Muslims to worship in. If there were no schools in the world, who would enter a mosque and worship there?"[103]

It was a crisis not because the morals of individuals were at stake or because sin was widespread but because immoral acts led to dereliction of duty to the community, which had come to be the locus of Jadid reform. A correspondent for *Shuhrat* calculated that at a recent Feast of the Sacrifice (*Id-i qurbān*), Muslims of Tashkent spent 100,000 rubles on alcohol and prostitutes. "If this is not progress, what is?" the writer asked. "But what kind of money was this? This was money enough to educate millions of children, to bring them from bestiality to humanity, to produce thousands of servants of the nation [*millat khādimi*]."[104] Narcotic addicts, lampooned in a play by Hāji Muin, were similarly immoral not so much because Islamic law forbade the use of narcotics but because they wasted time, money, and human resources.[105]

102. Nusratullah ibn Qudratullah with Hāji Muin, *Toy* (Samarqand, 1914).
103. Abdullah Awlāni, *Birinchi muallim* (Tashkent, 1912), 30.
104. Dimashqi (pseud.), "Musulmānlarda ichkulik balāsi," *Shuhrat,* 11 December 1907; the issue was also taken up in "Ichkulik balāsi," *Tojjār,* 13 January 1908.
105. Hāji Muin Shukrullah, *Koknāri* (Samarqand, 1916).

THE POLITICS OF ADMONITION

Locating morality in the public realm provided a new vision of the rights and responsibilities of different groups in society. In showing the mirror of admonition to society, the Jadids asserted a claim to cultural and moral leadership in it. Their knowledge of the path to a better future qualified them to lead the society. This was, of course, profoundly subversive to the authority of the established elites in society, who derived their authority from their mastery of the past and their role in the compromises with Russian authorities. What ensued as a result of the emergence of a Jadid voice in society was a struggle for leadership in which the fundamental stakes were cultural. The struggle was over the definition of Central Asian Muslim culture: How was it to be defined and by whom? It was not simply a struggle for cultural capital; the Jadids' challenge put the very definition of this capital in question. This politics was every bit as real, and more important, than the politics entrenched in formal institutions of state.

The Jadids commonly asserted that their society rested on the twin pillars of the wealthy (*aghniyā*) and the learned (*ulamā*), for whom they professed great respect if they did their duty to society. But they also bore the blame when problems arose. "The number of those imprisoned in the mire of pederasty, alcohol, and gambling has increased recently," wrote a concerned *Āyina* reader from Awliyā Atā, "because our leaders [*ulugh wa kattalarimiz*] and our qāzis have done nothing to counter these ills."[106] As we saw, the wealthy were open to criticism for wasting their wealth on extravagant feasts rather than using it to benefit the nation. The ulama fared no better. None of the portraits of ulama in Jadid literature is particularly flattering. In *The Feast,* the neighborhood imām makes an attempt to dissuade the merchant from wasting his money on the feast by arguing that such acts are forbidden by the shariat, but quickly backs down when someone makes a pointed reference to his livelihood depending on the goodwill of the *bāy*.[107] Hāji Muin's protagonist in his play, *The Oppressed Woman,* a new-method teacher, makes the following speech:

> In the old days, the common people were subservient [*tābi'*] to the ulama, but unfortunately now the ulama are subservient to the people and have become

106. Begi In'ām oghli, "Awliyā Atādan," *Āyina,* 10 May 1914, 562.
107. Nusratullah, *Toy,* 11–12.

flatterers. For this reason, a number of forbidden things such as pederasty, drinking, and ill treatment of [multiple] wives are growing daily. . . .

[Aside:] In this respect, the fault lies with our ulama, not the people. It is because of this that they say, "*fasād ul-ālim fasād ul-ālam* [The corruption of the learned is the corruption of the world]." . . . Ah! O God, grant our ulama justice and discernment![108]

Ulama hostile to reform were, for the Jadids, ignorant of Islam, venal, weak-willed, and concerned only with their own material well being. This was especially the case with criticisms of Bukhara. Fitrat's Indian Traveler found it offensive that the ulama in Bukhara charged high fees for affixing their seals and signatures on documents. Shariat was for sale in Bukhara. The Traveler puts the matter in historical perspective for a Bukharan interlocutor:

The activities of your self-proclaimed ulama are the reason for the extinction of your nation. But there's no need to grieve, brother, since your ulama aren't the only ones like this. The fact is, ulama all over the Muslim world in the last three centuries have committed similar crimes. Until yesterday, the majority of ulama among Turks and Tatars, and in Iran and India, like yours, all drank the blood of oppressed people. But these nations scrutinized matters before you have done, and they overthrew the ulama from their pedestal. Quickly they distinguished real scholars from mullās who only worshipped their own bellies; they placed crowns on the heads of the former and trampled the latter underfoot.[109]

Ishāns, connected with the world of Sufism and its related "superstitions," received even shorter shrift. Every ishān in Hamza's writing is a mean-looking glutton who takes a new wife every year, while the Tashkent poet Shawkat Khāndayliqi let them have it thus:

Why are there so many dogs in Bukhara in the winter, but so few in the summer?
In the summer, they all become ishāns and go to the country, that's why.[110]

It was in this context that the rest of society responded to Jadid criticism. The opponents of the Jadids were motivated by very real concerns: They were defending nothing less than a social order that privileged them. The Jadids put to question not just the credentials of the ulama but also the compromises the latter had worked out with the colonial regime,

---

108. Hāji Muin b. Shukrullah, *Mazluma khātun* (Samarqand, 1916), 23–25.
109. Fitrat, "Bayonoti sayyohi hindî," 26.
110. Quoted in A. Jalolov, *Inqilobiy dawr ōzbek adabiyoti wa Shawkat ijodi* (Tashkent, 1988), 58.

which ensured them a status as intermediaries between the local population and Russian officialdom. Much of the social landscape within
which the qadimchi operated was the product of Russian rule and the
compromises forced by it.

Many simply ignored the Jadids, although this was increasingly difficult to do at least in the urban centers. Others responded in kind. The
main arguments against the Jadids are encapsulated in the following attack by a Tashkent Tatar on other Tatars that doubtless was read as ap-
plying equally to local Jadids:

> How have they awakened [the nation]? To wearing narrow trousers, patent-
> leather shoes, and short jackets . . . to wasting money on all sorts of music
> and useless things, money that could be used to benefit the nation. . . . Our
> esteemed writers say, "The new method has arrived, the western sun has
> arisen, everyone has received the light, has arisen and become human." Why
> don't you show us a teacher who is a perfect Muslim, who works for the re-
> juvenation of religion [ahyā-yi din] and who explains it to common people?
> But you cannot. . . . This method of Yazid [usul-i Yazid] of yours will cause
> poor Muslims to be left without faith; [it] will cause women to discard their
> veils.[111]

The anonymous author went on to berate the Jadids for their duplicity
and insincerity (their concern for the nation exists only on their tongues,
not in their hearts, and is motivated by the need to sell their newspapers). Other arguments were more pointed. Sayyid Ahmad Wasli, the
Samarqand *mudarris* who had considerable sympathies for the Jadid
cause, wrote that one of the major shortcomings of the Jadid project was
its constant criticism of the ulama. "New-method teachers are merely
teachers of reading and writing; for them to criticize the teaching of the
ulama was a great impropriety [buyuk adabsizlik], especially when most
of them had never even attended such lessons. If they had only stuck to
teaching," Wasli added, "all of Turkestan would have phonetic-method
schools by now." [112] The point was made more forcefully by an author
in *al-Islāh* as few months later. Praising the *Sadā-yi Turkistān* and the
Sadā-yi Farghāna for their intentions, the author found it

> unfortunate that in every single issue, these esteemed newspapers accuse the
> ulama, the pillars of the faith of Islam, of every kind of ignorance, indeed of
> foolishness, and insult them by attacking the path shown by the noble shariat
> as ignorance or error. Rather, [these newspapers] are published in the spirit

111. Turkistānlik bir Noghāy Mullā, "Yāngi fikrchi, eski fikrchi," *TWG,* 7 January
1910.
112. Wasli, "Jarida wa usul-i jadida," *SF,* 6 November 1914.

of our Europeanized youth who, without regard to divine commandments [*amr-i haqq*] or the requirements of the shariat [*hukm-i shar'*], claim to be the renewers of the epoch. . . .

All of them are ignorant, [men] of unopened eyes and unsound intellects, who have wasted their lives in maktabs and madrasas for none of their lessons seems to have done them any good.[113]

Generational conflict was never far below the surface. After all, the most common appellation for the Jadids was *yāshlar*, "the youth." Hamza's *A Poisoned Life* was as much about the relations between the generations as about ignorance. It is a tale of eighteen-year-old Mahmudkhān, "most open-minded . . . [and] nation-minded [*millatparast*]," and seventeen-year-old Maryam khānim, the daughter of a craftsman who "although educated in the old maktabs had read novels, newspapers, and magazines under the influence of her love for Mahmudkhān, . . . a slave of the nation [*millat jāriyasi*]." They are in love and plan to open a school, but their wishes are quashed by their parents. Mahmudkhān's father refuses outright to marry his only son to the daughter of a poor craftsman. Maryam's "ignorant and money-worshipping" parents, on the other hand, have promised her hand to a sixty-year-old ishān who already has six wives. The result is disastrous, and both young people take their own lives rather than acquiesce to the dictates of their parents. Hamza attempts to portray them as victims of ignorance and martyrs to the nation, but the most memorable lines in the play involve the two protagonists cursing their ignorant (*jāhil*) and loveless (*shafqatsiz*) parents for riding roughshod over their wishes.[114] The generational aspect of conflict was prominent also when the qadimchi turned tables on the Jadids and, after Behbudi's *Patricide* began touring, began calling the Jadids "patricides."

All the major sites of Jadid reform—the new-method school, the periodical press, the theater—were criticized by the ulama, and the Jadids spent considerable energy trying to justify their enthusiasm for new cultural practices. The newspaper aroused deep suspicion. Early in its career, the *TWG* found it prudent to remind its readers that "reading or listening to a newspaper does not harm religion, but rather it informs [the reader] of all manner of things."[115] But the suspicions lingered. In 1906, an article by Munawwar Qāri (who himself had proper creden-

113. Khālmuhammad Toraqulov, "Talab-i islāh," *al-Islāh*, 15 June 1915, 336–338.
114. Hamza, *Zaharli hayot, yokhud ishq qurbonlari* (1916), in his *Tŏla asarlar tŏplami*, III: 15–41.
115. "Ma'lumnāma," *TWG*, 8 January 1874.

tials as an *ālim*) criticizing the old-method maktabs in the first issue of *Taraqqi* so irked the ulama of Tashkent that they sent a delegation to the city administrator requesting him to suspend publication of the newspaper.[116] Although the delegation did not achieve its aim, the newspaper was soon shut down for other reasons.

Similarly, the Jadids' use of music and theater provoked heated debate, with many traditionalist ulama, and even some of the more conservative Jadids, criticizing it on Islamic grounds. Music and theater had, of course, long existed in Central Asia, but they both occupied an ambiguous place in the cultural tradition. The Jadids' insistence that their theater was different only compounded their problems, since they could never shake off the ambiguities of *maskharabāzlik* and had to deal with suspicions over what they insisted was new. The two issues that came to the fore involved women and music.

Women acted on the stage in Tatar plays staged in Tashkent. This was cause for scandal, especially among the local population. In 1910, a Tashkent Tatar who happened upon a benefit performance was dismayed by what he saw ("What benefit will come from girls dancing shamelessly with unrelated men?").[117] When Central Asian Jadids began staging their own plays, they avoided the problem by having men play all roles on stage. A dual-track system developed in which outside plays could have women on stage, but not locally produced ones. For instance, when *The Patricide* first played in Tashkent in February 1914, the merchant's wife was played by Abdussami Qāri Ziyābāev, but a woman played a female role later in the evening during the Transcaucasian comedy *Khor khor*.[118] Apparently, even local troupes could include women when putting on performances of imported plays.

The questions over music were less easily dodged. Music was widely used by the Jadids: not only were theatrical performances accompanied by music, but most fundraising cultural evenings also featured performances of folk and traditional music. As we have seen, Hamza and Awlāni also wrote poetry specifically for music. The Jadids' open use of music in nonreligious contexts rendered them vulnerable to the charge of introducing illegitimate innovations into Islam. Because of these associations, the theater aroused the opposition of many who were generally supportive of Jadid reform. Nor was such criticism restricted to the

116. For later comment on the incident in *Taraqqi*'s columns, see Mullā Zulfiqār, "Madrasalargha āid," *Taraqqi,* 5 July 1906.
117. Tāhir Sami'ullin, "Ibratnāma," *TWG,* 7 February 1910.
118. Tāziljānbāev, "Tāshkanda [sic] milli tiyātir," *Āyina,* 22 March 1914, 324.

printed page. Before the first Tashkent performance of *The Patricide*, a number of ulama and merchants attempted to have the city authorities ban the play, failing which they sought to buy out the troupe by offering to pay an amount larger than what the performance would have raised. According to a contemporary observer, these men sought to prevent the performance because they feared that the actors, including many new-method teachers, would henceforth be counted as maskharas and excluded from polite company.[119]

This debate is most clearly documented in a polemic between Wasli and Behbudi, perhaps the most enthusiastic proponent of theater among the Jadids of Turkestan, over the permissibility of theater from the Islamic point of view. Wasli saw theater as completely contrary to the shariat:

> Now, among the things forbidden by the shariat are games and amusements. Basically, they destroy [personal] dignity and credit, waste one's time and life, and keep [one] from one's duties as a human being. They also bring [with them] calamities such as spendthriftness. . . . If other forbidden [things] such as musical instruments, singers, gambling, and women are added to these games, they become doubly forbidden and bring heavenly retribution upon the head of the community. . . . Obscenities (*fuhushiyāt*) are not entirely without some profit, and I am afraid that if the custom of considering permissible every forbidden thing which has some good in it takes hold, obscenities too will gradually flourish.[120]

By thus condemning music, Wasli was also condemning the new phenomenon of musical soirées and benefit concerts, which had become increasingly important to the Jadid cause.

In his response, Behbudi cited hadith and instances from the life of the Prophet to argue that music and games were permissible provided they did not contain obscenity. He acknowledged that theater was an innovation (*bid'at*), but, he argued:

> Innovation is that which did not exist in the time of the Prophet. Innovations that have arisen since then are of two kinds: If an innovation brings benefits to the faith and the community [*din wa millat*], it is called a good innovation [*yakhshi bid'at*]; if it brings harm . . . , it is called a sinful innovation [*gunāh bid'at*]. The Patricide is also an innovation, but we consider it a good innovation because it admonishes the audience. It enjoins good and forbids evil by showing the audience as a warning the murder and abasement that come from being caught in drunkenness and obscenity. Indeed, the theater is a place for preaching and exhortation [*majlis-i wa'z-u nasihat*].[121]

119. Salihov, *Ozbek teatr*, 74–79.
120. Mudarris Wasli, "Shariat-i Islāmiya," *SF*, 21 November 1914.
121. Behbudi, "Tiyātir, musiqi, she'r," *Āyina*, 18 December 1914, 111–114.

Behbudi also pointed out that Wasli himself wrote poetry incorporating rather racy themes of love and drink, which, although they followed received patterns, were not permitted by the shariat.

Wasli denounced theater as a wasteful pastime because it threatened to bring into public use behavior that had hitherto lain on the fringes of the acceptable. By putting women on the stage and having men act as people they were not, by openly acknowledging, indeed exhibiting, practices that were immoral, and by using music to appeal to the audience, Jadid theater threatened to upset the rules of proper deportment according to which the traditional elites had negotiated their life struggles. Wasli's support of the new method did not extend to this radical redefinition of acceptable behavior.

The debate over the permissibility of music continued after the polemic between Wasli and Behbudi came to an end. It was given a new lease of life by Russian officialdom. The Tatar singer Kamil ul-Mutigi Tuhfatullin sought permission to tour Turkestan in 1915 for a series of concerts to benefit various war-related causes. In a fit of zeal, acting Governor-General F. V. Martson referred the matter to the Muslim Spiritual Administration in Orenburg, whose opinion about the permissibility of the concert he sought, even though Turkestan lay beyond the board's jurisdiction. The matter leaked to the press and debate began anew, this time in the pages of al-Islāh. In response to a reader's question, a certain Fazlulwahhāb Qāri of Marghinān declared all use of music and song as harām. Ashurali Zāhiri, a teacher in a Russonative school in Kokand who had studied in Bukhara, joined the fray. He took on the author on his own turf, citing evidence from the requisite texts and discussing quotations from the hadith in the Arabic to show that none of the hadiths used by Fazlulwahhāb were trustworthy. Music and song were not harām, but mubāh (permissible), and their use in the time of the Prophet was attested to in historical accounts.[122] Zāhiri's intervention did not end the matter, of course, but it was a sign that many Jadids could take on their critics on their own terms. At the same time, the ulama found themselves debating issues in print, in a public forum where the rules of entry were not of their making.

122. Ashur Ali Zāhiri, "Shariat-i Islāmiya wa musiqa, yāki Fazlulwahhāb Qārigha raddiya," al-Islāh, 15 January 1916, 51–53; Zāhiri, "Ashāb-i karam, tābi'in wa mujtahidin-i azzāmning musiqa wa naghmātga nazarlari," al-Islāh, 15 February 1916, 104–110.

CHAPTER 5

Knowledge as Salvation

The merchant Ghāzi-bāy was an ignorant person who neglected to educate his son Abdulqahhār. Instead of sending him to school, he married him off at the age of sixteen to Maryam. Out of ignorance, Abdulqahhār fell into bad habits and soon managed to waste away his fortune on drinking and gambling. When all was lost, he pawned his house and disappeared, leaving Maryam to care for herself and their two children. But Maryam was intelligent and knew the value of knowledge, and despite all the hardship—she had to go from door to door, doing menial labor for neighbors—gave her son Alimjān the beginnings of education. Alimjān was a kind, studious child who went to the mosque regularly instead of playing in the street. Then one day Ahmadjān, a friend, took Alimjān to the new-method school he attended. The teacher was very kind to Alimjān and admitted him to the school, waiving tuition and providing him with the necessary school supplies. Given his mother's good training, Alimjān flourished, finishing two grades in one year. At the examination, he outshone his peers and, by answering all the questions posed by visiting dignitaries, brought credit to himself, the school, and the new method. In time, he graduated and was given a job as secretary by a merchant who had attended the final examination. Alimjān's knowledge and diligence won him the trust of the merchant, who gave him his daughter in marriage. In the meantime, Alimjān got word that his father was alive, eking out an existence in a hovel in Tashkent. Alimjān went to Tashkent to rescue his father (spending the sixteen hours on the train journey from Kokand reading) and thus reunited the family. Alimjān's father-in-law conveniently died soon afterward, leaving his fortune to Alimjān, who, along with his family, lived happily ever after, thanks entirely to knowledge.[1]

Such was the new happiness of which Hamza Hakimzada wrote in his "national novel" in 1915. This view of knowledge as the panacea for all ills, individual and social, as a font of happiness, wealth, and progress, was the point of departure for all Jadid thinking. But it was also clear to the Jadids that existing maktabs and madrasas were not producing such knowledge. Reform had to begin with the schools, the most crucial aspect of which was the adoption of the phonetic (or new) method (*usul-i jadid*) of teaching the alphabet. The creation of schools that would teach by the new method became the centerpiece of Jadid reform and, indeed, provided the movement its name.

The reform of the maktab (and the attempted reform of the madrasa) aroused extreme passions in Muslim society. Opposition to the Jadids is usually dismissed as the fanatical reaction of obscurantists opposed to all change, but taking the opposition—and the ensuing debate over the meaning of culture—seriously allows us to appreciate the extent and mechanism of change advocated by the Jadids. The knowledge that the Jadids celebrated came off the printed page and was predicated on the acquisition of functional literacy. This view of knowledge threatened to undermine existing practices surrounding the transmission of knowledge and the patterns of cultural and moral authority they engendered. Knowledge, and its place in society, was being redefined in the debate over the new method.

The Jadids' cult of knowledge also placed them firmly in the mainstream of the enlightenment project. The faith in the power of knowledge to transform societies was shared by the rulers of Russia and those sent to administer Turkestan, as well as Russian society in general, which also sought answers to its problems in knowledge and education. "Only knowledge can conquer this region spiritually," Kaufman once told Ostroumov. "Neither weapons, nor legislation can do this, but the school,

---

1. Hamza Hakimzāda Niyāzi, *Yāngi saādat (milli romān)* (Kokand, 1915). This basic plot is to be found in numerous Jadid works of verse and prose; see also Sadriddin Ayni's epistolary novel, *Khānadān-i khushbakht*, in his *Tahzib us-sibyān* (Samarqand, 1911); Abdulhamid Sulaymāni [Cholpān], "Dokhtor Muhammadyār," serialized in *ST*, 1914. The ultimate source of this vision was a novel by Gasprinskii, *The Muslims of the Abode of Happiness* (*Darürrahat Müsülmanlari* [Bahchesaray, 1906]), which was translated into Persian by Fitrat in 1916 (*Musulmānān-i Dār ul-rāhat* [Bukhara, 1916]).

and only the school, can."[2] This faith in the power of knowledge and education remained with Kaufman's successors, even when they abandoned policies he had initiated. The same faith in the power of knowledge, however, also produced a fear of the wrong kind of knowledge, which could exacerbate the "fanaticism" of the natives. Kaufman's worries about the malign influence of sedentary Muslims over the nomads and his successors' concerns about the influx of "pan-Islamic" ideas from the Ottoman empire shared this fear. As a promoter of an enlightenment suitable for Russian state interests and a jealous watchdog over rival forms of it, the state saw itself as a significant actor in the realm of education. Indeed, the earliest efforts to transform Central Asian society through education came from the state, and it is here that we begin our examination.

EDUCATING THE NATIVES

The dismal record of Russian educational institutions in attracting students from the local population led to a reappraisal of Kaufman's policy upon his death. In 1884, the new governor-general, N. O. Rozenbakh, seeking a different ploy to get Muslims to send their children to Russian schools, came up with the idea of "Russo-native schools" (*russko-tuzemnye shkoly*), in which Russian and traditional Muslim education would coexist. In the morning, a Russian teacher would teach Russian and arithmetic, while a *dāmlā* would give lessons identical to those in the maktab in the afternoon.[3] The course of study was four years, by the end of which students were expected to be able to write and speak Russian. Reading lessons in the fourth year introduced students to Russian geography and history.[4] Local notables were pressed into service in

2. N. P. Ostroumov, *Konstantin Petrovich fon-Kaufman, ustroitel' Turkestanskogo kraia: Lichnye vospominaniia N. Ostroumova* (Tashkent, 1899), 54–55.

3. The parallels with the Russo-Tatar schools that had begun to appear in the Volga region in the 1870s can be misleading. Muslim religious instruction in the Tatar schools was admissible, but possible only if paid for by the community (although this requirement was often bypassed). In the first year of the school, instruction was in Tatar, but gradually Russian became the sole language of teaching; see A. Kh. Makhmutova, *Stanovlenie svetskogo obrazovaniia u Tatar* (Kazan, 1982), ch. 2. The Tatar precedent seems not to have figured in the debates in Tashkent over the introduction of Russo-native schools; see K. E. Bendrikov, *Ocherki po istorii narodnogo obrazovaniia v Turkestane (1865–1925 gody)* (Moscow, 1960), 181–185.

4. Bendrikov, *Ocherki*, 308–309. A formal curriculum was drawn up only in 1907; a copy is in TsGARUz, f. 47, op. 1, d. 903, ll. 4–5.

this novel intervention in local cultural life, and the first Russo-native school opened in Tashkent in the house of Said Karim-bāy, Said Azim's son, in December 1884.[5] Notables were asked to provide funding and students. Most of the students of the first school in Tashkent were children of local notables, who also served as patrons of these schools, charged with promoting the school in society. Annual examinations were public occasions to which local dignitaries were invited to see for themselves the benefits of the new school. High-ranking officials acted as chief examiners, and graduates received prizes for completing the course of studies. (Abdullah Qādiri received a gold watch from the governor-general himself upon his graduation in 1912.) Yet the treasury remained reluctant to release any funds for these schools, leaving many of the first schools dependent on local revenues. The first school in Tashkent received 700 rubles from the treasury and 1,300 rubles from the city, while the rooms were donated by Said Karim-bāy.

The schools had a shaky beginning, as parents refused to send their children to them. In the first few years of their existence, it was even common for notables to pay children of the poor to attend, the police bearing the responsibility for finding the children.[6] In many locations, schools were supported by special levies (maktab puli), which served to heighten their unpopularity.[7] The situation changed by the turn of the century. With the growth in the economy, many more people encountered Russian and came to see it as an important skill. Table 5 shows the significant increase in the number of such schools in the first decade of the twentieth century. The growth was greatest in Syr Darya oblast, where the number of such schools almost doubled in the last six years of the old regime.

The primary goal of the schools was to impart functional skills in spoken and written Russian, and over the years the Russian sections of these schools became their real focus. Although many observers remained skeptical, a graduate of the four-year course was supposed to have acquired a facility in reading and speaking Russian and to be able to write basic bureaucratic or business documents.[8] The "native" part, on the other hand, was meant to gain the trust of the local population by assuring it that the school would transmit the knowledge that parents

5. TWG, 31 December 1884.
6. V. Nalivkin, Tuzemtsy ran'she i teper' (Tashkent, 1913), 104.
7. A.E. Izmailov, Prosveshchenie v respublikakh sovetskogo Vostoka (Moscow, 1973), 44. In Semirech'e, this tax was the only source of revenue for Russo-native schools: D. Aitmambetov, Dorevoliutsionnye shkoly v Kirgizii (Frunze, 1961), 50–51.
8. A copy of the academic program as revamped in 1907 is in TsGARUz, f. 47, op. 1, d. 903, l. 2–40b; see also TWG, 5 November 1915; 8 November 1915.

TABLE 5   RUSSO-NATIVE SCHOOLS IN TURKESTAN

		Students			
Year	Schools	"Native"	Russian	Total	Number Graduated
1886	4	116	—	116	—
1891	22	375	51	426	25
1896	28	650	51	701	15
1901	45	1490	89	1579	79
1906	87	2364		2364	—
1909	98	2975	102	3077	—

SOURCE: V. T. Kocharov, *Iz istorii organizatsii i razvitiia narodnogo obrazovaniia v do-revoliutsionnom Uzbekistane (1865–1917 gg.)* (Tashkent, 1966), 68–69.

expected from a maktab, a point Russian officials took care to emphasize repeatedly. "Remember," Governor-General Teviashev told the audience while inaugurating a new school in 1905, "that the education administration by no means hinders your religious customs and allows your children to study religion in this school in exactly the same manner that you studied it in your schools."[9] Native teachers were, therefore, left free to teach as they pleased. Sporadic attempts to establish a standardized curriculum produced no tangible results. By the turn of the century, many native teachers had begun to use the phonetic method to teach the alphabet and to use textbooks. In 1902, at Ostroumov's initiative, the local educational administration commissioned Said Aziz Khoja, a "native" teacher in one of the Tashkent schools, to write a textbook especially for the first year to replace the Tatar manuals that had hitherto been used.[10] The resulting text, *Ustād-i awwal* (The First Teacher), was the first new-method textbook to be published in Central Asia. A reader for the second year followed two years later.[11] The native section imparted basic literacy in Turkic (or Persian in a few schools in Samarqand) and the ability to recite the Qur'an and to answer questions

9. Quoted by Ostroumov, "Musul'manskie maktaby i russko-tuzemnye shkoly v Turkestanskom krae," *ZhMNP*, n.s., 1 (1906): otd. narod. obraz., 148.

10. Iuldash Abdullaev, *Ocherki po metodike obucheniia gramote v uzbekskoi shkole* (Tashkent, 1966), 107–118. Said Rasul Khoja (1866–1938), a native of Tashkent, learned Russian on his own initiative while a madrasa student and therefore found employment in the first Russo-native school to open in Tashkent. B. Qosimov, "Reformator pedagog, ma"rifatparwar," *Sovet maktabi*, 1967, no. 5, 76–79.

11. On the creation of these textbooks, see Abdullaev, *O metodike*, 107–126.

about religious obligations and rituals.[12] While many schools had two or three Russian teachers, all made do with only one "native" teacher, so that often by the fourth year "native" instruction amounted to no more than a half-hour a day.[13]

Over time, local administrators came to attach high hopes to these schools. Writing in 1909, Governor-General P. I. Mishchenko saw them as "the best means for promoting Russian citizenship [grazhdanstvennost'] and language" among the natives. His suggestion of increasing their budgetary allocations in view of the political benefits they were likely to accrue fell victim to the paucity of resources, however, and was never realized.[14] To the end of the old regime, numbers of Russo-native schools remained small, and only one offered more than the basic four years of instruction. Yet, they were the most likely channel for the local population to learn Russian.[15] At the same time, there remained considerable dissatisfaction about their efficacy. N. S. Lykoshin, a longtime administrator, felt that "the Sart merchant considers it sufficient if his son, after graduating from [a Russo-native] school, can write the address in Russian or a letter or a simple business telegram; but the development of the child does not go beyond this in a direction desirable to us."[16] Even so, the numbers of students graduating remained small; only forty-seven students finished the four-year course in 1910, and sixty-three in 1913, when Tashkent's schools were the most successful in the whole province.[17] The situation was far worse in Ferghana, where as many as seventeen of the twenty schools did not graduate a single student in 1907, and three schools in the oblast continued to exist without producing a single graduate among them after 1903.[18]

THE NEW METHOD

The growth in the numbers of Russo-native schools after the turn of the century was part of a broader phenomenon that included the emergence

12. This is what children were examined for at the public annual exams; see, e.g., TWG, 19 May 1911, 10 April 1914.

13. TWG, 8 September 1910; 19 May 1911.

14. TsGARUz, f. 2, op. 2, d. 369, ll. 10–11.

15. Several Russo-native schools also offered evening courses in Russian for adults; cf. Aitmambetov, Dorevoliutsionnye shkoly, 75.

16. N. S. Lykoshin, Pol zhizni v Turkestane (Petrograd, 1916), 58.

17. TWG, 20 May 1910, 23 May 1913.

18. A. Mukhammadzhanov, Shkola i pedagogicheskaia mysl' uzbekskogo naroda XIX–nachala XX v. (Tashkent, 1978), 74; A. F. Ardashirov, "Russko-tuzemnye shkoly v dorevoliutsionnom Andizhane," Uchenye zapiski Andizhanskogo gospedinstituta, no. 6 (1957): 123–124.

of new-method schools beyond the purview of officialdom. Indeed, Mishchenko's enthusiasm for Russo-native schools was provoked at least in part by his concerns about the growth of new-method schools in Turkestan. Pioneered in the Crimea by Gasprinskii, who opened the first such school in 1884, new-method schools were the staple of Muslim reform in the European parts of the Russian empire. By the turn of the century, these schools dominated elementary education among the Tatars, and new-method madrasas were being founded in Ufa and Kazan. In Turkestan, the first new-method schools appeared in the early 1890s, usually among the Tatar communities in Turkestani cities, but they had spread among the local population as well by the turn of the century. By the time Mishchenko wrote, these schools had become the object of concern for officialdom as well as the focus of the biggest debate in Muslim society.

Scholars have been too content to see the new-method school as the creation of Gasprinskii's genius alone. In fact, the new-method school was part of a secular trend toward functional literacy and the organization of general schooling in which new domains of cultural practice were elaborated. Such practices had first appeared in Western Europe, and they came to Central Asia from two sources. The first was Russia, where concern with elementary schooling had emerged by the middle of the nineteenth century. This experience was reflected in the Russo-native schools, with which new-method schools shared many characteristics. Many "native" teachers (Hāji Muin in Katta Qorghān, Sayyid Ahmad Ajzi in Samarqand, Āshur Ali Zāhiri in Kokand, Said Rasul Rasuli in Tashkent) were prominent in Jadid circles, and many of the younger Jadids attended Russo-native schools. The second, more relevant, source was the Ottoman empire, where, for reasons very similar to those in Russia, low rates of literacy among the empire's Muslim population had come to be a pressing concern in Ottoman circles by the early 1860s. In the ensuing debate, non-Ottoman Muslims, such as the Iranian statesman Mirzā Malkum Khān and the Azerbaijani Mirza Fathali Akhundov (Akhundzadeh), both of whom were in Istanbul at this time, took an active role. The diagnosis varied. For Malkum Khān and Akhundov, the cause was the difficulty of the Arabic script, and the remedy a reform of the script. Others, such as the poet Namık Kemal, felt that poor methods of teaching the alphabet were to blame for low rates of literacy and that more efficient methods of instruction would solve the problem.[19]

19. Hamid Algar, *Mīrzā Malkum Khān: A Study in the History of Iranian Modernism* (Berkeley, 1973), 82–95.

Gradually the phonetic, or new, method (*usûl-i cedid*) for teaching the alphabet won official favor when the authorities passed a law making elementary education compulsory.[20] This debate was known among Muslim elites in the Russian empire and had even made it to the pages of *TWG,* which in 1876 published an article (unfortunately anonymous) propounding the need for a more efficient method of teaching the alphabet.[21] Said Rasul Khoja, a teacher in Tashkent's first Russo-native school and author of *Ustād-i awwal* (The First Teacher), the first new-method primer in Central Asia, wrote in its preface: "After this [kind of] *First Teacher* became popular in Istanbul, and the advantages of imparting instruction with it in the maktab became known . . . , the scholars of Kazan translated it into their own language [and started using it in their maktabs]. . . . The advantages of this way of teaching were also realized at some Russian schools in Tashkent."[22] Gasprinskii himself was understandably reluctant to draw attention to the Ottoman antecedents of the school he pioneered, since that would have laid him open to official suspicion, but the circumstantial evidence is overwhelming. But while there can be no doubt about the Ottoman pedigree of the new-method school, it was more than simply a transplant. In the Ottoman empire, the new method was introduced in a network of state-sponsored and state-funded schools (although financial constraints kept funding levels low);[23] in the Russian empire, on the other hand, such schools existed in the often tenuous space provided by the state to the "confessional" schools of its religious minorities. The organization and support of such schools remained the concern of society, rather than the state, with all the attendant problems.

DISOWNING THE MAKTAB

The new-method school acquired such a central position in Jadid reform across the Russian empire because political realities allowed it. As "confessional" schools, maktabs had existed in the semi-public niche allowed by the state to religious communities. A reform of these schools could be carried out through purely civic initiative in considerable freedom from government control. But the reform also arose from a profound dissatis-

---

20. Bayram Kodaman, *Abdülhamid Devri Eğitim Sistemi* (Ankara, 1991), 63.
21. Anon., "Ta'lim-i ulum khususida," *TWG,* 5 February 1876.
22. Said Rasul Khoja Said Aziz Khoja oghli, *Ustād-i awwal* (Tashkent, 1902), 1.
23. Osman Ergin, *Türkiye Maarif Tarihi,* 5 vols. (Istanbul, 1977), IV: 460–475.

faction with the state of the maktab. Judged by the needs of the age, the maktab was found wanting. Hāji Muin's 1916 play *Old School, New School* opens in a maktab, "dark as a dungeon with a stove in the middle; a bastinado hangs on the wall; on one side lies a filthy container of water, on the other side, on a torn carpet, sits the teacher, wearing several layers of dirty clothes, short-tempered and with the looks of an opium addict." [24] The teacher is more concerned with food (he sends a pupil off to get tea) and gifts (he insistently asks for his weekly gift of food from the parents of another pupil) than with the welfare of the children in his charge, who learn absolutely nothing. Chaos reigns in the school, as fights break out between children frequently and provoke intemperate physical punishment from the teacher.

New conditions demanded schools where children could acquire literacy, a basic knowledge of "arithmetic, geography, history, especially the history of Islam," as well as "religious obligations [*wājibāt-i diniya*], i.e., proper recitation of the Qur'an, questions of faith . . . prayers, fasting, hajj, and almsgiving." [25] This valorization of functional literacy as a transposable skill was connected with the new ubiquity of the written word made possible by print. As I argued in Chapter 1, the juncture of orality and literacy at which the maktab existed rendered functional literacy less than a necessity. Now that literacy came to be a highly valued skill, the absence of literacy instruction became the maktab's biggest liability. Similarly, the complaint, repeatedly made, that poor children wasted several years of their lives in the maktab without *even* acquiring the rudiments of literacy bespoke a newfound sense of efficiency. The maktab was fully imbricated in the rhythm of everyday life, in which the teacher's qualifications in the maktab lay in his knowledge and piety acquired through interaction with a recognized master. "Teaching" as such was not a separate domain of practice, nor was "learning" to be measured by such means as examinations and grades. Now this became lack of method and organization, and hence a major shortcoming of the maktab.

The new method involved teaching the alphabet using the phonetic method instead of the syllabic method used in the maktab. Instead of memorizing the names of the letters, the emphasis here was on teaching children the sounds that the letters represented; the aim was to impart

24. Hāji Muin b. Shukrullah, *Eski maktab, yangi maktab* (Samarqand, 1916), 3.
25. Munawwar Qāri, "Bizni jahālat, jahl-i murakkab," *Taraqqi—Orta Azyaning umr guzārlighi,* 14 June 1906.

the ability to read and write rather than an "implicit" knowledge of certain canonical texts. The texts used in new-method schools were specially devised primers that introduced pupils to the alphabet, with the most commonly used letters coming first and letters representing the specifically Semitic phonemes of Arabic being left to the last. Beyond literacy, new-method schools also sought to teach such "contemporary" (*zamāncha*) subjects as arithmetic, geography, science, and history.

The new method made both the Russo-native and Jadid schools qualitatively different from the maktab. This fact was underscored by the insistence of new-method teachers on calling themselves *muallim*, after Tatar and Ottoman fashion, rather than *dāmlā* or *maktabdār,* the terms traditionally used in Central Asia for teachers in maktabs. The physical appearance of new-method schools was also different. The new school in Hāji Muin's play "accords with the rules of public health. Maps hang on the walls. On one side, the teacher sits on a chair behind a table and next to a blackboard. Across from him, behind two desks, sit four students. . . . As the curtain rises, the children rise to their feet and greet the teacher." [26] Desks, chairs, maps, and globes became fetishes of the new-method schools. The very act of sitting on chairs in orderly rows, with the teacher standing facing the class, rather than sitting on the floor in a circle around the *dāmlā,* meant, for the Jadids, a leap from the disorder and backwardness of the maktab to the scientific order of the school. A pedagogical manual written by Gasprinskii (and apparently well known in Central Asia) came complete with a diagram of the ideal classroom, with windows, maps, globes, blackboard, and desks neatly laid out in rows.

THE SCHOOLS

If so far this description of new-method schools seems like a Foucauldian delight, we need to remember the many ways in which such ideals did not become reality. It is impossible to determine the exact number of new-method schools in Turkestan, for although the new-method school was a more tangible entity than the maktab, with records of admissions and enrollments, the discrepancies between archival figures and unofficial information are substantial. Many schools quickly folded for lack of interest on the part of parents, active opposition from them, hostility of the state, or financial problems. Others existed unofficially, beyond

26. Hāji Muin, *Eski maktab,* 40.

the domain of the bureaucracy, especially after 1912, when new legislation sought to control them.

The first new-method schools in Turkestan were opened by Tatars for their own use. The first school for Turkestanis for which we have concrete evidence was opened in Andijān by Sultān Murād-bāy, owner of a cotton-cleaning factory, who hired a Tatar teacher to teach the children of factory workers,[27] but it was not until the turn of the century that these schools became widespread. Munawwar Qāri opened the first new-method school in Tashkent in 1901,[28] and by late 1903 the city was reported to have more than twenty such schools.[29] Abdulqadir Shakuri started the first school in the Samarqand area in 1903,[30] while the first schools in Kokand also opened in the first years of the century.[31] The actual numbers of these schools are difficult to determine, though. Mandatory registration began only in 1912, and even then many schools escaped the state's notice. The wide range of figures to be found in bureaucratic correspondence of the day indicates that officialdom had little idea of the precise number of schools in existence. According to official figures, there were thirteen schools with 1,100 students in the old city of Tashkent and thirteen in Kokand.[32] Yet, the inspector of schools in Ferghana oblast reported twenty-three new-method schools in his jurisdiction in February 1910, but only "about twenty" three years later.[33] However, according to a correspondent to *Āyina,* Kokand then had thirty-one schools with 3,000 students, making it the leading city in Turkestan.[34] In 1914, the Samarqand area had at least a half-dozen substantial schools.[35] These figures, in all likelihood, understate the number of schools in existence for the contemporary press gives the impression that new schools were being opened frequently. We might also consider the evidence of the textbooks. The last decade of tsarist rule saw the

27. A. F. Ardashirov, "K voprosu o roli novometodnykh maktabov," *Uchenye zapiski Andizhanskogo gospedinstituta,* no. 6 (1957): 131.

28. Sirojiddin Ahmad, "Munawwar Qori," *Sharq Yulduzi,* 1992, no. 5, 107.

29. *Turkestanskie vedomosti,* 2 November 1903, 552.

30. Muallim Mullā Abdulqādir Samarqandi, "Ajā'ib bir zamān emish," *Tojjār,* 2 October 1907.

31. A report from the Ferghana oblast educational establishment to the governor-general from 1913 provides details on four of the most important schools in Kokand, the first of which opened "ten to twelve years ago" (TsGARUz, f. 1, op. 31, d. 943, ll. 570b–58).

32. Sh. Ismoilov, "XIX asrning okhiri, XX asr boshlarida Turkistondagi yangi usul maktablari," *Obshchestvennye nauki v Uzbekistane,* 1976, no. 2, 56–58.

33. TsGARUz, f. 19, d. 35019, ll. 18–180b (for 1910); f. 1, op. 31, d. 943, l. 65 (for 1913, reported by the governor of Ferghana to the governor-general).

34. Mullā Ishāq Jān, "Jawāb," *Āyina,* 4 January 1914, 257.

35. *Āyina,* 6 September 1914, 1105–1106.

publication of scores of textbooks locally, many of which went into several editions. Since publishing was largely a commercial enterprise, we can safely assume that enough demand existed for publishers to put these textbooks on the market. The usual print run for local publications was 1,000 copies. Therefore, it seems reasonable to assume that new-method schools numbered in the hundreds in Central Asia during the last decade of the old regime. At the very least, it is quite clear that by the beginning of the second decade of the twentieth century new-method schools had become a constant feature of urban life in Turkestan.

New-method schools varied a great deal in size, organization, and stability. Some, such as Munawwar Qāri's in Tashkent and Abdulqādir Shakuri's in Samarqand, had over a hundred students, but many—perhaps the majority—had far smaller enrollments and existed in spare rooms in teachers' or patrons' houses. The novelty of some schools did not extend beyond the use of the phonetic method to teach the alphabet, whereas others offered four years of general elementary education.[36] The scarcity of financial and material resources remained the most formidable obstacle. They may have come from reasonably prosperous backgrounds, but few Jadids possessed the resources required for establishing schools. Several Jadids opened schools in their own houses, but others depended on the cooperation of those who had the means and the public authority to support their efforts. Many schools were founded by merchants and other notables, either in their own houses or in rooms especially constructed for the school. In Tashkent, the Imdādiya benevolent society provided a subsidy of fifty rubles per month to some schools.[37]

The practice of charging tuition brought its own ambiguities, for such frank exchange of knowledge for money went against the *adab* of knowledge (in the maktab, we will recall, the teacher received gifts of food or clothing from the parents, but almost never money) and was distasteful to many parents, but it also laid teachers open to the charge of being interested only in the money. This caused deep anxieties among the Jadids, who claimed to be "servants of the nation" first and foremost. The ambiguity was never resolved, since teaching was the main source of livelihood for many new-method teachers. Jadid publications carried many

36. See, e.g., reports of annual examinations at a school "with old-method order but new-method form" (*usul-i qadima tartiblarinda wa usul-i jadida suratinda*) in *TWG*, 15 July 1910; 26 June 1911. Such schools were quite widespread, but it is impossible to establish their numbers.

37. Gr. Andreev "Novometodnye maktaby," *Turkestanskie vedomosti*, 21 October 1915.

cautionary tales about the corrupt teachers for whom even new-method teaching was a source of private enrichment rather than a way of serving the nation.

Hopes of creating an organized system of schools remained unfulfilled. A shortage of teachers similarly bedeviled new-method schools. Until 1912, Tatars taught in many schools, but this practice became hazardous after new regulations went into effect that year. One solution was to send students to Tatar schools in European Russia for a higher education and to start summer teacher training courses locally,[38] but available resources again fell woefully short. Many new-method schools in Turkestan remained one-man shows in which the only teacher was an autodidact whose commitment to reform often outweighed his ability to teach. Ironically, although the Jadids insisted that maktab teachers were ignorant of the science of education, few if any in their own ranks had a higher education, let alone pedagogic training. Jadid textbooks, too, were the work of amateurs, very committed and dedicated, but amateurs nevertheless. For the same reasons, several attempts to impose a uniform curriculum came to naught because there existed no institution that could enforce uniform standards. An attempt in Kokand to teach according to a common program failed because few teachers could teach all the subjects included in the syllabus.[39] The Jadids of Central Asia could not bring any uniformity or system to their schools down to 1917.

THE ADVENT OF SCHOOLING

The program in Table 6 accompanied twelve identical applications for permission to open new-method schools in Tashkent submitted in June 1910. Unfortunately, it does not provide any information about the allocation of time in the classroom (and even if did, it could not be taken as a true indication of what went on in the classroom, since dodging the Russian school inspector was not very difficult). In the more established new-method schools, instruction took place four or five hours a day, six days a week.[40] The first year was largely devoted to learning the alphabet. By 1917, teachers in Central Asia had a choice of at least a dozen locally

38. N. Y., "Muallimlar tayyārlamaq usuli," *Āyina*, 19 April 1914.
39. Ozbek, "Maktab masalasi," *Āyina*, 28 December 1913, 234–235.
40. See, for instance, the teaching plans of several Andijān schools in Ardashirov, "K voprosu," 157–159.

TABLE 6   ACADEMIC PROGRAM FOR NEW-METHOD SCHOOLS, 1910

	Subject	Texts
Year I	reading and writing	Munawwar Qāri, *Adib-i awwal*
	prayer	
Year II	reading and writing	Munawwar Qāri, *Adib-i sāni*
	prayer	
	religious instruction	Munawwar Qāri, *Hawā'ij-i diniya*
Year III	reading	Mominjān Muhammadjānov, *Nasā'ih ul-atfāl*
	[moral instruction]	Sufi Allah Yār, *Sabāt ul ājizin*
	recitation of the Qur'an	Munawwar Qāri, *Tajwid*
	religious instruction	Munawwar Qāri, *Hawā'ij-i diniya*
	sacred history	Hanafi, *Tarikh-i anbiyā*
	geography	Fatih Kerimi, *Mukhtasar jughrāfiya*
		Hadi Maksudi, *Dunya ma'lumāti*
	arithmetic	Ināyatullah Mirzājān oghli, *Hisāb mas'alasi*
Year IV	reading	*Adabiyāt* (poetry)
	recitation of the Qur'an	Munawwar Qāri, *Tajwid*
	ethics	Fakhriddinov, *Nasihat*
	sacred history	Hanafi, *Tarikh-i anbiyā*
	arithmetic	Ināyatullah Mirzājān oghli, *Hisāb mas'alasi*
	Arabic	Maksudi, *Durus*
	Persian	Abdulqādir Shakuri, *Jāmi' ul-hikāyāt*

SOURCE: TsGARUz, f. 47, d. 1148, ll. 3–25.

produced primers to use in the classroom. Said Rasul Khoja's *Ustād-i awwal* (The First Teacher) was used in Jadid schools, but it was eventually displaced by Munawwar Qāri's *Adib-i awwal* (The First Writer, 1910).[41] The next few years saw the appearance of several other primers, including several in Persian. These books had much in common: They introduced the Arabic alphabet in stages, giving each letter its phonetic value, and providing exercises in joining the various letters. These led to exercises in forming words and, toward the end of the year, whole sentences. Certain primers contained passages for reading.

In the second year, students read longer passages in readers specially designed for children. The passages were largely in prose, but textbooks were also liberally sprinkled with verse. These texts differed from those used in the maktab in that they were specially written for children in their native language using a simple vocabulary. Although the readings remained didactic in intent, they now included fairy tales or stories about animals. Munawwar Qāri's *Adib-i sāni,* for instance, contains forty-five passages of literary, scientific (*fanni*), and moral content. The "scientific" passages provide basic information such as the months of the year in the lunar calendar, as well as the Arabic, Russian, and Ottoman solar calendars,[42] or word lists of animals, items of clothing, geographical terms, and so forth. The ethics lessons deal with common Jadid themes such as the superiority of knowledge over wealth, the status of teachers, the sad fate of a habitual liar, and notions of generosity, miserliness, and wastefulness. Thus, the story of a rich man who refuses to give a circumcision feast for his son because it would become wastefulness (*isrāf*) if he invited only his rich friends, and donates the money instead to schools and madrasas was recounted with approval.[43] In another story, a rich man who would not send his son to school because tuition cost one ruble per month deprives his son of the ability to tell right from wrong. As a result, the son becomes a wastrel and spends his entire fortune. The moral: "Such is the fate of the wastrel and of the wealth of the miser."[44] The genealogy of these textbooks remains to be examined. The most immediate model was provided by Tatar textbooks, but these were themselves

41. For a critical survey, see Hāji Muin, "Alifbālarimiz," *Hurriyat,* 19 January 1918; 22 February 1918. An extensive bibliography of pre-1917 textbooks and primers is in Adeeb Khalid, "The Politics of Muslim Cultural Reform: Jadidism in Tsarist Central Asia" (Ph.D. diss., University of Wisconsin-Madison, 1993), 448–454.

42. Munawwar Qāri ibn Abdurrashid Khān, *Adib-i sāni,* 3rd ed. (Tashkent, 1912), 13–14.

43. Ibid., 44.

44. Ibid., 40–42.

deeply influenced by Russian pedagogical tools. Said Rasul Khoja also
indicates an Ottoman connection, with its roots in French models. In
style and format, the new primers of Central Asia replicated developments in European pedagogy.

In subsequent years, primers were supplemented by collections of poetry written by various Jadid authors specifically for use in schools.
Unlike the mystical poetry of the maktab, these poems propagated the
basic message of Jadid reform, such as the fallen state of Turkestan, the
need for knowledge, the excellence of schools, and a passion for the nation. Often these poems were written to the tune of newly respectable
folk tunes and meant for recitation or singing. By 1913, weekly poetry
lessons were common in many schools.[45] This was a major change from
the maktab, where singing and profane poetry (let alone the singing of
profane poetry) had no place. Munawwar Qāri also introduced physical
exercise at his school, but the experiment did not last long. Physical exercise of this kind contravened the conventions of *adab,* and many parents, even those convinced of the superiority of the new method, could
not countenance it. Many parents also feared that physical training
would inevitably lead to conscription of their children into the army and
therefore began to withdraw them from the school.[46]

Elementary Arabic was taught in some schools, but the teaching of
Russian was still the exception rather than the rule in new-method
schools, the result of a combination of parental suspicion and a lack of
capable teachers. Munawwar Qāri started teaching Russian in his school
in 1911,[47] and four years later it was being taught twelve hours a week
by a Russian teacher.[48] The curriculum of new-method schools often included lessons in hygiene and elementary science, for which Tatar textbooks were used. Arithmetic was commonly taught, and some schools
even taught geometry in higher grades. Locally published textbooks for
elementary arithmetic became available in 1913, but Tatar manuals,
themselves translations of Russian textbooks, continued to be used for
higher classes.

Jadid criticism of the maktab went beyond its inefficiency and disorder and questioned the very suitability of its texts for young children.

45. Cf. Bobrovnikov, "Russko-tuzemnye uchilishcha, mekteby i medresy v Srednei
Azii, *ZhMNP,* n.s., 46 (1913): 66–70; Andreev, "Novometodnye maktaby v Turkestane,"
Turkestanskie vedomosti, 11 December 1915.
46. Andreev, "Novometodnye maktaby v Turkestane," *Turkestanskie vedomosti,* 21
October 1915.
47. Application dated 11 February 1911, in TsGARUz, f. 47, d. 1149, l. 4.
48. Andreev, "Novometodnye maktaby," *Turkestanskie vedomosti,* 21 October 1915.

Abdullah Awlāni echoed Munawwar Qāri when he wrote: "Everyone knows that the books used in the Muslim schools of Turkestan, such as *Chār kitāb, Sabāt ul-Ājizin,* Fuzuli, Nawā'i, Khoja Hāfiz, Bedil, and *Maslak ul-Muttaqin,* are, one and all, books of poetry. Some of them are concerned with difficult problems of dogma and practice [*e'tiqādāt wa amaliyāt*], . . . [and] as most of them are in Persian, it is impossible for young children to benefit from them, or even to understand them. Teaching these books is like reaching for the stars while sitting on the ground. . . . Even if [the children] understand the meaning of these apparently romantic poems, what good do they do?"[49] Others went further and claimed that romantic poetry memorized in the maktab actually spoiled the morals of little children and was the cause of widespread pederasty in Central Asia.[50]

Children needed books specially designed for them that paid attention to their levels of comprehension and provided material they would find interesting. "It would be more beneficial to pupils just embarking on the study of literature," Munawwar Qāri once suggested to Hamza, "if you included short, interesting tales, such as those about the actions of people and animals, in short tales accessible to the faculties of children, rather than [dealing with] difficult topics such as . . . honor, courage, nation, and nationalism, or other such dry admonitions. . . . Experience shows that pupils are troubled not by the size of our present books of literature but by the difficulty of their vocabulary and subject matter."[51]

A Russian orientalist visiting Munawwar Qāri's school in 1915 noted that punishments meted out to children were very mild and that teachers used the polite form of speech in addressing the children.[52] The Jadids' horror of physical punishment, repeated on numerous occasions by other writers, stemmed from the same sources as their new-found disgust with mystical poetry. This was the Jadids' discovery of childhood.[53] The maktab treated young boys essentially as men on a small scale. For

49. Abdullah Awlāni, *Adabiyāt, yākhud milli she'rlardan* (Tashkent, 1909), quoted in A. Bobokhonov and N. Mahsumov, *Abdulla Awloniyning pedagogik faoliyati wa ta"limtarbiya tŏghrisidagi fikrlari* (Tashkent, 1966), 45.

50. Hāji Muin ibn Shukrullah, "Jawānbāzlikning sabablari," *Āyina,* 31 May 1914, 637; Alimcan el-İdrisi, "Buhara'da Tahsil," *Sirat-ı Müstakim,* 8 October 1909, 111–112, made the same argument about madrasas in Bukhara.

51. Munawwar Qāri to Hamza Hakimzāda, 1 January 1916, in *Hamza Hakimzoda Niyoziy arkhivining katalogi,* 2 vols. (Tashkent, 1991), II: 286–287.

52. Andreev, "Novometodnye maktaby v Turkestane," *Turkestanskie vedomosti,* 28 October 1915.

53. Philippe Ariès, *Centuries of Childhood,* trans. Robert Baldick (New York, 1962).

the Jadids, childhood was a special period of life, marked off from the
rest of life, a period in which the obligations and gravity of adulthood
did not apply. However, such a period also provided the opportunity for
molding and training the intellect, morals, and even the body of the child,
all the subject of the new, "scientific" discipline of pedagogy.

DESACRALIZATION

Concerns with morality were ubiquitous in new-method schools. Moral
and ethical messages were never concealed below the surface in these
readings, nor did moral education stop with such reading passages.
Several textbooks published in Central Asia during this period were directly concerned with imparting purely ethical and moral advice. With
names such as *Adablik oghlān* (The Boy Who Has *Adab*) and *Nasā'ih
ul-atfāl* (Advice to Children),[54] these textbooks harked back directly to
the *adab* tradition of the maktab. Reading passages in these books described ideal modes of behavior and deportment. A well-mannered child
"listens carefully, with all his soul, without looking to either side, to the
teacher or the assistant [*khalifa*] when they teach."[55] The same text of-
fers, as an example to be followed, the story of a little boy who is woken
up by his father in the middle of the night, when the latter wakes up of
thirst. The father sends the child to fetch water but falls back to sleep before his return. The child stands quietly at his father's bedside with the
water until he wakes up again.[56]

Religious instruction took up a substantial part of school time. The
topics covered by the syllabus were quite traditional. The most commonly used textbook on Islam was the *Hawā'ij-i diniya* (Religious Requirements) by Munawwar Qāri. Its three parts treated belief, ritual, and
Islamic injunctions on social and commercial practices in the form of
questions and answers. Children also learned to read the Qur'an according to the principles of *tajwid* (for which new textbooks also appeared),
and they memorized passages from it, as well as learning to recite the five
daily prayers. The use of mystical poetry continued and prayer was mandatory in new-method schools. School events began with the recitation of
the Qur'an and the evocation of blessings on the Prophet.[57]

---

54. Muhammadjan Qāri ibn Rahimjān, *Adablik oghlān* (Tashkent, 1912); Mominjan
Muhammadjanov, *Nasā'ih ul-atfāl* (Tashkent, 1912).
55. Muhammadjān Qāri, *Adablik oghlān*, 7.
56. Ibid., 3–4.
57. For example, the final examination for the 1912–13 school year at Abdulqādir
Shakuri's school in Samarqand began with worship (*salāt*), invocation of blessings on the

The numerous continuities with the maktab can be deceptive, though. Concerns with morality might seem little different from the kind of moral training and obedience to older men that was imparted in the maktab, but morality was now taught through specially created texts, not under threat of physical punishment. Similarly, religious tenets were conveyed to pupils not through mimetic practice but from especially designed textbooks in the vernacular; pupils were also expected to *understand* the meaning of the religious acts they were learning. In setting lessons aside for religion, the new-method schools began the process of marking off Islam from the rest of knowledge. In the maktab, all knowledge was sacral and tenets of Islam pervaded everything taught. In new-method schools, Islam became an object of study, knowledge of which could be acquired in the same way as all other knowledge. The Jadids thus constituted the domain of "religion," as a result of which certain practices and spaces now became exclusively "religious." Other domains of practice, by the same token, were desacralized and firmly placed in the realm of the "nonreligious."

This approach is clearly seen in the construction of "sacred history" as a field of study in new-method schools. The "tales of the Prophets" (*qisas ul-anbiyā*) were a respected genre in Muslim tradition, and Rabghuzi's thirteenth-century text was widely circulated throughout the Turkic world. However, the immediate inspiration for including sacred history in the curriculum came from Russian schools, which had always included sacred history in their syllabus. The Jadids sought to create a Muslim equivalent of this modern phenomenon.

> All nations, whether Christians or Jews, teach the history of their religion and the lives of the prophets in their schools. Every Christian and Jewish student learns the guidance and formation of his religion and becomes acquainted with historical events. This is the cause of the growth of religious and national zeal and sentiment [*ghayrat-u hammiyat-i diniya wa milliya*].
> . . . The Europeans and [students] in the organized schools of Russia also study other religions [including] the history of Islam. A Christian student knows more about the history of Islam than a Muslim student.[58]

Muslims students must know more about the origins of their religion, and

---

Prophet (*mawlid*), recitation from the Qur'an (*qiraat*) as well as of national poetry (*milli she'r*), and recited supplication to God (*munājāt*). The religious ambiance of these schools could not be doubted, but the recitation of modern poetry was indicative of a growing concern with the community. *Samarqand,* 24 May 1913.

58. Mahmud Khoja Behbudi, *Mukhtasar tarikh-i Islām* (Samarqand, 1909), 2.

this knowledge should be structured in the same way as in corresponding disciplines developed by Europeans. Behbudi and Fitrat published textbooks on the history of Islam, and Awlāni wrote a history of the prophets, little different from the *qisas* genre in its content, but written in a vernacular style comprehensible to school-age children. In the process, Islam itself began to be historicized, with far-reaching consequences.

Similar assumptions underlay the Jadids' critique of the madrasa. The madrasas of Bukhara and their professors became the butt of criticism and ridicule in the press all over the Turkic world. Again, the most influential critique came from Abdurrauf Fitrat in the form of a debate between a Bukharan mudarris, in India on his way to hajj, and a European sympathetic to Islam and extremely learned in it. The European asks the Bukharan about the curriculum of Bukharan madrasas and is appalled at the list of commentaries and supercommentaries that he hears: "I didn't think I'd ever hear such nonsense [*khurāfāt*] even in my dreams. What a waste of time the people of Bukhara are engaged in! After spending twenty-seven years of their lives in a futile place, they start teaching the same empty and meaningless subjects. But when do they study the most important subjects such as tafsir, hadith, and fiqh?"[59] As we saw in Chapter 1, the madrasa was the site of the reproduction of a knowledge of Islam mediated through several layers of glosses and commentaries, in which the practice of commentary and interpretation *was* Islam. That set of practices had become a bundle of nonsense and sophistry now, since real knowledge lay in the scriptural sources of Islam. This new textual view of Islam subverted the interpretive practice that was the foundation of Bukharan madrasas and thus opened the way for a new understanding of Islam itself. The point was to acquire a "true" knowledge of the pristine textual sources of Islam, bypassing the glosses and commentaries, which now came to be seen as nothing more than centuries' worth of corruption and a source of moral and social decline.

There were other problems with the madrasa, too. For all his years spent studying Arabic grammar, Fitrat's mudarris cannot speak Arabic properly. (By using phonetic transcription of standard Bukharan [mis]-pronunciation of Arabic, Fitrat makes a point of highlighting the mudarris's poor Arabic.) The European, who has studied it through the new method, can speak Arabic fluently and corrects his interlocutor in several places. Elsewhere, madrasa teachers and students were criticized for

---

59. Fitrat Bukhārā'ī, *Munāzara-yi mudarris-i bukhārāyī bā yak nafar-i farangī dar Hindustān dar bāra-yi makātib-i jadīda* (Istanbul, 1911), 17.

their lack of interest in the affairs of the nation and their selfish opposition to those who had the interest of the nation at heart.[60] Fitrat's Indian traveler finds professors having affairs with their students.[61]

The Jadids' disdain for traditional ways of knowing Islam was rooted in this fundamental transformation of their worldview. In their desacralized universe, where all phenomena were liable to rationalist explanation, correct understanding of Islam required not insertion in a chain of authoritative masters but mastery of the textual sources of Islam in the original, now available in print. Hence the emphasis on fluency in Arabic and the acquisition of hadith, tafsir, and fiqh. In 1916, Fitrat published *The Guide to Salvation,* an ethico-didactic tract in which he sought the justification for all Jadid exhortations in the Qur'an itself. The text is peppered with quotations from the Qur'an in Arabic, which alone for Fitrat provide the true measure of the merit of social and individual endeavor.[62] These new emphases denigrated the cultural possessions of the traditionally learned and were thus profoundly subversive of their authority. They also opened up access to the practice of interpretation to those outside the ranks of the madrasa-educated elites. As the seventeen-year-old Maryam tells the sextogenarian ishān who has married her, "I am educated and know religion better than you."[63]

The Jadids may not have been "secularists," for they constantly sought justification for their arguments from Islam, but their understanding of Islam was situated squarely in a desacralized world defined by progress through history. The shariat and true Islam were entirely compatible with the needs of the age, as we saw, and could only be brought about through modern knowledge. The implementation of Islamic law was never an issue in the politics of the Muslim nation; that attitude toward the Islamization of law belongs to a later generation. At the same time, theological debate was conspicuously absent from Central Asian Jadidism. The Jadids doubtless followed the debates of other modernist Muslims, such as Rizaeddin Fakhreddin, the Islamists in the Ottoman empire, and Muhammad 'Abduh and his followers in Egypt, but we have no evidence of any local debates that went beyond the permissibility or other-

60. M. Sh., "Mullālarimizda daraja-yi fikriya," *ST,* 15 January 1915.

61. Fitrat, "Bayonoti sayyohi hindî," ed. Kholiq Mirzozoda, *Sadoi Sharq,* 1988, no. 6, 33.

62. Abdurrauf Fitrat, *Rahbar-i najāt* (Bukhara, 1915); cf. "Rohbari najot," ed. Muhabbat Jalilova, *Sadoi Sharq,* 1992, no. 7–8, 16–59; no. 9, 8–54.

63. Hamza, *Zaharli hayot* (1916), in his *Tŏla asarlar tŏplami,* ed. N. Karimov et al., 5 vols. (Tashkent, 1988–1989), III: 27.

wise of the new method or the theater. The Jadids' priorities tended to be the concerns of the community rather than of the faith.

STRUGGLES OVER SCHOOLING

The debate surrounding the new method is not easy to chronicle. Unlike the copious critique of the maktab produced by the Jadids, critics of the new method did not appear in print very often, and we are left to glean the nature of those criticisms from the Jadids' criticism of their critics in newspaper debates. Opponents of the new method also appear, in heavily caricatured form, in Jadid literature and drama.

The fundamental criticism of the new method was that it contravened customary practices surrounding the transmission of knowledge. If the possession of those practices made one a member of the Muslim community, then their contravention was construed by many as an act of secession from that community. As Fitrat's mudarris put it simply, "These schools turn our children into infidels [kāfir]." [64] Nor was this merely a literary topos: in December 1913, the imām at the Ulugh Bek mosque in Samarqand declared in a Friday sermon that the new method of education and learning Russian were against the shariat and that those who sent their children to a new-method school were infidels. [65] In 1914, a new-method school in the Maddāhi quarter of Samarqand was prevented from opening by residents who would not allow a "Russian school" in their midst, [66] while in late 1916, posters bearing a similar condemnation appeared in Bukhara. [67] These schools also did away with the texts traditionally used in the maktab, which popular opinion held to have been established as part of the canon by Imam Abu Hanifa (the founder of the Hanafi school of fiqh) himself. [68] New-method schools were considered unacceptable also because they used a simplified alphabet and because children sat on benches, "like Russians." [69] The new body language inculcated in new-method schools provoked, not surprisingly, a great deal of debate and hostility toward the Jadids. The Jadids' denigration of the standard texts of the maktab as nonsense and sophistry, and their re-

---

64. Fitrat, *Munāzara*, 37.
65. Mahmud Khoja [Behbudi], "Bizni hāllar wa ishlar," *Āyina*, 18 January 1914, 200–202.
66. *Āyina*, 14 January 1915, 154–155.
67. Abdurrauf Fitrat, "Jahilana taassubgha misal," *Shura*, 15 January 1917, 34.
68. Munawwar Qāri, "Bizni jahalat."
69. Hāji Muin, *Eski maktab*, 42.

placement of these texts by primers and textbooks, also provoked suspicion. In the tradition of the maktab, the written word possessed a sacred aura; the use of lighthearted stories about animals and of songs in the new-method curriculum offended many sensibilities.[70] Customary practices had been valorized into immutable tradition partly as a result of the Russian conquest and now served as markers of the local Muslim community and of the status of elites within it. The maintenance of such markers was especially important to the notables created by Russian rule itself if they were to act as intermediaries between two distinct communities. Jadid reform, and most specifically the new-method school, threatened to undermine the status quo.

The Jadids argued for the legitimacy, and indeed the superiority, of their method through recourse to the nation, Islam, and science. Fitrat's response to the charge that new-method schools turn children into infidels was to claim that, on the contrary, these make children "perfect Muslims and well-trained patriots [mu'addib watanparwarān]."[71] At the same time, the Jadids argued that it was the maktab that failed to transmit "proper" Islamic knowledge to children. Fitrat was more caustic in 1917 in his response to the anonymous posters in Bukhara; pointing to the poor grammar and spelling of the posters' text, he wrote: "Even if the backwardness of Bukharans in commerce, morals, science, and industry . . . is not obvious to the writers of the posters, it is obvious to others. . . . Even when we see the scientific wonders of the world, such as the telephone, the telegraph, or the railway, we do not have anybody who can learn their secrets. We do not even have people who, having graduated from a madrasa, could write posters . . . correctly."[72] Munawwar Qāri argued that it was simple ignorance (jahl) to think that the canon used in the maktab had been created by Abu Hanifa because poets like Fuzuli, Sufi Allāh Yār, and Bedil had not been born in Abu Hanifa's time.[73] The Jadids also pointed to the example of other Muslim countries where the phonetic method had long been in use.[74] As for sitting on benches, Hāji Muin invoked the authority of modern science to

70. This is scarcely peculiar to Turkestan or to Muslim society. Ben Eklof (Russian Peasant Schools: Officialdom, Village Culture, and Popular Pedagogy, 1861–1914 [Berkeley, 1986], ch. 9) has described very similar reactions to new schools among Russian peasants, who had only disdain for primers that made children read such lighthearted stuff, but nothing useful or "beneficial."

71. Fitrat, Munāzara, 23.

72. Fitrat, "Jahilana taassubgha misal," 34.

73. Munawwar Qāri, "Bizni jahalat."

74. Fitrat, Munāzara, 23; Munawwar Qāri, "Bizni jahalat."

argue that it was far more sanitary and hygienic than sitting on the ground because children were thus protected from the harmful moisture of the ground.[75]

In the end, though, the best argument for the new method was its efficacy in imparting functional literacy, which had increasingly become more valued. Consequently, the Jadids borrowed from Russo-native schools the custom of making the annual examinations a public occasion to which local notables were invited to see for themselves the achievements of the new system. Visitors could ask children questions, and the children recited prayers and read from the Qur'an to impress skeptics. Such occasions, complete with printed invitations and elaborate notices in the press (including the *TWG*), became important public events in the consolidation of Jadidism as a social phenomenon.

OFFICIAL SUSPICIONS

The state, once it had decided to intervene in local cultural life, proved to be very jealous of its turf and wary of initiatives from other sources. As early as 1871, Said Azim-bāy had petitioned Kaufman for funds to enable the teaching of Russian script in certain madrasas. The suggestion aroused some interest in Kaufman but died a natural death in the labyrinths of bureaucracy.[76] Similarly, in 1892, Ismail Bey Gasprinskii "took the liberty" of sending Governor-General Vrevskii a brief printed memorandum he had prepared the previous year for a functionary of the Ministry of Internal Affairs, identified only as Vashkevich, who had been sent to the Crimea to report on the possibility of reorganizing the religious and educational administration of the region's Muslims. The only reason Gasprinskii gave for this approach was that he knew that Vrevskii was "interested in everything that pertain[ed] to the Muslim school,"[77] but he obviously hoped that his views would at some level influence official policy. In the memorandum, Gasprinskii suggested that the "weak urge among Muslims to learn Russian, explained usually by their fanaticism or their isolation," stems from rather different reasons. The traditional maktab was so time consuming that it left children no time to devote to Russian; the solution was to make the teaching in the

75. Hāji Muin, *Eski maktab*, 42.
76. On this episode, see Bendrikov, *Ocherki*, 68–70.
77. Gasprinskii to Governor-General, 5 June 1892, in TsGARUz, f. 1, op. 11, d. 806, l. 1.

maktab more efficient, which would free up time necessary for learning Russian. The note described Gasprinskii's own successful experience in this regard:

> Close study of this question showed me that the entire six-year wisdom of the maktab may be managed in two years if certain order is brought about and the *hoja*s (maktab teachers) are given clear, organized elementary guides for teaching reading and writing. The three or four years thus saved may be devoted to the teaching of Russian *right there in the maktab* without transgressing the way of life of the Muslims. . . . For this it is necessary to popularize the new method of teaching and new-method maktabs, so that later the same person, best of all a *hoja* or *mulla,* could teach Arabic, Turkish, and Russian.[78]

For Gasprinskii, the solution lay in the creation of "higher madrasas," reformed madrasas, funded where possible from waqf funds, where Russian language and principles of law and pedagogy would be taught; such madrasas would serve as channels for obtaining religious and pedagogical positions.

Much of this did not apply directly to Turkestan, where no spiritual administration existed, but it was still a very modest proposal, couched in terms that officialdom would understand. It sought justification for the new-method maktab not in the backwardness of Muslim society and the need for self-improvement, as was to become the norm in Central Asian Jadid rhetoric in the following decades, but in the need for Muslims to learn Russian. This was where Gasprinskii hoped his proposal might strike a chord with Turkestan authorities, exercised by the lack of interest among the local population in learning Russian. Nevertheless, the memorandum encountered much hostility in Tashkent. The governor-general's chancellery passed the memorandum on to two local orientalist-administrators, Ostroumov and V. P. Nalivkin, for comment. Nalivkin found Gasprinskii's main point, the need for Muslims to learn Russian, to be "incontestable," but felt that very similar actions had already been undertaken by the administration itself; Gasprinskii's attention was not welcome because he did not know local conditions and his primer, written in Crimean Tatar, was of little use in Turkestan. "It would be lamentable," Nalivkin concluded, "if in the matter of the enlightenment of the natives of Turkestan Russian authorities turned for help to Tatars in general, and to a Tatar such as Mr. Gasprinskii in particular. As editor of the Crimean Tatar newspaper *Terjüman,* Mr. Gasprinskii has, over

78. TsGARUz, f. 1, op. 11, d. 806, ll. 2–3.

the course of many years, distinguished himself by a direction so anti-Russian that there remains no possibility of believing his readiness to serve Russian affairs. In the note presented by him, I see nothing more than an attempt to secure . . . some influence in the affairs of the Muslims of Turkestan." [79] Ostroumov, too, was appalled at the temerity of an *inorodets* to meddle in a question of state: "In the matter of the education of *inorodtsy* in Russia, we need the direction of a Russian member of the Ministry of Education, not that of a Tatar *inorodets,* vehemently defending the inviolability of *inorodets* way of life with all its peculiarities. . . . It would be absurd!" [80] Not only was Gasprinskii meddling in affairs of the state, but he was a Tatar. The memorandum was therefore put to rest in the files of the bureaucracy. Gasprinskii traveled to Central Asia himself the following year and met officials in Tashkent, as well as Amir Abdulahad of Bukhara, but with little result. [81] He opened Samarqand's first new-method school in the house of a Tatar merchant, but the school soon ran into trouble; a year later, when Gasprinskii wrote to Ostroumov, asking him to intercede, the school had still not received official sanction. [82]

Official Russian reaction to Jadid schools stemmed from a long tradition of thinking about Muslim affairs in the empire. State officials and policy makers since Il'minskii and Pobedonostsev had been wary of a Muslim community (and *inorodtsy* in general) that, led by a modern-educated intelligentsia instead of the traditional religious elite, would demand its rights on a political plane. The Jadids represented political awakening and separatism. For conservatives such as Ostroumov, who set himself as the enlightener of the local population, any unsanctioned attempt to spread enlightenment was by definition a political act contrary to Russia's state interests. At bottom was a tension, never resolved, in official thinking between the universality of the enlightenment and the strategies dictated by empire. Knowledge was the antidote to fanaticism, to be sure, but it had to be the right kind of knowledge, officially sanctioned and monitored, for otherwise knowledge and modern education could become dangerous political phenomena, leading to political or even "separatist" claims. In this sense, the Jadids were the true believers

79. Ibid., ll. 6–7ob.

80. Quoted in Bendrikov, *Ocherki,* 254.

81. This episode is treated in detail by Edward J. Lazzerini, "From Bakhchisarai to Bukhara in 1893: Ismail Bey Gasprinskii's Journey to Central Asia," *Central Asian Survey,* 3, no. 4 (1984): 77–78. See also Bendrikov, *Ocherki,* 253–256.

82. Gasprinskii to Ostroumov, 19 November 1893, TsGARUz, f. 1009, d. 50, l. 19.

in the universality of enlightenment; Gasprinskii's denial of Muslim fanaticism subverted the colonial order and therefore rendered him suspect
for pursuing the enlightenment project too far. In another memorandum
of 1901 on "the progressive movement among Tatars," Ostroumov had
taken to task all Tatar publicists for harboring anti-Russian sentiments.[83]
The solution was to foster organic change in the madrasa while fostering
officially supervised education "in the spirit of Russian state interests,"
using administrative regulations, inspections, and censorship to ensure
compliance.

All these fears seemed to be vindicated in 1905, when maktabs and
madrasas remained immune from the political activity that seized all
other educational establishments of the empire. The revolution produced
a honeymoon between officialdom and traditional maktabs and madrasas. In an article in the *Journal of the Ministry of Education*, Ostroumov waxed lyrical about the particular attention to strong discipline
and obedience paid in the madrasas of Central Asia, which he compared
to Orthodox seminaries of old Russia.[84] After 1905, therefore, the state
came to favor the old-style maktab more and more. As the minister of
internal affairs wrote in a 1913 circular to governors of all provinces of
the empire with a Muslim population, the traditionalist ulama, "being
motivated purely by religious conviction, are, without realizing it themselves, . . . allies of [the state] Power in the struggle with the undesirable
(from the state's point of view) nationalization of the Muslim school."[85]

In Turkestan, however, real concern with Jadid activity emerged only
in 1908, when the education administration received an application for
permission to open a new-method school. The school opened by Gasprinskii had left little trace in the files of the bureaucracy, and others had
long existed without any permission being requested or granted. In the
best traditions of Russian bureaucracy, the request was denied because
no clear guidelines existed for schools that, unlike confessional schools,
would also provide instruction in nonreligious subjects. An interdepart-
mental correspondence regarding the status of these schools ensued,
which resulted in Governor-General A. V. Samsonov writing to the min-

83. Ostroumov, "Po voprosu o narozhdaiushchemsia vo srede tatarskogo naseleniia
Rossii progressivnogo dvizheniia," 30 January 1901, TsGARUz, f. 1, op. 31, d. 123,
ll. 8–13.

84. Ostroumov, "Madrasy v Turkestanskom krae," *ZhMNP*, n.s., 7 (1907): otd.
narod. obraz., 20ff.

85. Circular from Minister for Internal Affairs, 22 September 1913, TsGARUz, f. 1,
op. 31, d. 943, l. 3.

ister of education for guidance on the question in September 1911.[86] Once word was received from St. Petersburg, Samsonov issued a circular on 25 January 1912, outlining the new regulations that were to govern new-method schools in Turkestan down to 1917. The new regulations allowed new-method schools to be opened with due permission from the Inspectorate of Education in Tashkent.[87] Applications were to be accompanied by a lesson plan and a list of textbooks to be used.[88] It was to be strongly recommended to each applicant that Russian be taught in the school. Most important of all, these schools were brought under imperial legislation of 27 October 1907, which required teachers in elementary schools for the *inorodtsy* to be either Russian or else belong to the same nationality (*plemia,* literally "tribe") as the students.[89] The law further required that teachers be properly certified according to legislation dating from 1892, which restricted certification to those who had completed their education in the Russian empire.

The new legislation was directed especially against the Tatars who were prominent among teachers in new-method schools. Jadid teachers were in short supply in Turkestan, and founders of new-method schools in the region often found it more convenient to hire Tatars, even though they did not speak the vernacular, than to find potential teachers locally. The law was meant to cripple the fledgling new-method schools of Turkestan by depriving them of their surest supply of teachers. Henceforth, each community was to produce teachers from among its own numbers, or else be dependent on Russo-native or Russian schools. These regulations created grave difficulties for Jadid schools by providing the state any number of pretexts for closing them, although the enforcement of these regulations remained, as ever, subject to individual zeal. As a matter of fact, the law forbidding teachers to teach children of other nationalities had already been enforced by city authorities in Kokand in December 1910. Seven schools were closed down in Kokand despite the

86. TsGARUz, f. 47, d. 1148, l. 54.
87. TsGARUz, f. 47, d. 1149, ll. 10–100b. These regulations have also been published in, *inter alia,* A. Mukhammadzhanov, *Shkola i pedagogicheskaia mysl' uzbekskogo naroda XIX–nachala XX v.* (Tashkent, 1978), 79–80.
88. In practice, it seems, an application for a new school also required information about the place where the teacher received his education (or the books he used for self-study) as well as his domicile. The application was to be submitted to the local *pristav* (prefect), who would then investigate the admissibility of the schools as well as the political reliability of the teacher before granting permission (Mahmud Khoja [Behbudi], "Maktablargha rukhsat ālmāq tariqasi," *Āyina,* 17 May 1914, 574–576).
89. "Vysochaishe utverzhdany Pravila o nachal'nykh uchilishchakh dlia inorodtsev," enacted by P. fon-Kaufman, Minister of Education, in TsGARUz, f. 19, d. 35019, l. 51.

intercession of Russian and German members of the Kokand chamber of commerce (*birzhevyi komitet*) on behalf of local notables.[90] On 23 January 1911, when parents of the affected children petitioned the governor of Ferghana to allow the Tatars to continue to teach, the governor disallowed the petition because "the same, and even better, results may be obtained in Russo-native schools, about the opening of which the petitioners may present an application with an undertaking to take the expenses upon themselves."[91] Even greater problems arose in Semirech'e, which had a small, mixed urban population of Tatars, Ozbeks, and Qazaqs, and where practically every school was ethnically mixed. The inspector in Przheval'sk was indulgent (he was highly impressed by the academic achievements of students he had inspected in such schools), but the one in Vernyi closed down six schools.[92]

The fear of the new-method schools also took the form of constant suspicion about the textbooks used in them. In September 1911, the education administration in Tashkent sent out a circular asking local officials to investigate reports that certain Jadid textbooks contained passages from the "oppositional" newspapers of 1906–1908.[93] Although no such passages were found, S. M. Gramenitskii, director of schools in Syr Darya oblast, suggested tightening censorship over textbooks used in new-method schools.[94] This would, of course, have been an impossible undertaking considering that the local administration had only a few bureaucrats trained in local languages. There were numerous expressions of the sentiment that these schools could not be outlawed because of the "fanatical" nature of the local population, or, more realistically, because such an action would serve only to push them underground, and hence render them more difficult to control.[95] Wary of phenomena it did not understand, and yet unwilling to ban them outright, the state chose instead to keep them on a short leash.

90. TsGARUz, f. 19, d. 35019, l. 630b; Bobrovnikov, "Russko-tuzemnye uchilishcha," 71–73.

91. The petition with 351 signatures and the governor's reply is in TsGARUz, f. 19, d. 35019, ll. 63–630b.

92. TsGARUz, f. 47, d. 1149, ll. 38, 48–51, 69–75.

93. TsGARUz, f. 47, d. 1148, ll. 59, 62.

94. Ibid., l. 161.

95. See, e.g., the opinion of the Inspector of Schools of Ferghana oblast, 1 February 1910, in TsGARUz, f. 19, d. 35019, l. 90b; also S. M. Gramenitskii, *Polozhenie inorodcheskogo obrazovaniia v Syr-Dar'inskoi oblasti* (Tashkent, 1916), 71–72.

CHAPTER 6

Imagining the Nation

Awaken, o beloved nation
   so that the love I have given won't go to waste
My thoughts are always tied up in the love of my nation
   pale-faced and red-eyed, this is my picture.

                                        Tawallā, 1914

The nation (*millat*) was the locus of Jadid reform, and sentiments such as these by Tolagan Khojamyārov Tawallā suffuse the work of practically every Jadid writer. For the Jadids, their concern for the nation set them apart from others in their society who recognized only particular, selfish interests. However, such concern was something new: Traditional Central Asian visions of history had revolved around dynasties or tribes. Now new understandings of the world engendered new notions of identity. But if the nation was central to Jadid thought, its boundaries and the manner in which it was to be delineated remained in a state of flux, for the nation was imagined in complex ways that at first sight appear mutually contradictory. Nonetheless, all of them were modern, and all of them helped define how the Jadids acted in the world both before and after 1917.

Despite the overriding importance attached to questions of identity in current writing on Central Asia, pre-Soviet identities remain poorly understood. Most writers writing outside the Soviet paradigm hold one of two views about pre-Soviet identity of Central Asians. One asserts that Central Asians before 1917 lacked all forms of identity except the religious. As late as 1926 the renowned Russian orientalist V. V. Bartol'd could write, "The settled peoples of Central Asia are in the first place Muslims and think of themselves only secondarily as living in a particular town or district, to them the idea of belonging to a particular stock is of no significance."[1] Alexandre Bennigsen and Chantal Lemercier-

---

1. W. Barthold, "Sart," *Encyclopedia of Islam*, 4 vols. (Leiden, 1913–1936), IV: 176.

Quelquejay, whose work has been enormously influential, extended this to the Jadids as well: "In Turkestan and the two protectorates of Bukhara and Khiva, . . . the national movement . . . assumed, after the defeat of Russia by Japan, a fundamentally pan-Islamic character. . . . Educated for the most part in the conservative *medresehs*, the young reformist intellectuals moved rapidly towards the left. Their nationalism, inspired by the teaching of Jamaleddin al-Afghani, was fundamentally hostile to Russia and the Russians."[2] In a more blunt formulation, this becomes a situation where as late as 1917, "Muslims were victimised by their own backwardness [and] ethnic or tribal rivalries. . . . Their political development hardly embraced the idea of class or of nation, being centred round Islam and the tribe or clan."[3] One hesitates to attach a label to a view so characterized by absences, but one might call it the "Muslim" view.

The second view, particularly popular in Turkey but also widely held in European and North American academe, might be labeled "Turkist." It holds that Central Asians were part of a single "Turkish" nation that extended from "the shores of the Bosporus to the sands of Kashgar," that all Turkic languages were essentially one mutually intelligible language, and that relations between various Turkic-speaking groups were characterized solely by respect, solicitude, and a will to unity.[4] Rooted in the hopes of Crimean and Volga Tatar intellectuals (the most prominent of whom was Gasprinskii), this notion of Turkic solidarity was popularized by Turkic émigrés in republican Turkey, whose claims have too often been taken at face value.

Both these views see the emergence of distinct nations in the 1920s as the result of imperial fiat, a classic case of divide and rule, imposed by an omnipotent regime on a helpless victimized population. They both also share the view that Central Asian identities were focused elsewhere and that Central Asians were only passive participants in larger dramas being played out elsewhere.

2. Alexandre Bennigsen and Chantal Lemercier-Quelquejay, *Islam in the Soviet Union,* trans. Geoffrey E. Wheeler and Hubert Evans (London, 1967), 47. The authors present no evidence for their categorical assertion of the overriding influence of Afghani in Central Asia; they also exaggerate the "leftist" or revolutionary stance of the Jadids.

3. Stephen Blank, "The Contested Terrain: Muslim Political Participation in Soviet Turkestan, 1917–19," *Central Asian Survey* 6, no. 4 (1987): 48.

4. This position has never been explicitly formulated, but is often taken for granted; see, e.g., Nadir Devlet, *Rusya Türklerinin Millî Mücadele Tarihi (1905–1917)* (Ankara, 1985). Its popularity (and the passion that it arouses) is evident to anyone who has attended a gathering of Central Asian studies or seen the question debated on the Internet.

For its part, Soviet scholarship offered a different narrative of Central Asian identities. It asserted the "objective" existence of nations since time immemorial. History was the process of the elaboration and refinement of these national identities through processes such as ethnogenesis. This obviously romantic idea had, from the beginning, formed the basis of Bolshevik (and hence Soviet) understanding of the "national question."[5] This view of things, "naturalized" by the existence of statistical data on each nation, is also often adopted by many writers abroad without much curiosity about the origins of either the nations or the data.[6] Despite the often bitter polemics between the holders of the "national" and "Turkist" views, the two share certain fundamental assumptions. They both take for granted the ontological existence of nations, the assumption that nations are "sociohistorical organisms," sharing common origins ("ethnogenesis") and united by common "historical destinies." The difference is simply that whereas the Turkist view insists on the existence of a single "Turkish" nation, the "national" view holds that there are several Turkic nations. The collapse of the Soviet Union has done little to challenge the belief in the reality of the nation among intellectual and political elites in formerly Soviet lands.[7]

All three views, for different reasons, largely ignore how Central Asians imagined their community and how those views evolved over time. This is especially true of the debates of the tsarist period. Yet, those debates are crucial to understanding the transformations of the 1920s. Attention to them allows us to question primordial discourses of identity by examining how such notions evolved over time in concrete historical circumstances. The aim in this chapter is to rescue history from

5. For an excellent examination of this fundamental trait of the Soviet polity, see Yuri Slezkine, "The USSR as a Communal Apartment, or How a Socialist State Promoted Ethnic Particularism," *Slavic Review* 53 (1994): 414–452.

6. For a critique of this literature, see John Schoeberlein-Engel, "Identity in Central Asia: Construction and Contention in the Conceptions of 'Özbek,' 'Tâjik,' 'Muslim,' 'Samarqandi,' and Other Groups" (Ph.D. diss., Harvard University, 1994), 44–72.

7. The use made of such "organismic" views of the nation (and national destiny) by political elites in the newly independent countries of the former Soviet Union is not simply a matter of political calculation. Rather, it represents a dominant paradigm widely shared in the (formerly) Soviet world that remains strong in academic circles as well. A lengthy debate on questions of nationality and national identity in the Moscow journal *Etnograficheskoe obozrenie* (Anthropological Survey) between 1994 and 1996 produced views that ranged from asserting the "objective reality" of ethnicity (S. A. Arutiunov, "Ethnichnost'—ob"ektivnaia real'nost'," *Etnograficheskoe obozrenie*, 1995, no. 5, 7–10) to an attempt to replace "ethnos" or "nation" with "socio-historical organism" as "the most important category of historical science" (Iu. I. Semenov, "Sotsiosial'no-istoricheskie organizmy, etnosy, natsii," *Etnograficheskoe obozrenie*, 1996, no. 3, 3–13).

the hegemony of the nation by showing how the nation itself is the product of history.

All nations are imagined, but they may be imagined in a number of ways. Benedict Anderson has drawn our attention to the ways in which new means of communications and new regimes of power make possible new ways of imagining community.[8] However, his insistence that nationalism emerges only with the demise of broader notions of community diverts attention from the many different ways in which the nation may be imagined. Print, the census, and the globe made it possible for the Jadids to see themselves as citizens of a modern, interconnected world, of a community of Muslims within it, and of a community of Turks that overlapped with the community of the world's Muslims. As I show below, these various visions of the world coexisted, sometimes in a state of tension, until well after 1917.

PREMODERN IDENTITIES

"There is no Persian except in the company of a Turk, [just as] there is no cap unless there is a head to put it on" (*Tatsïz Türk bolmas, bashsïz börk bolmas*), went a Turkic proverb recorded by the eleventh-century lexicographer, Mahmud al-Kāshghari.[9] Maria Eva Subtelny has rightly used this to investigate the symbiosis of Turkic and Iranian (or Tajik) elements in Central Asia.[10] I wish to go further and suggest that the mutual dependence to which the proverb refers may be seen at a more fundamental level. Only the existence of a Persian made a Turk a Turk, and vice versa. The symbiosis of Turkic and Iranian in Central Asia was not the coagulation of two preexisting wholes; rather, it was the very encounter that shaped the two components of the symbiosis. Without the opposition, each side of the symbiosis remained a variegated expanse.

Iranian speech varied greatly, although the emergence of a high literary tradition had ensured a great degree of standardization of the written language, which tended to mask the differences in regional usages. The language was always referred to as *Fārsi*, Persian, and never as *Tājik*. The differentiation of speech was much greater on the Turkic side, which

---

8. Benedict Anderson, *Imagined Communities*, 2nd ed. (London, 1991), 12–19.

9. Mahmūd al-Kāšyarī, *Compendium of the Turkic Dialects (Dīwān Luɣāt at-Turk)*, ed. and trans. Robert Dankoff, 3 vols. (Cambridge, 1982–1985), II: 103.

10. Maria Eva Subtelny, "The Symbiosis of Turk and Tajik," in Beatrice Forbes Manz, ed., *Central Asia in Historical Perspective* (Boulder, Colo., 1994), 45–61. I owe the reference to the proverb to Subtelny.

extended far beyond Central Asia to Anatolia and the Balkans in the west, the Volga and the Urals in the north, and the Gobi desert in the east. This vast array of dialects, gradually merging one into another, was united only in opposition to Iranian. In the period after the fifteenth century, two literary standards (Ottoman and Chaghatay) emerged, but their impact on spoken dialects was minimal, for skill in the literary form of either Turkic or Persian was a sign of culture and virtuosity, not a source of national pride. Indeed, a saying current in the late nineteenth century even asserted that "Arabic is honor, Persian baseness, [and] Turkic dirt" (*lisān-i arabi sharāfat, lisān-i fārsi qabāhat, lisān-i turki najāsat*).[11] Each language had its appropriate range of use. Arabic was entrenched in the madrasa, whereas Persian remained the language of the chancery in Kokand and Bukhara until their respective ends (only in Khiva was Turkic used extensively in the chancery). Thus, there was no paradox involved in the fact, embarrassing to both Iranian and Turkic nationalists today, that Firdawsi composed his immortal *Shāhnāma* under the patronage of Mahmud of Ghazna, a Turk. At the everyday level, Iranian speech in Transoxiana acquired Turkic lexical and grammatical elements, while Persian models imbued all literary Turkic. Bilingualism was widespread even in the countryside, and the cultural capital of any cultivated individual included a knowledge of the high traditions in both idioms.

As labels for population groups, too, "Turk" and "Tajik" operated only on the most general level. Contrasted to "Iranian," "Turk" denoted all groups of Turkic speech in Central Asia, but it also had more specific uses. After the last wave of Turkic migration into Transoxiana during the Shaybānid conquest, "Turk" came to be used exclusively for the older Turkic population of the region; the newcomers were called "Ozbek." This narrower sense of "Turk" survived down to 1917.[12] Other tribal conglomerates, such as the Qazaq, the Qïrghïz, and the Türkmen, retained their distinctive identities, rooted in myths of origin that defined them against other groups in Transoxiana. There were also smaller, more localized groups (such as the Moghuls of eastern Bukhara and the Qurama of the Chirchik valley) that did not fit the various tribal federations neatly and therefore remained distinctive. Moreover, the "ethnic" sense of "Turk" and "Tajik" did not coincide with language use. It was quite

11. Quoted by V. P. Nalivkin, "Shkoly u tuzemtsev Srednei Azii," *Sbornik materialov dlia statistiki Samarkandskoi oblasti, 1887–1888 gg.*, 1 (1889): 300–301.

12. B. Kh. Karmysheva, "Etnograficheskaia gruppa 'Tiurk' v sostave uzbekov," *Sovetskaia etnografiia*, 1960, no. 1, 3–22.

possible for groups to identify themselves as Ozbek while speaking *only* Persian, as was the case with many Ozbeks in Bukhara.[13] In 1949, the anthropologist Belqis Karmysheva found groups in Baljuwān who claimed descent from "Turk" tribes but spoke only Persian and considered themselves "Tajiks of Turkic descent [*Tadzhiki roda tiurk*]."[14]

Urban dwellers, many of whom did not use tribal designations, were referred to variously as "Tājik," "Sārt," or "Chaghatāy," regardless of speech. The usage of these terms was neither constant nor universal (as nineteenth-century scholars were to find out to their chagrin), but varied over time and place. The term "Sart" was not used in Bukhara, for example, where the term "Chaghatay" had currency. Although Russian scholars were to distinguish between the two on the basis of language, the relation between Sart and Tajik, often mentioned as synonymous in Timurid sources, was far more complex. As late as 1880, Sulaymān Efendi, the shaykh of the Bukharan Naqshbandi lodge in Istanbul, described "Sart" to his Ottoman audience as "tribes of Tajik and Persian origins living in Turkestan; also called Tat."[15] In practice, Sarts and Tajiks were marked as different by their urban status, not by common origin or language. A nineteenth-century history from Kokand used Sart (*sartiya*) to oppose the sedentary population of the khanate to the nomadic (*ilātiyya*).[16] To paraphrase John Schoeberlein-Engel, seeing the Sarts as an ethnic group or a nationality is analogous to seeing all town-dwellers of southern Europe as a nationality.[17] Nor did these label exhaust the diversity of the urban population, where groups such as Sayyids and Khojas asserted their distinctiveness on the basis of their sacred descent, even though they spoke the same language as their neighbors. The same held true, at the other end of the social spectrum, of the Loli, the "gypsies" of Central Asia, whose identity was defined by their profession.

13. O. A. Sukhareva, *Bukhara: XIX–nachalo XX v. (Pozdnefeodal'nyi gorod i ego naselenia)* (Moscow, 1966), 129–139.

14. B. Kh. Karmysheva, *Ocherki etnicheskoi istorii iuzhnykh raionov Tadzhikistana i Uzbekistana* (Moscow, 1976), 76.

15. Şeyh Süleyman Efendi Buharî, *Lûgat-i Çağatay ve Turkî-yi Osmanî* (Istanbul, 1298/1880–1881), 178.

16. T. T. Beisembiev, *"Tarikh-i Shakhrukhi" kak istoricheskii istochnik* (Alma Ata, 1987), 78.

17. Schoeberlein-Engel, "Identity in Central Asia," 141 (who makes this observation in examining a definition of Tajiks as the settled population of Central Asia). On Sarts as a social, rather than an ethnic, entity, see also Bert G. Fragner, "The Nationalization of Uzbeks and Tajiks," in Andreas Kappeler et al., eds., *Muslim Communities Reemerge: Historical Perspectives on Nationality, Politics, and Opposition in the Former Soviet Union and Yugolslavia* (Durham, N.C., 1994), 15.

Individuals felt themselves to be Ozbek or Turk or Tajik not through some abstract sense of belonging to a national group but through the concrete fact of being born in a family that was located socially in a ramified structure of relationships conceived in kinship terms. Tribal designations were far more significant to individual identity than broader categories such as "Turk" or "Tajik." There is no reason to assume that individuals classified by court chroniclers as "Turk" would have felt any affinity for each other, or that divisions between Turk and Tajik or Ozbek and Sart mentioned in the literary sources implied anything but divisions among the court elites. Among the sedentary population without tribal divisions, geographical designations played a similar role. Thus, the sedentary Turkic-speaking population of Khwārazm, called "Sart" in Khwārazm, were called "Urganji" (after the town of Urgench) in Bukhara.

Group identities in pre-Russian Central Asia presented a complex mosaic of fragmented identities intimately intertwined with the social and economic fabric of the land. Community was not conceived of as an organism. Nor were the various identities mutually exclusive: One could be a Sart, a Khoja, and a Turk at the same time. Genealogical explanations were used to assert the origins of groups or social practices; but there is little reason to take these explanations at face value (as indeed they have been by numerous scholars, who all too easily assimilate them into theories of "ethnogenesis"). Arguments based on the organic unity of populations with common genetic descent are hazardous enough at the best of times; they have even less applicability in Central Asia, with its centuries of migration, warfare, and social dislocation.

ISLAM AND THE NATION

The Jadids defined the nation in a number of ways. Take, for instance, this appeal addressed by the editor of *Tojjār* to his "compatriots" (*watandāshlar*):

> In our time there is not a single nation that doesn't have tens or hundreds of newspapers and magazines in its own language, for the twentieth century deems any nation not having publications in its own language savage and uncivilized by time itself. . . . O compatriots! . . . By virtue of the manifesto granted by our emperor on 17 October 1905, we too acquired ten or fifteen newspapers and magazines and thus became aware of the world. . . . But because these newspapers and magazines were in Turkish or Tatar [*turkcha tātārcha*], and not in the pure language of Turkestan, it was generally not possible for the Muslims of Turkestan to benefit from them. . . . Now it is ob-

vious to any intelligent person that the solution to this is of course to publish a newspaper in the language of Turkestan, that is, in Chaghatay.[18]

The "we" refers in the beginning to the Muslims of the Russian empire, but then is quite explicitly narrowed to refer only to the "Muslims of Turkestan." At other times, Jadid authors referred only to "Muslims," but again the context made it clear that the intended audience did not comprise Muslims generally but only the Muslims of Central Asia. Similarly, when the protagonist in Hāji Muin's play *Old School, New School* declaims, "At present, we Turkestanis are not sufficiently acquainted with religious and worldly knowledge,"[19] he clearly has in mind the Muslim population of Turkestan, local Jews and all recent settlers being implicitly excluded from the intended audience. Reference to the Muslims of Turkestan abound in Jadid writing of the period. If the Jadids were nationalists, they were so on behalf of a nation defined in both territorial and confessional terms.

The nation was rooted historically. It is significant that the history taught in new-method schools of Turkestan was that of Islam, not Turkestan or the Turks. The prior golden age of the nation with which the Jadids identified was that of Islam, or more precisely, of the glorious empires built by Muslim dynasties. Jadid writings are replete with references to this earlier age, which served both to highlight the degradation of the present as well as to justify the reforms they advocated. Thus, Nushirvan Yavushev claimed that madrasas in the glory days of Islam offered a full curriculum of worldly as well as religious sciences.[20] Usually, however, the historical legacy was delineated more precisely. The names of Bukhāri, Fārābi, Ibn Sinā, and Ulugh Bek were invoked to highlight the past of a Central Asian Muslim nation.

This community had all the characteristics of a nation. We find the expression "Muslim language" (*musul'manskii iazyk, musulmān tili*) in both Jadid and official Russian discourse. Ingeborg Baldauf, the only scholar to have remarked upon this phenomenon, confuses the issue needlessly when she writes: "I do not dare to answer the question whether the introduction of a 'Muslim language' along with the existence of a 'Muslim nation' is to be regarded as a homage to the romantic identification of a nation with its tongue, and *vice versa*. We might,

18. "Matbuāt ālami, yāki sabab-i ta'sis-i ghazita-yi 'Tojjār'," *Tojjār*, 21 August 1907.
19. Hāji Muin b. Shukrullah, *Eski maktab, yangi maktab* (Samarqand, 1916), 27–28.
20. N. Y., "Eski musulmān madrasalarinda nimalar oqulur edi?" *Āyina*, 15 February 1914, 256–259.

however, regard the *musulmon tili* as a 'pseudo-language.'"[21] There was
nothing pseudo about the Muslim language. The expression again was
a product of Russian usage. For Russian bureaucrats, anything written
in the Arabic script or incomprehensible to all but the few trained orientalists among them was "Muslim." Thus, the administration granted
separate licenses to booksellers for the sale of books *po-musul'manski*
("in Muslim"), regardless of the language. This usage was adopted by
the local population, although it clearly meant the language of the Muslims of Turkestan. The newspaper *Tojjār* proclaimed on its masthead
that it was published in "the Muslim language" (*musulmāncha*). But
this usage was obviously understood in a strictly local context, as *a* language of the Muslims of Central Asia, for the same newspaper claimed
in its first issue to be filling a gap created by the fact that the ten or fifteen
newspapers that appeared in the wake of the October Manifesto of 1905
were all "in Turkish or Tatar [*turkcha tātārcha*] and not in the pure language of Turkestan."[22] The Muslims of Turkestan were a nation, but
that nation was not defined by its language in the romantic mold.

And the uses of the nation were entirely secular. As with any other
nation, the Muslim nation of Turkestan existed alongside many others,
and its essence was political rather than religious. The "others" could be
conceived as religious or national entities, although given the realities of
the time, the two tended to coincide. Jadid authors constantly pointed
to the Jewish and Armenian communities as both sources of danger and
models for emulation.

> We Muslims have been left behind in everything. In matters of trade we are
> the prisoners of Jews. There's no place more important than unskilled labor
> or salaried work left for us local Muslims. Drivers, carriers, diggers, watch-
> men, in short, those performing menial labor are all Muslims, but their em-
> ployers, the owners of large buildings, the masters of the stores are all Jews.
> The small Jewish nation [*millat*], without any protectors, has taken all trade
> in its own hands.
>
> We do not complain of the Jews, to whom we have no enmity. They have
> achieved this status through their own energy and expertise. Bravo! The fault
> is our own. We did not take the path taken by the Jews in trade and we did
> not learn the things learned by the Jews.[23]

For Hamza, the "most basic reason for their [Jews' and Armenians'] being able to command so much wealth so quickly . . . is their knowledge of

21. Ingeborg Baldauf, "Some Thoughts on the Making of the Uzbek Nation," *Cahiers du monde russe et soviétique* 32 (1991): 82.

22. "Matbuāt ālami, yāki sabab-i ta'sis-i ghazita 'Tojjār'."

23. 'A., "Tijāratimiz wa maktab," *Turān,* 30 December 1912.

the languages of Russia, and, indeed, their having perfected their knowledge of commerce in organized schools and universities."[24] These communities proved to the Jadids the truth of their general assertion that knowledge was the key to progress. At the same time, they were the perfect example of a Darwinian world in which survival was assured only by disciplined effort.

In many Jadid writings, the distinction between Islam as a faith and Muslims as a community disappears completely. Behbudi once urged his compatriots to educate their children to become "judges, lawyers, engineers, teachers, the supporters and servants of the nation, . . . who would work for the true faith of Islam."[25] This was the new language of group survival, of progress and modernity. Similarly, Tawallā had in mind the progress and prosperity of the nation of Muslims when he titled a collection of his poetry *The Splendour of Islam*. Russian bureaucratic practices, which emphasized religious affiliation as a significant marker of classification, contributed to self-identification in this form. Although the nation of "the Muslims of Turkestan" was connected to other Muslim communities in the Russian empire and beyond, it remained a delineated, territorial entity in which ethnic identities were clearly subordinate to a more general, *patriotic* identity. The desacralization of Islam and the absence of theological debate, both noted above, meant that the Jadids' priorities tended to be the concerns of the community rather than of the faith.

Such secular confessional nationalism was hardly unusual at the turn of the century, as the rise of Zionism attests. In the Muslim world it arose in a variety of contexts, the dissolution of the Ottoman empire, in which the nationalisms of its subjects in Europe were all fueled by fervent anti-Muslim feelings, being the most significant. Ottomanist intellectuals, such as the Lebanese Druze Amir Shakib Arsalān, looked to Islam to provide a rallying point in their struggle against imperialism. In a different political context, the highly secularized Muslim elites of India found in Muslim "communalism" a node of politically significant loyalty. After 1917, the Tatar Mirsaid Sultangaliev was to advocate class war in defense of a proletarian Muslim nation.[26]

24. Hamza, "Muallim afandilarimiza ulugh rijamiz," *SF,* 25 October 1914.
25. [Behbudi], "Āmālimiz yā inki murādimiz," *Āyina,* 7 December 1913, 155.
26. William L. Cleveland, *Islam against the West: Shakib Arslan and the Campaign for Muslim Nationalism* (Austin, 1985); Alexandre Bennigsen and Chantal Lemercier-Quelquejay, *Les mouvements nationaux chez les musulmans de Russie: le «Sultanga-lievisme» au Tatarstan* (Paris, 1960); Alexandre Bennigsen and S. Enders Wimbush, *Mus-*

The line separating the Muslims of Turkestan from those of other areas could be porous. In 1904, Tatar public figures began organizing a political movement that sought to represent all the Muslims of the empire in one organization. Although Turkestan and Bukhara remained largely marginal in this movement, the idea that the Muslims of the Russian empire belonged to one community was often invoked. Behbudi could claim, for instance, that "we Muslims constitute the second largest nation [*millat*] in the Russian empire." [27] The affinity the Jadids felt with Muslims elsewhere in the world is obvious from the intellectual milieu in which they lived and worked.

But this was a very different matter than the "pan-Islam" whose dread filled the hearts of colonial officials all over the Muslim world. Russian officialdom spent a great deal of time worrying about pan-Islam and the dangers it posed to the stability of the empire. It located its sources in the "fanaticism" of Muslims, which needed only a spark to ignite. That spark could come, many in Russia feared, from agents of the Ottoman sultan, and the Okhrana, the tsarist secret police, assembled a vast archive on the subject. Its agents saw Turkish emissaries everywhere they looked, although none were ever apprehended. The kernel of truth on which these fears were based was provided by Ottoman attempts under Abdülhamid II to forge links with Muslim populations in the colonies of European powers primarily to provide his empire some diplomatic leverage. But the success of that enterprise was vastly circumscribed, and Ottoman intrigue does not explain the phenomena that worried the Okhrana.

Pan-Islamic sentiment was undoubtedly significant in Central Asia before 1917, but its sources lay not in the fanaticism (inherent, yet malleable by malign forces such as Turkish emissaries) of the Muslim masses, as colonial officials feared, but in Muslim elites' encounter with modernity. Pan-Islam was not (and could not have been) the result of manipulation from outside. During the last two decades of the tsarist regime, Russian officialdom was seized with the fear of "Turkish emissaries" roaming the empire and sowing seeds of fanaticism and separatism among its Muslim population. Yet, in those years the Ottoman empire faced immense problems externally and political instability domestically. It did not have the resources necessary to mount such an operation, and Ottoman archives

---

lim *National Communism in the Soviet Union: A Revolutionary Ideology for the Colonial World* (Chicago, 1979).
    27. "Sharq āqshāmindagi nutq," *Āyina*, 2 April 1915, 285.

have yielded no evidence of it ever having been mounted.[28] Nor was it a throwback to some primordial sentiment traceable to the teachings of the Qur'an. Rather, pan-Islamic sentiment was rooted in modernity, which made it possible for the first time to imagine a community encompassing all the Muslims of the world. We have already seen the wide circulation of the printed word among Muslim elites throughout the world, which allowed new links to be forged. The Jadids belonged to perhaps the last generation of Muslim intellectuals who could communicate with each other without the use of European languages. Muslim newspapers of the period frequently quoted each other. The Jadid press (especially in the freer period of 1906–1908) gives evidence of a fascination with Muslims all over the world. There are numerous stories about the spread of Islam in Europe and extensive, optimistic coverage of an imminent explosion of interest in Islam in Japan, the one non-European power to have asserted its presence in the world.

This sense of unity was given a very visible form by modern geography and cartography. The novelty of this sense of the world is often not appreciated. Bernard Lewis, among others, writes that in the "Muslim world view the basic division of mankind is into the House of Islam . . . and the House of War. . . . The one consists of all those countries where the law of Islam prevails, that is to say, broadly, the Muslim Empire; the latter is the rest of the world." [29] But the fact remains that the "House of Islam" was never imagined in a geographical sense, and the legal theory did not by itself bring about a consciousness of unity. (In any case, there is little evidence that legal theories influenced political and diplomatic practice as directly as Lewis asserts.) Rather it was globes, atlases, and postcards bearing maps of the Ottoman empire or the route of the Hijaz railway that allowed the Muslim *ummah* to be imagined as a geopolitical entity for the first time in history. Munawwar Qāri's geography textbook, which provided a country-by-country account of all the major countries of the world, also included statistics on the number of Muslims in each country.[30]

Yet, this was very different from the pan-Islam that Abdülhamid II sought to use as a diplomatic tool against European powers, since it did not automatically serve Ottoman state interests, nor was it instigated by

28. Hakan Kırımlı, *National Movements and National Identity among the Crimean Tatars (1905–1916)* (Leiden, 1996), 190–191.

29. Bernard Lewis, *The Muslim Discovery of Europe* (New York, 1982), 60–61.

30. Munawwar Qāri, *Yer yuzi* (Tashkent, 1913).

Ottoman agents. Nevertheless, as the last Muslim state left in the high age of European imperialism, the Ottoman empire took on a great symbolic value to Muslims living under colonial rule, and its travails, especially during the second constitutional period, provoked sympathy among Muslims worldwide. The wars in North Africa and the Balkans were assiduously followed by the Muslim press of Russia (including the *TWG*) and provoked much angst. We have not had the means to enter the private world of the Jadids during this period, but a personal letter from Sadriddin Ayni I found serendipitously provides a first glance. Writing to a friend in March 1913, while Balkan armies laid siege to Edirne, Ayni has this to say: "The news from the war is very bad. . . . [But] the second war is altogether more cheerful than the first. Even women are present in the service of the wars and the soldiers. The unbelievers are united in their attempts to destroy the Muslim world, whether through war or through peace. The difference is that if they destroy it through peace, the Muslim world will be destroyed disgracefully [*razilāna*]; if they destroy it by war, we will be martyred with honor [*nāmus*]." [31] Ayni sent along pictures from the press of Şükrü Paşa, the defender of Edirne, and a group of Tatar women doctors who had volunteered to serve in Ottoman field hospitals. He also wrote an ode to Şükrü Paşa in Turkish. The same sense of impending doom was evoked three years earlier by Fitrat, who concluded his *Debate* with an impassioned appeal to the amir to act before "the enemies of our faith of Islam conquer all Muslims . . . and demand that we renounce our religion . . . and replace our imāms with priests, our call to prayer with bells, and our mosques with churches." [32]

Before we rush to declare these statements expressions of age-old Islamic fanaticism, we might do well to remember that the language of honor used here would not have been alien to anyone in Europe at that time. Nor should we forget that the anti-Muslim sentiment that had fueled every Balkan nationalism was commonplace in contemporary Europe. The plea to do something before all mosques are turned into churches evokes this experience, which was very current to people in Istanbul. Moreover, pan-Slavic sentiment was widespread in Russia during the Balkan wars, as numerous societies emerged to aid the struggle

31. Private letter dated 10 Rabiʿ II 1331/7 March 1913, in the possession of Dr. Elyor Karimov, Tashkent, to whom goes my gratitude for allowing me to quote from it.
32. Fitrat Bukhārāyī, *Munāzara-yi mudarris-i bukhārāyī bā yak nafar-i farangī dar Hindustān dar bāra-yi makātib-i jadīda* (Istanbul, 1911), 65. This plea was excised from the Turkic translation published legally in Tashkent in 1912.

of fellow Slavs against Muslim oppression, and anti-Muslim sentiment remained an integral part of official Russia's self-perception.[33] Nor was the role of print incidental in understanding how a Bukharan mudarris came to write poetry in honor of a foreign general defending a city the author had never seen. Pan-Islam was located squarely in the twentieth century.

For the mass of the population, Islam continued to be embedded in everyday practices mediated by men or women of learning. Pan-Islam as a phenomenon of the reading or hearing public remained a matter of elite concern. Different elites in different Muslim countries looked at Muslim unity through the prism of their own struggles (within their own society as well as with colonial authorities). No organizational structure for pan-Islamic unity ever existed.[34] In Central Asia, it was rooted in the anxieties of the Jadids themselves, which alone shaped their activities. More importantly, even for the intellectual elites, pan-Islam was never the sole identity or course of political action.

ROMANTIC NATIONALISM

The idea that humanity is divided into discrete nations united by a language and common descent through history arrived in Central Asia in full force from two different directions. In the eighteenth century, the Russian state had become interested in knowing more about its subjects. By the middle of the nineteenth century, the major axis of classification had come to be the nexus of race, nationality, and language. From the beginning, Russian officialdom had looked to anthropology to render Central Asia comprehensible by classifying its inhabitants. These new classifications, created to understand and control the local population, became integral to bureaucratic practice in Central Asia, and from there entered local understandings of identity.

33. On the eve of world war in 1914, an official publication claimed: "The majority of the people of the East were Muslims or inclined to this faith (Tatars, Kirgiz, Bashkirs). Sometimes among them appeared emissaries of the Turkish sultan. Already in the seventeenth century, Russia's role as the main and most dangerous enemy of the Mahomedan world had been defined, and therefore the Mahomedan world attempted to unite for a more successful struggle with Russia." S. M. Seredonin, "Istoricheskii ocherk zavoevaniia Aziatskoi Rossii," in *Aziatskaia Rossiia*, 2 vols. (St Petersburg, 1914), I: 26.

34. The several international Muslim congresses did, after all, not amount to much; see Martin Kramer, *Islam Assembled: The Advent of the Muslim Congresses* (New York, 1986). The first such congress, held in Cairo in 1907, at the initiative of Gasprinskii, failed to excite even the Okhrana; the disappointingly slim dossier is in GARF, f. 102, op. 238, d. 289.

The same understanding of community underlay the vision of the various nationalist movements in the Russian and Ottoman empires, even though the political aims of these movements were often diametrically opposed to those of officialdom. Romantic ideas appealed to Turkic intellectuals in the two empires, who began to reimagine their histories toward the end of the nineteenth century. Given the nature of the romantic nation, and the fact that they tapped into common sources (new findings in history, Turkology, and anthropology)[35] and common sensibilities (enthusiasm for romantic nationalism under the influence of pan-Slavism and pan-Germanism), these groups soon discovered mutual affinities, and the idea of a broader pan-Turkic nation emerged. The study of these various Turkisms (Tatar and Crimean nationalisms in Russia and Turkism in the Ottoman empire) has been long been overshadowed by an emphasis on the purely political side of pan-Turkism, with the result that the complex connections and contestations between them are poorly understood.[36] The writings of Turkic émigrés from Russia in the Ottoman empire, such as Yusuf Akçura, Ağaoğlu Ahmed and Hüseyinzade Ali, brought the most extreme versions of the two currents together in pan-Turkism, which professed the goal of the political unity of those who belonged to the Turkic race/nation. Such pan-Turkism, however, was not synonymous with the variegated discourse of Turkism. Pan-Turkism may have had limited success as an intellectual movement, but the more basic idea of the affinity of various Turkic groups, and the knowledge of their Turkness, rapidly suffused all notions of identity in the Turkic world.

Central Asia was of great importance to Turkists, both as the original homeland of the race/nation (the Turan celebrated most famously by Ziya Gökalp as "the homeland of the Turks, neither Turkey, nor Turkestan / but a great and eternal land: Turan"),[37] and also as the home of a large Turkic population. Turkist intellectuals in both empires (although in vastly different conditions) produced a vast corpus of litera-

35. The most concise account of the origins of Turkism in nineteenth-century discoveries in orientalism and Turkology remains that of Ziya Gökalp, *Türkçülüğün Esasları* (Ankara, 1923), 5–10.

36. The British Admiralty's *A Manual on the Turanians and Pan-Turanianism* (London, n.d. [1918]) remains an iconic text in any discussion of pan-Turkism down to today. The brief account in Jacob Landau, *Pan-Turkism*, rev. ed. (London, 1995), chs. 1–2, is deeply flawed and peppered with factual and interpretive inaccuracies. The only comprehensive account of Turkism in both empires is again by a participant: Akçuraoğlu Yusuf [Yusuf Akçura], "Türkçülük," in *Türk Yılı 1928* (Ankara, 1928), 288–459. See also Paul Dumont, "Le revue *Türk Yurdu* et les Musulmans de l'empire russe, 1911–1914," *Cahiers du monde russe et soviétique* 15 (1974): 315–331.

37. Ziya Gökalp, "Turan," *Kızıl Elma* (Istanbul, 1914), 7.

ture that depicted Central Asia as part of a much larger community marked by race and language. This literature was widely read in Central Asia, and although no Central Asians contributed to it, its fundamental premises seeped into Jadid thinking about community and shaped the manner in which they imagined the world and their place in it.

SART AND TAJIK

The romantic idea of the nation wreaked havoc on older notions of community and identity. Armed with an understanding of the world that saw it divided into discrete groups, amenable to rigorous, "scientific" classification if only sufficient "objective" data could be obtained, Russian officials and scholars proceeded to find the objective reality behind every label they encountered in their new domains. The enumeration and classification of the population that ensued created new understandings of old labels. The complexities of Central Asian identity were nowhere better demonstrated than in the case of the "Sarts." The career of this label in the half-century of Russian rule demonstrates the forces at work in shaping identities in Central Asia.

For reasons that remain unclear, "Sart" became the term most commonly used by the Russians to denote the sedentary population of Central Asia after the conquest. It was used in several different ways. "In common parlance and every day life," a German geographer wrote in 1914, "the Russians use 'Sart' in much the same way as British colonists would speak of 'niggers.' It is applied to all and sundry 'natives' whose dress does not single them out at once (Jews, Turkmen, Kirghiz) or who are not evidently foreigners (Europeans, Afghans, Chinese, Hindu, etc.)." [38] Officials and scholars sought to use the term in a more precise manner, to apply it only to the "real" Sarts. The precise demarcation of the community united behind the label remained in question, but officials and scholars never doubted that the acquisition of sufficient objective information would provide the answer. The Sarts existed as an organic entity; the problem was to define them precisely. The answers could be sought in the realms of science or history, but not social practice, for how the people defined themselves was of very little importance to the concerns of "science." For physical anthropologists, craniological measurements provided a key to the Truth that was often clouded by social

38. W. Rickmer Rickmers, *The Duab of Turkestan: A Physiographic Sketch and Account of Some Travels* (Cambridge, 1913), 5

conventions of naming. Similarly, although orientalists exhaustively examined the etymology of the term and its occurrences in historical texts, they did not deign to look at how the term was used in actual practice (but then that has never been the concern of orientalism).

The earliest Russian observers often saw no difference between the terms "Sart" and "Tajik." Iu. D. Iuzhakov, arriving in Central Asia with the armies of conquest, reported that the two terms were synonymous and both referred to the sedentary population of the region. His informants, most likely Tatar or Qazaq interpreters, had apparently told him that this population had descended from Jews and Iranians, an explanation he found convincing. Iuzhakov felt he knew the natives well enough to report, "In their terrible greed for money and their thievery, they exceed even the Jews. In their manners, the tone of their conversations, their cowardice, in the pettiness of their interests, and in the complete absence of political tact, they are, precisely, Jews." The fact that some Sarts spoke "their own language . . . a mixture of Turkic and Persian in which the Turkic element strongly predominates," whereas others spoke a variety of Persian, was not of sufficient importance for him to override the common genetic origins as a marker of identity.[39] The stereotypes Iuzhakov used continued to be invoked down to the end of the old regime, but the linguistic distinction, so unimportant to him, soon emerged as all-important, and "Sart" came to be applied in Russian bureaucratic practice exclusively to the Turkic-speaking parts of the sedentary population of Central Asia, while "Tajik" was reserved for those of Iranian speech, the widespread bilingualism ignored for being too cumbersome.

Such a definition of "Sart," which distinguished Sarts from Tajiks on the one hand and other Turkic-speaking Central Asians on the other, proved difficult to establish in practice. Science came to the rescue. A. Bogdanov used craniological data to argue that Sarts and Ozbeks were distinct peoples.[40] The anthropologist N. A. Aristov suggested a narrower definition of "Sart" to rescue the term from popular misuse. Real Sarts were, for Aristov, "sedentary Turks and Turkicized natives who have already lost their tribal way of life and the tribal divisions connected with it," and the term should only be applied to them.[41] The notion of

39. Iu. D. Iuzhakov, "Sarty ili Tadzhiki, glavnoe osedloe naselenie Turkestanskoi oblasti," *Otechestvennye zapiski* 173 (1867): 398–400.

40. A. Bogdanov, "Antropometricheskie zametki otnositel'no turkestanskikh inorodtsev," *Izvestiia Obshchestva liubitelei estestvoznaniia, antropologii i etnografii,* 1888, no. 5, 85–87.

41. N. A. Aristov, "Zametki ob etnicheskom sostave tiurkskikh plemen i svedeniia ob ikh chislennosti," *Zhivaia starina* 6 (1896): 429. Precisely this notion has been resurrected

"Turkicization" also evoked racial admixture (already foreshadowed in Iuzhakov), which proved compelling to the romantic imagination and soon became a characteristic trait of the Sarts.[42] Orientalists, on the other hand, sought the answer in philology. Perhaps the most influential view was formulated by Bartol'd. For Bartol'd, "Sart" was an old Turkic term, of Sanskrit origin, meaning "merchant," which in the post-Mongol period came to be used as a synonym for "Tājik" in referring to bearers of the Persian Muslim culture of the towns, in opposition to the nomadic Turkic culture of the steppe. The distinction between Turk and Tajik was of little interest to the Ozbek conquerors of Central Asia, and after the sixteenth century, "Sart" distinguished the sedentary population of the conquered territory from the conquerors and their allies. Gradually, "under the influence of the conquerors," the town-dwellers began to call themselves Sart, "but the tribal differences between Turks and Tajiks were so great that the representatives of both peoples could not call themselves by the same name. Since the majority of the settled population now spoke Turkic, urban Turks began to be called 'Sarts,' in contradistinction to not just the nomads, but also the Tajiks."[43]

This approach was in many ways typical of the orientalist enterprise. The etymology of the term "Sart" was the key to the business of understanding who the Sarts were. Similarly, if the term appeared in historical sources, then Sarts must exist as "a people," and today's Sarts must have something to do with the Sarts mentioned in those sources. Much of Bartol'd's evidence comes from a few scattered references in historical sources, all produced at court and usually referring only to court elites, which he sees as proof of his fundamental assumption that stable labels refer to stable communities, which retain their organic unity through the ages.[44]

---

in the only post-Soviet discussion of the Sarts: O. M. Bronnikova, "Sarty v etnicheskoi istorii Srednei Azii (k postanovke problemy)," in *Etnosy i etnicheskie protsessy: pamiati R. F. Itsa* (Moscow, 1993), 151–158.

42. This explanation especially found wide acceptance in more popular works; see, e.g., A. Kruber et al., eds., *Aziatskaia Rossiia: illiustrirovannyi geograficheskii sbornik*, 3rd ed. (Moscow, 1910), 189; or V. I. Masal'skii, *Turkestanskii krai* (St. Petersburg, 1913), 392–393.

43. V. V. Bartol'd, "Eshche o slove 'Sart'" (1895), in *Sochineniia*, 9 vols. (Moscow, 1963–1977), II/2: 310–314; see also Barthold, "Sart," 175–176.

44. This is also the approach taken by Yuri Bregel ("The Sarts in the Khanate of Khiva," *Journal of Asian and African History* 12 [1978]: 120–151), who on the basis of literary references to a division of notables among "Sarts" and "Uzbeks" in Khiva concludes that Sarts "were definitely considered by the Uzbeks as a different ethnic group, a

One person not daunted by the complexity of the problem was Ostroumov. In a work titled *Sarts: Ethnographic Sketches,* he reviewed the "scientific" literature on the question for forty pages, but then concluded simply that "Sarts are the sedentary natives, predominantly of the Syr Darya and part of the Ferghana oblasts."[45] (Ostroumov clearly never paused to wonder at the neat coincidence of ethnic distribution with recently created administrative boundaries.) What Ostroumov thought was important, however, because his control of the *TWG* and his stature as an orientalist allowed him to elaborate a Sart language, distinct from Ozbek and other Turkic dialects, as a literary language. Russian orientalism knew the Turkic speech of the sedentary population of Transoxiana as "Sart," and in addition to Ostroumov's exertions at the helm of *TWG,* grammars and dictionaries of the Sart language made their appearance.

"Sart" also appeared as a category in the all-Russian census of 1897. The census made a brave attempt to reduce the empire's ethnic complexity to the simplicity of numbers. Although the census did not have a category for "nationality" as such, it did classify people according to native language, which was believed to be the primary attribute of a nation. The purpose was largely defeated in Central Asia. The census counted Ozbeks and Sarts separately but left a large part of the population classified simply as "Turkic" (*tiurkskii*) (see Table 7). This could have been an attempt to distinguish between "Ozbek" and "Turk"—the census does not make this clear—but since the same classification was used in other regions of the empire for very different groups of Turkic speakers, it confounded not only local statistics but also those at the all-Russian level.[46] (There were other instances of less than consistent usage: In some tables, Tatars were counted separately, but in others they appeared only as speakers of "Turko-Tatar languages." In any case, "Tatar" covered the Turkic languages of the Volga, Urals, Crimea, and

---

different people." Bregel's insistence that the Sarts were distinguished by a specific political position defined "by the role of their [sic] leaders in the government" makes it seem as if the Sart notables who laid claim to certain positions at court actually *represented* other Sarts in the affairs of government. This betrays a misunderstanding of the nature of both power and community in premodern Central Asia, for there is no reason to believe that Sart notables felt any affinity for, or were capable of mobilizing, peasant Sarts in the rest of the country.

45. N. P. Ostroumov, *Sarty. Etnograficheskie materialy (obshchii ocherk),* 3rd ed. (Tashkent, 1908), 3.

46. See comments by Guido Hausmann in Henning Bauer et. al., *Die Nationalitäten des Russischen Reiches in der Volkzählung von 1897,* 2 vols. (Stuttgart, 1991), I: 244–245.

TABLE 7   CLASSIFICATIONS USED BY THE 1897 CENSUS

	Ferghana	Syr Darya	Samarqand	Total
Tajik	114,081	5,558	230,384	350,023
Sart	788,989	144,275	18,073	951,337
Ozbek	153,780	64,235	507,587	725,602
Turk	261,234	158,675	19,993	439,902
Kirgiz	201,579	952,061	63,091	1,216,731
Tatar	852	5,257	450	6,559
Russian	8,140	31,900	12,485	52,525
Others	43,559	116,437	7,958	167,954
Total	1,572,214	1,478,398	860,021	3,910,633

SOURCE: *Pervaia vseobshchaia perepis' naseleniia Rossiiskoi Imperii, 1897 g.,* vols. 83, 86, 89 (St. Petersburg, 1905), table 13.

The basis of classification was native language. "Kirgiz" included both Qazaq and Qïrghïz; "Tatar" included Volga, Crimean, and Transcaucasian ("Azerbaijani") speech.

Transcaucasia.) Nevertheless, enumeration produced new understandings of community. To say that in 1897 in the three core oblasts of Turkestan there were 951,337 Sarts who were only Sarts and nothing else transformed the meaning of the term by abstracting it from the contours of local relations and oppositions.

It is difficult to judge whether the official use had any resonance among the population itself. To be sure, official favor for the term "Sart" led to its use, especially in bureaucratic contexts, and the *TWG* helped popularize the new understanding of the term. This usage was also accepted by Tatar writers, who found the notion of racial admixture as the explanation for the origins of the group quite compelling. The Jadids of Central Asia, however, were resolutely opposed to the label.

Criticism of the official use of the term came as early as 1893, when concern that Russian functionaries should learn local languages led to the creation of language courses for them. One of the languages scheduled to be taught was Sart. Sher Ali Lapin, whom we will encounter again in Chapter 8, an interpreter in the chancellery of the governor of Samarqand oblast and a Qazaq himself, argued in a lecture that "there is neither a Sart people, nor a Sart language." Rather, the word was a contraction of *sarï it,* "yellow dog," a derogatory appellation used by Qazaq and Qïrghïz nomads for all sedentary people, regardless of origin. "We have no basis for calling the language of the Sarts 'Sart,' since the language of the Sarts includes both Tajik and the language of the sedentary Ozbeks; therefore the language should be called . . . the Ozbek language, in the dialect of the sedentary Ozbeks."[47]

Lapin was taken to task by Bartol'd, then working on his doctorate in Tashkent, who was surprised that "Mr. Lapin decided to speak with such aplomb about things with which he apparently has not the slightest acquaintance." Rejecting the explanation of the origin of the term put forward by Lapin as mere folk etymology, Bartol'd fixed the explanation in the proper realm of high culture, citing references to the term in the literary and historical sources of the post-Mongol period.[48] When Lapin had the temerity to reply in print, Bartol'd heaped further condescension on him. Writing in *Turkestanskie vedomosti,* where Lapin had responded, Bartol'd presented a long list of faulty citations and misquotations committed by Lapin, before concluding: "In printing Mr. Lapin's article, the editors proceeded from the opinion that the inclination to scientific work on the part of a native in any case represents a gratifying phenomenon that must be supported by every means. No one disputes this; but no one expects native writers to attain at once the scientific standards established by European science as a result of long experience."[49] Having crushed the native beneath the weight of the long experience of European science, Bartol'd went on to indulge in orientalism's fetish with literary etymologies, elaborating in the process his theory of the origins of Sart. No more was heard from the native side for a decade and a half.

When the issue arose next, it was taken up with the Tatars, who used the term routinely. In 1911, Behrām-bek Dawlatshāev, the highest-ranking interpreter in Bukharan service, broached the topic in *Shura,* perhaps the most respected magazine in the Tatar world. "Are we Sarts or Turks?" he asked the editors in the regular question-and-answer section of the magazine. Turkestan means "the land of the Turks," he asked, "so why is it that we are called 'Sarts'? Is it that in earlier times Turks lived in this 'land of the Turks,' but later left it, leaving their name behind? If so, then where did the people called 'Sart,' that is, us, come from and when? . . . And how is it that we inherited Turkic literature? Did the Turks

47. Quoted in Bartol'd, "O prepodavanii tuzemnykh narechii v Samarkande" (1894), in his *Sochineniia,* II/2: 303–304.
48. Ibid.
49. Bartol'd, "Vmesto otveta g-nu Lapinu" (1894), in *Sochineniia,* II/2: 308–309.

leave it to us? Or did we take it, and the land, from them by force?"[50]
And so forth. No Tatar writer responded, but Behbudi joined in with a
lengthy article in which he argued that the origins of the word "Sart"
were unknown and that it was used pejoratively only by the northern
neighbors of Central Asia (Qazaqs and Tatars, from whom the Russians
took it). "Upon asking Qazaqs 'Whom do you call a "Sart,"' I usually
received the answer, 'Those who travel around our steppe' (meaning all
traders)." The term was not used by those labeled "Sart" themselves,
Behbudi further argued: "Those who have no interaction with the Russians or are unfamiliar with the press think it is the Russian word for
'Muslim.'" Finally, Behbudi noted, there were ninety-two tribes in Turkestan, but none was called Sart.[51]

Behbudi was backed by his friend Baqā Khoja, who in a long article
denied the existence of a Sart people. "The inhabitants of Turkestan,
that is, Turan and Transoxiana, are, from the point of view of race and
nationality [jinsiyat wa qawmiyat], predominantly Turks and Tajiks."
The opposition of Turk and Tajik had become a metaphor among "oriental poets," but neither old Arabic, nor Persian histories, geographies,
or dictionaries contained the word "Sart." Quoting Russian authors in
the original, he went on to show the many, often contradictory, explanations given for the word. "To call the Ozbek Turkic inhabitants of the
five oblasts of Russian Turkestan and the khanates of Bukhara and
Khiva 'Sart' is an injustice, the despotism of opinion, the cause of doubt
and division; [in short,] a huge mistake."[52]

The same conclusions were reached by Dawlatshāev when he himself
answered the question he had raised. The matter was simple: "We Turkestanis are Turkic Ozbeks who belong to more than one hundred tribes
[awmāq] of the Mongol people [qawm] and the Turkic race [urugh]."
The proof was simple and lay in the Turkic speech and literature of the
region, as well as in its ruling dynasties. The 92 tribes "renowned from
olden times to the present" had increased to over 100, he argued, and he
appended a list of 111 tribal names then current. "Now, if foisting the
name 'Sart' on [the population of] Turkestan, composed of 'more than
a hundred Turk-Mongol tribes,' whose history, literature, language, and

50. *Shura*, 15 August 1911, 504.
51. Mahmud Khoja bin Behbud Khoja, "Sart söze mäjhuldur," *Shura*, 1 October 1911, 581–582.
52. Samarqandi Baqā Khoja bin Sayyid Hādi Khoja, "Sart söze asïlsïzdïr," *Shura*, 15
December 1911, 754–757.

customs are Turkic, is not an injustice, what is?"[53] The debate flared up again, but this time in Behbudi's *Āyina,* in early 1914, in response to an article by the young Bashkir historian Ahmed Zeki Velidi in which he spoke of "Sarts." Behrām-bek Dawlatshāev again expressed his displeasure with "those writers who, not knowing that we Turkestanis belong to over a hundred Turkic tribes, call us 'Sart,' as well as those who, knowing full well that we are Turks, call us 'Sart' by way of insult."[54] Two weeks later, *Āyina* published an open letter with seven signatures expressing displeasure over the use of the term "Sart" when "everyone knows that the population of Turkestan is composed of Ozbek, that is Turkic, Tajik, that is, Persian [*Fārs khalqi*], and Arab (Khoja) groups."[55] Behbudi took this opportunity to republish the 1911 articles from *Shura* in modified form.[56]

Beyond such "ethnographic" debates, "Ozbek" also appeared occasionally in Jadid literature as synonymous with the nation. In a poem published in 1916, for instance, Hamza used *Turkistān eli* ("the people of Turkestan") and *Ozbek eli* ("the Ozbek people") interchangeably in exhorting the nation to "not sleep in this age of progress."[57]

Not everyone in Central Asia shared the Jadids' position. Not surprisingly, *TWG* took the lead in criticizing the Jadids. A student from Osh wrote in 1913 to criticize those who wanted to protest the use of the term on two counts. First, "Sart" was not a pejorative term but rather carried connotations of "royal descent" and "philosopher." Second, the author asked if a change in terminology would make the people of Turkestan stronger or more developed?[58] Other writers argued that this search for roots was a form of nationalism and divisive of the Muslim community and that labels were not important, since "the name of the renowned and developed *Nemets* [German] nation comes from the word *nimoi,* which means 'mute.' But they respect this name and do not worry about changing it. They have not lagged behind because of this name, but are the most developed; the cause for their renown is not their name, but their good morals."[59] An author, writing under the pseudonym "Sart,

53. Behram-bek Dawlatshaev, "Türkistanlïlar," *Shura,* 1 January 1913, 12–15.
54. Behrām-bek Dawlatshāh, "Sārt masalasi," *Āyina,* 19 February 1914, 300.
55. "Tashkanddan gila=opka," *Āyina,* 1 March 1914, 354.
56. "Sart sozi majhuldur!" *Āyina,* 22 March 1914, 314–315; 29 March 1914, 338–340; 5 April 1914, 362–365; 12 April 1914, 386–388; 19 April. 1914, 478–480.
57. Hamza, "Dardiga darmon istamas," in *Tŏla asarlar tŏplami,* ed. N. Karimov et al., 5 vols. (Tashkent, 1988–1989), II: 29–30.
58. Mirzā Qādirjān Qābiljānbāyev, "Haqqāniyat," *TWG,* 10 January 1913.
59. Mullā Ālim, "Po povodu pis'ma o slove 'Sart'," *TWG,* 20 January 1913.

son of Sart [*Sart oghli sart*]," contended that "we Sarts do not hate the name, since our faith does not consider names and lineages important." [60]

Nevertheless, the Jadids' opposition to the term "Sart" was significant for various reasons. In disowning it, the Jadids were as far from the pre-Russian usage of "Sart" as a social marker as were Russian scholars and functionaries, but whereas the latter searched for the nation hiding behind the label, the Jadids rejected it because, they argued, there was no nation there. Nations were objective identities, but their objectivity was defined by race; hence the concern with biological origins, which made Tajiks into Iranians and Khojas into Arabs. The fact that Behbudi, with his cosmopolitan tastes, moderate politics, and Muslim education, was so prominent in demanding the use of the "proper" names for the people of Central Asia indicated how far Turkism had crept in around the edges into local discourses of identity. "In our age, the 'national' [*milliyat*] question has taken precedence over the question of religion among Europeans," wrote a writer who unfortunately remained anonymous, "so there is no harm if we too occasionally discuss the 'Sart' question, which is considered a national question, and thus remember our nation." [61] Indeed, the Tatar writer Abdurrauf Muzaffar made the point, quite popular in Ottoman circles at the time, that "religion exists only on the basis of the nation and national life. . . . A religion without a nation is destroyed." [62]

It is equally important that criticism of the use of "Sart" was directed against Turkist authors. The discourse of Turkism was polyphonic, and the debate described above was an attempt by Central Asian writers to define their own version of Turkism. More significant, especially with hindsight, is the fact that the distinction between "Ozbek" and "Turk" disappears entirely. The ninety-two tribes mentioned by Behbudi were the ninety-two tribes of the Ozbek confederation in the aftermath of the Shaybāni conquest of Transoxiana and did not encompass the entire Turkic-speaking population of the region. No wonder, then, that they turn into "more than one hundred tribes" in the hands of Dawlatshāev. Ozbekness became, for the Jadids, a defining feature of the Turkic-speaking population of Central Asia. We are reminded of Wickmer's ob-

---

60. Sart oghli Sart, "Otvet zhurnalu 'Aina'," *TWG,* 27 April, 1 and 4 May 1914. The pseudonym is significant, since this form was popular with Turkist authors in the Ottoman empire.

61. "Sārt sozi maʿlum bolmādi," *Āyina,* 19 July 1914, 923.

62. A. Muzaffar, "Din millat, millat milliyat ila qāimdir," *ST,* 26 November 1914; 2 December 1914; 10 December 1914.

servation that "Sart" was used to denote all "unmarked" Turcophone groups of Central Asia. In Jadid parlance, that meaning of "Sart" was being translated into "Ozbek." This also applied to the name of the language, which was often equated with Ozbek in this period. In the early 1920s, all the "marked" groups of Central Asia (Türkmen, Qazaq, Qïrghïz, and, eventually, Tājik) were carved away from Turkestan, and the remaining Turcophone population became the modern Uzbek nation. The roots of these momentous changes are to be found in local discourses before 1917. The modern nations of Central Asia were not simply the work of an imperial Soviet regime bent on dividing its subject populations, the better to conquer them; rather, their origins lie in new ways of imagining the world and Central Asia's place within it. Similarly, the abolition of the term "Sart" in the early Soviet period was not "evidence of [the] ignorance of those who governed Turkestan at that time," as Yuri Bregel snidely claims, but rather the outcome of very real politics surrounding Central Asian identity in a revolutionary age.[63]

The insistence on the "proper" identification of peoples led to the disaggregation of the sedentary population along newly drawn ethnic lines. The most difficult disentanglement was that of the Tājiks. The longstanding dichotomy of Turk and Tajik was invested with new meaning. Now the difference was seen to reside in the realm of nature and was described in a new language, such as in this description of the Tajiks of Bukhara that appeared in *Shura:* "Although the Tajiks are Iranian and their language Persian, their religion is Sunni. Their name emerged from their animosity toward the Shi'is. . . . Their faces are straight, their women renowned for their beauty. They are assiduous and masters of commerce, but [also] deceptive and have low morals."[64] The low levels of morality and general effeteness of the Tajiks, taken whole cloth from contemporary European anthropology, appear quite frequently in Jadid writing. Criticisms of the maktab often carried an anti-Iranian subtext. A Jadid schoolteacher complained that although old-style maktab teachers "are Turks, [they] do not know their mother tongue and do not teach it, but rather look upon it . . . with hatred. Instead, they waste the poor children's time with Persian fairy tales and puzzles, whose harmfulness in the present day is quite obvious."[65]

63. Bregel, "The Sarts of the Khanate of Khiva," 121n.
64. "Bukhara mamleketi," *Shura,* 1 February 1910, 101.
65. Dāda Mirzā Qāri, "Muallim wa shāgirdlar," *Āyina,* 14 December 1913, 183–4.

This re-visioning of identity remained an exercise in *exclusion,* since we have little evidence of any parallel assertion of Iranian or Tajik (or Aryan) identity among the Iranophone population of Central Asia. The few instances in which romantic notions of Iranianness appeared in print were all connected with the Turkist enterprise. The Transcaucasian editor of *Bukhārā-yi sharīf* published a language tree that placed Persian in its "proper" Aryan context. In another issue we read: "There are [between] 10 million and 12 million Muslims in Turkestan, Transoxiana, Bukhara, and Khiva. Approximately 7 million of them are Ozbeks, Turkmens, and Qïrghïz Qazaq, who belong to Turanian nations [*umam-i tūrāniya*], and are Turks; their national language is Ozbek or Chaghatay Turkic. The remaining [sic] 2 million are Tajiks, who belong to the Aryan nations [*umam-i āriyāniya*], and are of Iranian origins; their literary language is also Persian." [66] Beyond this, however, there was little discussion of Tajik or Iranic identity in Central Asia until well into the 1920s.

WATAN

Patriotism (*watanparwarlik*) was also an important virtue for the Jadids. Abdullah Awlāni placed it in the realm of nature when he suggested that even animals and birds love the place where they are born. Because of this natural feeling, Arabs continue to live in their blistering hot deserts and Eskimos in the cold north, "just as we Turkestanis love our homeland more than our lives." [67] In its traditional meaning, the term *watan* meant merely one's birthplace. By the period under consideration, however, it had been attached to the nation, although its boundaries remained ambiguous. The Jadids used the term in many different ways. The most common use of "watan" was to denote Turkestan in the Russian administrative sense of the term. At other times, its extent was vaguer, incorporating the protectorates and even Chinese Turkestan, and after the outbreak of war in 1914 "watan" often meant the Russian empire. But these were all purely territorial designations. The millat and the watan defined each other in the most common designation of the nation, the Muslims of Turkestan. Similarly, the term "Turān," which became quite popular in the early twentieth century in Central Asia (it was borne by three different newspapers, and Awlāni used it for

66. B. Kh., "Amārat-i Bukhārā," *Bukhārā-yi sharīf,* 28 March 1912.
67. Abdullah Awlāni, *Turki Gulistān, yākhud akhlāq* (Tashkent, 1914), 36.

a reading room and a theater troupe he organized) did not carry the baggage attached to it by Turkists elsewhere. Rather, in Central Asia it signified "Russian Central Asia" (Turkestan, Bukhara, and Khiva), as when Behbudi wrote of "the 20 million Muslims in Russia, of which half are us Turānis." [68]

But romantic discourses had begun to encroach on this notion and to impart to it a new meaning. In its extreme formulation, this new understanding of Turkestan as the homeland of the Turks differed markedly from its premodern usage (which in Persian had connoted the land where Turks, as opposed to Iranians, predominated, just as there was an Arabistan and a Hindustan), for it now came with claims of political primacy (and ultimately sovereignty) and cultural hegemony for the nation to whom the homeland "belonged." As such, it was profoundly subversive of the symbiosis of Turks and Iranians that had existed in Transoxiana for several centuries. This was explicitly stated by the Istanbul Turkist journal *Türk Yurdu,* which criticized the fact that *Bukhārā-yi sharīf* was being published in Persian "when [Bukhara's] people are entirely Turks and children of Turks [*Türk oğlu Türk*]." [69] Elsewhere, the same journal expressed the hope that "since the Bukharans are all Turks, the situation [of Persian being the official language] will change in the near future. The official language and the publications of [this] Turkic state will of course be Turkic, and the Persian language will be used, to an extent proportionate to their numbers, only for the few Tajiks who have immigrated from Iran." [70] This argument was reproduced almost intact by Dawlatshāev, who claimed that Turān, the land north of the Amu Daryā, had always been Turkic, and that the prevalence of Persian speech, limited in any case only to the three cities of Bukhara, Samarqand, and Khujand, was the result of forced migrations of Iranian population by the Turkic Ozbek khans of Bukhara in previous centuries, and of the high esteem for Persian literature among urban sophisticates. [71] The claim was preposterous, of course (and perhaps because of this it has resonated ever since in nationalist discourses in Central Asia) but, given the basic premises of the new notions of identity, logical in its own way. Nevertheless, it is important to keep in mind that although the essential Turkicness of Turkestan was thus asserted, it did not automatically imply that it was

68. "Sadā-yi Turkistān, Sadā-yi Farghāna, yākhud Turānning ekizik=tuwwām farzandlari," *Āyina,* 12 April 1914, 392.
69. "Buhara-yı Şerif Gazetesi," *Türk Yurdu,* 1 (1912): 376.
70. "Turan Gazetesi," *Türk Yurdu,* 2 (1912): 631.
71. Dawlatshaev, "Tükistanlïlar," 14.

the homeland of *all* Turks or that all Turks had equal claims to it. The Central Asians might be Turks, but for the Jadids they were so on their own terms. Even as they discovered common ties with other Turkic peoples, the Jadids drew lines marking themselves off from them.

LANGUAGE

If the rhetoric of the homeland marked Central Asians off from other Turks and Muslims implicitly, debates over language did so quite explicitly. At bottom lay the brand-new idea that (as a local author put it) "every nation takes pride in its language."[72] Language had never served as a marker of identity in Central Asia, and the idea that an individual should work and feel pride in his or her native language would have been incomprehensible a generation earlier. Romantic notions of nationhood were partly the cause, but the real change came with schooling. If functional literacy was a desired goal, it had to be achieved only in the child's native language. A central point in the Jadids' criticism of the old maktab was that a number of texts used in it were in Persian, which the children could not understand. The need for textbooks written in the vernacular led to the elaboration of a modern literary Central Asian Turkic language.

The fact that the maktab did not teach language as such now came to be seen as a major shortcoming. Before it could be taught as a subject, however, language had to be abstracted from lived experience and rendered into an object of study. This process began with the publication in 1916 of a volume on orthography by Āshura Ali Zāhiri.[73] At the same time, the Jadids hoped to simplify the written language and bring it closer to speech. The process was not simple, of course, as models, both lexical and grammatical, were borrowed indiscriminately from Tatar and Ottoman.[74] Jadid authors began to use new letters to represent the phonemes /ŋ/ and /v/. But the trend toward simplification by ridding the language of borrowings from Persian and Arabic, common to all Turkic languages of the period, and underlain again by romantic notions of authenticity, was less successful in Central Asia than anywhere else. Authors commonly doubled more arcane (Arabic and Persian) words

72. S.A., "Har millat oz tilidan fakhr etar," *Āyina*, 21 June 1914, 836–838.

73. Āshur Ali Zāhiri, *Imlā* (Kokand, 1916).

74. A.K. Borovkov, *Uzbekskii literaturnyi iazyk v period 1905–1917 gg.* (Tashkent, 1940).

with their more popular (Turkic) equivalents, using the sign of equality as a punctuation mark, but there was little interest in a more thorough-going purification of the language.[75]

The logic of simplifying and rendering the written language closer to the spoken led to the crystallization of distinct literary standards. The history of the transition of numerous Turkic dialects from speech to print languages is a contentious matter. Turkists insist that all Turkic languages are essentially a single language, arguing that the distinction between Turkic and Turkish does not exist in Turkic languages and that the distinctions between the "dialects" have been imposed by the divide-and-rule policies of the Soviet regime. The argument is specious, since it misrepresents the situation until the nineteenth century and refuses to acknowledge the transition from spoken to print language undergone by all Turkic languages since then.

Historically, *Turki/Turkcha* referred not to a single language but to a range of dialects sharing a common grammatical structure. Until the nineteenth century, two literary standards coexisted, each with its own orthographic conventions and rules of syntax. However, because literary standards were as much about virtuosity as about communication, their connection with spoken speech was minimal. The roots of the Turkist contention lie in the late nineteenth century, when Gasprinskii, motivated by the hope of bringing about the unity of deed, thought, and language (*Ishte, fikirde, dilde birlik,* in his words) among the Turks of the world, sought to create a common literary language out of the numerous dialects that had begun to appear in print. This hope became a fundamental plank of Turkist thought, for if Turks were a single nation, then they had to share a common language. *Terjüman,* written in a simplified form of Ottoman, was widely read throughout the Turkic world, but the rapid rise of Tatar as a literary language at the end of the century put paid to the hope of creating a common Turkic language. The Transcaucasian press also retained peculiarities of local speech in its orthography. Written in the Arabic script, which concealed differences in vowels, all these variants remained mutually comprehensible in written form, but clearly local variants had emerged as full-fledged languages. The market and the ideal of schooling in the vernacular (with the emphasis on comprehension and literacy) combined to create new literary languages out of mere dialects. For literary languages are not a product of nature but are cre-

75. Indeed, Behbudi ridiculed very modest suggestions in *ST* for the purification of language; see his "Til masalasi," *Āyina,* 2 April 1915, 274–277; 16 April 1915, 306–311.

ated historically through complex interactions of states, markets, and academies. Ultimately, the best analogy for the development of the Turkic languages is to be drawn with the manner in which imperial courts, national markets, and (later) academies marked off ranges of Romance dialects into the national languages of today. Some, such as French, Spanish, and Italian, became "national" literary languages, while others, such as Catalan and Provençal, remained (at least until recently) dialects. The Soviet period was different in the systematic manner in which languages were delineated one from another, but the process had begun well before 1917.

In Central Asia, where the spoken language was close to the literary standard of Chaghatay Turkic (which has the same relation to the Uzbek of today that Ottoman has to modern Turkish), the debates about the creation of a common language around a modified Ottoman, so dear to Gasprinskii, had little appeal. The only trace of this debate in the Jadid press of Central Asia is a short piece by Hāji Muin. Titled "On Language Unity," the piece is notable more for its brevity and casual tone than for its content. There was little to indicate that the article addressed a burning issue of the day. Hāji Muin wrote: "In my opinion, the first step in this direction would be to replace the words not understood by most Turks with those understood by all." He went on to provide a list of words that Tatar authors might replace with their Chaghatay equivalents.[76] The problem would be solved if the Tatars deferred to Central Asians.

The language of Central Asia might have been called "Turkic" (*turki, turkcha*), but it was always qualified as "Turkestan Turkic" (*Turkistān shewasi, Turkistān shewa-yi turkiyasi*). Similarly, primary school textbooks in Central Asia were avowedly written in "Turkestani Turkic" (*Turkistān shewasida, āchiq tilda*), as was prominently displayed on their title pages. This was to be a common language for all of Turkestan but *not* one common to all of Turks of the world. Local authors whose writings bore Tatar or Ottoman influences were criticized for not writing in Central Asian Turkic. A reader criticized Awlāni on this count: "Only a person who knows Ottoman [*usmānlicha*] can understand his poems. Now, at least Ottoman is a delicious and very literary dialect [*lehja*]; but what do we have to do with Tatar, which neither our literati, nor our stu-

76. Hāji Muin ibn Shukrullah, "Til birlāshdurmāq haqqinda," *Āyina*, 4 January 1914, 259–260.

dents know?"[77] There were instances when local newspapers refused to print articles because they were not in the local language.[78] Reviews of theatrical performances published in the Jadid press often criticized Transcaucasian Muslims and (especially) Tatars, who were prominent in the first years of modern theater, for declaiming in their own languages, which, according to the reviewers, were not easily understood by the audience.[79]

But what was the "Turkestan Turkic" to be? Behbudi's *Āyina* was published, according to the Turkic inscription on the title page, in "Turkic and Persian [*turki wa fārsi orta shewada*];" the Russian inscription on the same page, however, described those languages and "Ozbek and Persian [*na uzbekskom i persidskom iazykakh*]." Much as the Jadids had come to see the "unmarked" Turkic population of Central Asia as Ozbek, so they saw its Turkic speech as Ozbek. The roots of modern Uzbek predate the Soviet regime.

THE MUSLIMS OF TURKESTAN

"Of course," Behbudi concluded his article criticizing the use of the term "Sart," "they will ask, 'What should we call you if we can't call you Sart?' The answer is very easy: the Ozbeks of Turkestan, the Tajiks, Arabs, Turks, Russians, Jews of Turkestan. If they say, 'We're unable to distinguish the Turks, Arabs, and Persians [*Fārsi*] of Turkestan from one another, and need a name common to all,' we say, 'Write "the Muslims of Turkestan [*Turkistān musulmānlari*]."'"[80] The Muslims of Turkestan constituted the Jadids' nation. It was a secular nationalism in which concern for the welfare of Muslims firmly took precedence over questions of religious doctrine. Jadid affinities extended beyond Central Asia, and the Muslims of Central Asia were part of larger communities (the Muslims of Russia and the Muslims of the whole world), nonetheless the politically significant identity remained the local, territorial one. The Muslims of Turkestan were to form the most significant node of solidarity in 1917.

77. Rasuli, "Shāir wa milli she'rlarimiz," *Āyina*, 14 February 1915, 214. Such disdain for Tatar was not unusual; Behbudi once called it "a corrupt and base dialect": "Khātirāt-i Farghāna," *Shuhrat*, 8 January 1908.

78. See, for example, the editorial response to M. Mirzā Hamidzāda (probably a Transcaucasian Muslim) in *SF*, 9 October 1914.

79. "Samarqanda [sic] tiyātir," *Āyina*, 1 February 1914, 262; "Bukhārāda milli tiyātir," *Āyina*, 22 March 1914, 326; "Katta Qorghānda tiyātir," *Āyina*, 29 March 1914, 349.

80. Mahmud Khoja [Behbudi], "Sārt sozi majhuldur," *Āyina*, 19 April 1914, 480.

At the same time, romantic notions of community had seeped deep into Central Asian discourses. The Jadids professed profound interest in their "national" origins. Acts of implicit exclusion came to define the Muslims of Turkestan primarily as Turks, and those Turks primarily as Ozbeks. However, these acts remained implicit until late 1917, when events forced a changed. In the meantime, the territorial, confessional, and national identities coexisted, as the following "Categories of Islam," taken from Munawwar Qāri's primer for new-method schools, show: "Arab Turk Fārs Ozbek Noghāy Tātār Bāshqurd Persiyān [sic] Cherkes Lezgin Tekke Turkman Afghān Qāzāq Qirghiz Qipchāq Tungān Taranchi Hanafi Shafi'i Māliki Hanbali Ja'fari. All of them believe in the existence and unity of God and the prophecy of Muhammad, on whom be peace."[81]

81. Munawwar Qāri, *Adib-i awwal* (Tashkent, 1912), 30.

CHAPTER 7

Navigating the Nation

The recentering of social vision on the nation brought with it new responsibilities and new claims to leadership. The Jadids claimed to be motivated by the good of the nation, while their criticism of various groups in society emanated from the perception that these groups were not playing their proper role in the development of their community. Jadid authors routinely decried the selfishness and parochialism of their opponents, whether wealthy merchants who spent their money on extravagant feasts or traditionalist ulama who opposed the new method. More pertinently, it was the Jadids who, in the name of the nation, claimed the authority to define social roles and obligations for the new age. If the Jadids were important to the nation, so too was the nation important to them.

Overtly political action directed at the state occupied only a small part in the struggles of the Jadids before 1917. The possibilities for such action remained slim, even after 1905, as Turkestan's colonial position dictated its marginalization from the empire's experiment with quasiconstitutionalism. When the greater self-assurance of the Jadids by 1914 led many of them to engage in politics, their strategies were defined by the twin needs of working within the existing legal framework and of asserting their claim to speak for the nation in the political realm. The nation of the Jadids was located at a specific point in Turkestani society, which their universal claims sought to hide. The Jadids' own position in society thus shaped their political action in fundamental ways.

THE LOCATION OF THE NATION

In attempting to locate the nation of the Jadids in society, we might begin by examining more closely their dire warnings about extinction and destruction. Whose survival was at stake? Quite clearly, there was no threat to the physical existence of the population of Central Asia in the way that was conceivable for, say, the Crimean Tatars. There was also no pressure of assimilation through proselytization or forced conversion, as had been the case with the Volga Tatars (which had left a deep imprint on Tatar Jadidism). Rather, the fear was of something else. For Behbudi, it was "imperative [that we] reform our schools, our shops, our workshops, our madrasas, [in short] everything, according to the needs of the age. Otherwise, we will lose everything and nothing will be left for us except menial labor."[1] This fear of immiseration appears again and again in Jadid writing. The extinction that the Jadids warned about was the extinction of the elites of Muslim society.

The challenge therefore was to create an elite that could participate in the new imperial economy. The clearest expression of this again comes from Behbudi, who as a man of substance and consequently moderate tastes in politics realized the need to work through the system, a position that his generally cautious approach to politics tended to confirm. "We Muslims constitute the second largest nation [*millat*] in the Russian empire," he claimed at a fund-raising event during the First World War, "but unfortunately, in the affairs of government . . . we are one of the smallest. . . . In order to benefit from the state and to enter government office, we must send our children to government schools."[2] Elsewhere, Behbudi suggested that money spent by the wealthy on ostentatious feasts would be much better spent providing children with an education that would allow them to become "judges, lawyers, engineers, teachers [*zamāna maktabdāri*], the supporters and servants of the community, i.e., deputies to the State Duma, technicians to reform our workshops [*milli sanaatkhānalarimiz*], people who have studied the science of commerce to help us in commercial establishments and banks, i.e., men of commerce, [as well as] to develop people who, in city dumas and in the zemstvos to be introduced in the future for the Russian homeland [*watan*], would work for the true faith of Islam, for the weak and the poor."[3]

1. Behbudi, "Ihtiyāj-i millat," *Samarqand*, 12 July 1913.
2. "Sharq aqshamindagi nutq," *Āyina*, 2 April 1915, 285.
3. [Behbudi], "Āmālimiz yā inki murādimiz," *Āyina*, 7 December 1913, 155.

Other Jadids might have held a less rosy picture of the possibilities, but they shared Behbudi's basic attitudes. We need only recall the happiness brought by knowledge to characters in the fiction of Cholpān and Hamza (see Chapter 5) to understand this basic vision of success. Participation in the imperial mainstream thus became the Jadids' fundamental political goal.

Such elites would be able to undermine the Russian-native dichotomy that had framed Central Asian life since the conquest. The solution was not assimilation or Russification, however, but the modernization of Turkestani society. The new elite was to be modern but also Muslim and Turkestani. Jadid authors criticized those in Central Asia who aped Russian ways simply for the sake of imitation. Ubaydullah Khojaev once wrote that "wearing Russian dress in the way of education or official service is harmless, even required. It is a different matter when people put on a suit to look like Russians or to speak with Russian girls."[4] (Of course, the distinction was hard to make, and many of the Jadids' opponents did not make it at all; for them, the Jadids were no different from the dandies criticized by the Jadids.) Similarly, the Jadids were at one with Russian officialdom in exhorting Central Asians to learn Russian,[5] but they also criticized those who used Russian words indiscriminately in vernacular speech. Abdullah Awlāni even elevated "preservation of the language [*hifz-i lisān*]" to the status of a moral trait: "Learning Russian, the language of the state, is as necessary for our life and happiness as bread and food, but it is essential to keep it in its own place. Mixing [words] up like kedgeree cooked in linseed oil destroys the spirit of a language.... [and] the loss of the national language is the loss of the soul of the nation."[6]

This was also why new-method schools were so essential. Russo-native schools offered a similar (or, as officialdom insisted, better) curriculum, but the Jadids' enthusiasm for them was always equivocal (even when some of them taught in such schools). Although Turkestani Jadids did not always share the harsh views of these schools held by Tatars, who saw in them a missionary plot, they nevertheless felt that Russo-native schools devoted inadequate time to teaching articles of the Muslim faith and taught "Russian to seven-year-old children who do not even know their

4. Response to A. Muhammadov, "Kiyum masalasi," *ST*, 24 May 1914.
5. M. R., "Luzūm-i dānistan-i zabān-i khārijī," *Bukhārā-yi sharīf*, 12 April 1912; Mir Muhsin Shermuhammadov, "Ahwālimizgha bir nazar," *TWG*, 19 January 1914; "Rus lisānining ahamiyati," *ST*, 17 May 1914.
6. Abdullah Awlāni, *Turki Gulistān, yākhud akhlāq* (Tashkent, 1914), 45.

own language." [7] Future members of the elite had to master their own faith and language before they could join the battle in the wider world.

Reform required resources that only money could buy. "In today's world, bravery resides in wealth . . . because people are necessary in order to have sovereignty; people require skills; skills require knowledge; and knowledge requires money." [8] And it worked both ways, for wealth was a sign of success in the new economy, the just desert for effort and zeal. Jadid authors came to see the existence of millionaires as the sign of the progress of the community to which they belonged. Upon arriving in Baku on his way to Istanbul in 1914, Behbudi noted with approval that "in terms of the extent of Muslim wealth, this is the second city in Russia. Here there are several Muslims who own property and capital worth 100 million rubles; Muslim millionaires number more than 100, and the number of those worth half a million is even greater. There are thousands of Muslims worth 100,000 [rubles], while those whose capital is worth between 20,000 and 30,000 rubles number in the tens of thousands. Most of the property in this city is in the hands of Muslims. May God increase [their wealth]!" [9] Behbudi's numbers are, of course, exaggerated, but his fascination with the numbers of wealthy Muslims was widely shared by his contemporaries (and in later decades used as damning evidence of the Jadids' bourgeois nationalism). The wealth of individuals was the wealth of the community and could (and should) be put to the communal good. For Awlāni, all members of a society were interconnected: "The rich man depends on the poor, the poor on the rich; the teacher on the student, the student on the teacher; the parents on the child, and the child on the parents." [10] At first sight this differs little from views long held in the Muslim tradition, but Awlāni made service to the nation the yardstick for judging all actions. The proper functioning of society required that all its members recognize their duties to the nation. In more developed nations, these mutual dependencies were clearly recognized, and the Jadid press pointed to government expenditures on education or health in various countries, or to acts of organized philanthropy, as evidence of this. When Mirzā Sirāj toured Europe, he saw the fact that the theater he visited in Berlin cost 100 million marks to build,

7. "Turkistān maktablari," *ST,* 22 April 1914; similar opinions were expressed by Behbudi, who usually bent over backward to advocate the learning of Russian (*Samarqand,* 9 May 1913).

8. Awlāni, *Turki Gulistān,* 23.

9. Mahmud Khoja [Behbudi], "Sayāhat khātiralari—II," *Āyina,* 21 June 1914, 834.

10. Awlāni, *Turki Gulistān,* 54.

or that tens of millions of marks were spent on the construction alone of the university in the same city, as evidence of the zeal of the people of Germany.[11]

Such views of society and social responsibility might be naive, but do they make the Jadids the ideologues of a nascent bourgeoisie, the chauvinist bourgeois nationalists of Soviet lore? The nation as imagined by the Jadids was, as we shall see, narrowly based in certain urban groups, and its core was provided by the wealthy. However, the wealthy were to be celebrated only as long as they fulfilled their duties to their community as defined by the Jadids. This they did only seldom, and far more prevalent in Jadid literature are criticisms of the wealthy for *not* fulfilling their duties properly. Ultimately, the Jadids' claim to leadership was in their own right. It was as intellectuals that the Jadids sought to set the direction for their society. "It is well known," wrote Awlāni, "that the progress and exaltation of every nation comes from valuing the service of those who serve it with their lives, money, and pens. By celebrating the brave scholars and poets of the past with stipends, statues, and the pen, [other nations] increase the courage and zeal of those who work [for the glory of the nation]."[12] The assertion of moral authority by new intellectuals had its problems. Awlāni found his own situation rather different, for he complained that "unfortunately, we [Turkestanis], far from valuing such people, scorn them and even call them infidels [*takfir qilmak*]."[13] If the nation was a phenomenon of the modern age, a fact the Jadids well recognized, then it needed modern leadership, which only the Jadids could provide. They were to make this claim a significant feature of their bid for leadership in 1917.

The rhetoric of the nation served to conceal the Jadids' own position in their society and their vision of its functioning. That rhetoric precluded discourses of class, of which the Jadids had the greatest suspicion. Behbudi wrote of the Social Democratic party in 1906: "Our present epoch is not propitious for carrying out their program. . . . Their wishes appear fantastic and joining this party is extremely dangerous for us Muslims."[14] The radical transformation of society advocated by this

---

11. Mirzā Sirājiddīn Hāji Mirzā 'Abdurra'ūf, *Safarnāma-yi tuhaf-i Bukhārā*, ed. M. Asadiyān (Tehran, 1992, [orig. 1911]), 117, 120.

12. Awlāni, *Turki Gulistān*, 53.

13. Ibid.

14. Al-Hāji Mahmud Khoja walad-i Qāri Behbud Khoja, "Khayr ul-umur awsatihā," *Khurshid*, 11 October 1906. This suspicion marked Jadid thinkers throughout the Russian empire; Musa Jarullah Bigi, the prominent Tatar Jadid, expressed very similar sen-

party would be highly intrusive of Muslim society, its cultural practices and its solidarities, and, in the process, would jeopardize the Jadids' claim to lead reform. Of course, the predominance of Russians in the industrial work force in Turkestan, and the complete unwillingness of Russian socialist parties to attract their "native" co-workers to their cause, meant that Behbudi's fears remained largely groundless. Meanwhile, the older solidarities of craft guilds had been severely disrupted by the advent of capitalism. By the turn of the century, guild lodges (*takiya*) were reported to be in disuse.[15] Caught in this transformation, Muslim artisans and craftsmen could not formulate a voice of their own.

Although the Jadids spoke of "the 10 million Muslims of Turkestan," and although the settlement of Russian and Ukrainian peasants in the Qazaq lands of Semirech'e and the Steppe krai had become a political issue of sorts, the rural population remained virtually invisible in their writings. The silence is revealing enough, but the one piece in the Jadid repertoire to address the issue is even more so. The first issue of the Bukharan newspaper *Turān* carried "An Address to Our Peasant Brothers," in which the anonymous author wrote: "O peasant brothers, o children of the land [*watan*], you are a pure and sincere people who, unaware of the world, spend your time in hard labor. . . . If you did not exist, our affairs would be in ruin. May God give you power and abundance. Amen. But our duty is to teach you and to open schools for you and to give you all possible help. . . . It is an obligation for us city dwellers to ensure that you are not oppressed."[16] On a less positive note, many writers criticized "shameless lazybones," such as storytellers and Sufi adepts (*qalandar*s), who lived off the gullibility of others.[17] Even more telling is a discussion of the fruits of knowledge in Hamza's *New Happiness*: "All unskilled peoples, such as drivers, tea shop owners, bakers, gamblers, thieves, sweepers, cobblers, watchmen, water carriers, doormen, and others like them, are uneducated. Educated people, even if young, are teachers, owners of large shops, clerks in good places, well dressed and

---

timents when taking stock of the Muslim political movement in 1915: *Islahat esaslari* (Petrograd, 1915), 200.

15. V. P. Nalivkin et al., "Kratkii obzor sovremennogo sostoianiia i deiatel'nosti musul'manskogo dukhovenstva, raznogo roda dukhovnykh uchrezhdenii i uchebnykh zavedenii tuzemnogo naseleniia Samarkandskoi oblasti s nekotorymi ukazaniiami na ikh istoricheskoe proshloe," in *Materialy po musul'manstvu*, vyp. 1 (Tashkent, 1898), 33.

16. "Dehqān qardāshlarimizgha khitāb," *Turān*, 11 July 1912.

17. Abdulhakim Sārimsāqov, "Qalandarlar yākhud tanballar," *ST*, 4 April 1914; anon. (Sārimsāqov?), "Qalandar, maddāh (wā'iz), luli, wa gadāylarimiz, yāki musulmānlik nāmini bolghātguchi be-'ār tanballarimiz," *Āyina*, 14 June 1914, 805.

respected everywhere."[18] This was a far cry from Narodnik-style popu-
lism. The nation included the peasants, but they had little to contribute
to it. Only urban folk (and then, of course, only a few of them) were qualified to lead the nation in the battlefield of modern life.

The Jadid nation was coexistent with the reading (and hearing) public described in Chapter 4. Within that public, the Jadids were engaged
in a struggle of elites for the right to lead the nation. As such, the Jadid
vision of the nation was elitist, although this elitism was never fully articulated as a doctrine (as, for instance, was the case with the Young
Turks)[19] but rather the logical conclusion of the Jadids' position in their
own society and the political constraints in which they operated. The
same political constraints softened that elitism, for new-method schools
(in many of which tuition was waived for poor children) were a far more
egalitarian instrument of elite formation than the creation of universities
(as in Muslim India with the Aligarh movement of Sayyid Ahmad Khān).
Such struggles were an integral part of the establishment of the hegemony of the nation. Partha Chatterjee has argued that in colonial situations, nationalist elites have to declare the sovereignty of nationalism in
native society before engaging the colonial state in a political struggle
for independence.[20] In Central Asia, that first struggle for sovereignty
had not been resolved by 1917.

WOMEN AND THE NATION

A critique of the position of women in Central Asian society formed an
integral part of the Jadid project. In common with modernists elsewhere
in the Muslim world, the Jadids of Central Asia criticized the practice of
polygyny, the poor treatment of women, and their lack of education.
Again, the Jadids sought legitimacy for these criticisms from an understanding of "pure" Islam acquired through modern education, but it was
the nation, not religious reform, that drove them.

A proper assessment of the place of the "women's question" in Jadid
thought is made difficult by our sketchy knowledge of changes affecting
urban women's lives during the tsarist period. The lot of urban women
was difficult in Central Asia: In the late nineteenth century, za'ifa
("weak") and nāqis ul-aql ("deficient in judgment") were common terms

18. Hamza Hakimzāda Niyāzi, Yāngi saādat: milli romān (Kokand, 1915), 21–22.
19. M. Şükrü Hanioğlu, The Young Turks in Opposition (New York, 1995), 203–208.
20. Partha Chatterjee, The Nation and Its Fragments (Princeton, 1992).

for "woman" in learned usage. The impact of the Russian conquest on local gender relations is difficult to gauge. As we have seen, the immediate result of the conquest was the valorization of traditional practices as hallmarks of local Muslim identity. It is likely that the need to assert respectability and propriety in the new conditions led to an increase in the seclusion of women. Several other factors tended to heighten the role of respectability as a status marker. The new wealth accumulated in the cities, which led to the marathon feasts often criticized by the Jadids, created new demand for it (it likely also made polygyny into a form of conspicuous consumption), while the appearance of legal prostitution further made respectability significant. (Most of the prostitutes counted in the census of 1897 were Central Asian; Russian and Tatar women remained a minority in the profession.)

We know even less about the Jadids' personal lives or their private attitudes toward women. Hamza married a Russian woman who converted to Islam and seems to have played a small role in Jadid activities (she was invited to the annual examinations at new-method schools).[21] We also have a photograph, although of unknown date, of Munawwar Qāri with his wife, who is unveiled.[22] Our main source, therefore, are the Jadids' writings. These are marked by a great sympathy for women and a concern for bettering their position. Again, the inspiration came from Tatar and Ottoman debates. Magazines by and for women, such as *Âlem-i nisvan* (Women's World), edited by Gasprinskii's daughter Shafika Hanum in Bahchesaray, and *Suyüm Bike,* which appeared in Kazan from 1913 to 1917, had created a women's voice in the new discourses of the nation then being articulated. Veiling had disappeared among the Tatars by the turn of the century, and Tatar women in Central Asian cities were visible symbols of the change local Jadids wanted to bring about in their society; and to the extent that women had a voice in this debate, Tatar women were also agents of reform.

Women wrote poetry, of course, and in 1914 the Kokand poet Ibrāhim Dawrān published an anthology of verse written by women. Some of the poets included in the anthology had lived in the nineteenth cen-

21. *Hamza Hakimzoda Niyoziy arkhivining katalogi,* 2 vols. (Tashkent, 1990–1991), II: 10.

22. The photograph is reproduced in *San"at,* 1990, no. 12, 9. Soviet sources provide some information on individual women's lives: *Islam i zhenshchiny Vostoka: istoriia i sovremennost'* (Tashkent, 1990); *ÖSE,* I: 343–44, s.v. "Anbar Otin"; ibid., IV: 39, s.v. "Dilshod otin." See also Marianne R. Kamp, "The Otin and the Soviet School: The End of Traditional Education for Uzbek Girls," paper presented to the annual meeting of the American Association for the Advancement of Slavic Studies, Boston, 1996.

tury, but most were contemporaries. The anthology had a marked reformist character, with numerous poems lamenting the difficult position
of women in Central Asian society, exhorting women to acquire knowledge, and calling on men to enable women to do so.[23] Women, especially
Tatar women, also wrote in the press, particularly in *Sadā-yi Turkistān,*
which debated the women's question at some length. The themes as well
as the mode of argument remains embedded in a nationalist discourse
on women.

"In case you do not know [already], know clearly: We too are human
beings and Muslims [*biz insān bālasi insān, musulmān bālasi musulmān-
dirmiz*]," wrote a woman schoolteacher from Tashkent, "and as such we
need, and have the right to, education." Similarly, Zuhuriddin Fathiddinzāda of Bukhara wrote in an article entitled, "Women's Rights":
"Women are the mothers of all humanity: Prophets, messengers, kings,
scholars, writers, and poets are all children of these esteemed mothers."
Therefore, he argued, citing the Qur'an, Islam had accorded equal rights
("apart from a few partial exceptions") to them. "But we leave them
without education, we marry off fourteen-year-old girls to old men of
sixty or seventy for money, and we lock women up in dungeonlike houses
as if they were thieves. Is this justice? Is this equality? Is this the condition
of women who are the lights of civilization [*madaniyat chirāghi*]?"[24]

All these themes appear in Jadid literature and theater. In Abdullah
Awlāni's comedy, *Is It Easy to Be a Lawyer?,* the only sympathetic character is a woman who comes seeking divorce from her abusive husband.
Dawrān-bek, the Russian-trained lawyer who is Awlāni's protagonist, is
agitated:

> O cruel civilization! When will you take root among us Turkestanis? When
> will you liberate us from this dungeon of ignorance? Until we start domestic
> education and enlighten our women, such terrible things will continue in our
> midst. Instead of being married to a man of her own choice, one she had seen
> and wanted, she was given off, like an animal . . . to a cruel man. The whole
> life of this innocent has passed in suffering, sorrow, and distress. . . . Now to
> abolish such terrible things from our midst, we must expend all our might in
> the way of educating our women and acquainting them with knowledge and
> civilization [*maārif wa madaniyat*].[25]

23. Ibrāhim Dawrān, *Ashʿār-i niswān* (Kokand, 1914). I have not been able to locate
a copy of this book, but it is discussed (with extensive quotations) by Tŏkhtamurod
Jalolov, *Özbek shoiralari,* 3rd ed. (Tashkent, 1980), 125–173.
24. Zuhuriddin Fathiddinzāda, "Huquq-i niswān: musāwāt," *ST,* 12 November 1914.
25. Abdulla Awloniy, *Advokatlik oson mi* (1916), in *Toshkent tongi,* ed. Begali Qosimov (Tashkent, 1979), 312–313.

Hāji Muin's play, *The Oppressed Woman*, describes the evils of polygyny. Ozāqbāy is a rich merchant contemplating taking a new wife: "New wives bring back a man's lust and make his mouth water. Now I too have to take a fourteen-year-old for a wife and enjoy life. This [present] wife of mine has borne three or four children and is approaching thirty. There's no joy left in life with her." He is egged on in his thoughts by Ishān Bābā, a man who has performed the hajj seven times and appears on stage with a long string of prayer beads. A new-method teacher, on the other hand, tries unsuccessfully to dissuade Ozāqbāy. Polygyny is permissible, he argues, only if the husband can treat all his wives justly and equally, which is never possible in practice. Ozāqbāy's present wife, Tunsuq Āy, is a devoted mother and a loving wife who insists that their fourteen-year-old son attend a new-method school. She is devastated by the news that Ozāqbāy is contemplating taking a new wife, but her feelings are of as little consequence as the imprecations of the teacher, and Ozāqbāy, on the strength of his wealth, finds himself an eighteen-year-old wife. But the new wife, Suyar Āy, spells disaster from the beginning. After six months of this menage, Suyar Āy accuses Tunsuq Āy of theft; Ozāqbāy believes the allegation and in a fit of anger begins beating his first wife. The play ends in tragedy: Ozāqbāy discovers the error of his ways ("I didn't take a second wife, I took on a calamity"), but Tunsuq Āy is already mortally ill and dies in the last scene.[26]

The biggest cause of Jadid concern, however, was the fact that women were denied education. Zuhuriddin Fathiddinzāda's argument that women's right to knowledge was granted by Islam itself was repeated again and again by other writers and accompanied by exhortations to *men* to educate women.[27] Not only were women being denied a right granted by Islam itself, but doing so was bringing irreparable harm to the nation. "The progress and civilization of a nation is dependent upon the educational, moral, and intellectual progress and civilization of women,"[28] because of the crucial role of women as mothers of the next generation. "In the hands of ignorant [*jāhila*] mothers, the young, innocent children of the nation grow up untrained, unclean, and deprived of delicacy and morals. Full of meaningless tales and superstitions heard from the mouths of their mothers, children's brains become insensate, like roses pulled up from their

26. Hāji Muin b. Shukrullah, *Mazluma khātun* (Samarqand, 1916).

27. See, e.g., Hamza, "Erlar wa qizlar laplari," in his *Tŏla asarlar tŏplami,* ed. N. Karimov et al., 5 vols. (Tashkent, 1988–1989), II: 31; many poems in *Ash'ār-i niswān* also take this view.

28. "Khānimlar tāwushi," *ST,* 11 July 1914.

roots. Removed from reason and reality, they incline toward unnatural suppositions." [29] The solution, of course, was education: Child rearing was a science just as engineering or accountancy, and in civilized nations, it was taught to women in schools. [30] The nation demanded changes in the status of women, and the nation's needs were to determine what the new status was to be.

The nation also demanded a strong, stable family, for that alone could provide the preconditions for progress. This was the fundamental reason behind the Jadids' opposition to polygyny. In *The Oppressed Woman,* the second wife disrupts the tranquillity of the family and distracts attention from the education of Ozāqbāy's fourteen-year-old son. Taking child brides or very early marriage similarly made for insecure families and inadequate upbringing. The idea of the monogamous family as the bastion of the nation was introduced to Central Asia by Behbudi, who, in a long series of articles on "Family Health," expounded the latest wisdom on the matter extracted from contemporary Ottoman and Arabic manuals. Marriage was a natural instinct for human beings, but its place in society must be clearly understood. Puberty introduces thoughts and ideas that, if left unchecked, could cause great harm; therefore civilized Muslims make their children read books explaining these dangers. Semen has to be used in the right manner, for "just as it is incorrect to use it before its time, so it is to delay its use." [31] Late marriage or bachelorhood were equally harmful, and Behbudi cited statistics from France and Holland to prove that most "crimes, murders, and sins" are committed by unmarried men and women. Sex outside of marriage creates limitless disease and is, moreover, a sin. Similar, only greater, dangers lurk behind other misuses of semen and lust: adultery, pederasty, masturbation, and excessive intercourse of any kind weaken the body, deaden the brain, and make it impossible to develop one's intellectual faculties. [32] Similarly, Awlāni, saw "lust [as] a valuable treasure. If used in a legal manner [*surat-i mashru'a*], it becomes the alms of the body, indeed the center of life itself.... If used improperly, it represents the embezzlement of a trust ... [which] destroys virtue and ruins life." [33] Fitrat wrote a full-length book, appar-

29. Nushirvān Yāvushev, "Khātun-qizlarimizga bir nazar," *ST,* 3 June 1914.

30. Tāshkandlik bir muallima, "Turkistān muslimalari tarfidan bir sadā," *ST,* 20 May 1914; Zuhuriddin Fathiddinzāda, "Huquq-i niswān," *ST,* 10 December 1914.

31. Behbudi, "Hifz-i sihhat-i āila," *Āyina,* 13 September 1914, 1127–1129.

32. Behbudi, "Hifz-i sihhat-i āila," *Āyina,* 27 September 1914, 1172–1173; 4 October 1914, 1196–1197; 16 October 1914, 1218–1120.

33. Awlāni, *Turki Gulistān,* 65–66. The societal aspect is foregrounded here as well, for Awlāni presents, by way of the consequences of improper use of lust, the example of

ently no longer extant, called *Family, or the Duties of Housekeeping,* in which he set out to define the true Islamic (*shar'i*) manner of taking a wife, performing the ceremony of marriage, and raising children, as well as the rights and obligations of spouses as prescribed by Islam. He was especially critical of polygyny, on which he took the usual modernist position, seeing it as permissible, but only under conditions that are impossible to fulfill in normal life. Practiced in the absence of the required conditions, polygyny only caused grave moral harm.[34]

The invocation of the norms of scripturalist Islam should not blind us to the real source of this new sexual morality, which lay squarely in contemporary bourgeois Europe. Behbudi's Ottoman and Arabic sources banked heavily on contemporary European medical science and reproduced whole cloth the sexual morality that underpinned it. (Not only did Behbudi cite crime statistics from France and Holland, but he also reproduced in great detail the tale of a fifteen-year-old English boy whose addiction to masturbation could not be cured by anything other than marriage.)[35] Modernist Muslim discourses on women invoked the authority of science as quickly as they invoked that of the shariat, but their concerns were strictly circumscribed by the broader interests of the nation.

The impact of this discourse on actual social practices was minimal. Traditionalists rebutted Jadid claims about the equality of women's rights with equally authoritative verses from the Qur'an.[36] The connection of the debate with Tatar practices also had its disadvantages; and although Jadid authors could point to Tatar (and Istanbul) women as proof that the changes they advocated were the norm among other ("more civilized") Muslims, their opponents could dismiss the whole argument as one more example of the Jadids aping the Tatars, who, for many, existed at the outer limits of Muslimness. Sayyid Ahmad Wasli, a Samarqand mudarris with substantial Jadid credentials, parted company with other Jadids on this issue. He was happier publishing doggerel in honor of veiling ("The veil is a beautiful treasure for women and girls/the veil is the curtain of chastity on the face of shame and honor,"

"many of our youth . . . [who] fall victim to the oppressive disease of syphilis" and spend their hard-earned money (and waste their precious lives) in finding a cure.

34. Abdurrauf Fitrat, ʿĀʾila, yākhud wazāʾif-i khānadāri (Bukhara, 1916); my discussion is based on a review by Hāji Muin (in *Hurriyat,* 22 September 1917) and an advertisement for the book that reproduced its table of contents (*Hurriyat,* 28 November 1917).

35. Behbudi, "Hifz-i sihhat-i āila," *Āyina,* 25 October 1914, 1241–1244.

36. "Mozhet li zhenshchina byt' kaziem," *TWG,* 15 July 1912; Bir Musulmān, "Zhenshchina ne ravna s muzhshchinoi," *TWG,* 20 Septmber 1912; "Sotrudniku gazety 'Sadai Turkestan'," *TWG,* 30 November 1914 (a direct response to Fathiddinzāda).

and so on[37]) than following the Tatars in their misguided ways: "[Turke-stani newspapers] take inspiration directly from Tatar life and therefore alienate the people of Turkestan. For example, if a Tatar writer describes Turkestanis as polytheists [*mushrik*], all local newspapers also start call-ing [Turkestanis] polytheists. Trying to imitate the Tatars, they are also call for letting loose our women [*khātun-qizlarimiz qāchmāsun dedilar*]. Therefore, the number of buyers for these newspapers is small."[38] A pseudonymous author wrote in *TWG* that the "freedom of Tatar women is nothing more than the freedom to go around barefaced and mix with unrelated men." All his suspicions were confirmed, he stated, when a Tatar family moved in next door: "The women do not cover their faces, do not pray, and have no idea of *adab* or proper manners."[39]

Regardless of what Wasli insinuated, the question of unveiling was never explicitly raised in Central Asia before 1917, and Jadid attitudes on gender issues remained conservative. In 1915, Abdulwahhab Muradi, a locally resident Tatar fired off another letter to *Shura* with the usual criti-cisms about the position of women in Turkestan and the lack of attention given to their education. No local newspaper has published anything on the issue, Muradi informed his Tatar audience, and *al-Islāh,* far from dis-cussing the need to educate women, has started to talk about veiling. Igno-rant women in a veil only bring harm, as the author himself had witnessed at a fair in Tashkent recently, where all sorts of illicit things happened un-der the veil.[40] In response, Zuhuriddin Fathiddinzāda, who had argued for the equality of women's rights, jumped to the defense of *al-Islāh* and Turkestan: "Sir! No Muslim journal (including *al-Islāh*) desires the un-veiling of women, and no son of Turkestan [*Turkistān bālasi*] (and the editorial team at *al-Islāh* is not exempt from this) would agree that his mother or sister should dress up her hair in the Paris fashion and prom-enade on boulevards in a *décolleté* dress."[41]

THE JADIDS IN POLITICS

Official Russia feared political awakening in the borderlands of the em-pire primarily for its potential for "separatism." The same fears that cul-

37. Wasli, "Tasattur-i niswān haqqinda," *al-Islāh,* 1 October 1915, 542–545.
38. Mudarris Wasli, "Jarida wa usul-i jadida," *SF,* 6 November 1914.
39. Bir Musulman, "Tātār khātunlārida hurriyat," *TWG,* 24 September 1915.
40. Abdulwahhab Muradi, "Türkistanda khanimlar," *Shura,* 1 November 1915, 659–660.
41. Bukhārāli Zuhuriddin Fathiddinzāda, "Turkistānda khānimlar," *al-Islāh,* 21 De-cember 1915, 730.

tural reform would inevitably lead to separatism (here made worse by the fanaticism of the local population and the intrigues of Ottoman emissaries) underlay the reaction of the local administration to the growth of Jadidism in Turkestan. Russian official discourse therefore treated Jadidism primarily as a political phenomenon, a view that historians, both in Russia and the Soviet Union and abroad, have tended to adopt. This fear was largely unfounded, though, for two fundamental reasons: There existed no institutional framework within which local political interests could be articulated, and Jadidism had not vanquished its opposition within Muslim society. Jadidism remained a cultural movement rather than a political movement asserting claims against the state. What little political activity the Jadids engaged in before February 1917 bore the marks of these constraints.

The elective offices introduced by the Provisional Statute of 1867, and largely retained by the legislation of 1886 (see Chapter 2) were not meant to, and did not, lead to the emergence of organized politics. Russian legislation intended these offices to mediate between state and society, not to articulate any political goals. As such, these offices remained the domain of the informal politics of personalities.[42] Such notables also monopolized the "native" seats in the Tashkent City Duma when the city was brought under the Municipal Legislation of 1870 (modified to restrict Muslim representation to only one-third of all seats).[43] Said Azim-bāy won election to the body early in its existence, and the seat stayed in the family for most of its existence.[44] The Tashkent City Duma did not serve as a forum for the articulation of political demands, Russian or Muslim.

The Jadids were a fledgling group when the revolution of 1905 created vast new possibilities for political action. Although they lacked any organizational basis or experience, they attempted to make use of the new freedoms in the cause of their reform. However, they could not always turn their energies into practical results. Although many writers exhorted their compatriots in the newly founded newspapers to make use of the new freedoms, they were unable to play a significant role in the brief period of political activity that followed.[45] Much of that activity in-

42. N. S. Lykoshin, *Pol zhizni v Turkestane* (Petrograd, 1916), 140–143.

43. F. Azadaev, *Tashkent vo vtoroi polovine XIX veka: ocherki sotsial'no-ekonomicheskoi i politicheskoi istorii* (Tashkent, 1959), 107–112.

44. Ibid., 114.

45. See, for example, Munawwar Qāri, untitled article, *Taraqqi—Orta Azyaning umr guzarlighi*, 7 March 1906; or Fazlullah Yunchi, letter, *Taraqqi—Orta Azyaning umr guzarlighi*, 22 March 1906.

volved petition campaigns waged by the established elites. However, these petitions seldom went beyond religious issues to the question of political rights of the Central Asian population.

A common demand in these petitions was the creation of a Muslim "spiritual assembly" patterned after the three that existed in European Russia, and whose creation in Turkestan had been opposed by Kaufman. In a petition signed by the notables of Kokand in December 1905, for instance, seven of the sixteen demands concerned the formation and functions of such an assembly, while another seven concerned the reform of the office of the qāzi. It also demanded complete freedom to import and publish locally books and periodicals. The petition thus sought to rescue the process of the appointment and removal of qāzis from the electoral principle and to return it to the ulama. The petitioners also wanted the qāzis to have jurisdiction over foreign Muslims visiting Turkestan and for them to have freedom from intervention by Russian courts in cases involving blasphemy. The last section of the petition, asking for the abolition of Section 64 of the Turkestan Statute of 1886 (which gave police officers sweeping rights of imprisonment without charge), was the only part of the petition with any directly political implications; it was also the only one to mention the term "Turkestan."[46]

Petitions for the creation of a "spiritual assembly" were no doubt political to the extent that they asserted local rights against the state and demanded a change in the structures of power. Purely religious demands could turn into political ones, as was the case with the Tatars' struggle to wrest control of the Orenburg spiritual assembly from the state. But whereas the Tatar movement sought to make the assembly entirely elective, and hence free of government control, the petitions in Turkestan were geared toward undoing some of the damage done to the moral authority of the ulama by Russian legislation. Hence the insistence on *revoking* the electoral principle in religious affairs in Turkestan and its replacement by the moral authority of the traditionally learned. In any case, such petitions often disappeared into the abyss of the bureaucracy without a trace.[47]

46. *Taraqqi—Orta Azyaning umr guzarlighi,* 10 January 1906.

47. Muslim notables of Semirech'e met in Alma Ata on 13 March 1906, to draft a petition demanding the creation of a "spiritual assembly" for Turkestan. The petition was handed to the military governor of Semirech'e on 4 April 1906, for transmission to Count Witte. Eight years later the petitioners were still waiting for a response: "Yettisu wilāyati Musulmānlarining iltimāsi," reprinted from *Vaqït* (Orenburg) in *Āyina,* 3 May 1914, 542–544.

THE ALL-RUSSIAN MUSLIM MOVEMENT

The October Manifesto of 1905 conceded the right of political assembly and popular representation to the population of the empire. The nascent elites of the Muslims of European Russia and Transcaucasia seized this opportunity to launch an empire-wide political movement that sought to speak in the name of all the Muslims of the empire in the newly granted institution of popular representation, the State Duma. Both in the All-Russian Muslim movement and in the Duma, however, Turkestan's participation remained minimal.

Existing scholarship has tended to endow the All-Russian Muslim movement with immense authority. Its creation, and the convocation of three congresses in the years 1905–1906, is seen as proof of the existence of a political and cultural unity among the empire's Muslim population. In fact, the movement was dominated by Tatar and Transcaucasian public figures, many of whom had received foreign educations, and the third congress was the only one to include delegates from Turkestan. That congress decided to create a political party (Rusya Musulmanlarïnïng Ittifaqï, Union of Russian Muslims) to work for the defense of the religious and cultural rights of the Muslims of the empire through the new quasiconstitutional means allowed by the October Manifesto.[48] As such, this congress marked the political victory of Jadidism among the Muslims of Russia and Transcaucasia, but it had little impact on Turkestan. The congress also decided to ally the movement with the Constitutional Democrats (Kadets) in mainstream Russian politics. This alliance was hardly surprising. Jadid thinking consistently saw the enlightenment of individuals as the true path for the progress of society. This individualistic thrust of their thinking gave the Jadids a natural affinity for political liberalism. The political program adopted by the Muslim Faction was hardly distinguishable from that of the Kadets except for a few clauses specifying Muslim religious rights.[49] Tatar and Transcaucasian Muslim elites could by now speak the language of Russian politics and engage the state (and other political parties) in a discourse of political rights that

48. On Muslim political activity in this period, see Musa Jarullah Bigi, *Islahat esaslarï*; A. Arsharuni and Kh. Gabidullin, *Ocherki panislamizma i pantiurkizma v Rossii* (Moscow, 1931), 23–33; Serge A. Zenkovsky, *Pan-Turkism and Islam in Russia* (Cambridge, 1960), ch. 4.

49. *Programma Musul'manskoi gruppy v 2-oi Gosudarstvennoi Dume* (St. Petersburg, 1907), art. 15n, 22–25, and 41, were the only parts of the document specific to the Muslim community.

required a vocabulary entirely different from the discourse of cultural
reform within Muslim society. In Central Asia, on the other hand, no
groups yet existed that could participate in such an enterprise. The dis-
parity between the language of the program of the Muslim political
movement and that of cultural debate in Turkestan is indicative of the
marginal position Turkestan occupied in the political movement. The
agenda of the political movement was set by the largely secular elites of
the Muslims of European Russia, with little contribution coming from
Turkestan. There were no Central Asian delegates at the first two congresses and only a few at the third,[50] where the question of creating a Muslim spiritual assembly for Turkestan received some attention.[51] Only one
Central Asian was elected to a commission of the congress.[52] In any
case, the congress's deliberations never took practical form, and the organs of empire-wide organization of the Muslim community remained
on paper only.

On 3 June 1907, Prime Minister P. Stolypin dissolved the Second
Duma and revamped electoral laws in an attempt to manufacture a more
pliant legislature. Representation of *inorodtsy* was cut drastically, and
Turkestan was completely disenfranchised. This coup also put an end to
the Muslim congresses, and their deliberations came to naught. The
state never allowed the Ittifaq to register as a political party[53] and in the
increasingly repressive political climate after 1907, even the purely cultural and educational activities of the body atrophied. Muslim political
activity was restricted to a small Muslim Faction in the Duma. Legal action had strict limits, as the attempt by members of the Muslim Faction
to organize a Fourth Muslim Congress with official permission showed.
The conference, convened in St. Petersburg in June 1914 to allow members of the Muslim Faction to discuss educational and religious issues
with their constituents, was attended by forty officially approved delegates, who met behind closed doors. In this era of restricted activity,
Turkestan again took a back seat. Now that the Muslim Faction in the

50. The available documents of the congress do not provide a complete list of participants. We know for certain of only two Turkestanis who attended the meeting: Mahmud
Khoja Behbudi (cf. Behbudi, "Qasd-i safar," *Āyina*, 24 May 1914, 598) and Aminjān
Ilhāmjānov, whose name appears on the list of officials elected by the meeting.
51. "Bizlargha ne lāzim?" *Khurshid*, 21 September 1906.
52. Aminjān Ilhāmjānov was elected to the fifteen-member Presidium, but his seems
to be the only Turkestani name on that or the three other commissions elected by the congress: *III- i Vserossiiskii Musul'manskii s"ezd* (Kazan, 1906), 2, 7, 11, 13–14; cf. A. Z. V.
Togan, *Bugünkü Türkili (Türkistan) ve Yakın Tarihi*, 2nd ed. (Istanbul, 1981), 348.
53. Alfred Levin, *The Third Duma: Election and Profile* (Hamden, Conn., 1973),
56–57.

Duma did not contain even a token Turkestani contingent, its concerns focused more and more on Tatar and Transcaucasian issues. Of the forty delegates invited to attend the Fourth Muslim Congress in 1914, only three represented Turkestan (and one of them was a Tatar), even though the agenda included the creation of a spiritual assembly for Turkestan.[54] Turkestani newspapers expressed their disappointment at this snub, but they could do little but bemoan the lack of qualified and committed individuals in Central Asia.[55]

TURKESTAN IN THE STATE DUMA

Turkestan's experience with the State Duma was similarly short-lived and marginal. Turkestan's representation in the State Duma was subject to special election rules, which were still being drafted when the First Duma opened in April 1906 in St. Petersburg.[56] It was dissolved well before elections could take place in Turkestan.[57] Turkestan did send delegates to the Second Duma: Seven "non-native" and six "native" deputies were elected from separate curiae. Not only was the local population vastly underrepresented, but the election of its deputies took place in four stages, rather than the two for the election for the Russian deputies.[58] The franchise was limited by strict property requirements as well as a knowledge of Russian.

The Jadids had great enthusiasm for the Duma, which they saw as a tribune of liberty and equality. Even Munawwar Qāri, far more skeptical of Russian officialdom than someone like Behbudi, wrote passionately of the need to elect worthy individuals as deputies of the nation.[59] The reality proved to be rather different. There existed no political parties among the local population of Turkestan at this time. The Union of Muslims projected by the Muslim congresses remained only a hope, and Rus-

54. The three delegates were Sher Ali Lapin, Said Nāsir Jalilov, and General Sahibgeray Yenikeev, a Tatar; cf. *Āyina*, 28 June 1914, 863. Because of its low profile, this congress has escaped most historians' notice, although it was covered in the Russian as well as the Muslim press at the time. Yenikeev's speech was reported by *Novoe vremia*, 19 June 1914.

55. *ST*, 6 June 1914.

56. "Polozhenie o vyborakh v Gosudarstvennuiu Dumu," *Polnoe sobranie zakonov Rossiiskoi Imperii*, 3rd ser., vol. 25 (St. Petersburg, 1907), no. 26662, art. 1, *prilozhenie*.

57. A. V. Piaskovskii, *Revoliutsiia 1905–1907 godov v Turkestane* (Moscow, 1958), 525–526.

58. *Sotsial'no-ekonomicheskoe i politicheskoe polozhenie Uzbekistana nakanune oktiabria* (Tashkent, 1973), 11.

59. "Millat majlisigha wakil kerak," *Khurshid*, 19 October, 1906; "Khālisāna bir arz," *Khurshid*, 12 November 1906.

sian political parties restricted their activity in Turkestan to the Russian population. Therefore, as in the elections to the Tashkent City Duma, most of the successful candidates from the local population came from the notables. Makhtumquli Nur Berdikhanov, the deputy from Transcaspia, belonged to the Akhal Tekke aristocracy and had actually taken part in the defense of Gök Tepe against Skobelev's armies in 1881 before going into Russian service.[60] Tāshpulāt Abdulkhalilov and Sālihjān Muhammadjanov, deputies from Samarqand and Ferghana oblasts, respectively, were merchants, while Töleuli Allabergenev, the deputy from Syr Darya oblast, was a Qazaq tribal chief.[61] In Tashkent the election descended into farce. The forty eligible voters met for the final election on 7 February to choose from two candidates. One of the candidates withdrew, leaving the other, Arif Khoja, a son-in-law of Said Azim-bāy winner by default. Later in the day, however, the presiding officer had doubts about the legality of election without voting, and therefore he convened the electors again the next day to confirm the winner by casting actual votes. At this time, Arif Khoja withdrew "for personal reasons," leaving the field open again. New candidates were hastily found, but to the consternation of the presiding officer, the election resulted in a tie, with both candidates receiving eighteen votes, and the decision was made by the drawing of lots. The winner was Abdulwāhid Qāri, the mudarris at Mirzā Abdullah madrasa in Tashkent.[62] He took no discernible part in the proceedings of the Duma, but his election made the Okhrana suspicious of him. Two years later, he was arrested for conducting "nationalist-separatist propaganda" among the local population and exiled to Tula province for five years.[63] Muhammadjan Tïnïshpaev (Tanyshbaev), a scion of the Qazaq aristocracy who held an engineering degree from the Alexander I Institute of Rail Transport in St. Petersburg, elected from Semirech'e, was the only one of the six with whom the Jadids might have felt strong affinity.[64]

60. "Chleny Gosudarstvennoi Dumy pervogo, vtorogo i tret'ego sozyva," section at the end of *Entsiklopedicheskii slovar' russkogo bibliograficheskogo Instituta Granat*, vol. 17 (Moscow, n.d.), 42; Togan, *Türkili*, 349.

61. Gosudarstvennaia Duma, *Ukazatel' k stenograficheskim otchetam: vtoroi sozyv; 1907 god* (St. Petersburg, 1907).

62. Gosudarstvennaia Duma, Vtoroi Sozyv, *Stenograficheskie otchety: 1907 god*, vol. 2 (St. Petersburg, 1907), 783.

63. TsGARUz, f. 461, op. 1, d. 1311, l. 70.

64. On Tïnïshpaev, see A. S. Takenov and B. Baigaliev, "Inzhener i istorik (o M. Tynyshpaeve)," in M. Tynyshpaev, *Istoriia kazakhskogo naroda*, ed. Takenov and Baigaliev (Alma Ata, 1993), 3–14.

Five of the six Muslim deputies from Turkestan sat with the Muslim Group in the Duma. (Tïnïshpaev, the only one of the six with a Russian education, was elected on a Kadet ticket.) Tïnïshpaev and Abdulkhalilov won election to the Agrarian Commission of the Duma, but otherwise Turkestani deputies left little mark on the proceedings. On 22 May 1907, in the only speech ever delivered at the Duma by a Turkestani Muslim, Abdulkhalilov criticized a bill submitted by the Ministry of Finance proposing a tax levy on unirrigated lands in Turkestan.[65] The speech drew applause from the center, but the Stolypin coup was less than two weeks away.

A MUSLIM VOICE IN TURKESTAN

To understand the real dimensions of Jadid political action in Central Asia, however, we have to lower our sights to the local level. Jadid concerns revolved around not separatism but a quest for *participation* in Russian political life; or, in the terms outlined in Chapter 4, it involved an attempt to overcome the split between the Russian and native publics through the entry of Muslims into the Russian sphere. Only by creating a Muslim voice in the Russian public could political claims be made on the state.

The fundamental problem remained that of resources. Not many Jadids had the command of Russian necessary for such participation, and the few Central Asians with Russian educations tended, as we saw in Chapter 3, to develop a different profile. Unlike the Jadids, who spoke in the idiom of Muslim cultural reform, the secular intellectuals spoke the language of modern Russian liberalism. Few of the Russian-educated intellectuals took part in Jadid activities such as teaching in new-method schools or publishing. The differences were by no means unbridgeable, however, and a rapprochement between the two groups is discernible after 1914, when many Jadids turned more and more to political action.

The bridge between the two groups was provided by Ubaydullah Khojaev (1886–1942). Born in Tashkent, Khojaev attended a Russo-native school. Upon graduation, he found work as translator for a Russian justice of the peace, whom he accompanied to Saratov when the latter was transferred there. Khojaev stayed in Saratov for several years, during which he acquired considerable legal training. He returned to Tashkent early in 1913 and set up a legal practice. At the same time, he became

65. Gosudarstvennaia Duma, Vtoroi Sozyv, *Stenograficheskie otchety*, II: 1037–1039.

involved in local Jadid affairs. He was a partner in the Umid Bookstore as well as the editor of the newspaper *Sadā-yi Turkistān*.[66] Khojaev began his public career in Tashkent. In February 1914, he sued the publisher of *Turkestanskii kur'er* on behalf of such local Jadids as Munawwar Qāri and Mirzā Hakim Sārimsāqov for publishing a poem they deemed blasphemous.[67] This was an attempt to assert the religious rights of the Turkestani population through channels provided by Russian law as well as a move by the Jadids to challenge the monopoly of the decorated notables as spokesmen for the local population vis-à-vis the state. Protestations of loyalty, of course, were seldom transparent. In 1914, as editor of *Sadā-yi Turkistān*, Ubaydullah suggested that Muslim society in Tashkent should celebrate the forthcoming fiftieth anniversary of the Russian conquest of the city: "The friendly Russian state took our city and our sovereignty from us. What harm came to us out of this? The Muslims of Turkestan have suffered no harm from the Russian government. On the contrary, our country has flourished." To celebrate the auspicious occasion, Khojaev suggested that society establish either a teachers' college or a new-method college [*āliya madrasa*] such as those that existed in Ufa and Orenburg.[68] After all, Gasprinskii had obtained permission to publish *Terjüman* only on the occasion of the centenary of the Russian annexation of the Crimea. In Tashkent, Khojaev's plea went unheeded, but it provides a crucial insight into the political strategy of the Jadids. By appropriating the discourse of the state, they sought to create a civic space in which the nation could organize itself, using toward that goal the institutions of the state to their advantage.

Khojaev also ran for election to the Tashkent City Duma in 1914. He used his newspaper to good effect, criticizing the general apathy surrounding the election even among the small electorate in a matter of such great importance. The duma was a forum in which the most respected men from each nation spoke in their nation's interest, for there "wealth does not matter, but carefully reasoned speeches attract attention."[69] He and a number of sympathizers ran on the basis of their claims to providing just that kind of service to the nation, with modest success. Khojaev was one of six new members elected that year.[70] He entered the new

66. Most of this information comes from the Okhrana dossier on Khojaev: TsGARUz, f. 461, op. 1, d. 2263, ll. 104–1080b; see also *Politicheskie deiateli Rossii 1917 g.: biograficheskii slovar'* (Moscow, 1993), 335, s.v. "Khodzhaev, Ubaidulla."
67. GARF, f. 102, op. 244, d. 74, ch. 84B, l. 104.
68. Ubaydullah, "Yubeligha hāzirlanuw," *ST,* 28 May 1914.
69. "Dumakhāna wa ghilāsnilar," *ST,* 30 September 1914.
70. "Ghilāsni sāylāwi," *ST,* 17 October 1914.

forum with enthusiasm, speaking out against arbitrary activities of the police in the old city and unlawful imprisonment of those searched.[71]

Such activities had increased after the outbreak of war in July 1914. The declaration of war had provoked the usual declarations of loyalty to the tsar from the decorated notables in Turkestan,[72] but the Jadid press, then at the moment of its greatest success, was not far behind. Khojaev, writing in *Sadā-yi Turkistān,* called for support of the Russian army, especially since it included "many of our coreligionists."[73] Behbudi reminded his readers of the need for patriotism during this hour of difficulty for "the Russian state [which] is home for us Russian Muslims." This patriotism could take the form of "help to the state in cash or kind, to the extent possible."[74] The message was also conveyed through patriotic poetry. In his "Prayer for the Emperor," Hamza declaimed:

> Give your lives to the Land, be an example
> Find success, o tiger-hearted armies
> Long live the nation, long live our Emperor

The tiger-hearted armies were encouraged to "raze Hungary to the ground/conquer and destroy German cities."[75] Hamza was hardly unusual. Ibrāhim Dawrān wrote an ode "To Our Soldiers" and Mir Muhsin asked the Kaiser, "Who's the Coward?"[76] The Russian empire was unequivocally the homeland (*watan*) and, as such, the recipient of all the obligations due to a homeland.

The situation was complicated by the entry into war of the Ottoman empire in October, especially as the Ottoman government sought to play the pan-Islamic card. The Şeyhülislâm declared the war to be a holy war (*Cihad-ı Mukaddes*) in which aid to the Ottoman empire was incumbent upon all the Muslims of the world. In his *fetvâ* (legal opinion), the Şeyhülislâm also answered "Yes" to the following question: "Is it absolutely forbidden to Muslim subjects of the aforementioned [Entente] powers, at war with the Muslim government, to fight against the armies of the Muslim government even if they were coerced with threats to their life and even of the destruction of their families; and if they do so, do

---

71. "Shahr dumāsinda," *ST,* 2 December 1914.
72. "Vsepoddaneishii adres tashkentskikh musul'man," *TWG,* 3 August 1914.
73. Ubaydullah, "Watan muhāfazasi," *ST,* 2 September 1914.
74. Behbudi, "Watanparwarlik kerak," *Āyina,* 16 August 1914, 1018–1022.
75. Hamza, "Padishāh hazratlarina duā," in *Āq Gul* (Kokand, 1914), cf. Hamza, *Tŏla asarlar tŏplami,* II: 22–24.
76. Dawrān, "Bizim askarlarga," *ST,* 22 September 1914; Mir Muhsin, "Kim nāmard," *TWG,* 11 September 1914.

they deserve . . . the fires of hell?"[77] The C.U.P. regime had chosen, under German pressure, to place a greater burden on pan-Islam than Abdül-hamid had ever done in his three decades at the helm. Ironically, the decision to seek the fetvâ was motivated by the same assumptions about the nature of Muslim opinion that underlay European fears of pan-Islam: that it was monolithic in its religious motivation, and that it could be molded (and manipulated) by Ottoman proclamations. The reality was quite different.

True, the Balkan wars had created a groundswell of sympathy for the Ottoman empire in Central Asia, which carried over into the world war. Central Asia was rife with rumors, all dutifully transcribed by Okhrana agents, of an Afghan invasion of Central Asia, and many prayed for Ottoman successes with German help. Many in Central Asia, especially members of the traditionalist religious elite, openly expressed their antagonism to the Russian cause in the war. Russian authorities stepped up their vigilance, resulting in an upsurge in arbitrary searches and arrests. The Jadids, however, figure nowhere in the Okhrana's catalogue of its fears and anxieties. The Ottoman empire no doubt was the focus of the Jadids' sympathies, but those sympathies did not override the political realities they faced at home. The process of building a civic space for Central Asian Muslims could not be sacrificed at the altar of quixotic support for the Ottoman cause. "There is nothing to be done," Behbudi wrote of the entry of the Ottoman empire in the war, "except to express sorrow that the fires ignited by the Germans have engulfed Russia and Turkey. . . . We, the Muslims of Turkestan, are subjects of Russia and co-religionists of the Turks. Our common religion and common race [ham-din wayā ham-uruqlikimiz] cannot hinder our friendship with Russia, because this war is not a religious war, but one for political gain, indeed a German war."[78] The "friendship" here was, of course, a euphemism for the civic space Central Asian society enjoyed under Russian rule, but even that space (which made Jadid reform possible) would be threatened if the state was provoked by overt opposition to the war. "It should be well understood that any ignorant and impolite action would destroy our fifty-year friendship."[79] Behbudi went on to wish that the Turks had never entered the war, but since they had been duped by the Germans,

77. "Cihad-ı Mukaddas İlani ve Fetvâ-yı Şerif," İslâm Mecmuası, 6 November 1914, 440–441.
78. Behbudi, "Rusiya wa Turkiya arasinda harb," Āyina, 6 November 1914, 3.
79. Ibid., 4.

he advised his readers to "remain peaceful and help the wounded to the extent possible," because "the war between Turkey and Russia is 3,000 to 5,000 *chaqirim* away from us and it will stay there. . . . One should not trust the word of those who, knowing nothing about history, geography, or politics, claim to be ishans or divines. Those who want to know [about the war] should read the telegraph and newspapers, read the books of history and geography, and look at the map of the world to acquaint themselves with . . . the warring states."[80] The "ishans and divines" were obviously those in Central Asia who hoped for liberation from Russian rule through the war. Behbudi here was arguing, on the basis of his new-method knowledge, that such hopes were not justified by the geopolitics of the war. The war was too far away to benefit Turkestan; a look at the map also told Behbudi that rumors of an Afghan intervention in Central Asia in the name of Islam were mere fantasies (Behbudi could not have known that the German and Ottoman high commands were to try to make them come true in the following years). Since liberation by Ottoman arms was not a possibility, Behbudi urged his readers to value the "friendship" of Russia.

Nor was this the personal opinion of Behbudi alone. Most Jadids displayed the caution he suggested. The police reports from the period meticulously record countless rumors, many of them outlandish, overheard by agents, but none of them mention anyone active in Jadid reform except Munawwar Qāri. Instead, the Jadids began organizing a number of events to raise funds for wounded soldiers and their families. Over the three years of its existence, Jadid theater was staged at least as often to raise funds for the war effort as for Jadid cultural activities. The most popular causes with Turkestani Jadids were a field hospital for Muslim soldiers and aid to the victims of war on the Kars front. Patriotic, pro-war sentiment continued to be expressed in Jadid poetry and journalism after the Ottoman entry into the war.

The war came to Central Asia in June 1916, when, faced with two years of disasters in the battlefields, the government decided to revoke Central Asians' exemption from military service and to levy troops for work at the rear. Since no records of births existed, lists of men to be conscripted were to be drawn up by volost administrators enjoying considerable discretionary powers. Both the decree and the manner of its proposed implementation provoked hostility from the beginning. Throughout the sedentary regions of Turkestan, crowds gathered at volost offices

80. Ibid.

demanding the destruction of the lists and the revocation of the decree. These gatherings were accompanied by mob justice, in which volost administrators and accompanying troops were attacked and killed. In Jizzakh uezd of Samarqand oblast, such opposition turned into open revolt, as insurgents destroyed railway and telegraph lines and attacked Russian settlements. But it was in the nomadic areas of the Steppe krai and Semirech'e that the colonial peace was shattered most dramatically. There, Qazaq and Qïrghïz nomads refused to be conscripted and went on the offensive. Unlike in the core oblasts of Turkestan, where native functionaries were often the target of the rebels, in the nomadic areas resentment over massive state-sponsored settlement over the previous decade made Russian settlers the focus of attack. These attacks were accompanied by flight by large numbers of nomads (as well as the sedentary Dungans) into Chinese territory.[81]

Russian control could be reestablished, and then tenuously, only by reinforcements from Russia, who, along with armed settlers, repaid the atrocities with usurious interest. At the height of the uprising, A. N. Kuropatkin, an old Turkestan hand, was appointed governor-general of Turkestan. He arrived in Tashkent resolved to set matters right using the methods he had used in Andiján in 1898. Land where "Russian blood had been spilt" (in the Przheval'sk, Pishpek, and Jarkent uezds in Semirech'e, and in Jizzakh uezd in Samarqand) was confiscated. Kuropatkin also contemplated separating Russian and "Kirgiz" (the generic Russian term used to denote both Qazaq and Qïrghïz nomads) populations in large parts of Semirech'e, cleansing the area around the Issiq Köl and the Chu River of its Qazaq and Qïrghïz population, and creating a "Kirgiz"-only uezd in the Narïn region. In more practical terms, Russian soldiers and settlers wreaked vengeance on those nomads who remained behind. Those who had fled to Chinese territory, where they spent the winter in miserable conditions and were preyed upon by Chinese officials, returned to find their crops destroyed, their grazing land taken over by Russian settlers, and their cattle lost en route. The total Russian losses were substantial, although they were concentrated mostly in Semirech'e (a total of 2,246, of which 2,108 were in Semirech'e), but in typical colonial fashion, native casualties far outnumbered them. According to early So-

81. The only substantial narrative account in English of this episode is the dated work by Edward D. Sokol, *The Revolt of 1916 in Russian Central Asia* (Baltimore, 1954). Of the several accounts in Russian, the most comprehenisve is Kh. Tursunov, *Vosstanie 1916 goda v Srednei Azii i Kazakhstane* (Tashkent, 1962).

viet figures, in Przheval'sk oblast, 70 percent of the Qazaq and Qïrghïz population, and 90 percent of the cattle, died. In Semirech'e as a whole, 20 percent of the population, 50 percent of the horses, 39 percent of the cattle, 55 percent of the camels, and 58 percent of the sheep were lost.[82] The atrocities continued well into the summer of 1917.

The fact that the Jadids were not involved in the uprising is not surprising. They had no presence in the rural areas, let alone the nomadic territory where the uprising was the strongest. What is surprising, however, is their enthusiasm for recruitment and their dismay at the uprising. Ubaydullah Khojaev was involved in the process and chaired the Tashkent city committee for recruitment.[83] Others sought to cooperate with the authorities. Tawallā welcomed Kuropatkin upon his arrival in Tashkent, at the height of the uprising, with a poem in *TWG*.[84] When the first batch of one thousand conscripts left Tashkent on 18 September 1916, the ceremonies included patriotic poetry recited by members of Awlāni's Turān theatrical troupe and students of new-method schools. (The latter were rewarded with 100 rubles and candy by the city's governor.)[85] The new volume in Hamza's series of *National Songs*, published in November 1916, was entirely dedicated to poetry in support of the war effort. The refrain of his poem "A Sincere Prayer" was quite unequivocal: "O compatriots, be true to our King / until even our lives are sacrificed."[86]

This is strange behavior for pan-Islamists or nationalists. It becomes impossible to explain if we insist on seeing Turkestani society as a monolithic whole in its response to colonial rule. Rather, we have two different strategies located in very different parts of society. The nomads and peasants of Turkestan, operating along the solidarities of tribe and clan, sought to drive the Russians (functionaries and settlers) out of their lands. The Jadids sought to use the conscription edict as an opportunity to establish a Central Asian Muslim presence in mainstream Russian life. Behbudi for one had long seen Turkestan's exemption from military service as a practice of exclusion;[87] the 1916 edict, born of necessity, was a chance to overcome this exclusion and, by contributing to the war ef-

82. Sokol, *The Revolt*, 146, 159.
83. TsGARUz, f. 1, op. 31, d. 1144, ll. 5, 370b.
84. *TWG*, 21 August 1916.
85. "Istoricheskii den' v Tashkente," *TWG*, 24 September 1916.
86. The text is in Hamza, *Tŏla asarlar tŏplami*, II: 66.
87. Behbudi, "Askar mas'alasi," *Samarqand*, 28 June 1913; Behbudi, "I'ānat kerak, kongulli askar kerak," *Āyina*, 23 August 1914, 1042–1044.

fort, stake out a place in Russian political life after the war. Indeed, the mobilization in itself was a political issue, even before the ensuing uprising made it a matter of empire-wide importance. While he helped organize the mobilization, Khojaev also traveled to Petrograd along with the Andijān millionaire Mir Kāmil-bāy and Khojaev's friend Vadim Chaikin, a Social Revolutionary, to invite a delegation from the State Duma to visit Turkestan and examine the situation themselves. The quest was successful, and a two-member delegation, consisting of Kutlugmurad Tevkelev, the chairman of the Muslim Faction, and the Social Revolutionary deputy Aleksandr Kerenskii (who was born in Tashkent), toured the province in August. Upon his return, Kerenskii gave a two-hour speech, highly critical of Russian policy in Turkestan, in a closed session of the Duma. At the same time, Khojaev's success in bringing two worthies from Petrograd increased his influence in Tashkent. Russian officials noted with concern that many people in Tashkent had begun to think of him as an aristocrat and had begun to address him directly with their grievances as someone enjoying great power.[88]

The alliance between Khojaev and Chaikin provided one of the few instances in prerevolutionary Turkestan of political collaboration between members of the Russian community and the native population, but it is a good example of Jadid strategy in this tumultuous period. Its origins remain unclear. When *Sadā-yi Turkistān* collapsed due to financial problems in May 1915, Khojaev moved, his membership in the Tashkent City Duma notwithstanding, to Andijān, where he started a legal practice. By summer 1916, Khojaev was on friendly terms with several Russians of Social Revolutionary persuasion, such as Vadim Chaikin and I. Ia. Shapiro. Chaikin had been arrested in Kursk province in June 1908, for agitating among the peasants, for which he had spent five years in exile in Yakutia. In 1916 he worked with his brother Anastasii, who as an "honorary citizen" had far more solid credentials.[89] Shapiro was a lawyer who had a long history of antigovernment activity and who had first been arrested in Kharkov in 1904.[90] After the events of the summer of 1916, they launched the Andijān Publishing Company as a joint-stock venture, in which Ubaydullah Khojaev was apparently a shareholder. The company hoped to publish two newspapers, one in Russian and one in Turkic, called *The Voice of Turkestan*, although finan-

88. TsGARUz, f. 461, op. 1, d. 2023, ll. 12, 190b, 250b.
89. TsGARUz, f. 1, op. 31, d. 1144, ll. 30b–40b.
90. TsGARUz, f. 461, op. 1, d. 2023, l. 24.

cial constraints meant that only the Russian version (*Turkestanskii golos*) ever saw the light. The Ghayrat Company of Kokand was also interested in publishing the Turkic version (to be called *Sadā-yi Turkistān*), and negotiations were under way between the two organizations in November 1916. Preparations were far advanced, for in December 1916, Cholpān, on behalf of the editorial board, solicited the customary poem in praise of the new newspaper from Hamza.[91] The Russian version remained a Russian newspaper, catering to local Russian society but, unusually, providing comment favorable to Muslim positions on issues such as Russian settlement in Semirech'e.[92] The activities of this group went beyond publishing, however. The offices of the newspaper had become the meeting place for local Jadids, who counted among their numbers merchants, interpreters, and booksellers.[93] In 1916, they launched a campaign of petitions and denunciations against corrupt local officials, as a result of which a number of officials were dismissed. Again, as with the lawsuit over blasphemy, the purpose of this campaign was to assert the presence of the group in local society by forcing the administration to play according to its own rules. The campaign was successful enough to attract the notice of oblast authorities, who, not surprisingly, did not share this view of accountability. The governor of Ferghana oblast, took a dim view of the situation and the people involved. What he had on his hands was a "local party called 'Taraqqiparwar,' which covers itself in pan-Islamist ideas, but which in reality pursues the goals of profit through blackmail, vile slanders, graft, intrigues, and lies." These unscrupulous individuals—corrupt interpreters, slimy lawyers, self-serving members of the Russian community, and Jews—had "terrorized" the population and succeeded to the extent that "power had passed from the hands of the administration to this group." The governor recommended exiling the whole group from Turkestan.[94] The matter was still being investigated when revolution broke out in the streets of Petrograd.

OF NATIONAL INTEREST

Jadid political strategies aimed at the creation of a Muslim voice in Turkestan and of Muslim participation in the imperial mainstream. To this

91. *Hamza arkhivi katalogi*, II: 23–24; TsGARUz, f. 1, op. 31, d. 1144, l. 340b.
92. Togan, *Türkili*, 355–356.
93. TsGARUz, f. 1, op. 31, d. 1144, l. 20.
94. Military Governor, Ferghana, to Governor-General, Turkestan, 12 December 1916, in TsGARUz, f. 461, op. 1, d. 2023, ll. 5–10.

end, they sought alliances with sympathetic Russians in their midst and
attempted to work for the state. The continuation of this strategy during war and insurgency was the only choice open to the Jadids, who had
no roots in the countryside that would allow them to launch a popular
movement of armed resistance against the colonial regime. Indeed, as the
foregoing should have made clear, they had no interest in doing so even
if they had the resources. The logic of a modernist, urban, intellectual-
led political movement and that of rural insurgency remained fundamentally incongruent. Rather, their ultimate hope remained that politically
cautious participation would bear fruit and produce political concessions after the war from which the nation, and the Jadids as the nation's
leaders, would benefit. National interests do not exist beyond the competing parochial interests of the social agents that compose the nation,
but are articulated in the struggles of those groups.

Ultimately, the strategy was unsuccessful. Russian officialdom mis-
took the striving for inclusion for separatism, and the campaign against
corrupt functionaries became, in its eyes, terrorism. Jadid involvement
in the mobilization of 1916 was either easily forgotten or else ascribed
to the opportunism of ambitious individuals. The revolution of 1905
had not dented autocracy's will to exclude all social groups from matters of political import in the colonial periphery that was Turkestan.
Turkestan might be defined by the "fanaticism" of its inhabitants, but
the ambitions of its modern elites were equally, if not more, dangerous.
Official hostility proved insurmountable. That was only half the battle
for the Jadids, however. Equally significant was conflict within their society. Officials investigating the dark deeds of Khojaev and his associates
in Andiǧān had no trouble finding people in Andiǧān and elsewhere to
fill its dossiers with denunciations of the group.[95] The nation was deeply
divided just as revolution in distant Petrograd hurled it into a new era
of political opportunity.

95. TsGARUz, f. 276, d. 916.

CHAPTER 8

1917: The Moment of Truth

The Russian revolution of February 1917 arrived in Turkestan by tele-gram and took everyone by surprise. Overnight, the political order in place for a half-century disappeared. Groups scrambling to organize in the new order followed the example of events unfolding in Petrograd, but since social tensions in Turkestan had little in common with those of distant Petrograd, the politics of the new era were fully embedded in the colonial realities of Turkestan. The familiar patterns of dual power appeared in Turkestan, too, as executive committees of the Provisional Government appeared side by side with soviets of workers', soldiers', and peasants' deputies within the first few days of the revolution, but both sides represented the Russian population. Far more significant was the divide between Russian and Muslim politics, as the Russian-native dichotomy that had framed Central Asian life since the conquest became a significant political vector.

The revolution also transformed the nature of Muslim politics in Turkestan. Overnight, the struggle over culture, confined to a restricted public space and fought over schools and newspapers, was transformed into an explicitly political struggle to be decided by the vote. This put the Jadids in a difficult position, for it was quite clear that their struggle for authority within their society had just begun. Strategies that worked in the struggles of urban elites did not always succeed in the era of mass mobilization. As the conflict between the Jadids and their opponents came into the open, it shaped the reactions of both sides to the opportunities opened up by the revolution. The Jadids embraced the promise of liberal constitutionalism embodied in the February revolution and, in keeping with their political strategies of the tsarist period, sought to maximize Turkestan's participation in Russian life, a hope reiterated by Jadid writers throughout the year. Their opponents sought to protect the local specificities that marked Turkestan's position in the empire and upheld their position within Turkestani society.

For the Jadids, 1917 was a turning point. The emergence of open politics pitched them in unforeseen directions. They struggled on two fronts: for the defense of their nation's interests against the colonial aspirations of the Russian population of Turkestan, and for control of their nation's destiny against many opponents in their own society. Before the year was out, many of them found themselves experimenting with running a government. Their lack of success led to a fundamental shift in both the premises of their reform and the political strategies they were willing or able to employ. The year 1917 marked a shift from the politics of admonition to those of mobilization, while the nation for whose benefit the Jadids acted in politics came to be imagined increasingly as an ethnic entity, with the rhetoric of Turkism firmly being foregrounded. As we will see in the Epilogue, both of these shifts were of paramount importance in understanding the politics of the early Soviet period.

COLONIAL REVOLUTION

A. N. Kuropatkin, the recently appointed governor-general, put the matter in its imperial context when he confided to his diary on 6 March: "Nothing special has happened yet, but we can expect anything, even terrorist acts, which are especially dangerous in Asia where we Russians form a third [sic] among the 10 million strong native population."[1] His first instinct, therefore, was to suppress the news of the revolution in Petrograd, but his efforts at concealment were unsuccessful, and the news became widely known through unofficial channels in Tashkent early the next morning.[2] On 2 March, Russian workers of the Central Asian and Tashkent railways organized a soviet, which in turn elected a Tashkent Soviet of Workers' Deputies on 3 March. Soldiers at the Tashkent garrison followed two days later and organized a Soviet of Soldiers' Deputies

1. "Iz dnevnika A. N. Kuropatkina," *Krasnyi arkhiv,* no. 20 (1927): 60.
2. *Istoriia Tashkenta s drevneishikh vremen do pobedy fevral'skoi burzhuazno-demokraticheskoi revoliutsii* (Tashkent, 1988), 286.

on 5 March. The same day, the Tashkent City Duma called a meeting of all public organizations, which proceeded to elect a nineteen-member Executive Committee of Public Organizations with V. P. Nalivkin, a moderate Menshevik in spite of his long career as a functionary in Turkestan, as chair.[3] All the trappings of dual power were in place in Tashkent.

The initial assumption among all sectors of Russian society was that the revolution would not question their supremacy in Turkestan and that it would remain a largely Russian affair, as had been the case in 1905. The earliest efforts to organize public life in Tashkent therefore made no attempt to include the native population. The public organizations represented in the Executive Committee were all organizations of Russians in the Russian part of Tashkent, and dual power was at first a purely Russian affair. The token presence of "natives"—Ubaydullah Khojaev and Tāshpolād Nārbutabekov were coopted into the Tashkent Executive Committee to represent the old city—only served to underscore this assumption. On 6 March, Kuropatkin addressed separate assemblies of Russians and Muslims, assuring the latter (in an abridged version of his speech to the Russian assembly) that "under the new order of life in Russia their lives, too, will be easier than before."[4]

But this was not to be a repeat of 1905. The rise of the reading and listening public over the previous decade and, more importantly, the war and the uprising of 1916, had politicized local society, and in March 1917 the proclamation of the new order was universally celebrated as the dawn of a new age of liberty, equality, and justice. A long poem, "The New Freedom," by the Tashkent poet Sirājiddin Makhdum Sidqi, published in an enormous edition of 10,000 copies on 12 March, provides a glimpse at how the revolution was received in this distant colony of the Russian empire. "Praise be that the epoch of freedom has arrived. The sun of justice has lit the world. . . . The time of love and truth has come. . . . Now, we have to set aside our false thoughts; . . . the most important aim must be to give thought to how we will live happily in the arena of freedom."[5] A few weeks later, Sidqi published another narrative poem giving an account of the revolution in Petrograd with a print run of 25,000. Here again, Sidqi's fundamental theme was liberty: The events in Petrograd, which he recounts in considerable detail, were the

3. P. A. Kovalev, *Revoliutsionnaia situatsiia 1915–1917 gg. i ee proiavleniia v Turkestane* (Tashkent, 1971), 217.

4. "Iz dnevnika," 60.

5. Sirājiddin Makhdum Sidqi, *Tāza hurriyat* (Tashkent, 1917), 2.

culmination of a long struggle by the people of Russia for liberty that
dated back to the Pugachev revolt in the 1770s. The verse format of the
pamphlet bridged the gap in intelligibility by translating the episode into
a form fully accessible to the local population.[6]

Sidqi's call for action was echoed by many others in Turkestan. The
newly established newspaper *Rawnaq ul-Islām* declared that "it . . . [was
now] necessary to pass from the epoch of words to the era of deeds."[7]
Even Behbudi broke his composure and in a moment of excitement criticized the old regime, in which "missionaries, or rather men wishing to
destroy us and our sacred shariat," had subordinated the shariat to the
Turkestan Statute.[8] And indeed, in the very first days of the new order,
a number of organizations appeared among the Muslim population. The
Jadids played a crucial part in this period of organization. As early as
5 March, activists in the old city of Tashkent formed a committee to "explain the meaning of the revolution to the Muslim population and to prepare it to take advantage of the new political situation."[9] On 9 March,
a public meeting in old Tashkent, presided over by Ubaydullah Khojaev
and Munawwar Qāri, attracted 20,000 people.[10] Another, even larger
public meeting on 13 March at the main mosque elected by acclamation
four deputies to the Tashkent Executive Committee. The meeting also
elected a separate commissar for the old city and resolved to elect a
forty-eight–member committee to administer it. This committee met the
following day and chose the name Tāshkand Shurā-yi Islāmiya (Tashkent Muslim Council) for itself. In due course, the Shura decided to send
delegations to other cities in Turkestan to initiate organizations, induct
new members, and raise funds.[11] But similar meetings, perhaps on a less
spectacular scale, took place in almost every city of Turkestan.

The Tashkent Shura, which in contemporary Russian sources was
commonly translated as the "Soviet of Muslim Deputies," was clearly
intended to be the counterpart of the soviet in the Russian city. In the
long run, this audacious bid to secure self-administration did not suc-

6. Sidqi, *Buyuk Rusiya inqilābi* (Tashkent, 1917). Sidqi's poems are only one example
of a minor literary explosion unleashed by the February revolution in Turkestan. For obvious reasons, this corpus has received no scholarly attention.

7. *Rawnaq ul-Islām* (Kokand), no date (April 1917), no. 5.

8. Mahmud Khoja Behbudi, "Bizga islāhāt kerak," *Najāt*, 17 April 1917.

9. D. I. Manzhara, *Revoliutsionnoe dvizhenie v Srednei Azii 1905–1920 gg. (Vospominaniia)* (Tashkent, 1934), 36.

10. *Najāt*, 23 March 1917. The figure of 20,000 was most likely exaggerated, but it
nevertheless indicates a completely unprecedented scale of mobilization.

11. *Najāt*, 26 March 1917 *UT*, 25 April 1917; *Tirik soz* (Kokand), 2 April 1917.

ceed, and the Shura came to be a coordinating committee of Muslim organizations in Tashkent. By the summer, when other organizations had
emerged beyond its ambit and, eventually, in direct opposition to it, it
had become one Muslim organization among many in Tashkent. But in
March, it served to assert a Muslim presence in the politics of the most
important city in Turkestan, and it tapped the widespread enthusiasm
aroused by the revolution.

This enthusiasm was also reflected in the rebirth of the vernacular
press. The first month of the new order saw a number of newspapers
launched in Tashkent, Samarqand, and Kokand. However, the biggest
coup was the takeover of the *TWG* by a group of Jadids in mid-March.
In pursuance of demands by social organizations that both *TWG* and its
parent publication, *Turkestanskie vedomosti,* be given over to the public (*obshchestvo*),[12] the Tashkent Executive Committee of the Provisional
Government organized a public meeting on 12 March to discuss the fate
of *TWG.* The meeting, with Nalivkin in chair, convened in the Teachers'
Seminary, which since its inception in 1879 had been headed by N. P.
Ostroumov, who was present as editor of *TWG.* In attendance were
Munawwar Qāri, Ubaydullah Khojaev, and a host of other Tashkent
Jadids. Ostroumov resigned as editor before the meeting began, and his
permission to leave was granted. Nalivkin, speaking in Turkic, decried
"the extremely constrained position" of the vernacular press that had
existed until then but expressed hope for a better future "now that there
are no secrets between the government and the Muslims." The evening
ended with Munawwar Qāri being elected the new editor of the newspaper, which was renamed *Najāt* (Salvation).[13]

Ostroumov might have thought the world had turned upside down.
The same bewilderment is clear in a letter sent to a Tashkent newspaper
by N. S. Lykoshin, the orientalist and longtime Turkestan hand who until recently had been governor of Samarqand oblast. Lykoshin drew his
readers' attention to "the transformation in the worldview of our natives," who never had even as many popular rights as those expressed
in the Novgorod *veche.* The difference between Russian and native had
to be established, even if only through an appeal to the hoary myths
of eleventh-century Novgorod. "These people lived for centuries under

12. TsGARUz, f. 1, op. 8, d. 528, ll. 16–160b.
13. Gr. Andreev, "Soveshchanie po reorganizatsii 'Turkestanskoi Tuzemnoi Gazety,'"
Turkestanskie vedomosti, 16 March 1917; "Tarikhi majlis, yākhud Āstrāumof ornida
Munawwar Qāri," *Najāt,* 19 March 1917.

the despotic administration of their khans and amirs, under the severe statutes of their strict religion. . . . Our natives were never citizens; they were always only members of the general Muslim religious community, regardless of which state they happened to live in." Their incapacity to become citizens was clearly demonstrated in 1916, when, "presented with the demand to raise troops, our natives responded not as citizens, but simply as people in whom the instinct for self-preservation was much stronger than [the sense of] duty. . . . Disorders erupted in the region, Russian blood flowed, and punitive expeditions were called up." Once "pacified" (and Lykoshin knew all about the "pacification," for he had been responsible for the suppression of the uprising in Jizzakh, one of the bloodier episodes in the uprising), the natives had turned to other unsavory practices, such as the campaign of petitions against functionaries launched by "the secret society 'Taraqqiparwar.'" It was in these conditions that the natives entered Russian political life. "The administration explained to the natives the recent events, but of course it was not possible to explain everything completely. The native mass heard nothing sensibly, and understood nothing sensibly. Only it became clear that with the change in the government, our native population was also given the same rights as the other citizens of our fatherland. . . . This our practical natives understood very well and, not thinking apparently of the *obligations* of Russian citizenship, turned all their attention to the most rapid realization of their new rights." Lykoshin's ire was raised by events in Samarqand, where the organizers of the first executive committee, formed on 5 March, had coopted two Muslims (one of whom was Behbudi) as its members. At its first meeting, however, the committee had decided that the Muslim population should elect its own deputies. A mass meeting held two days later had resurrected the petition campaign and, in addition to calumniating various members of the administration, had been impertinent enough to ask that taxes raised in old Samarqand not be spent on the Russian part of town and that Muslims be granted not two, but fifty-eight of the ninety seats in the executive committee.[14]

Lykoshin's views were not necessarily typical of the Russian population, but the unease at the prospect of the transformation of natives into citizens was widely shared. Once the bewilderment had worn off and it became clear that the Provisional Government intended to extend full citizenship to Turkestan and to grant its Muslim inhabitants the fran-

14. N. S. Lykoshin, "Grazhdane tuzemtsy!" *Turkestanskii kur'er,* 19 March 1917.

chise on the same basis as other citizens, Russian organizations acted to protect their privileged status in the region.[15] This took the form of a demand at the Regional Congress of Executive Committees in April to create separate dumas for the Russian and "native" parts of cities in Turkestan, each controlling separate budgets. This attempt to protect the privileges that had been assured under the old regime (the Tashkent Duma was assured a two-thirds Russian composition) and to protect the interests of the Russian population from the impact of democracy clearly pitted the Russian community against the local population. In mid-summer, this issue took a different form, as local Russians demanded the creation of a special electoral unit for the Russian population of Turkestan in the elections to the Constituent Assembly to ensure that the local Russian population was not drowned in the sea of local voters. Both these demands directly contradicted the principle of universal and equal franchise and were contested by Muslim representatives.

The Russian left, which had a considerable presence in Turkestan (the region had returned several socialist deputies to the Second Duma), did not differ markedly in this respect from the rest of Russian society. A Soviet of Soldiers' and Workers' Deputies had emerged in Tashkent at the very beginning of the revolution. Given the situation in Turkestan, it was by definition a Russian institution. The labor movement in Turkestan had always been a Russian affair, with little effort to propagandize the "natives." In the conditions of empire, even Russian workers were a prosperous elite in Turkestan, since "belonging to the industrial proletariat in [this] tsarist colony was the national privilege of the Russians."[16] For the labor movement, native society with its dark Asiatic masses signified little more than the panorama of backwardness that socialism was to conquer. It had failed to protest against the atrocities committed against the local population in 1916. For its part, the Muslim artisans were organized along very different principles. The struggles of the Russian labor movement would scarcely have been intelligible to them even if the Russians had made any effort to be inclusive.[17] The case of the soldiers

---

15. In April, the Provisional Government ordered new elections for all existing municipal dumas (including that of Tashkent) on the basis of universal suffrage (Robert Paul Browder and Alexander F. Kerensky, eds., *The Russian Provisional Government, 1917: Documents,* 3 vols. [Stanford: Stanford University Press, 1961], I: 261–262). It also introduced dumas into other cities in Turkestan.

16. G. Safarov, *Kolonial'naia revoliutsiia—opyt Turkestana* (Oxford, 1985 [orig. Moscow, 1921]), 110.

17. Ibid., 83 et passim. For a similarly harsh appraisal of the Russian labor movement and the early Soviet regime in Turkestan, see the opening pages of S. Ginzburg, "Basma-

was even more obvious: Even the most humble Russian soldier in Turkestan was a member of an occupying force and derived his identity on the colonial fringe from that fact. Moreover, many of the soldiers stationed in Turkestan in February 1917 were recent arrivals, having been sent just the previous autumn to quell the uprising against recruitment. Russian peasants, mostly armed settlers competing with the local population for land and water, were also quick to organize soviets. The majority of them lived in Semirech'e, where the bloodshed from the previous year continued well past the revolution.[18] The soviets' claim to power thus violated the principle of autonomy of Turkestan on both "national" and territorial grounds, but their monopoly over armed force in the region at a time when all constituted authority was disintegrating ensured that they emerged as very significant political actors.

MUSLIM POLITICS

Many of the local Muslim organizations founded in the first weeks of the revolution were concerned primarily with cultural or educational issues, while others had more overtly political aims, although the two sets of goals were rarely separable. The Splendor of Islam Society (Rawnaq ul-Islām Jamiyati) in Katta Qorghān, for instance, aimed to "acquaint the people with the present situation and to send people to the villages to spread ideas of citizenship [ghrāzhdānliq] and knowledge, in order to prepare our brothers for the Constituent Assembly and to reform our schools."[19] Along with the mushrooming of organizations went the adoption, no matter how superficially, of new norms of procedure. On 22 March a meeting of the prominent ulama of Kokand began with the election of a chair and a secretary to record the minutes of the proceedings.[20] Agendas were drawn up for meetings and minutes diligently kept and promptly published in the press. The revolution had produced new forms of sociability among the local population that the tsarist regime had done its utmost to curtail. Although the more ambitious among

---

chestvo v Fergane," in *Ocherki revoliutsionnogo dvizheniia v Srednei Azii: sbornik statei* (Moscow, 1926)

18. Marco Buttino, "Turkestan 1917, la révolution des russes," *Cahiers du monde russe et soviétique*, 32 (1991): 66–67, 70–71.

19. *UT*, 5 May 1917, 3. Very similar aims were expressed by the Muslim Education Society in Samarqand (*Samarqand anjuman-i maārif-i islāmiya jamiyatining mukhtasar proghrāmasi* [Samarqand, 1917], 2–7).

20. *Tirik soz*, 2 April 1917.

them could still comment with dismay that most of the new organizations remained mere societies or circles,[21] there was little question that the nature of politics had changed irrevocably in Turkestan.

For the Jadids, the revolution was a summons to action, and they acted to realize their long-held wishes. The organizational activity of the first weeks of the revolutionary era bore the marks of cultural struggles of Central Asia. The enthusiasm that led to the reemergence of the periodical press was replicated in other areas of Jadid concern. Munawwar Qāri organized a commission in early March to work toward creating a common program for all Muslim schools in Turkestan and to suggest ways of introducing the teaching of Russian into them.[22] New-method teachers formed unions in Tashkent and Kokand and, in true revolutionary fashion, convened a Turkestan Teachers' Congress, which met in Tashkent on 20 May.[23] Over the summer, the Jadid-led Turkestan Central Council organized teacher training courses in Tashkent, which paralleled similar initiatives in Samarqand.[24] Abdullah Awlāni went as Turkestan's delegate to the All-Russian Muslim Teachers' Congress in Kazan in August 1917, where he was elected to the presidium.[25]

The revolution opened up entirely new domains to competition among Muslim elites of Turkestan. Now the state came to occupy a central place in their thinking about the future; the politics of admonition gave way to the politics of mobilization, and votes took the place of exhortation. They sought to use the freedoms allowed by the revolution to ensure full participation for Turkestan in the political life of the Russian republic (which had been a basic political goal of the Jadids before the revolution). The possibilities seemed limitless now. The fundamental task was to ensure that the nation knew how to take advantage of them. Exhortations to unity and action abounded in the Jadid press, and they were combined with warnings about the dangers of not seizing the opportunity provided by the revolution: "[If we let this moment go,] it will be an enormous crime, a betrayal of not just ourselves, but of all Muslims. . . . We will leave a bad name behind in the history of Turkestan. God forbid, we will be accountable both to coming generations and to our ancestors and will receive retribution both in this world and

21. "Turkistānda tashkilāt masalasi," *Kengash*, 11 July 1917.
22. Ibrāhim Tāhir, "Maktab wa madrasalar islāhi," *UT*, 5 May 1917.
23. "Turkistān muallimlar isyizdi," *UT*, 24 May 1917.
24. *Kengash*, 25 July 1917; *Hurriyat*, 18 July 1917.
25. *Kengash*, 20 August 1917.

afterlife. O Muslims of Turkestan! . . . Let this time not pass!"[26] The Jadids also asserted their claim, implicit in their rhetoric of the previous decade and a half, to lead their society in the new era. Their possession of modern knowledge, especially of the Russian language, gave them the necessary qualifications for that role. Conversely, the Jadids commonly asserted that the traditional educations of the ulama had left them incapable of understanding, let alone making use of, the opportunities offered by the new turn of events.

The emergence of open politics brought the Jadids in cooperation with those Russian-educated Central Asian intellectuals who had played little or no role in the politics of cultural reform. Tāshpolād Nārbutabekov, a lawyer, was from the beginning very prominent in Muslim politics. The revolution found Mustafā Choqāy in Petrograd, where he worked in the offices of the Muslim Faction at the State Duma. He took the first train to Turkestan. Also taking the train was the young Bashkir historian Ahmed Zeki Velidi (1894–1970), who had spent some time in Central Asia several years earlier doing his research. Until August, when Bashkir politics claimed his attention, he played a very visible role in organizational matters. Delegations from Kazan and Transcaucasia arrived to help local Jadids organize, and some of their members ran for office. A number of lines dissolved in 1917, and the Jadids became part of a broad coalition of groups whose major common characteristics were their youth and a will to participate in the liberal politics of the revolution.

The Jadids' claim to leadership was contested by other groups in society. Tensions appeared at the outset. The induction of Khojaev and Nārbutabekov into the Tashkent Executive Committee on March 6 led to grumbling in the city about "why have the youth [*yāshlar*] entered the committee when no ulama, functionaries, or merchants were included?" The Jadids were able to contain conflict on this occasion by going door to door over the next few days and putting the matter before the public meeting of 13 March, which in addition to ratifying the election of these two, elected two more representatives (both Jadids) to the committee.[27] But much tougher struggles lay ahead. The Jadids retained control of the Tashkent Shura, but many other organizations, especially outside the

26. Muallim M. H., "Bukun qāndāy kun?" *Kengash* (Kokand), 15 April 1917, 12. For other expressions of such anxiety, see Shākirjān Rahimi, "Eng zor wazifalarimiz," *Najāt*, 23 March 1917; Ābidjān Mahmudov, editorial in *Tirik soz*, 2 April 1917; Mirmuhsin Shermuhammadov, "Hurriyatdan nechuk fāidalanamiz," *Najāt*, 9 April 1917.

27. "Tāshkandda hurriyat harakatlari," *Najāt*, 23 March 1917.

capital, appeared far beyond their purview. Many revolved around personalities, in effect transforming the informal politics of colonial Turkestan into the formal politics of the revolutionary era. Tashkent Jadids hoped to create a network of organizations covering all of Turkestan, but no coordinated effort ever came about. The title "Shurā-yi Islām" proved quite popular, but the various shuras in Turkestan had little in common with the Tashkent organization. In Samarqand, the local shura was the organization of the ulama, many of whom were inimical to the Jadids. The three organizations in Āq Masjid represented various factions of local notables.[28] But the most intriguing story came from Andijān.

Representatives of the Tashkent Shura arriving in Andijān walked into the ancient rivalry between two local millionaires, Mir Kāmil-bāy and Ahmetbek Temirbekov. Mir Kāmil interfered in the meetings of the newly established organization (in one instance, his minions forced all Tatars present to wear a *chalma* (turban), and expelled those who refused),[29] while Temirbekov refused to have anything to do with the Tashkent delegates. Instead, he asked the local executive committee for permission to start "his own" Shurā-yi Islām. When permission was not granted, he named his organization Hurriyat (Liberty). By late May, though, numerous other organizations had come into existence and joined together to form a Ferghana Oblast Soviet of Deputies of Muslim Organizations. On 20 May, this soviet, in conjunction with the Turkestan Soviet of Soldiers' and Workers' Deputies, managed to have Mir Kāmil exiled from Turkestan and Temirbekov sent off to Tashkent. They were allowed to return in mid-July, but only on condition that they not interfere with public affairs until the election of the Constituent Assembly.[30]

Moderate Jadids emphasized unity in their attempts at organization. When Munawwar Qāri organized the school commission in March, he invited maktab teachers to participate, clearly an attempt to build bridges with more conservative groups. The Union of Teachers in Kokand similarly took a conciliatory stance toward the ulama. As the editorial in the first issue of its magazine asserted, the community needed the ulama for guidance in religious affairs just as much as it needed open-minded, Russian-speaking, modern-educated people to take the helm in the po-

28. Mustafa Çokay, *1917 Yılı Hatıra Parçaları* (Ankara, 1988), 17–19.

29. *UT*, 20 May 1917, 4.

30. "Protokol zasedaniia S"ezda Andizhanskikh obshchestvennykh musul'manskikh uezdno-gorodskikh organizatsii ot 14–17oe iiulia 1917 goda," TsGARUz, f. 1044, d. 24, ll. 26–27ob.

litical realm.[31] However, other aspects of Jadid activity worked against this attempted conciliation. One of the Jadids' first organized efforts after the revolution was a campaign against corrupt or incompetent qāzis. This was clearly a continuation of the campaign pursued the previous winter by Ubaydullah Khojaev and Vadim Chaikin, but now it tapped into the general revolutionary sentiment against the old order. The Tashkent Shura called for the re-election of all qāzis who had been serving for more than three years, and two days later it resolved to form a committee to "dismiss those old functionaries whose continued employment is harmful" in the new era.[32] In Kokand, one of the first acts of the local shura was the dismissal of several qāzis.[33] Many of these functionaries, and especially the qāzis among them, were to form the backbone of the opposition to Jadids that emerged by late spring.

The high point of the political movement came early, when it organized the First Turkestan Muslim Congress, from 16 to 22 April, in Tashkent. Although the congress was not representative in the strict sense of the word (Muslim organizations from all over Turkestan were invited to send delegates with mandates, but more than 100 delegates arrived on their own out of a sense of civic duty),[34] the mere fact of its convening only seven weeks after the fall of the autocracy was remarkable. The congress opened in the mansion of the governor-general with typical revolutionary pomp, as representatives of the Provisional Government, Turkestan Congress of Executive Committees, and Turkestan Soviet of Soldiers' and Workers' Deputies greeted its inaugural session.[35] The elections to the presidium of the congress signified a victory for the Jadids: Munawwar Qāri was elected president, and Ubaydullah Khojaev, Mustafā Choqāy, Nārbutabekov, Islam Shahiahmedov, and Zeki Velidi were among those elected to the presidium.[36] The congress also elected a twelve-member delegation to attend the forthcoming All-Russian Muslim Congress organized by the Muslim Faction of the Duma in Moscow and decided to establish a Turkestan Muslim Central Council (Turkistān Milli Markaz Shurāsi) as its standing executive organ.[37] Although this organ did not begin work until 1 June, it was to provide an invaluable institutional base

---

31. Muallim Hakimjān Mirzākhānzāda, "E'tizārga e'tizār," *Kengash,* 15 April 1917, 14.

32. *Najāt,* 26 March 1917; 9 April 1917; 15 April 1917.

33. Muallim Shākir al-Mukhtāri, *Kim qāzi bolsin* (Kokand, 1917), 2; *UT,* 5 May 1917.

34. *UT,* 25 April 1917.

35. *Turkestanskie vedomosti,* 22 April 1917.

36. *UT,* 25 April 1917.

37. *Kengash,* 31 August 1917.

for the Jadids; through it, the Jadids could claim to speak in the name of all Muslims of Turkestan. The sixteen-point program for the congress included a wide array of questions dealing with the political future of Turkestan, ranging from the attitude toward the new government, the forms of state organization, food supply, and land and water rights, to questions of education reform.[38]

Yet, even the euphoria of the occasion could not hide the acute tensions within Muslim society. The congress was sharply divided on the question of autonomy. All had celebrated the dawn of freedom, and all could agree on the desirability of autonomy, but different groups had very different ideas about the meaning of these terms. The ulama were wary of a redefinition of culture that undermined their position as its authoritative interpreters. The Jadids' eagerness to use the opportunities afforded by the revolution to seek full participation for Turkestan in the new order also threatened to collapse the walls that sustained the ulama's status within the community. The ulama's response to the revolution therefore took the form of an attempt to maximize the space allowed by the regime to the regional and cultural peculiarities of Turkestan and to attempt to cordon off as much of their society as possible from the depredations of the new universalist order inaugurated by the revolution. In practical terms, it meant demands for broadening the competence of Muslim courts to new areas of criminal and personal law, which would have placed the ulama in greater control of Muslim society.[39] The ulama were less concerned with participation in mainstream imperial life, for while they could reach accommodation with outsiders, they had no patience for those within their own society who sought to undermine their authority.

Non-Russians in the country widely assumed that the democratic Russia of the future would provide some sort of autonomy for its various nationalities. As various groups across the empire organized politically and sought to be recognized as future autonomous subjects, they debated the choice between territorial and cultural forms of autonomy (the latter would have guaranteed nationalities such cultural rights as those of language, education, and representation, without attaching those to a territory). The debate came in this form to Turkestan. Most Jadids favored cultural autonomy, for they feared that without outside help they

38. *UT*, 25 April 1917; see also Browder and Kerensky, eds., *Russian Provisional Government*, I: 420–421.

39. Çokay, *1917 Yılı*, 49.

would be swamped by the enormous influence the ulama wielded in Turkestan and thus be marginalized in public life. Behbudi, along with Zeki Velidi, vehemently opposed this position and insisted that the congress vote for territorial autonomy. They were successful, and the congress voted in favor of a democratic federative republic for Russia with Turkestan enjoying wide territorial autonomy.[40] The Jadids' fear of territorial autonomy turned out to be justified, although a different resolution at the congress would hardly have mattered.

Conflict came into the open by late spring. In Kokand, Hamza had early got into trouble with his peers, when an article he wrote in the Kokand magazine *Kengash* (Counsel) provoked criticism for its generally harsh tone.[41] In Tashkent, the Turān party (*toda*), under the leadership of Abdullah Awlāni, consistently took a more radical line than the Shura. It began by requisitioning, in true revolutionary fashion, the offices of the municipal chief of Tashkent for use as its headquarters (a rare, perhaps unique, instance of such revolutionary initiative from a Muslim organization).[42] In July it was instrumental in hosting a delegation from the Turkic Federalist Party based in Ganjä in Transcaucasia. But it was an article by Mir Muhsin Shermuhammadov in the second issue of its newspaper *Turān* that brought matters between the Jadids and their opponents to a head. Mir Muhsin, recently returned from a year at the new-method Galiye madrasa in Ufa, expressed the usual Jadid criticisms of traditional education. These sentiments had been repeated *ad nauseum* by Jadid writers and orators since the turn of the century, but now certain ulama seized upon it as a show of strength. Mir Muhsin's criticism of a medieval tract on Arabic grammar was deemed blasphemous by the qāzi of the Sibzār section of Tashkent, and although Awlāni apologized publicly in the next issue of the newspaper, Mir Muhsin was arrested and sentenced to death for apostasy.[43] The sentence far exceeded the qāzi's

---

40. Contemporary reports (e.g., *Najāt*, 23 April 1917) unfortunately do not provide details of this debate. Behbudi recounted his views several months later: "Turkistān mukhtāriyati," *Hurriyat*, 19 December 1917; A. Z. V. Togan, *Hâtıralar: Türkistan ve Diğer Müslüman Doğu Türklerinin Millî Varlık ve Kültür Mücadeleleri* (Istanbul, 1969), 152–153; see also Ahlullah Khayrullah oghli, "Türkistanda birinchi 'qurultay,'" *Shura*, 15 July 1917, 323–324.

41. The article in question seems never to have been published, but the debate it provoked became public when Hamza complained in a different newspaper that he had been censored in a manner worse than he had experienced in the imperial period; see Hamza, "E"tizor," in *Tôla asarlar tôplami,* ed. N. Karimov et al., 5 vols. (Tashkent, 1988–1989), IV: 269. For *Kengash*'s response, see Mirzākhānzāda, "E'tizārga e'tizār," 14.

42. *UT*, 7 July 1917.

43. "Shāyān-i ta'assuf wāqealar," *UT*, 31 May 1917. This incident caused comment in the Tatar press as well; see *Shura*, 15 June 1917, 286–287.

competence, but what was truly at stake was not blasphemy but an assertion by the ulama of their power within Muslim society as well as a
challenge to the new Russian authorities. Ultimately, Mir Muhsin was
rescued by the police from the Russian quarter and his sentence was
"commuted" to eighteen months' imprisonment. Mir Muhsin managed
to escape and with financial help from friends among the Jadids returned
to Ufa, but the absence of widespread protest against this action was
proof that the ulama retained moral and religious authority among the
population at large, surely a disturbing sign for the Jadids.

As disagreements deepened, the ulama in Tashkent split from the
Shura and formed their own organization, the Ulamā Jamiyati (Society
of Ulama). Again, the new principle of sociability is worth noting, for
the Ulamā Jamiyati was a modern organization quite distinct from the
ulama's traditional modes of association. Although technically not a political party, the Ulamā Jamiyati often functioned as one, as is clear from
its actions during the rest of the year, when it mounted political campaigns, ran candidates for office, held conferences, and published magazines. Nor was it merely a trade union for the ulama; it was a political
organ representing the interests of all traditional elites in Turkestani society. It was headed not by a religious dignitary but by Sher Ali Lapin, a
Russian-educated Qazaq who had spent years in Russian service as an
interpreter and was currently a lawyer.[44] Nor was the Jamiyat averse to
forming alliances with Russian parties of the right and the left, as its
progress through the year showed.

The campaign for elections to the Tashkent Duma, set for late July after the Russians had dropped their demand for segregated dumas, pitted
the Jadids directly against the ulama in a test of political strength.[45] An
offer by the Shura to field a joint slate of all Muslim groups in the city was
rebuffed by the ulama, who saw little need to cooperate with their rivals.
The Shura responded with a pamphlet that severely criticized "certain
mullas and old functionaries who have united with foreign enemies who
do not wish Muslims to achieve progress and take their affairs in their
own hands and [who therefore] oppose the Shurā-yi Islāmiya."[46] Here
and throughout the campaign, the Shura stressed that its candidates

44. TsGARUz, f. 47, d. 2769, passim; Çokay, *1917 Yılı,* 18–19. Hélène Carrère
d'Encausse ("The Fall of the Czarist Empire," in Edward Allworth, ed., *Central Asia: A
Century of Russian Rule* [New York, 1967], 216), assuming the Ulamā Jamiyati to be a
purely clerical organization, automatically promotes Lapin to "a mullah."

45. Togan, *Hâtıralar,* 163–165.

46. Tāshkand Shurā-yi Islāmiyasi, *Khitābnāma* (Tashkent, 1917), 2.

would be able to function fruitfully in the duma because they had modern educations and were fluent in Russian. The purely traditional education of the ulama, the pamphlet went on to argue, rendered them ignorant of the times and of contemporary politics, and led them to be taken in by mischief makers (*fitnachilar*). The pamphlet also asserted the credentials of the Shura's candidates, many of whom were learned in traditional knowledge.[47]

The ulama's response was brief and caustic. In the few months of freedom, they stated in their response, the ulama of Tashkent had heard several criticisms from "inexperienced youth [*yāshlar*] . . . who had not received a complete religious or worldly education." The ulama had refused to field a joint slate because they knew who would be on that list and "which children [*bālalar*] would gain control of the public affairs of the Muslims of Tashkent. Keeping in mind the great importance of the duma, the ulama saw no public good coming out of cooperation in this matter with such youth."[48] The list of candidates put forward by the Ulamā Jamiyati was dominated by members of the religious elite.[49]

Two different bases of authority were at stake here. The Shura based its claim to authority and leadership on its superior knowledge of the current situation and its claim to be able to function fruitfully in the Duma and, later, in the Constituent Assembly. The ulama derived their authority from their possession of traditional knowledge still greatly valued by society. Their condescension about the inexperience of youth also tapped into the great respect accorded to age in Central Asia. Ultimately, the ulama's claims to leadership proved more authoritative as they won the election by a landslide, gaining an absolute majority in the new duma, while the Jadids could scrape together only eleven seats. Voting was strictly according to national lines, with much of the Russian vote going to the Socialist Revolutionaries (see Table 8).

Once elected, the Tashkent Duma found it difficult to accomplish much in the chaotic situation of the summer except to provide further evidence of the tensions that existed between the ulama and the Jadids. The election of a new chairman for the duma produced the first crisis. The Ulamā Jamiyati had no hesitation in putting forward as its candi-

47. Ibid., 5, 13.
48. Ulamā Jamiyati, *Haqiqatgha khilāf tārqatilgan khitābnāmagha jawāb wa ham bayān-i ahwāl* (Tashkent, 1917), 2, 5–7.
49. "V obshchestve mull," *Turkestanski kur'er*, 2 July 1917, in *Pobeda oktiabr'skoi revoliutsii v Uzbekistane: sbornik dokumentov* (henceforth *PORvUz*), 2 vols. (Tashkent, 1963–1972), I: 153.

**TABLE 8   TASHKENT CITY DUMA
ELECTION RESULTS, 1917**

List	Votes	Seats
Social Democrats	2,946	5
Social Revolutionaries	15,753	23
Ulamā Jamiyati	40,302	62
Union of Houseowners	1,124	2
Union of (Muslim) Construction Workers	477	1
Radical Democrats	1,569	2
Russian Jews	466	1
Soviet of (Russian) Public Organizations	1,156	2
(Russian) Construction Workers	18	—
Shurā-yi Islāmiya	7,160	11
Union of Shop Assistants	173	—
Cossacks	376	1
Party of People's Freedom	315	1
Society of Native Jews	360	1
Union of Soldiers' Wives	27	—
Progressive Women (Russian)	21	—
Total	72,241	112

SOURCE: *Kengash,* 6 August 1917

date Lykoshin, whose amazement at natives becoming citizens we noted above. However, strong protest from other parties led to his nomination being withdrawn, to be replaced by that of A. K. Iakhimovich, whose politics were described by a disgruntled Jadid newspaper report as "to the right of the Kadets." [50] Iakhimovich was finally elected chair in late August, signifying an alliance between the ulama and conservative Russians.

The issue of schools provided the ulama another opportunity to humiliate the Jadids. The ulama elected five of their number to the eight-member commission formed in August to inspect schools in the city, and

50. *UT,* 27 August 1917, 3.

one place went, ex officio, to the head of the duma. For the other two places, the Shura nominated Munawwar Qāri, the founder of the largest new-method school in Tashkent and widely recognized as the leader of the Jadid movement in the city. In a public insult to Munawwar Qāri and the Jadid cause, the ulama voted him down and instead elected two Russian socialist members of the duma to the commission.[51] The ulama deemed even radical Russians preferable to the Jadids in questions of cultural policy, an indication of how far apart the two sides had drifted over the summer.

Tashkent provided only the most telling example of a conflict that raged throughout Turkestan. First blood had been shed in mid-April during a confrontation in Namangān, although details of the incident are extremely sketchy.[52] In June, a meeting of the notable ulama of Kokand, called on the initiative of a qāzi who had been dismissed earlier in the year, decreed that Musa Jarullah Bigi, the renowned Tatar modernist *ālim*, and Ayaz Ishaki, the Tatar writer, were both infidels whose books should be gathered and burnt. The assembled ulama also demanded that they should have the right to supervise and censor all books and newspapers published in Turkestan.[53] Attitudes were also influenced by events in Bukhara, where the amir had mustered conservative forces against the Jadids. In May, a certain Mullā Khālmurād Tāshkandi, a conservative scholar in Bukhara, had obtained a fatwā decreeing all Jadids of Turkestan and Bukhara to be "enemies of the Islamic faith."[54]

The question of women's place in the new era proved to be a major source of conflict. The Provisional Government granted the franchise to all citizens of Russia over the age of twenty, regardless of sex. This momentous change upset all existing calculations in Turkestan. The Jadids welcomed these new rights and set about registering women voters. They saw the right to vote as a boost to the position of women, but they also deemed women's votes to be crucial to the success of Muslim candidates in an election based on proportional representation. They succeeded in

51. "Duma jivilishi," *UT*, 23 August 1917. In a few weeks, the commission decided to coopt four experts to help it in its work, and elected Munawwar Qāri as one of the four. But the ulama still managed to elect two teachers of old-method schools. "Maktab kāmisiyasi," *Kengash*, 8 September 1917.

52. I have encountered several indirect references to this incident: TsGARUz, f. 1044, d. 1, l. 36; see also a letter signed by representatives of two Andijān organizations expressing dismay at the activities of "the Protopopovs of Turkestan": "Turkistān Protāpāpavlari," *UT*, 14 June 1917.

53. "Khoqand ulamāsining qarāri," *UT*, 13 July 1917.

54. "Bukhara v 1917 godu," *Krasnyi arkhiv*, no. 20 (1927): 110.

securing a resolution of the April congress in favor of "giving" women the vote,[55] and in July they garnered the help of Tatar women in registering women voters. As a conciliatory measure, the Jadids approached the ulama for a fatwā on whether it was permissible for women to vote if separate polling facilities existed for them and they encountered no men in the process. For the ulama, the choice between ensuring the electoral strength of the Muslim community and relinquishing their vision of a Muslim society built on gendered patterns of authority was clear-cut. They ruled that women's right to vote contravened Islamic laws and was therefore impermissible. Eventually, some Muslim women did vote, but the issue proved highly divisive throughout Turkestan. Behbudi, ever the moderate, suggested that the Jadids yield on this question for the sake of "national" unity, although in a different context he rued the fact that women's votes were crucial in assuring Muslim control of the new organs of self-government.[56] This kind of unity was achieved in Katta Qorghān at least, where women simply did not vote in the elections.[57]

Class was conspicuously absent from this intense political conflict, which was played out in the language of the nation and of its culture. The local urban workforce had plenty of grievances: It had suffered the consequences of the rapid transformation of the local economy under the impact of cotton and had been adversely affected by the severe economic crisis that hit Turkestan after the outbreak of the war. But it was in a period of transition, in which older patterns of organization such as the guilds were dissolving and new forms of solidarities had not emerged. The political language of the Russian labor movement remained unintelligible to Muslim artisans operating in a very different moral economy.

Artisans did begin to organize, and a Soviet of Muslim Workers' Deputies was formed in Tashkent in June at the initiative of Muslim soldiers returned from duty in the rear of the front.[58] A Union of Muslim Toilers (Khoqand Musulmān Mehnatkashlar Ittifāqi) appeared in Kokand on 25 June, and a Muslim Artisans' Union (Sannāʿ ul-Islām) organized in Andijān with as many as 1,500 members.[59] Although Soviet historiography made much of the existence of Muslim labor organizations, it is unlikely that they shared much with the Russian soviets, which in turn made little effort to proselytize among the natives. A number of organizations

55. *Najāt*, 28 April 1917.
56. Behbudi, "Bayān-i haqiqat," *UT*, 12 June 1917; *Hurriyat*, 3 July 1917.
57. M. Khojayev, "Katta Qorghān," *Hurriyat*, 29 September 1917.
58. *PORvUz*, I: 281.
59. *Hurriyat*, 18 July 1917, 4 August 1917.

of Muslim artisans were headed by Jadids. The Tashkent Soviet of Muslim Workers was led by Abdullah Awlāni and Sanjar Asfendyarov, a
Qazaq medical doctor who was active in the Shura and who was to be
prominent in the Kokand Autonomy. Its journal, despite its proletarian
title (*Ishchilar dunyāsi* [Workers' World]), differed little from any other
Jadid publication.[60]

The most prominent class-based Muslim organization existed in Samarqand, where by July, Muslim politics had split between an organization called the Shurā-yi Islāmiya, dominated entirely by the ulama,
and a Muslim Executive Committee, which included members from "the
merchants and all other groups."[61] In August, a public gathering established the Samarqand Labor Union (Samarqand Zehmat Ittifāqi), which
fielded a full slate of candidates for the municipal elections held on 8 September. Eschewing the rhetoric of Muslim unity, it openly stressed the
specific needs of the poor.[62] Many candidates on the list were workers,
but among its organizers was Sayyid Ahmad Ajzi, and it acquired the
support of the Jadids of the city and of their newspaper, *Hurriyat* (Liberty). Behbudi stood aloof, however, while Wasli campaigned actively
against it. The campaign turned nasty, as the ulama declared supporters
of the Ittifāq to be infidels and threatened anyone who voted for them
with eviction from his neighborhood. Violence broke out on the day of
the election, in which eight supporters of the Ittifāq were badly injured.[63]
In the event, the Ittifāq won only 1,796 votes and four of the seventy-five
seats. The Shurā had entered the election in a coalition with the (Russian) Householders' Union, and their joint list (on which there were
twenty-five Russians) won fifty-five seats.[64]

It was obvious to the Jadids that they needed outside help. Their
domination of the Central Council gave them an institutional base from
which they could claim to speak on behalf of the indigenous population
of Turkestan, and in doing so, they could look for support to two outside sources that held considerable promise. A liberal democratic Russia

60. Its first issue included an article (in Ottoman) on universities in Japan, two articles
on the history of early Muslim dynasties, complete with tables on the titles and reigns of
Umayyad and Abbasid caliphs, and a piece of political commentary borrowed from *UT*.
61. Mufti Mahmud Khoja Behbudi, "Samarqandda milli ishlar haqqinda," *Hurriyat*,
28 July 1917.
62. E.g., "Samarqand Ishchilar Ittifāqining bayānnāmasi," *Hurriyat*, 25 August 1917.
63. S. Siddiqi, "Har asbāb oz ishi uchun yirāghlikdur," *Hurriyat*, 29 August 1917;
H. M. Shukrullah, "Shurā-yi Islāmiya wa sāylāw," *Hurriyat*, 19 September 1917. The list
of those injured is in *Hurriyat*, 12 September 1917.
64. "Shahr dumāsi," *Hurriyat*, 19 September 1917.

willing to recognize the principle of national rights while upholding a commitment to secularism and civil liberties could provide a cushion against the more reactionary demands of the ulama (as had clearly been demonstrated in the Mir Muhsin case). Similarly, incorporation into an all-Russian movement for Muslim unity under the modernist leadership of the Tatars, among whom Jadid reform had succeeded to a far greater extent, might have allowed the Jadids of Central Asia the moral and political support they needed to implement their reform, as well as providing a broader sphere of action at the all-Russian level. Yet, in the chaotic conditions of 1917, both these sources of support melted away, leaving the Jadids to wage their struggles by themselves.

The support of democratic Russia had great potential, and the early signs were hopeful. When the Tashkent Soviet of Soldiers' and Workers' Deputies placed Kuropatkin under arrest on 31 March, Petrograd approved the action and, recalling Kuropatkin, appointed a Turkestan Committee of nine members (five Russians and four Muslims, none of them from Turkestan) to govern the region until the Constituent Assembly could meet and determine its political status. The committee began with great enthusiasm and high hopes, holding its first meetings on the train to Tashkent as its members prepared to take on the challenge of governing a distant colony.[65] It was welcomed upon its arrival in Tashkent on 13 April by a throng of thousands. Troops played the "Marseillaise," and children from new-method schools sang "national" songs in the committee's honor.[66] But the euphoria evaporated almost immediately, as the Kadet background of its members led to opposition from the Turkestan Soviet, leading six of them to resign within weeks.[67] For much of the summer, the committee was inactive, although Nalivkin became its acting chair. Attempts to resurrect it continued down to October, but the committee was never a force to be reckoned with.

The All-Russian Muslim movement proved equally disappointing. participation in a larger Muslim community whose overall leadership was firmly in the hands of fellow Jadids appeared to Turkestani Jadids to be a guarantee against the influence of ulama at home. But the movement had tried, ever since its inception in 1904, to reconcile varied interests. Its Tatar leadership had hoped to use it as a vehicle for extending Tatar leadership to a wider constituency, hopes that were renewed in

65. Minutes of the meetings of the committee are in TsGARUz, f. 1044, d. 1.
66. *Najāt*, 17 April 1917.
67. TsGARUz, f. 1044, d. 1, ll. 173–1730b.

1917. The Kazan Muslim Committee sent a six-member delegation to Tashkent to help the local population organize for the awesome possibilities opened up by the revolution. Their natural affinities lay, of course, with the Jadids, but the venture proved ineffective from the beginning. The members of the delegation arrived one at a time, and although they were welcomed loudly,[68] the leadership of the Shura had ambivalent feelings toward them. The delegation spent considerable energy on organizational matters, but local leaders were suspicious of the uninvited guests, who understood little of the local realities but felt called upon nevertheless to give advice.[69] Differences came to the fore quite quickly; three of the members resigned and returned to Kazan by early June,[70] and another two returned at the end of August.[71] The All-Russian Muslim Congress at Moscow also proved unsuccessful in the long run. The fanfare of the occasion could not hide basic differences, and the conference turned into a contest between the Tatars and the rest over the question of autonomy: Mainstream Tatar opinion favored national-cultural autonomy, while almost everybody else voted in favor of territorial autonomy. Although, after lengthy debate, the congress passed a compromise resolution that recognized both forms of autonomy,[72] the confrontation cost a de facto Tatar withdrawal from the movement. The Second All-Russian Muslim Congress, held in Kazan in July, was an all-Tatar affair, its exclusivity underscored by its organizers' refusal to avoid a conflict with a Qazaq congress in Orenburg.[73]

Transcaucasian politicians attempted to fill the space vacated by the Tatars after June. The Ganja-based Türk Adäm-i Märkäziyät Firqäsi (Turkic Federalist Party)[74] sent a four-member delegation to Tashkent in June to establish a local organization of the party with the aim of form-

68. *UT,* 13 May 1917, 3.

69. The malaise was mutual; Abdullah Battal Taymas, one of the Kazan representatives, looked back on his visit as a waste of time: *Rus Ihtılâlinden Hâtıralar* (Istanbul, 1947), 39.

70. "Qazan hay'atining isti'fāsi," *UT,* 7 June 1917, 4.

71. "Qazan hay'ati," *UT,* 27 August 1917, 4.

72. Browder and Kerensky, eds., *Russian Provisional Government,* I: 409.

73. The proceedings of the Moscow congress are in *Butun Rusya Müsülmanlariniñ 1917nchi yilda 1–11 Mayda Mäskävdä bolghan umumi isyizdining protaqollarï* (Petrograd, 1917). See also Serge A. Zenkovsky, *Pan-Turkism and Islam in Russia* (Cambridge, 1960), 141–153.

74. On the Türk Adäm-i Märkäziyät Firqäsi, see Tadeusz Swietochowski, *Russian Azerbaijan, 1905–1920: The Shaping of National Identity in a Muslim Community* (Cambridge, 1985), 86, 90. *Adam-i markaziyat* is literally "decentralization," but the party's own publications translated it as *Tiurkskaia federativnaia partiia,* and I have followed that in translating the name into English.

ing a bloc of autonomist movements in the Constituent Assembly.[75] The delegation began by building bridges with the ulama and exhorting the Jadids to greater caution.[76] Its members traveled to various cities in Turkestan, establishing local cells and raising money. They seem to have achieved considerable success in garnering a consensus around the idea of autonomy, for in early September the party published its program, signed by fourteen men from several cities of Turkestan, including Munawwar Qāri and Behbudi.[77] Yet again, the ulama of Tashkent remained aloof, and not a single one of them appears among the signatories of the program.

The crisis deepened further in September, when the Jadids and the ulama held separate congresses. The Shura had called the second Turkestan Muslim Congress for early September to discuss the activity of the Central Council, the questions of land, water, and food supply, and the political future of Turkestan.[78] The ulama effectively sabotaged the congress by vehemently criticizing it in a pamphlet as a conference of atheists.[79] The congress opened with barely 100 delegates, instead of the 500 expected, and almost no ulama in attendance. It nevertheless heard a proposal, drafted by Islam Shahiahmedov, a graduate of the law faculty in Petrograd, outlining a plan for far-reaching autonomy for Turkestan. Shahiahmedov saw Turkestan enjoying territorial autonomy in a federal Russia. It was to have its own duma with authority in all matters except external affairs, defense, posts and telegraphs, and the judiciary. The region was to enjoy complete autonomy in the economic realm, including control over mineral and water resources. The project also called for the equality of all citizens of Russia, regardless of religion, nationality, or

75. Members of a delegation from Baku had attended the meeting of the Central Council on 26 June and been coopted into it: *Kengash,* 28 July 1917.

76. The first issue of its newspaper, *Turān,* published an article lavishing praise on the ulama: "A number of complaints have arisen since the beginning of Freedom because of discord between the ulama and the youth [*yāshlar*]. Gentlemen, even a little prudent reflection would force us to admit that today the ulama are our spiritual fathers and the supporters of our faith. If we youth deny their existence, we will be guilty [*gunāhgār*] for all time" ("Jahālat yuzindan i'tilāfsizlik," *Turān,* 1 September 1917). The next issue of the newspaper published a similarly laudatory article about the ulama: "Al-'ulamā' warsat ul- anbiyā'," *Turān,* 6 September 1917.

77. This document has been published in modern Uzbek by Ahmadjon Madaminov and Said Murod, eds., "Turkistonda khalq jumhuriyati," *Fan wa Turmush,* 1990, no. 7, 6–8; for an English translation and commentary, see Hisao Komatsu, "The Program of the Turkic Federalist Party in Turkistan (1917)," in H. B. Paksoy, ed., *Central Asia Reader: The Rediscovery of History* (Armonk, N.Y., 1994), 117–126.

78. See *Kengash,* 31 August 1917, for the agenda of the congress.

79. *Kengash,* 12 September 1917.

class, the freedoms of assembly, religion, and conversion, and the abolition of censorship and the passport system. The congress recommended
broad dissemination of the project for discussion before being put to a
vote at the next conference.[80] The congress also passed a resolution on
questions of "education and civilization," which called for universal,
compulsory, free elementary education in the vernacular, the organization of a hierarchy of new-method schools and teachers' colleges, and the
creation of a university. All education was to be funded by the state but under Muslim control. Russian was to be introduced only in middle school.
Madrasas were also to be reformed and regulated.[81] Finally, a resolution
called for the establishment of a shariat administration (*mahkama-yi
shar'iya*) in each oblast, but with the crucial proviso that the electoral
principle be maintained and that its members be "educated and aware
of contemporary needs" (*zamāndan khabardār, ilmlik kishilar*).[82]

The ulama met in their own congress a week later, a huge affair with
over 500 delegates from the five oblasts of Turkestan as well the Turgay
and Ural'sk oblasts of the steppe region. The congress unanimously resolved itself to be in favor of a federative democratic republic, with Turkestan having its own duma with jurisdiction over issues of land and water, as well as its own militia. It also called for a halt to the creation of
land committees and the socialization of land. None of this was drastically different from the form of autonomy the Jadids' congress had heard
the previous week. The crucial difference lay in the ulama's resolution of
the questions of religion and women. The congress resolved that "the affairs of religion and of this world should not be separated, i.e., everything from schools to questions of land and justice should be solved according to the shariat." Similarly, "Women should not have rights equal
to those of men, but everyone should have rights according to one's station as adjudged by the shariat."[83] (Of course, since the only people capable of interpreting the shariat were the ulama themselves, this guaranteed the entrenchment of their authority in the new regime.) Finally, the
congress called for the Muslims of Turkestan to maintain unity and suggested that this unity be embodied in a new party to be called the Ittifāq
ul-Muslimin (Union of Muslims), which should replace all existing or-

80. *Kengash*, 13 September 1917; the text of the draft resolution in autonomy is in
UT, 7 and 10 September 1917.
81. *Turān*, 21 September 1917.
82. *Turān*, 14 September 1917.
83. "Ulamā isyazdining qarārlari," *UT*, 30 September 1917.

ganizations such as the Shurā-yi Islāmiya.[84] This was nothing less than a call for the abolition of the organizational infrastructure of Jadidism in Turkestan, an aggressive assertion by the ulama of their power. Each side now saw itself as the sole legitimate representative of the community and sought to act on its behalf.

BREAD AND REVOLUTION

Ultimately, the fate of the region was decided by its Russian population, which enjoyed a monopoly on armed force rooted directly in the fact of empire. Much more than political supremacy was at stake in Turkestan in 1917. By that spring, Turkestan was in the midst of a severe economic crisis, and famine was already a possibility. The grain shortage had afflicted the whole empire since the outbreak of the world war,[85] but it afflicted Central Asia with special force. The area under cotton had increased dramatically once the war began, making Turkestan dependent on grain imported from European Russia. The destruction wrought by the uprising of 1916 and its suppression had further disrupted agricultural production. In 1917, the rains failed and the ensuing draught crippled the grain harvest, just as political instability rendered shipments from European Russia unreliable. By autumn, when Cossack forces besieging Orenburg cut off the most direct route from Russia, Central Asia was in the grips of a full-scale famine. The struggle for political power in 1917 and the following years was played out against the backdrop of famine and the collapse of the imperial economic order.[86] Maintaining the political supremacy of the Russian community in Central Asia had become, quite literally, a matter of life and death, since only such control could assure the settlers privileged access to food. As Marco Buttino has

---

84. "Tāshkandda ulamā siyazdi," *UT*, 30 September 1917.

85. Lars T. Lih, *Bread and Authority in Russia, 1914–1921* (Berkeley, 1990).

86. Until recently, scholarship on Central Asia has failed to take adequate notice of the famine or the economic crisis that preceded it. For recent attempts to right the balance, see Richard Lorenz, "Economic Bases of the Basmachi Movement in the Farghana Valley," in Andreas Kappeler et al., eds., *Muslim Communities Reemerge: Historical Perspectives on Nationality, Politics, and Opposition in the Former Soviet Union and Yugoslavia* (Durham, N.C., 1994), 277–303; Marco Buttino, "Study of the Economic Crisis and Depopulation in Turkestan, 1917–1920," *Central Asian Survey* 9, no. 4 (1990): 59–74; Buttino, "Politics and Social Conflict during a Famine: Turkestan Immediately after the Revolution," in Buttino, ed., *In a Collapsing Empire: Underdevelopment, Ethnic Conflicts and Nationalisms in the Soviet Union* (Milan, 1993), 257–277.

persuasively argued, the actions of the Russian inhabitants of Central Asia in 1917 were motivated by this imperative.[87]

In March, the Provisional Government proclaimed a monopoly on grain and established a network of food supply committees at every administrative level to oversee the distribution of food among the population. Turkestan, however, was exempted from this monopoly, largely because the situation there had become so dismal that the government did not want to add to the liabilities it was taking on. The food supply committees became an arena of overtly political conflict between Russians and Muslim, as various organizations struggled for control of them. The Muslim congress in April passed two resolutions on the food supply question. The first called for all grain currently in Turkestan and that which was to be imported to be distributed among the population in proportion to the weight of each community in the local population. As an operational tool, the conference called for the creation of a network of bakeries under the control of local food supply committees to ensure proper distribution. The second resolution called for the dissolution of all existing food supply committees and for their reelection, giving the local population proportional representation on them.[88] The resolutions were largely ignored, but the question remained a major issue throughout the year. When in early June the Syr Darya oblast food supply committee decided to reconstitute itself, the representation was by organization. The Tashkent Soviet got ten seats out of forty-one, but only four members were guaranteed to be Muslims.[89]

While these struggles continued, many Russians, especially soldiers and (newly armed) workers organized in soviets, sought other ways of intervening in the distribution process. Many Russians in Tashkent were convinced that the inhabitants of the old city had stockpiles of grain and that Muslims merchants were hiding these in order to push food prices up. The requisitioning of food from hoarders and speculators had perfect revolutionary credentials, and groups of Russian soldiers began routinely to indulge in the practice. Buttino notes several waves of req-

87. Marco Buttino, "'La terra a chi la lavora': la politica coloniale russa in Turkestan tra la crisi dello Zarismo e le rivoluzioni del 1917," in Alberto Masoero and Antonello Venturi, eds., *Russica: Studi e ricerche sulla Russia contemporanea* (Milan, 1990), 277–332; Buttino, "Turkestan 1917," 61–77.

88. "Muhim qarārlar," *UT,* 25 April 1917, 3.

89. "Āziq masalasi," *UT,* 14 June 1917, 3–4. Three of the four Muslim seats were to go to representatives of organizations of Muslim peasants and one to a Muslim member of the Tashkent Duma.

uisitions in the old city in Tashkent, as well as similar incidents in Samarqand and Skobelev.[90] But matters acquired a different shape in early September around the Feast of the Sacrifice (*Id-i qurbān*), which fell on 10 September that year. On that day, soldiers from two regiments arrived at the railway station and began confiscating all grain in possession of the passengers, many of whom were peasants from villages around Tashkent who had come to town to sell their animals and buy grain for the holiday. Matters escalated rapidly, and the following day a vast meeting of soldiers formed by acclamation a provisional revolutionary council, which proclaimed the overthrow of both the Provisional Government and the Turkestan Soviet and took power in its own hands.[91] Contemporary observers explicitly noted the connection between the food crisis and this putsch, but it has ever since been misrecognized as part of the revolutionary upsurge throughout the empire in the aftermath of Kornilov's march on Petrograd.[92]

The other political issue of the summer that had a clear Russian-Muslim dimension was the continuing bloodshed in Semirech'e, and the timing of the putsch was probably connected to it. If requisitioning of food provided good revolutionary cover for protecting the interests of the urban Russian population, the soldiers' soviets provided impeccable revolutionary credentials for carrying out devastating warfare in the countryside against the nomadic population. The issue came to the fore in Muslim politics in Tashkent. It had occupied the Turkestan Committee substantially, to the extent that two of its members, Shkapskii and Tinïshpaev, spent most of their sojourn in Turkestan in Vernyi, inspecting the carnage. In April, the Shura and the Soviet had agreed to form a joint commission to investigate the situation in Semirech'e, but it took until 15 June for the commission to leave Tashkent.[93] In July, reports by its members, returning individually, began to appear in the Muslim

90. Buttino, "Turkestan 1917," 69–70. At times, "requisitioning" extended to other commodities as well. On 31 July, soldiers in Kokand commandeered two cartloads of draperies, which they planned to sell off. The goods belonged to solid merchants of the city, who approached the Turkestan Soviet, more moderate than its local counterparts, which directed that the goods be returned, otherwise the perpetrators "would be accountable according to the law" (*PORvUz*, I, 201). We do not know whether the Turkestan Soviet's writ bore fruit or not.

91. Buttino, "'La terra a chi la lavora'," 318–326; Buttino, "Turkestan 1917," 72.

92. The incident was reported prominently in the Provisional Government's *Vestnik*, where the connection with food riots is made explicitly (see Browder and Kerensky, eds., *Russian Provisional Government*, I: 422–424).

93. "Yedisu haqqindagi nimāyish," *UT*, 18 July 1917.

press, and several Muslim organizations began to plan a demonstration in support of the Muslims of Semirech'e.[94]

The demonstration came off spectacularly on 18 August. A massive procession, carrying banners and red flags left the old city and marched through to the streets of Russian Tashkent to the governor-general's mansion. Nalivkin, then acting chair of the largely moribund Turkestan Committee, addressed the crowd in Turkic, laying the blame for the events on Russian settlers. But the demonstrators wanted more. According to the report in *Ulugh Turkistān*, Nalivkin was heckled: "We did not come here to listen to past history. Give us a clear answer. . . . It's been six months since freedom was declared, but the government hasn't given a thought to them [the Muslims of Semirech'e]. This is because the blood flowing in Semirech'e is Muslim and Turkic blood." A clear answer was not forthcoming, and the demonstration moved off after two hours to Kaufman Square, the center of Russian Tashkent, to listen to more speeches.[95]

The episode was remarkable for several reasons. For all the setbacks the Jadids had suffered recently, this demonstration showed that they retained the ability to put masses of people on the streets. The ulama do not seem to have taken an active part in it, but they did not obstruct it either. The Shura's major demands were substantial: that fresh troops be sent to stop the carnage and that half of them be Muslim, that arms given to the settlers at Kuropatkin's command be taken back, that refugees returning from Chinese territory be allowed to settle on their own lands, that Cossack regiments sent to Semirech'e be withdrawn, and that a Muslim representative be added to a Provisional Government delegation being sent to the area.[96] But it was the physical presence of large numbers of Muslims in the Russian city in an overtly political cause that upset the balance and led to the panic that culminated in the putsch of 12 September.

This putsch won less than unanimous support locally. The Provisional Revolutionary Committee had acted against not just the authority of the Provisional Government but also that of the Turkestan Soviet, whose much more moderate leadership was forced to flee to Skobelev in Ferghana, where it continued to denounce this usurpation of power.[97] The putsch was also denounced by various Muslim organizations, the Jadid conference resolving that "Muslims will never accept the acquisition of

94. "Yedisuda dahshatli hāllar," *UT*, 19 July, 26 July, 9 August 1917.
95. "Yedisu Musulmānlari haqqinda buyuk nimāyish," *UT*, 23 August 1917.
96. *Kengash*, 14 July 1917; 20 August 1917.
97. *PORvUz*, I, 328–330.

power by a single party in a democratic Russia."[98] Ultimately, however, the putsch was unsuccessful because not every group among the local Russian population supported it. Petrograd was able to quell the rebellion by rushing loyal troops from Kazan under the command of Major General B. A. Korovichenko, who was able to restore order. Korovichenko began a fresh round of all-party negotiations for rejuvenating the Turkestan Committee while attempting to reassert the authority of the center. However, the coincidence of interests between the various groups that had opposed the putsch proved evanescent. As the legitimacy of the Provisional Government declined throughout the empire, the commitment to constitutional procedure on the part of Tashkent Russians, never very strong to begin with, rapidly gave way to concern for survival. As preparations began for the elections to the Constituent Assembly,[99] the second congress of soviets in October elected a far more radical regional soviet that had fewer qualms about taking power by force. When the Tashkent Soviet took power on October 23, after fours days of fighting, the regional soviet did not oppose it.

It is crucial to realize that the conquest of power by the Tashkent Soviet preceded the Soviet victory in Petrograd and was largely unconnected to it. The roots of the October "revolution" in Turkestan lay in the balance of power between the forces represented in the soviets (predominantly soldiers and settlers) and the rest of society ("privileged" Russians and natives) as it existed on the ground. The struggle might have been clothed in the language of revolution then fashionable throughout Russia, but its reality was very different than in Petrograd. Contemporary observers in Central Asia saw the two takeovers as separate. The revolution in Petrograd was not without its possibilities, as we shall see, but the assumption of power by the soviets in Tashkent was of much greater practical import.

Contrary to the general impression in the literature, the Soviet takeover in Tashkent did not galvanize the Muslim population to united political action.[100] The positions of the two sides were too far apart for that, and few saw the takeover as the end of politics. The pattern of parallel responses continued. The ulama convened a general Muslim congress in the second week of November, to which no Jadids were invited,

98. *Turān*, 21 September 1917; see also *UT*, 30 September 1917.

99. *Turk eli*, 15 October 1917.

100. Hélène Carrère d'Encausse, "Civil War and New Governments," in Allworth, ed., *Central Asia*, 225, asserts that the "refusal [of the Soviet to share power] welded the unity of all the Muslim political groups," which united around the Shura.

in order to discuss the question of relations with the new regime. The congress met when many Jadid leaders were out of town in the immediate aftermath of the fighting, and their absence led to the withdrawal of the delegation from Transcaspia.[101] After the initial chaos, however, the congress heard more than twenty speeches. Its final resolution, noting that "the Muslims of Turkestan . . . comprise 98 percent of the population," deemed it "impermissible to advocate the assumption of power in Turkestan by a handful of immigrant soldiers, workers, and peasants who are ignorant of the way of life of the Muslims of Turkestan."[102] Rather it decided to propose to the Soviet the creation of a new Turkestan Committee to govern Turkestan until the convening of the Constituent Assembly. The committee was to have twelve members, six from the present congress and three each from the regional congresses of municipal dumas and the soviets. The committee was to be responsible to a council of twenty-four, with the ulama's Muslim congress receiving fourteen seats. The congress elected a five-member commission, headed by Lapin, to convey these proposals to the Soviet.[103]

Even as a negotiating position, these proposals are remarkable. They indicate how secure the ulama felt in their leadership of the Muslim population and of the political weight of that population in the affairs of the region. At the same time, they indicate the continuity in politics perceived by the ulama, for the proposals were aimed at the creation of a new Turkestan Committee, the same process that Korovichenko had been attempting. The Soviet, of course, had no intention of sharing its power and curtly refused the offer. The resolution of the Bolshevik-Maximalist faction passed by the Soviet gives clear indication of its views on the matter: "The inclusion of Muslims in the organ of supreme regional power is unacceptable at the present time in view of both the completely indefinite attitude of the native population toward the power of the Soviets of Soldiers', Workers', and Peasants' Deputies, and the fact that there are no proletarian class organizations among the native population whose representation in the organ of supreme regional power the faction would welcome."[104] The language of class could easily conceal the national and colonial dimensions of the conflict.

101. "Musulmān krāevāi siyazdining bātafsil qarāri," al-Izāh, 28 November 1917, 269.

102. "15nchi noyābirda Tāshkandda bolghān musulmān krāevai siyazdining qarāri," al-Izāh, 28 November 1917, 266–267.

103. Ibid.; "Siyazdning qarāri," UT, 18 November 1917.

104. The text of this resolution is in A. A. Gordienko, Obrazovanie Turkestanskoi ASSR (Moscow, 1968), 309–310.

EXPERIMENT IN GOVERNMENT

While the ulama were negotiating with the Tashkent Soviet, several members of the Central Council had fled from Tashkent during the fighting and gathered in Kokand, where they convened their own "extraordinary" conference to address the new political situation. The Kokand conference was *not* convened as a result of the rebuff to the ulama by the soviet congress; rather, it was a counterpart to the ulama's conference of early November and was dominated by the Jadids and their sympathizers. Although conditions in Turkestan made travel difficult and the majority of delegates came from the Ferghana oblast,[105] the major figures in the Shura were all present when the congress opened on 26 November. Also present were large numbers of Russian and Jewish representatives of municipal and other public organizations from Turkestan (although most in fact came from Ferghana). The Jadids had veered into an alliance with moderate Russian forces in Turkestan.

After only brief debate, the congress passed the following resolution: "The Fourth Extraordinary Regional Muslim Congress, expressing the will of the peoples of Turkestan to self-determination in accordance with the principles proclaimed by the Great Russian Revolution, proclaims Turkestan territorially autonomous in union with the Federal Democratic Russian Republic. It entrusts the elaboration of the form of autonomy to the Constituent Assembly of Turkestan, which must be convened as soon as possible. It solemnly declares that the rights of the national minorities inhabiting Turkestan will be safeguarded in every possible way."[106] The congress elected an eight-member "provisional government of Turkestan," which was to be responsible to a fifty-four–member council. It elected thirty-two members from among those attending; eighteen of the remaining seats were to be filled by representatives of various non-Muslim parties and organizations while four seats were to go to representatives of municipal dumas.[107]

In following up on the resolutions of the September congress, the congress affirmed the Jadids' sense of continuity with the period since February. Nevertheless, speakers were also aware that the assumption of

---

105. J. Castagné, "Le Turkestan depuis la révolution russe," *Revue du monde musulman* 50 (1922): 47. Castagné was a French archeologist who spent several years in Turkestan.

106. *PORvUz*, II, 27; cf. Mustafa Chokaev, "Turkestan and the Soviet Regime," *Journal of the Royal Central Asiatic Society* 18 (1931): 407.

107. *UT*, 8 December 1917, 2.

power by the Soviet had altered the situation drastically. Mustafā Cho-qāy, who was elected foreign minister, spoke of "the absence of government in Russia today . . . [which] makes the convocation of the Constituent Assembly doubtful." [108] The congress linked Turkestan's future to a liberal democratic Russia and yet promised to convene Turkestan's own Constituent Assembly. In his speech, Behbudi stressed the necessity of having Turkestani delegates present at any peace conference in the future. [109] More practically, the congress decided, after lengthy debate, to join Kaledin's South-Eastern Union. Many speakers disputed the wisdom of an alliance with a Cossack force known for its counterrevolutionary tendencies as well as its avowed intention of "placing a cross over the Aya Sofya," but the union controlled rail routes to Russia, the only source for importing grain. [110]

This provisional government, which became known as the "Kokand Autonomy," was dominated by Russian-educated Muslim intellectuals, with whom the Jadids had cooperated all year. Muhamedjan Tinïshpaev served as prime minister and minister for internal affairs; the other ministers and their portfolios were Islam Shahiahmedov, deputy prime minister; Mustafā Choqāy, external affairs; Ubaydullah Khojaev, in charge of creating a people's militia; Yur Ali Āghāev, land and water affairs; Ābidjān Mahmudov, food supply; Abdurrahmān-bek Urazaev, deputy minister for internal affairs; and Solomon Gertsfel'd, finance. [111] The thirty-two members elected to the council included Sher Ali Lapin but no other members from the Ulamā Jamiyati. Indeed, the council was remarkable for its complete exclusion of the ulama. At the same time, the congress offered moderate Russians a disproportionate role in the proposed government in an attempt to distance them from the soviets. The congress and the government elected by it were thus characterized as a broad alliance of moderate forces of the region that excluded both the ulama and the soviets.

Events had pitched the Jadids into the unfamiliar business of running a government, but November 1917 was a singularly inauspicious time for embarking on such an experiment. As a symbolic gesture, the proclamation of autonomy was widely celebrated by the Jadids throughout Turkestan. It also attracted support from several Russian organizations,

---

108. *Vaqït,* 17 December 1917.
109. *Vaqït,* 21 December 1917.
110. Ibid.
111. "Muwaqqat Turkistān hukumatining a'zālari," *UT,* 13 December 1917, 1.

especially those of Ferghana.[112] Many others in Muslim society held out little hope for it, and many feared that it would lead to war.[113] The new government therefore called for demonstrations in its support throughout Turkestan. Demonstrations took place successfully in Andiján on 3 December and Tashkent on 6 December.[114] The Kokand Autonomy then called a second meeting in Tashkent on the following Friday, 13 December, which that year was the birthday of the Prophet. The second meeting was intended both as a show of support and a direct challenge to the Tashkent Soviet on its own turf. The second demonstration was supported by the Tashkent Duma, which had refused to accept its dissolution by the Soviet in early December.[115] The Soviet briefly debated participating in the demonstration under its own banners, but decided against it.[116] Instead, it decided to allow the demonstration to take place, but not to allow it into the Russian part of the city; it also placed Tashkent on war footing on the day of the demonstration.[117] A clearer admission of the geographic limits of its authority could not have been possible. In the event, the demonstration attracted tens of thousands of people from Tashkent and beyond, including many non-Muslims. The ulama in Tashkent had showed little enthusiasm for the Kokand Autonomy, but a group of them also joined the demonstration. The demonstration then marched into the Russian part of the city, where it quickly turned into a confrontation: It attacked the prison and freed political prisoners taken by the Soviet during its conquest of power the previous month. Russian soldiers fired into the crowd, killing several people, while many others were killed in the ensuing stampede.[118] The freed prisoners were recaptured and summarily executed.

Two weeks later, in a transparent attempt to garner "proletarian" credentials for itself, the Kokand Autonomy organized a Congress of Muslim Workers and Peasants in Kokand. It was attended by about 200 deputies who declared that the Kokand Autonomy was not a government of the bourgeoisie alone but was "composed of the best sections of our society." Few of those taking part were either workers or peasants, and

112. P. Alekseenkov, *Kokandskaia avtonomiia* (Tashkent, 1931), 35–36.
113. Behbudi, "Turkistān mukhtāriyati," *Hurriyat,* 19 December 1917.
114. *UT,* 10 December 1917; 16 December 1917.
115. *UT,* 8 December 1917; 10 December 1917.
116. *PORvUz,* II: 38.
117. Alekseenkov, *Kokandskaia avtonomiia,* 47–48; *PORvUz,* II: 59.
118. "Katta mitingh," *UT,* 10 December 1917; "Fājiali wāqea," *UT,* 16 December 1917; "Tāshkandda mukhtāriyat nimāyishi," *al-Izāh,* 25 December 1917, 277; cf. Safarov, *Kolonial'naia revoliutsiia,* 115.

among the presidium we find the names of Dr. Sanjar Isfendyarov, Abdullah Awlāni, and Piri Mursilzade, a member of the delegation from the Turkic Federalist Party.[119]

While the Kokand Autonomy could bring people out into the streets, it lacked the means to assert its power. Forming a standing army in a colony of occupation was of course difficult, and the uprising of the previous year had shown how unpopular the idea of conscription was in the area. The government invited Russian and Tatar officers and Ottoman prisoners of war quartered in the area to its side, but it could recruit only sixty-odd volunteers for the ranks. Its financial resources were equally scarce. Even a government with much greater coercive power behind it would have found it difficult to raise revenue in the region's crisis-ridden economy. The Kokand Autonomy found it impossible to levy taxes. Its writ did not even extend to Russian institutions in the new city. In January, P. G. Poltoratskii, the commissar for labor in the Soviet government, came to Kokand and "nationalized" the Kokand branch of the State Bank.[120] The government raised 3 million rubles through a loan, but they were spent quickly, and nothing more could raised.[121] And there was little outside help to be found in the chaotic conditions of that winter. The Kokand Autonomy sought cooperation from Ataman Dutov as well as the Alash Orda regime among the Qazaqs.[122] A mission dispatched to the amir of Bukhara produced predictably scanty results.[123] Help from beyond the borders of the Russian empire was out of the question. Tendentious claims of Soviet historiography notwithstanding,[124] the British were in no position to give any help. Indeed, the fear of pan-Islam paralyzed British thinking on Central Asian affairs throughout the period of Russian civil war, rendering it incapable of distinguishing be-

119. "Musulmān ishchi wa dehqān siyazdi," *UT*, 4 January 1918; *Vaqït*, 18 January 1918; *Hurriyat*, 9 January 1918.

120. Alekseenkov, *Kokandskaia avtonomiia*, 43–44.

121. Choqāy claimed that, although the sum was raised, the government could not find any arms to buy (Chokaev, "Turkestan," 408).

122. M. Tchokaieff, "Fifteen Years of Bolshevik Rule in Turkestan," *Journal of the Royal Central Asiatic Society* 20 (1933): 358.

123. Abdullah Receb Baysun, *Türkistan Millî Hareketleri* (Istanbul, 1943), 31.

124. The Kokand Autonomy was demonised early in Soviet historiography. To its sins of being a counterrevolutionary alliance of local and Russian bourgeoisies was added the accusation of being "an attempt of imperialist states, especially England and America, to come to the help of exploiter classes overthrown by the October revolution and to realize their aggressive plans of turning Turkestan into their colony and a bridgehead for an attack on Soviet Russia" (Kh. Sh. Inoiatov, *Otvet fal'sifikatoram istorii sovetskoi Srednei Azii i Kazakhstana* [Tashkent, 1962], 61).

tween various political currents in the struggle. In any case, the period in which the Kokand Autonomy existed was too early for any British action. In December 1917, a report received at the British consulate in Kashgar that the Kokand Autonomy was "doing great honor" to two *āqsaqqāl*s from Chinese Turkestan set off pan-Turkist alarms, and the British minister in Beijing unleashed a thunderous letter to the concerned authorities upbraiding them for their laxity.[125] The British did intervene, briefly and ineffectively, in Central Asia, but the Kokand Autonomy had ceased to exist long before then.

The end came in early February. Hostilities grew between the Kokand Autonomy, entrenched in the old city, and the Kokand Soviet, which controlled the Russian quarter and the citadel. Again, Soviet power was entrenched in the planned spaces of the colonial city. By February, Dutov's blockade of Orenburg was broken, and the Soviet in Tashkent could spare enough forces to Kokand. Anticipating the arrival of reinforcements, the Kokand Autonomy opened hostilities but was soon outgunned.[126] As the last Soviet scholar to write on the episode, P. Alekseenkov, stated in a matter-of-fact manner, "Not knowing exactly where the enemy was, the defenders of the citadel opened machine-gun fire on the old city." [127] After the machine guns came the burning and looting. The city burned for three days. Russian soldiers were in control of whatever power remained in Turkestan.

125. IOLR, L/P&S/10/721, 245.

126. The Kokand government did not leave any archives behind, and therefore its activities are shrouded in mystery. For details of the negotiations between the Autonomy and the Soviet, see M. Khasanov, "Al'ternativa: iz istorii kokandskoi avtonomii," *Zvezda Vostoka*, 1990, no. 7, 112–113.

127. Alekseenkov, *Kokandskaia avtonomiia*, 58.

Epilogue

THE TRANSFORMATION OF JADIDISM

The revolution marked a turning point in the history of Central Asian Jadidism. By 1917, the Jadids had been successful in asserting their presence as a new group in society and pursuing their claims to leadership in it. The advent of print (and later the use of theater) had allowed them to create a new public space from which older cultural elites were increasingly marginalized, their cultural capital slighted by the Jadids as being irrelevant to the needs of the age, and their commitment to the good of the nation questioned. The new knowledge brought in by print and reproduced in new-method schools led to new understandings of the world. The nation appropriated from dominant discourses of contemporary Europe was now used as a yardstick for measuring the utility of ideas and practices in Muslim society. Islam itself came to be abstracted from the social practices of religious scholars and anchored in sacred texts, access to which, the Jadids claimed, was open to anyone with the requisite knowledge. At the same time, the Jadids saw the welfare of Islam inextricably linked to the progress of Muslims. The Muslim community thus became a modern nation, with all the rights and obligations that went with it. Measured in terms of the number of new-method schools, publications, and theater, the Jadids' success was unquestionable before 1917. Central Asian cultural life in 1917 was very different from even a generation earlier.

Yet, Jadid success was very far from complete. The new public space was still minuscule, and the status and prestige of the older elites, though diminished, remained very strong in society at large. When the February revolution transformed overnight the old politics of cultural reform into one of mass mobilization, the Jadids found themselves on new, uncertain terrain. Their political strategies until then had been dictated by the constraints imposed on political activity by an autocratic colonial state. The promise of an inclusive liberal constitutionalism proffered by the Provisional Government marked a complete transformation of the political arena. The Jadids saw in liberal constitutionalism the promise for the fulfillment of their hopes for their nation, and as numerous pronouncements throughout the year show, they sought to work within that framework. This strategy failed, however: the Jadids were surprised by the vehemence of the opposition from within their society, just as the constitutional order collapsed under the weight of social radicalism. The new politics brought into the open deep conflicts that had existed ever since the rise of Jadidism but had remained confined to debate over culture. Through the course of 1917, the Jadids found themselves capable of organizing massive demonstrations but repeatedly failed to convert that support into votes. Rather, the ulama emerged as the leaders of the society, their claim confirmed, in many elections, by votes. The ulama's triumph was rendered moot, however, by the collapse of the constitutional order, which put an end to electoral politics and put power in the hands of members of the settler community.

But the struggle was far from over in Turkestan after the Soviet victory at Kokand. The three years following 1917 were a period of intense upheaval during which the entire social and political order in the former Russian empire was reconstructed in a multifaceted struggle of various social groups. For the Jadids the years were transformative of both their worldview and their strategies. They succeeded in becoming active agents in the contests over the reestablishment of state order in Central Asia, in which the future of Central Asia was defined. When the exclusionary policies of the Tashkent Soviet changed, under pressure from the central government, a remarkable concatenation of circumstances allowed the Jadids to first enter, and then briefly take over, the new institutions of power being created by the Soviet regime in Turkestan. Although the attempt was unsuccessful, the state had come to play a significant role in Jadid strategies. This marked a significant break from the tsarist period, when Jadid reform was formulated solely in society, often against the suspicions of an exclusionary state.

The experiences of 1917 went a long way toward defining the new strategies. The nation had let the Jadids down. Their vision of the good of the nation was clearly not shared by large parts of the urban population (the rural population had remained largely invisible in Muslim politics throughout the year). Although the Jadids continued to blame ignorance for the ills of their society,[1] and struggles in the realm of culture and education remained at the forefront of their agenda, they had realized that new methods were required in the new era. Years of exhortation had produced scanty results. The new era was to be one of action and institution building. At the same time, the emphasis on politics had come to stay, but liberal constitutionalism gave way to the politics of mobilization. As Soviet attitudes changed, the Jadids came to see the state not as an enemy but as an instrument of change. The new regime was quite different from the old and presented its own opportunities and constraints. Jadid strategies accordingly shifted in the years after 1917. The revolution provided the chance for a politicized and radicalized cultural elite to win control of the destiny of the nation it sought to change. In the process, the nation itself came to defined anew, as an ethnically charged patriotism came to be synonymous with a nationalism expressed in confessional terms.

TOWARD SOVIET POWER

In some ways, the carnage at Kokand made surprisingly little difference for the Jadids. Most delegates to the November congress remained active in public life in the immediate aftermath of the battle. Mustafa Choqāy represented "Autonomous Turkestan" at several all-Russian gatherings of anti-Bolshevik forces in 1918 and 1919, before going into exile through Transcaucasia.[2] The Kokand Autonomy had never been able to assert its power beyond the old city of Kokand, and therefore its fall did not affect any significant part of the population beyond Kokand. Nor did military conquest result in effective rule by the Soviets. The Soviet government in Tashkent had admitted its own limits in December when it had allowed the demonstration in support of the Kokand Autonomy to take place in the old city but refused it entrance into the Russian quarter. There matters stood for quite some time. The old city, with its laby-

1. Fitrat, "Maktab kerak," *Hurriyat*, 22 April 1918.
2. D. A. Amanzholova, *Kazakhskii avtonomizm i Rossiia* (Moscow, 1994), 100, 105, 122.

rinthine alleys and unfamiliar sights, remained alien to the new Russian power and largely beyond its control. The only manner in which Soviet power could be asserted in the old city was through requisitioning, carried out in brief armed sorties. These had picked up immediately after the Soviet takeover. The newspaper *Ulugh Turkistān* complained in early January of the numerous requisitions in recent days. "There was a time when people were dying every day of hunger in the old city, but the European inhabitants of the new city did not grieve. Now that the food supply is diminishing in the new city, they turn their gaze to the old city."[3] Beyond Tashkent the situation was chaotic still. Soviet power, to the extent that we can speak of it as a unitary entity, came to different places at different times, its fortunes varying greatly according to local conditions. In areas of Russian peasant settlement, Russian-dominated food supply committees took requisitioning in their own hands, often acting against the commands of the Tashkent regime. The establishment of Soviet rule in Turkestan ultimately became a matter of reestablishing the rule of the city over the countryside.[4]

The dislocation caused by the revolution also redefined the geopolitical situation in Central Asia. Although the Russian civil war did not officially begin until May 1918, the military situation in the empire had been uncertain at least since the autumn of 1917, and had seriously undermined the apparatus of colonial power established a half-century earlier. Soviet power was not established in any militarily meaningful way until 1920, when the central government, having emerged victorious in the civil war in European Russia, could send reinforcements to Central Asia. Until then, the Soviet regime in Tashkent remained vulnerable.

This geopolitical uncertainty was accompanied by a profound economic crisis. By 1918, the cotton economy was in utter ruin. Production had declined after a peak in 1916, and inflation, dating back to 1914, had rocketed in the revolutionary era (prices had increased by 466 percent in 1917, 149 percent in 1918, and 1065 percent in 1919, by which time they stood at 588 times the level of 1914).[5] Most significantly, how-

3. "Eski shahrda tintuw," *UT,* 4 January 1918.

4. The extremely complex politics of famine in Turkestan after 1917 are analyzed by Marco Buttino, "Politics and Social Conflict during a Famine: Turkestan Immediately after the Revolution," in Buttino, ed., *In a Collapsing Empire: Underdevelopment, Ethnic Conflicts and Nationalisms in the Soviet Union* (Milan, 1993), 257–277.

5. Safarov, *Kolonial'naia revoliutsiia: opyt Turkestana* (Oxford, 1985 [orig. Moscow, 1921]), 164.

ever, the famine of 1917 had assumed disastrous proportions over the winter. Over the next three years, the famine and the accompanying epidemics and armed conflict with the Russians devastated the local population of Central Asia. According to Marco Buttino's careful estimate, the indigenous rural population declined by 23 percent between 1917 and 1920. (The figure was 30.5 percent for 1915–1920, which included the destruction of the 1916 uprising.) The loss was offset only in very small part by a modest 8.3 percent increase in the urban population, and there was doubtless some emigration to other parts of the Russian empire as well as to China, Afghanistan, and Iran. But the majority of the decline in population is attributable to hunger and war.[6]

Such were the political realities faced by the Jadids in the spring of 1918. Many entertained hopes of foreign intervention against the Soviet regime. One émigré account, written a quarter of a century later, suggests that many Jadids were in contact with Ottoman authorities in Transcaucasia as well as Istanbul, hoping to attract military intervention.[7] Rumors of such action had reached P. T. Etherton, the British consul in Kashgar, who also reported in December 1918 that "a deputation of the leading merchants of Ferghana and Kashgaria, men of great wealth and influence, came to see me and expressed the hope that British intervention would eventuate, whilst at the same time they voiced the confidence of the people in any action the British might take."[8] The Ottoman foray into Transcaucasia ended quickly, and the British, for all their concern about the security of India, were wary of active involvement in an unstable situation while the war still continued in Europe. Armed resistance did not appear as an option to the Jadids.

The Jadids had little connection with the Basmachi revolt in Ferghana, which began in 1918 and continued for several years, by which time it had also spread to eastern Bukhara. Conventional wisdom connects the Basmachi to the destruction of the Kokand Autonomy. Soviet historiography saw in them the force of counterrevolution, acting in unison with every reactionary force in the region to nip Soviet power in the bud. Non-Soviet scholarship has generally accepted the romanticized émigré view of the Basmachi as a guerrilla movement of national libera-

---

6. Buttino, "Study of the Economic Crisis and Depopulation in Turkestan, 1917–1920," *Central Asian Survey* 9, no. 4 (1990): 64–69.

7. Abdullah Recep Baysun, *Türkistan Millî Hareketleri* (Istanbul, 1943), 31–34.

8. Etherton to Government of India, 9 December 1918, in IOLR, L/P&S/10/741, 211v–212.

tion.[9] Both views place a greater burden on the Basmachi than historical evidence can sustain. Instead, the revolt was a response to the economic and social crisis produced by the famine and the resulting "bacchanalia of robbery, requisitions and confiscations on the part of 'Soviet authorities.'"[10] Ferghana had been a turbulent area in the last decades of imperial rule, when the term *bāsmachi* was commonplace in *TWG*, whose pages were replete with accounts of banditry and murder in the region. The Basmachi represented one strategy of the rural population to cope with this dislocation.[11] The potential military threat that the Basmachi represented to Soviet power was recognized by many contemporaries, but always greatly overestimated. Both in terms of its organization and its goals (or rather the absence thereof), the movement was embedded in local solidarities, which remained alien to the more abstract visions of national struggle espoused by those who sought to coopt it to their goals.[12] We might do well to remember that Choqāy on more than one occasion disowned any connection between the struggle he had led and that of the Basmachi, who were little better than bandits in his opinion.[13]

The main political strategy of the Jadids came to focus instead on a struggle for participation in the new regime and its fledgling institutions. "Knowing that struggle in Turkestan was useless and could lead only to the ruin of the land," Choqāy wrote in 1923, "the core of the autonomists remaining after the defeat at Kokand called upon its supporters to work with existing authorities in order to weaken the hostility directed at the indigenous population by the frontier Soviet regime."[14] For reasons beyond their control, the Jadids were remarkably successful in this bid; in the process they outflanked the ulama in their quest for leadership of urban Muslim society.

9. Most recently by Baymirza Hayit, *Basmatschi: Nationaler Kampf Turkestans in den Jahren 1917 bis 1934* (Cologne, 1992).

10. S. Ginzburg, "Basmachestvo v Fergane," in *Ocherki revoliutsionnogo dvizheniia v Srednei Azii: sbornik statei* (Moscow, 1926), 134.

11. Richard Lorenz, "Economic Bases of the Basmachi Movement in the Farghana Valley," in Andreas Kappeler et al., eds., *Muslim Communities Reemerge: Historical Perspectives on Nationality, Politics, and Opposition in the Former Soviet Union and Yugoslavia* (Durham, N.C., 1994), 277–303.

12. The most quixotic of these attempts was that of Enver Pasha, who in 1921 briefly placed himself at the helm of the Basmachi in a bid to oust the Soviet regime from Central Asia. On this episode, see now Masayuki Yamauchi, *The Green Crescent under the Red Star: Enver Pasha in Soviet Russia, 1919–1922* (Tokyo, 1991).

13. *Bor'ba* (Tiflis), 12 February 1921; Chokaev, "Korni vozstanii v Bukhare," *Poslednie novosti* (Paris), 29 September 1923.

14. Chokaev, "Korni vozstanii."

MUSLIM COMMUNISTS

One of Lenin's first decrees had been directed "To the Toiling Muslims of Russia and the East," whose grievances the Bolsheviks sought to coopt. The policies of the Tashkent Soviet were, from this point of view, totally reckless and were challenged by the central government (which moved to Moscow in March 1918) early on. Yet, Moscow's influence was highly mediated. The civil war and the tenuousness of the Bolshevik hold on power in central Russia itself ruled out any direct intervention. Still, Turkestan's avowed adherence to Russia, an important pillar of its claim to legitimacy, gave Moscow some scope for moral suasion, which it sought to utilize to the fullest extent possible. The newly formed People's Commissariat for Nationality Affairs (or Narkomnats, in the revolutionary argot then coming into vogue) sent a mission with plenipotentiary powers to Turkestan to assert its will. The mission, composed of A. P. Kobozev and two Tatars, Y. Ibrahimov and Arif Klevleev, arrived in Tashkent in February 1918 and began the task of attracting Muslims into the new regime. Kobozev's tactics were straightforward: to support local Muslims almost indiscriminately against the Russians in control of the Soviet.[15] In a telegram to the Tashkent Soviet announcing the Kobozev mission, Stalin, then commissar for nationality affairs, informed the Tashkent Soviet that Klevleev was a former nationalist, but suggested that the new regime not be afraid of "the shadows of the past" and "attract to [Soviet] work other supporters of Kerenskii from the natives, to the extent that they are ready to serve Soviet power."[16] Kobozev's efforts bore fruit, and on the eve of the Fifth Turkestan Congress of Soviets in April, he was able to inform the Council of People's Commissars in Moscow that "white Muslim *chalma*s [turbans] have grown [in number] in the ranks of the Tashkent parliament."[17] Seven of the thirty-six members of the Central Executive Committee of the Turkestan Autonomous Federative Republic that was proclaimed by the congress were Muslims. Kobozev also pushed for the formation of a Commissariat for Nationality Affairs (Turkomnats) in the new autonomous republic, to which the Tashkent government acceded in June after much footdragging. This was the first in a series of institutions that provided Muslims access to the new power structure. The terms of reference of the Turkomnats were fairly

15. Safarov, *Kolonial'naia revoliutsiia*, 159.
16. Stalin to Kolesov, 7 April 1918, in *PORvUz*, II: 223.
17. Radiogram dated 16 April 1918, in ibid., 241.

modest. Its main function was to represent and defend the interests of workers of various nationalities (including non-Russian Europeans living in Turkestan). With the moral support of Moscow, however, it gathered considerable political power around it and became the mouthpiece of Muslim opinion within the party. By the autumn of 1918, all oblast-level executive committees of the Soviet regime had sections on nationality affairs.

Over the next few months, large numbers of Muslims flocked to the new institutions of power. The Bolsheviks finally formed their own party, the Communist Party of Turkestan (KPT), in June 1918. Archival research on the recruitment of Muslims into the party in its first years is still not possible, but all evidence suggests that large numbers of Jadids joined it as soon as it was possible. Klevleev was especially active in recruiting Muslims into the party and state apparatus. In May, he visited Samarqand, where he addressed a mass meeting in the Sher Dār madrasa organized by the Samarqand Labor Union. Later in the month, the union renamed itself the Muslim Soviet of Workers' and Peasants' Deputies of Samarqand uezd, and by August, a Muslim Workers' Communist Society (Musulmān Zehmatkash Ishtirākiyun Jamiyati) boasted 1,600 members in Samarqand. The Jadid newspaper *Hurriyat* had been adopted by the education section of the Samarqand Soviet as its organ.[18] In Tashkent, the Tatar Union reorganized as the Tatar Socialist Workers' Committee in June. Then, on 2 August, in a meeting held in the main mosque of Tashkent and chaired by Klevleev, it transformed itself into the Tatar section of the Russian Communist Party (Bolshevik).[19] A Soviet of Workers' and Peasants' Deputies had appeared in old Tashkent, and it provided an important channel for recruitment of Muslims. After Klevleev engineered new elections for its Executive Committee in June, it included the Bolsheviks Abdullah Awlāni and Said Akram Said Azimbaev and the Left Social Revolutionary Tawallā. By August, Tawallā had been elected to the Executive Committee of the Tashkent Soviet, as was Bashirullah Khojaev, the brother of Ubaydullah Khojaev and an old Jadid in his own right.[20]

The Jadids thus rapidly transformed themselves into Muslim Communists and asserted the claim, again, to speak in the name of the Muslims of Turkestan. "Muslim" also functioned as an identity label in the

18. Ibid., 235, 267, 289, 324–325.
19. Ibid., 303, 420–421.
20. Ibid., 333–334, 461–462.

early Soviet period. For the new regime in Moscow, "Muslims" represented a nationality alongside Ukrainians, Jews, and Georgians in the vocabulary of the Narkomnats. (In Turkestan, "Muslim" had the added benefit of being usable as a synonym for "native.") The ulama, who had contested the Jadid claim to leadership the previous year, proved far less adept at operating in the new political language and quickly lost the initiative they had gained in Muslim politics in 1917. The Jadids went on the offensive quickly. In early 1918, they organized a Fuqahā Jamiyati (Society of Jurists) comprising ulama sympathetic to reform, which was clearly meant to counter the influence of the ulama. Then in April the Tashkent Soviet of Muslim Workers' and Peasants' Deputies, essentially a Jadid organization, asked the City Soviet to arrest the "counterrevolutionary" ulama belonging to the Ulamā Jamiyati and to requisition the property belonging to the organization. The request was duly carried out, and the Jamiyat was abolished on 5 May for "not corresponding to the interests of the working people" and its organ, *al-Izāh,* was banned.[21] The Fuqahā Jamiyati did not last very long, but it had done its work. When it was dissolved in its turn for being "irrelevant to current problems," its property was turned over to Madaniyat (Civilization), a new educational society formed by Jadids.[22]

For their part, the new Muslim Communists assimilated the language of class that legitimated the new regime. The Tashkent Soviet, in using the language of class to assert the national rights of the region's European settler population, had highlighted the importance of the new language. The Kokand Autonomy had also sought "proletarian" legitimacy for itself by organizing a Muslim Workers' and Peasants' Congress. From then on, class and revolution entered Jadid vocabulary and over the next several years were repeatedly used to assert the rights of the local population. To be sure, most of the Muslims who entered the party in 1918 and subsequent years had not been active Jadids before 1917. The revolution had seen a major influx of new people into public life, and their numbers continued to increase, thus broadening the base of the politically active elite in Turkestan. The politics of these Muslim Communists, however, represented in many ways a direct connection with the main thrust of Jadidism. Education and enlightenment continued to hold a central place in their strategies. The burst of activity that took place in 1917,

21. Ibid., 203–204, 265.
22. "Maqsad-u maslak," *Bayān ul-haq,* 16 August 1918 (n.s.).

when the Jadids organized teachers' courses and published new textbooks, continued and by the middle of 1918 found a more receptive official environment. Kobozev and Klevleev ensured that the new Commissariat for Education became involved in Muslim education as well. This
provided a significant channel for the influx of Jadids into the new apparatus. Russo-native schools had been abolished in the summer of 1917,
and now a new network of "Soviet" schools began to emerge around existing new-method schools. In the summer of 1918, twenty new schools
were opened, and in 1919, in Tashkent alone, there were forty-eight
Muslim schools with 158 teachers and 9,200 students, a significant increase over the figures of the tsarist period.[23] (This was in addition to the
maktabs, which continued to exist.) Although details of the curricula of
these schools remain elusive, there is no doubt that these schools were a
direct continuation of the Jadids' new-method schools. The increase in
the number of schools was made possible by the presence in Turkestan
of Ottoman prisoners of war, many of whom were pressed into service
as teachers.[24] They brought with them curricular and political attitudes
that had little in common with those of the new regime. Ottoman Turkish was widely used in instruction, and the "national poetry" of the Jadids gave way to Ottoman martial songs and military drill.[25] Old textbooks were reprinted and new ones continued to appear in a very similar
mold. Textbooks such as Wasli's *Ortāq* (Friend) or Shākirjān Rahimi's
Sawghā (Present) scarcely differed, in tone or content, from any new-
method textbook of the past, even though they were published by Soviet
authorities.[26] In addition, several textbooks were translated from Russian or Tatar.[27]

The lithography-based publishing trade did not survive the revolution. The year 1917 had been the most prolific in Central Asian publishing, and the same activity continued into the first half of 1918, when
several new periodicals appeared. By the summer, however, the Soviet
regime had managed to nationalize all printing presses (the majority of

23. Rakhimi, "Prosveshchenie uzbekov," *Nauka i prosveshchenie,* 1922, no. 2, 41–
42; Safarov, *Kolonial'naia revoliutsiia,* 149.
24. This episode remains little known; the only substantial piece of documentation is
the reminiscences of Râci Çakıröz, one of the prisoners of war, in R. Çakıröz and Timur Kocaoğlu, "Türkistan'da Türk Subayları," serialized in *Türk Dünyası Tarih Dergisi* in
1987–1988.
25. Sh. Rahim, *Ozbek maārifning otkandaki wa hāzirgi hāli* (Tashkent, 1923), 18–19.
26. Wasli, *Ortāq* (Samarqand, 1918); Shākirjān Rahimi, *Sawghā* (Tashkent, 1919).
27. N. P. Arkhangel'skii, "Uchebnaia literatura na uzbekskom iazyke," *Nauka i prosveshchenie,* 1922, no. 2, 2nd pagination, 36.

which had existed in Russian parts of towns and for whom the printing of Arabic-script texts was a side operation), thus sounding the death knell of the book trade. The official monopoly on printing and publishing was in place, but again the only qualified personnel available were Jadids, and the new official press bore an uncanny resemblance to the Jadid press of old. The unofficial vernacular press had ceased to exist by mid-1918, to be replaced by *Ishtirākiyun* (Communists), the official organ of Turkomnats, which, as its Arabianate title indicates, retained a distinctly Muslim flavor. Jadid authors retained a commanding presence in the many such quasi-official newspapers that appeared throughout Turkestan over the next three years, as the officially sanctioned press became in those years a conduit for a Jadid voice.

But that voice had changed dramatically in the aftermath of the collapse of the old order. An ethnically charged patriotism rapidly came to characterize the Jadid rhetoric of the nation. In the first days of the revolution, the nation was universally defined as comprising the Muslims of Turkestan. Over the course of the year, the Jadid emphasis shifted gradually to Turkestan, which was now insistently seen as the homeland of the Turkic peoples. The ulama's appropriation of Islam was partially responsible for this, for it pushed the Jadids to cast their appeal increasingly in terms of ethnic nationalism. For Turkestani Jadids, the new conditions pushed to the fore the romantic notions of Turkicness that had been present in their rhetoric before the revolution. All through the year Jadid writers evoked Chinggis, Temur, and Ulugh-bek. Nowhere is this clearer than in the writings of Fitrat, who wrote a regular column in *Hurriyat* after becoming its editor in August 1917. In July, he wrote: "O great Turan, the land of lions! What happened to you? What bad days have you fallen into? What happened to the brave Turks who once ruled the world? Why did they pass? Why did they go away?"[28] This newfound Turkism was also reflected in Fitrat's language. Up until the revolution, Fitrat had published almost exclusively in Persian; in that year he switched to a highly purist form of Turkic. In September 1917, he published a reader for the fourth year of new-method schools (ostensibly for use in Bukhara) with a vocabulary so rigorously Turkist that Fitrat felt compelled to translate several words in footnotes. All the characters in the reading passages bear Turkic names.[29] In the spring of 1918, a news-

28. Fitrat, "Yurt qāyghusi," *Hurriyat*, 28 July 1917.
29. Fitrat, *Oqu* (Bukhara, 1917).

paper, *Turk sozi* (Turkic Word), was being published in Tashkent by an organization called Turk Ortāqlighi (Turkic Friendship). Over the next two years, the same mood was to lead to the elaboration of a Chaghatāy nationalism by a number of Jadid writers under Fitrat's leadership, grouped in the Chaghatāy Gurungi (Chaghatay Conversation).[30]

There were several sources of this new emphasis on Turkism. The abolition of censorship made possible the expression of hitherto unmentionable visions of identity. The most extreme expressions of Turkism still came from the Tatars, whose newspaper in Tashkent was called *Ulugh Turkistān* (Great Turkestan). In its first issue, Nushirvan Yavushev had claimed that the "30 million Turko-Tatars in Russia" were, "from the point of view of race, nationality, and language, tied to one another like the children of the same father and the branches of the same tree. Turkestan is the original homeland of the Turks. Therefore, no Turkic nation of Russia will stand back from helping our Turkestani brothers in their quest for autonomy. No Turkic son can forget that Turkestan is his own homeland."[31] This tenor was kept up throughout the year by *Ulugh Turkistān* and the Tatar press in European Russia.

The other source of this new Turkism was the Ottoman empire, where pan-Turkism had reached an apogee of influence during the war, the fetvâ depicting it as a holy war notwithstanding. Strict censorship imposed at the beginning of the war had excluded much of this rhetoric from Russia, but with the weakening of the Russian war effort by the autumn of 1917, such censorship waned. Ottoman victories in Transcaucasia in the spring of 1918 further heightened enthusiasm for Turkism among the Jadids. Yet, this was not the Ottoman-directed spread of pan-Turkism that Russian official had long feared (and that contemporary British intelligence services suspected). No evidence of direct Ottoman government support for Turkist or pan-Turkist groups in Central Asia has come to light. Rather, this enthusiasm for Turkism sprung from the radical mood of the Jadids. The most tangible connection between the Ottoman empire and Turkestan was the presence of several thousand Ottoman prisoners of war in Turkestan, who, in the chaotic circumstances of 1918, found themselves having to fend for a living. Yet their participation in

30. On the Chaghatāy Gurungi, see Hisao Komatsu, "The Evolution of Group Identity among Bukharan Intellectuals in 1911–1928: An Overview," *Memoirs of the Research Department of the Toyo Bunko*, no. 47 (1989): 122ff.; William Fierman, *Language Planning and National Development: The Uzbek Experience* (Berlin, 1991), 232–239.
31. N. Yavushev, "Turkistān āftānomiya āluw haqinda," *UT*, 5 May 1917.

local cultural life, although important, was hardly part of a centrally directed plot to disseminate pan-Turkist ideas.[32]

It is also important to note that this rigorous Turkism did not come at the expense of Islam, which continued to figure prominently in Jadid rhetoric. Consider the following appeal for unity among Muslims published in October 1917 by the Shura's Central Council: "Muslims! All hopes, all goals of us Turks are the same: to defend our religion [*din*] and our nation [*millat*], to gain autonomy over our land [*toprāq*] and our country [*watan*], to live freely without oppressing others and without letting others oppress us. Turkestan belongs to the Turks."[33] "Muslim" and "Turk" were still used interchangeably, but all the Muslims of Turkestan were now assumed to be Turks.

This shift toward Turkism was accompanied by a sudden turn to anticolonialism in Jadid rhetoric. This turn, first noticeable in the autumn of 1917, is largely to be explained by contemporary events. The Jadids had supported the Russian war effort in the hope of securing a voice in imperial politics after the war. The February revolution had changed little in this regard; however, by autumn Russia's commitment to the war, and the geopolitical calculations that underlay it, had unraveled. Upon taking power in Petrograd, the Bolsheviks immediately cast their appeal in antiwar and anti-imperialist terms. Their appeal to toiling Muslims, meant to rattle the governments of the Entente powers,[34] was followed by the publication of secret treaties signed during the war, many of which were at the expense of the Ottoman empire. The publi-

32. The main sources for our understanding of pan-Turkism have been contemporary British intelligence reports. Written in the heat of the moment, during a war that had a taken a turn that their authors often did not understand, these reports can easily exaggerate Ottoman influence in Central Asian affairs. They also assumed political manipulation behind every change of opinion among the "natives," who were usually assumed to not be able to think for themselves.

It is true that in the aftermath of the Ottoman collapse, both Enver and Cemal pashas found themselves in the Russian empire. But it is simplistic to assume that they were still chasing a pan-Turkist dream. Based on unprecedented access to Enver Pasha's private correspondence, Masayuki Yamauchi (*The Green Crescent under the Red Star*) has argued persuasively that Enver was motivated ultimately by a desire to recapture his political position in Anatolia. For much of his time in Soviet Russia, Enver sought ways in which he could upstage Mustafa Kemal (Atatürk) as the leader of the anti-Entente struggle in Anatolia by appealing to a mixture of anticolonial, anti-Entente, Muslim, and Turkic sentiments. It was only when he realized that the Soviet regime had little interest in backing him that he went to Bukhara and sought to rally the Bāsmachi against Soviet rule.

33. "Musulmanlar!" *Turk eli,* 15 October 1917.

34. The move achieved its goals, for the British were truly concerned and sought to ensure that news of the proclamation did not reach India or Egypt. The correspondence in this regard is in IOLR, L/P&S/11/130, file P4/1918.

cation of the treaties had a significant impact on Jadid thinking. For Fitrat, "it had now become clear who the real enemies of the Muslim, and especially the Turkic, world are."[35] The defeat of the Ottoman empire in 1918 further fueled anti-Entente sentiment, and anticolonialism (with an acutely anti-British ring) became a constant feature of Jadid rhetoric.

This marked a significant break from the Jadid admiration for the "developed" and "civilized" nations of Europe, which had withstood all evidence to the contrary. Fitrat, who had chosen Europeans as his mouthpiece in his exhortatory tracts earlier in the decade, wrote *Sharq siyāsati* (Politics of the East), a bitter denunciation of Europe's imperial record in 1919. "To this day, European imperialists have given the East nothing except immorality and destruction. Even though they came to the East saying, 'We will open schools of civilization and colleges of humanity,' they have opened nothing but brothels and winehouses." The European policy of "enslavement and destruction" was current everywhere in the East and the Muslim world and had reached new heights after the recent war. The British now occupied all Arab lands with the exception of Hijāz, which, Fitrat wrote, they were about to swallow. "They will make an Englishman who has falsely converted to Islam the caliph and thus turn 350 million Muslims into their eternal slaves." The only solution for Muslims, and for the people of "the East," was to seek the support of Soviet Russia, which had already fought the imperialist powers and which needed help from "the East" for its own survival. Most significantly, "Today it is necessary to drop everything else and take on the English. In order to do that, it is our responsibility to befriend every enemy of the English."[36]

The plight of their counterparts in Bukhara further drew the Jadids to the Soviet regime. Bukharan Jadids has sought to force the amir's hand in April 1917, but the move had backfired. The amir turned the matter into one of Bukharan sovereignty and Islamic purity and persecuted the Jadids, most of whom fled to Kagan and Turkestan, where they continued to plot and publish.[37] Their writings from this period are

35. Fitrat, "Yāshurun muāhidalari," *Hurriyat,* 28 November 1917.
36. Fitrat, *Sharq siyāsati* (N.p., 1919), 13, 37–47.
37. Accounts of the revolution in Bukhara are to be found in S. Ayni, *Bukhara inqilabi tarikhi uchun materiallar* (Moscow, 1922); Faizulla Khodzhaev, *K istorii revoliutsii v Bukhare* (Tashkent, 1926); Khodzhaev [Fayzulla Khojaev], *Bukhara inqilabinin tarikhiga materiallar* (Tashkent, 1930); Hélène Carrère d'Encausse, *Réforme et révolution chez les musulmans de l'empire russe,* 2nd ed. (Paris, 1981), 190ff.; Seymour Becker, *Russia's Pro-*

also marked by a conflation of revolution and national struggle. Abdullah Badri, who had written several plays before 1917, published two pamphlets in 1919 presenting the Young Bukharans (as the Bukharan Jadids had come to be known after 1917) to the peasant population of Bukhara. The amir appears not as the last surviving Muslim monarch in Central Asia, as Bukharan Jadids had seen him before 1917, but as a corrupt, bloodthirsty despot living off the toil of the peasants in his realm; other high-ranking dignitaries fare no better.[38] Fayzullah Khojaev, the leader of the Young Bukharans, writing in the first issue of the party's newspaper, *Uchqun* (Spark), connected the amir to imperialism, especially that of the British (who had forced the government of Turkey, the center of the Muslim world, to move to Anatolia and who had bombed Mecca and Medina). "Therefore, it is necessary for us," he concluded, "to destroy the cruel, bloodthirsty, and despotic amir [and his functionaries], and to form in their place a just and equitable government, so that poor peasants, artisans, and soldiers may live together in liberty and peace, like the children of the same parents. Thus, hand in hand with our coreligionists throughout the world, Afghans, Iranians, Indians, Arabs, and Turks, we will counter the English, accursed throughout the East, and their lackeys." Khojaev also concluded the need for assistance from Soviet Russia, "the tribune of justice and liberty in the whole world."[39]

But the conflation of class and nation allowed by anticolonialism could be used against Russian Communists in Turkestan just as easily as against the British. As the First Regional Conference of Muslim Communists, held in May 1919, noted, "The spirit and direction of the old privileged classes has not been removed decisively and . . . members of the former privileged classes as well as some self-styled Communists treat Muslims as subjects."[40] Another conference of Muslim Communists of Tashkent "consider[ed] it necessary to note that the primary hurdle to the Soviet construction of Turkestan is the mistrust shown by the

---

tectorates in Central Asia: Bukhara and Khiva, 1865–1924 (Cambridge, 1968), chs. 14–17; Reinhard Eisener, "Bukhara v 1917 godu," *Vostok*, 1994, no. 4, 131–144; no. 5, 75–92.

38. Abdullah Badri, *Yāsh Bukhārālilār kimlar?* (Moscow, 1919); Badri, *Yāsh Bukhārālilar bechāra khalq wa dehqānlar uchun yakhshimi, yamānmi?* (Moscow, 1919).

39. Fayzullah Khoja, "Bukhārāning yagāna āzādliq wa istiqlāl chāralari," *Uchqun*, 15 April 1920. The masthead of the newspaper proclaimed: "The liberation of the East is a matter of the People of the East themselves."

40. Quoted by Safarov, *Kolonial'naia revoliutsiia*, 151.

European proletariat toward the toiling Muslim masses, as a result of which the Muslim proletariat is sidelined in the construction of the new life."[41] Food supply committees, subordinated to the soviets by early 1918, became the most significant arena of political conflict, but the conflict soon spread to the highest organs of the party itself.

The process was set in motion by the highest authorities of the (newly renamed) Russian Communist Party (Bolshevik), or RKP(b), themselves, who by the spring of 1919 were stressing the need for "particular care and attention" toward "the remnants of national feelings of the toiling masses of the oppressed or dependent nations." This concern led to the formation in April 1919 of the Muslim Bureau (Musbiuro) of the Regional Committee of the KPT as the party analog of the Turkomnats.[42] Quite rapidly, the Musbiuro became autonomous of the Regional Committee of the KPT and began to assert its will quite openly. A Central Committee decree demanding that the indigenous population of Turkestan enjoy proportional representation in all state organs provided an opportunity for the Musbiuro to act. New party and Soviet congresses were hurriedly convened to act upon the new directive, and both elected new executive committees, both of which were dominated by Muslims. Turar Rïsqulov, a Qazaq from Awliya Ata, was elected president of both committees.

Muslim Communists made their most ambitious bid in January 1920, at the Fifth Regional Conference of the KPT, where they succeeded in passing a resolution changing the name of the KPT to the "Communist Party of the Turkic Peoples" and that of the Turkestan Republic to the "Turkic Republic."[43] This was accompanied by another resolution demanding wide-ranging autonomy for Turkestan. Rïsqulov had explicitly drawn a parallel with the Kokand Autonomy in describing to the congress the kind of autonomy the resolution hoped to institutionalize,[44] but the resolution, "On the Autonomy and Constitution of Turkestan," went much further. "In the interests of the international unity of toiling and oppressed peoples, to oppose by means of Communist agitation the

41. Quoted by U. Kasymov, "Iz istorii musul'manskikh kommunisticheskikh organizatsii v Turkestane v 1919–1920 godakh," *Trudy Tashkentskogo gosudarstvennogo universiteta*, n.s., no. 207 (1962): 10.

42. T. Ryskulov, *Revoliutsiia i korennoe naselenie Turkestana* (Tashkent, 1925), 121–127.

43. Safarov, *Kolonial'naia revoliutsiia*, 171.

44. V. P. Nikolaeva, "Turkkomissiia kak polnomochnyi organ TsK RKP(b)," *Voprosy istorii KPSS*, 1958, no. 2, 83.

strivings of the Turkic nationalities to divide themselves into different groups . . . and [their desire] to establish separate small republics; instead, with a view to forging the unity of all Turkic nationalities who have so far not been included in the RSFSR, it is proposed to unify them with the Turkic Soviet Republic, and wherever it is not possible to achieve this, it is proposed to unite different Turkic nationalities in accordance with their territorial proximity."[45] The juxtaposition of nationalist and Communist language was used again when Rïsqulov traveled to Moscow in May 1920 to present the Muslim Communist case to the highest party authorities after the resolution had been overridden, after some vacillation, by the recently appointed Turkestan Commission (Turkkomissiia) of the Moscow Central Committee. In a presentation to the Central Committee, Rïsqulov argued that there were only two basic groups in Turkestan, "the oppressed and exploited colonial natives and European capital."[46] He went on to demand, in the name of the KPT and the government of Turkestan, the transfer of all authority in Turkestan to the Central Executive Committee of Turkestan, the abolition of the Turkkomissiia, and the establishment of a Muslim army subordinate to the autonomous government of Turkestan.[47] In their substance, these demands harked back to the hopes of 1917, but they were now couched in the language of revolution. But class had been replaced, in the colonial situation of Turkestan, by nation; national liberation of the Muslim community could be achieved through Communist means and in the Soviet context.

SOVIET CENTRAL ASIA

The attempt to transform the KPT was, of course, defeated. The Turkkomissiia, shifting its attention to combating local nationalism, rescinded the resolution on autonomy as being "contrary to the principles of internationalist construction of the Communist Party." Instead, the Central Committee in Moscow passed its own resolution on the autonomy of Turkestan, which offered a strictly territorial autonomy to Turkestan. In June 1920, the Central Committee passed another four resolutions call-

45. Quoted in Safarov, *Kolonial'naia revoliutsiia*, 171; see also *Rezoliutsii i postanovleniia s"ezdov Kommunisticheskoi partii Turkestana (1918–1924 gg.)* (Tashkent, 1968), 70.
46. Quoted by Nikolaeva, "Turkkomissiia," 82.
47. Ibid., 85.

ing for stricter central control over Turkestan affairs. The Bolshevik victory in the Civil War and the massive presence of the Red Army in Turkestan made such resolutions meaningful. In September, party and Soviet congresses met to elect new executive committees that excluded Rïsqulov and his supporters and adopted the RKP(b) resolutions of July. This setback did not spell the end of Muslim participation in Soviet political life, though. The new central committees elected in September 1920 had a Muslim majority, and the people's republics formed in Khiva and Bukhara in that year were governed entirely by Muslims, mostly Jadids. The strengthened central position did not mean an unrestricted enforcement of a central will. The regime in Moscow had neither the means nor the resources for that. Indeed, ideologically committed to granting autonomy to all national groups within its domain, the regime was only too willing to accept the particularism of Central Asia. How that particularism was to be defined became the crucial question. The Turkic Muslim nation of the Jadids conflicted with the more narrowly defined ethnic nations supported by the Soviet regime (but also, increasingly, by many Muslims in Central Asia itself). Ultimately, with the "national delimitation" of 1925, ethnic nationalism supplanted broader Turkist visions of identity as the legitimate basis of autonomy. This process created new ethnographic knowledge, which made possible, but also legitimized, the new national identities.

By 1925, then, the political boundaries of modern Central Asia were largely in place. The political and cultural transformations they represent have only been briefly sketched here, but the involvement of the Jadids in the process cannot be overemphasized. Their adroit appropriation of the new language of class and revolution, perhaps most clearly visible in the resolutions passed by the Muslim Communists of Turkestan in January 1920, expressed what Alexandre Bennigsen has called "Muslim national communism," which was best developed by the Tatar Mirsaid Sultangaliev.[48] This was a new strategy called for by a new age. Prerevolutionary Jadidism had been fully imbricated in the imperial order, making use of the opportunities allowed by it while subject to its constraints. Hence the emphasis on self-improvement by the Muslim society with the hope of its inclusion in the imperial economy and the impe-

---

48. Alexandre Bennigsen and Chantal Lemercier-Quelquejay, *Les mouvements nationaux chez les musulmans de Russie: le «sultangalievisme» au Tatarstan* (Paris, 1960); Bennisgen and S. Enders Wimbush, *Muslim National Communism in the Soviet Union: A Revolutionary Ideology for the Colonial World* (Chicago, 1979).

rial political order. Muslim national communism was the Jadids' strategy for the new age ushered in by the revolution. After 1920, Soviet rule provided the new context in which Central Asian cultures were to be imagined. The regime was quite different from tsarist autocracy: Instead of exclusion, it offered mobilization, and it increased the reach of the state into spheres of activity autocracy had been content to leave alone. Its emphasis on enlightenment and progress was easily comprehensible to the Jadids, and its methods of mobilization and organization evoked their respect. The Jadids had not forgotten the lessons of 1917. They had found in the Soviet regime the outside support they had been unable to muster in that year.

Muslim national communism represented a new expression of the secular Muslim nationalism that had motivated the Jadids before 1917, now expressed in the language of revolution and combined, seamlessly in the minds of those involved, with anticolonial struggle.[49] The Jadids' commitment to revolution was genuine, and the language of class was not evoked simply out of cynicism; yet, the Jadids' understanding of both these concepts was their own. Scholars outside the former Soviet Union have wasted much energy in debating whether the Jadids were "true" Communists or not. The assumption that both "Jadids" (or "Muslims") and "Communists" are stable entities whose essential characteristics are mutually exclusive is of course untenable in the light of historical evidence. To a radicalized cultural elite, the mobilizational methods of communism appealed greatly, and the rhetoric of revolution provided a means for struggling with enemies both within and without society.

For much of the 1920s, the Jadids played central roles in the political and especially the cultural life of Central Asia. Fayzullah Khojaev was prime minister of the Bukharan People's Republic and then president of Uzbekistan, while Fitrat served as minister for education in Bukhara. Cholpān, Qādiri, Hamza, Munawwar Qāri, Awlāni, Ayni, Ajzi, and Hāji Muin, to name only a few of the most important figures, were all central figures in the worlds of letters, arts, and education all through the decade. They saw themselves creating a new civilization—modern, Soviet, Central Asian, Turkic, and Muslim all at once. They hoped to coopt the state to the work of modernization that exhortation alone had not achieved in the prerevolutionary era. As such, the Jadids in the 1920s

49. The transition from anticolonial pan-Islam to anticolonial socialism also proved easy for many Muslim Indians: see K. H. Ansari, "Pan-Islam in the Making of the Early Indian Muslim Socialists," *Modern Asian Studies* 20 (1986): 509–537.

were hardly the pawns of a monolithic Soviet regime; rather, they are best compared with fellow modernists in Iran and (especially) Turkey in the same decade who also used the newly established apparatus of a modern centralized nation-state to revolutionize society and culture.

But unlike their counterparts in Turkey and Iran, the Jadids' triumph was short-lived. By the late 1920s, the regime in Moscow had given up on the experimentation that had characterized much of that decade, and the Jadids' understanding of Soviet reality collided head on with the centralizing impulse of the new period. The results were catastrophic for the Jadids personally and for Jadidism as a cultural movement. Of the major figures, only Ayni died in his bed; most others met violent deaths at the hands of various enemies. Behbudi was the first to go, tortured to death in March 1919 by (appropriately enough, perhaps) the functionaries of the amir of Bukhara after they had apprehended him as he traversed Bukharan territory on his way, in all likelihood, to the Peace Conference in Versailles to plead the case of Turkestan. Hamza was killed by a mob in 1929 as he took part in a campaign against the veil. Munawwar Qāri, Cholpān, Qādiri, Hāji Muin, and Ubaydullah Khojaev all disappeared in the Gulag in the 1930s. By 1938, when Fitrat was executed and Fayzullah Khojaev, most famously of them all, mounted the podium at the Great Purge Trial in Moscow as part of the "anti-Soviet bloc of 'Rights and Trotskyites'" to face the fatal charges of counterrevolution and anti-Soviet activity, the Jadid generation had been obliterated. They were replaced by a new generation (the so-called Class of '38), whose education and worldview had been shaped entirely within the Soviet context.[50] Although this generation inherited many of the compromises of the 1920s and 1930s, it shared little else with the Jadids. It was a new political elite that over the next several decades came to entrench itself in the political structures of the Soviet Union. And although this new elite developed its own versions of (often virulent) nationalism, it had little in common with the visions of the Jadids. Given such a conjuncture of political interests between the new republican elites and the central regime, the memory of the Jadids was rapidly consigned to oblivion.

That oblivion has proved quite difficult to overcome. The process of reclaiming the memory began with the belated advent of glasnost to Central Asia, and in the heady days of 1991 and 1992, much was written

---

50. The term "Class of '38" was coined by Donald S. Carlisle, "The Uzbek Power Elite: Politburo and Secretariat (1938–83)," *Central Asian Survey* 5, no. 3/4 (1986): 99.

about the Jadids. But the Class of '38 survived in power (especially in Uzbekistan) and has sought to base its legitimacy in a nationalism that appeals to the safely distant past of the fourteenth and fifteenth centuries.
"Amir" Temur, Ulugh-bek, and Alisher Nawā'i are the new heroes of independent Uzbekistan, while the Jadids serve largely to symbolize the
martyrdom of the Uzbek nation at the hands of the colonial Soviet regime.
The Jadids have thus been appropriated by a nation imagined largely in
the Soviet period.

Select Bibliography

ARCHIVAL SOURCES

TSENTRAL'NYI GOSUDARSTVENNYI
ARKHIV RESPUBLIKI UZBEKISTAN, TASHKENT

f. 1	Kantselliariia Turkestanskogo General-Gubernatora
f. 2	Diplomaticheskii chinovnik pri Kantselliarii Turkestanskogo General-Gubernatora
f. 3	Rossiiskoe Politicheskoe agentstvo v Bukhare
f. 17	Syr-Dar'inskoe oblastnoe upravlenie
f. 18	Samarkandskoe oblastnoe upravlenie
f. 19	Ferganskoe oblastnoe upravlenie
f. 47	Upravlenie uchebnykh zavedenii Turkestanskogo kraia
f. 276	Kantselliariia Voennogo gubernatora Ferganskoi oblasti
f. 455	Tret'ii Inspektor narodnykh uchilishch Turkestanskogo kraia
f. 461	Turkestanskoe raionnoe okhrannoe otdelenie
f. 1009	Lichnyi fond N. P. Ostroumova
f. 1044	Turkestanskii Komitet Vremennogo Pravitel'stva

GOSUDARSTVENNYI ARKHIV ROSSIISKOI FEDERATSII, MOSCOW

f. 102	Departament Politsii Ministerstva Vnutrennikh Del

INDIA OFFICE LIBRARY AND RECORDS, LONDON

L/P&S/10	Departmental Papers: Political and Secret Separate Files

L'INSTITUT DES LANGUES ET CIVILISATIONS ORIENTALES, PARIS

L'Archive de Moustafa Tchokai Bey

CENTRAL ASIAN PRIMARY SOURCES

Abdulkarīm Bukhārī. *Histoire de l'Asie centrale par Abdoul Kerim Boukhary.* Ed. and trans. Charles Schefer. Paris: Ecole des Langues Orientales Vivantes, 1876.

Ajzi, Sayyid Ahmad Siddiqi. *Tarjima-yi mir'at-i ibrat.* Samarqand: Zarafshān, 1914.

Awlāni, Abdullah. *Birinchi muallim.* Tashkent, 1912.

——. *Turki Gulistān, yākhud akhlāq.* Tashkent, 1914.

Ayni, Sadriddin. *Tahzib us-sibyān.* Samarqand, 1911.

Badri, Abdullah. *Ahmaq.* Samarqand, 1915.

——. *Jawānmarg.* Samarqand, 1916.

——. *Yāsh Bukhārālilār kimlar?* Moscow: Yāsh Bukhārālilarning Maskaw kamiteti, 1919.

——. *Yāsh Bukhārālilar bechāra khalq wa dehqānlar uchun yakhshimi, yamānmi?* Moscow: Yāsh Bukhārālilarning Maskaw kamiteti, 1919.

Behbudi, Mahmud Khoja. *Mukhtasar tarikh-i Islām.* Samarqand, 1909.

Dānish, Ahmad Makhdum. *Traktat Akhmada Donisha "Istoriia Mangytskoi dinastii."* Ed. and trans. I. A. Nadzhafova. Dushanbe: Irfon, 1967.

Fitrat, Abdurrauf. *Bayānāt-i sayyāh-i hindi.* Istanbul, 1911.

——. *Hindustānda bir farangi ila bukhārālik bir mudarrisning birnecha masalalar ham usul-i jadida khususida qilghan munāzarasi.* Trans. Hāji Muin. Tashkent: Turkistān kutubkhānasi, 1914.

——. *Mukhtasar tarikh-i Islām.* Samarqand: Hāji Muin, 1915.

——. *Munāzara-yi mudarris-i bukhārāyī bāyak nafar-i farangī dar Hindustān dar bāra-yi makātib i jadīda.* Istanbul: Matbaa-yı İslâmiye-yi Hikmet, 1911.

——. *Oqu.* Bukhara: Marifat, 1917.

——. *Razskazy indiiskogo puteshestvennika: Bukhara kak ona est'.* Trans. A. N. Kondrat'ev. Samarqand: Behbudi, 1913.

——. *Sharq siyāsati.* N.p.: Yāsh Bukhārālilār Qomitāsining nashriyāt shu'basi, 1919.

Ghulāmuddin Akbarzāda. *Ta'lim-i sāni.* Tashkent, 1913.

Hāji Muin b. Shukrullah. *Eski maktab, yangi maktab.* Samarqand, 1916.

——. *Koknāri.* Samarqand, 1916.

——. *Mazluma khātun.* Samarqand, 1916.

Hamza Hakimzāda Niyāzi. *Milli āshulalar uchun milli she'rlar majmuasi.* 7 parts. Kokand, 1915–1917.

——. *Yāngi saādat: milli romān.* Kokand: Madārā, 1915.

Majmu'a-yi nurnāma. Tashkent, 1914.

Mirzā Badi' Diwān. *Majma' al-arqām.* Ed. and trans. L. M. Epifanova. Moscow: Nauka, 1976.

Mominjān Muhammadjānov. *Nasāih ul-atfāl.* Tashkent, 1912.

Muhammadjān Qāri b. Rahimjān. *Adablik oghlān*. Tashkent, 1912.

al-Mukhtāri, Muallim Shākir. *Kim qāzi bolsin*. Kokand, 1917.

Munawwar Qāri. *Adib-i awwal*. Tashkent, 1912.

———. *Adib-i sāni*. Tashkent, 1912.

———. *Yer yuzi*. Tashkent, 1913.

Nusratullah b. Qudratullah (with Hāji Muin). *Toy*. Samarqand, 1914.

Qādiri, Abdullah. *Bakhtsiz kiyāw*. Tashkent, 1915.

———. *Jawānbāz*. Tashkent, 1916.

Rahimi, Shākirjān. *Sawghā*. Tashkent, 1919.

Said Rasul Khoja Said Aziz Khoja oghli. *Ustād-i awwal*. Tashkent, 1902.

Sidqi, Sirājiddin Makhdum. *Buyuk Rusiya inqilābi*. Tashkent: Rawnaq, 1917.

———: *Tāza hurriyat*. Tashkent, 1917.

Tāshkand Shurā-yi Islāmiyasi. *Khitābnāma*. Tashkent, 1917.

Tawallā. *Rawnaq ul-Islām*. Tashkent, 1914.

Ulamā Jamiyati. *Haqiqatgha khilāf tārqatilgan khitābnāmagha jawāb wa ham bayān-i ahwāl*. Tashkent, 1917.

Wasli. *Ortāq*. Samarqand, 1918.

Zāhiri, Āshur Ali. *Imlā*. Tashkent, 1916.

MODERN EDITIONS

Awloniy, Abdulla. *Toshkent tongi: she"rlar, masallar, riwoyatlar, dramalar*. Ed. B. Qosimov. Tashkent: Ghafur Ghulom, 1979.

Chŏlpon. *Adabiyot nadur*. Ed. D. Quronov, Zamira Eshonova, and U. Sultonov. Tashkent: Chŏlpon Nashriyoti, 1994.

———. *Bahorni soghindim*. Ed. Ibrohim Haqqulov. Tashkent, 1988.

Fitrat [Abdurauf Fitrati Bukhoroî]. "Bayonoti sayyohi hindî." Ed. Kholiq Mirzozoda. *Sadoi Sharq*, 1988, no. 6, 12–57.

——— [Abdurauf Fitrat]. "Hind sayyohining qissasi." Trans. Hasan Qudratullaev. *Sharq yulduzi*, 1991, no. 8, 7–39.

——— [Abduraufi Fitrati Bukhoroi]. "Rohbari najot." Ed. Muhabbat Jalilova. *Sadoi Sharq*, 1992, no. 7–8, 16–59; no. 9, 8–54.

Hamza Hakimzoda Niyoziy. *Tŏla asarlar tŏplami*. Ed. N. Karimov et al. 5 vols. Tashkent: Fan, 1988–1989.

Mirzā Sirājiddin Hāji Mirzā ʿAbdurrauf. *Safarnāma-yi tuhaf-i Bukhārā*. Ed. M. Asadiyān. Tehran: Intishārāt-i Bū ʿAlī, 1992.

Qodiriy, Abdulla. *Kichik asarlar*. Tashkent: Ghafur Ghulom, 1969.

Tawallo. *Rawnaq ul-Islom*. Ed. Begali Qosimov. Tashkent: Fan, 1993.

PERIODICALS

Āyina. Samarqand, 1913–1915.

Bayān ul-haq. Tashkent: Madaniyat shirkati, 1918.

Bukhārā-yi sharīf. Kāgān, 1912–1913.

Hurriyat. Samarqand, 1917–1918.

al-Islāh. Tashkent, 1915–1917.
al-Izāh. Tashkent: Ulamā Jamiyati, 1917–1918.
Kengash. Kokand: Khoqand Muallimlar Jamiyati, 1917.
Kengash. Tashkent: Markaz Shurāsi, 1917.
Khurshid. Tashkent, 1906.
Najāt. Tashkent, 1917. Continuation of *TWG*.
Rawnaq ul-Islām. Kokand, 1917.
Sadā-yi Farghāna. Kokand, 1914–15.
Sadā-yi Turkistān. Tashkent, 1914–1915.
Samarqand. Samarqand, 1913.
Shuhrat. Tashkent, 1907–1908.
Taraqqi. Tashkent, 1906.
Taraqqi—Orta Azyaning umr guzārlighi. Tashkent, 1906.
Tirik soz. Kokand, 1917.
Tojjār. Tashkent, 1907.
Turān. Kāgān, 1912–1913.
Turān. Tashkent: Turān Jamiyati, 1917.
Turān. Tashkent: Turk Adam-i Markaziyat Firqasi, 1917.
Turk eli. Tashkent, 1917.
Turkistān wilāyatining gazeti. Tashkent, 1870–1917.
Uchqun. Tashkent: Yāsh Bukhārālilar Firqasi, 1920.
Ulugh Turkistān. Tashkent, 1917–1918.

PUBLISHED DOCUMENTS AND OFFICIAL SOURCES

Bigi, Musa Jarullah. *Islahat esaslarï*. Petrograd, 1915.
Browder, Robert Paul, and Alexander F. Kerensky, eds. *The Russian Provisional Government, 1917: Documents*. 3 vols. Stanford: Stanford University Press, 1961.
"Bukhara v 1917 godu." *Krasnyi arkhiv*, no. 20 (1927), 78–122.
Butun Rusya Müsülmanlärining 1917nchi yilda 1–11 Mayda Mäskävdä bolghan umumi isyizdining protaqollarï. Petrograd: Butun Rusya Müsülmanlarï Shurasï, 1917.
Dukhovskoi, S. M. *Vsepoddanneishii doklad Turkestanskogo General-Gubernatora Generala ot Infentarii Dukhovskogo: Islam v Turkestane*. Tashkent, 1899.
Ezhegodnik Ferganskoi oblasti. 3 vols. Novyi Margelan, 1902–1904.
Girs, F. K. *Otchet revizuiushchego, po Vysochaishemu poveleniiu, Turkestanskii krai, Tainogo Sovetnika Girsa*. St. Petersburg, 1883.
Gosudarstvennaia Duma. *Ukazatel' k stenograficheskim otchetam: Vtoroi sozyv, 1907 god*. St. Peterburg: Gosudarstvennaia tipografiia, 1907.
———. Vtoroi Sozyv. *Stenograficheskie otchety: 1907 god*. St. Petersburg: Gosudarstvennaia tipografiia, 1907.
Great Britain. Parliament. *Central Asia, No. 2 (1873): Correspondence Respecting Central Asia*. C. 704. London: HMSO, 1873.
Hamza Hakimzoda Niyoziyning arkhivining katalogi. 2 vols. Tashkent: Fan, 1990–1991.

"Iz dnevnika A. N. Kuropatkina." *Krasnyi arkhiv,* no. 20 (1927): 56–77.

fon-Kaufman, K. P. *Proekt vsepoddanneishego otcheta General-ad"iutanta K.P. fon-Kaufmana po grazhdanskomu upravleniiu i ustroistvu v oblastiakh Turkestanskogo general-gubernatorstva 7 noiabria 1867–25 marta 1881 g.* St. Petersburg: Voennaia tipografiia, 1885.

Krivoshein, A. V. *Zapiska glavnoupravliaiushchego zemledeliem i zemleustroistvom o poezdke v Turkestanskii krai v 1912 godu.* St. Petersburg, 1912.

A Manual on the Turanians and Pan-Turanianism. I.D. 1199. London: HMSO, n.d. [1918].

Materialy dlia statistiki Turkestanskogo kraia. Ezhegodnik. 4 vols. St. Petersburg, 1872–1876.

Obzor Ferganskoi oblasti za 1896 god. Novyi Margelan, 1898.

Obzor Samarkandskoi oblasti za 1905 god. Tashkent, 1906.

Osmanlı Devleti ile Kafkasya, Türkistan ve Kırım Hanlıkları Arasındaki Münasebetlere Dâir Arşiv Belgeleri. Ankara: Başbakanlık, 1992.

Palen, K. K. *Otchet po revizii Turkestanskogo kraia, proizvedennoi po Vysochaishemu poveleniiu Senatorom Gofmeistorom grafom K. K. Palenom.* 19 vols. St. Petersburg, 1910.

Pervaia vseobshchaia perepis' naseleniia Rossiiskoi Imperii, 1897 g. 89 vols. St. Petersburg, 1905.

Pobeda oktiabr'skoi revoliutsii v Uzbekistane: sbornik dokumentov. 2 vols. Tashkent: Fan, 1963–1972.

Polnoe sobranie zakonov Rossiiskoi Imperii. 2nd ser., vol. 42; 3rd ser., vol. 25. St. Petersburg: Gosudarstvennaia tipografiia, 1868, 1907.

Programma Musul'manskoi parlamentarskoi fraktsii v Gosudarstvennoi Dume. St. Petersburg, 1907.

Rezoliutsii i postanovleniia s"ezdov Kommunisticheskoi partii Turkestana (1918–1924 gg.). Tashkent: Uzbekistan, 1968.

Samarqand anjuman-i maārif-i islāmiya jamiyatining mukhtasar proghrāmasi. Samarqand, 1917.

Sbornik materialov dlia statistiki Syr-Dar'inskoi oblasti. 13 vols. Tashkent, 1891–1907.

Spravochnaia knizhka Samarkandskoi oblasti. 10 vols. Samarkand, 1894–1912.

Tāshkand shahrining orus chāstida istiqāmat etub masjid-i jāmi'imizga qawm bulub turghuwchi hamma ahl-i mahalla noghāy khalqiga ruski tātāriski ishkolāning pāpichitilstvāsining predsidātilidan dāklād. Tashkent, 1902.

III-i Vserossiiskii Musul'manskii s"ezd. Kazan, 1906.

Trudy Syr-Dar'inskogo oblastnogo statisticheskogo komiteta v 1887–1888 gg. Tashkent, 1888.

Ustav musul'manskogo obshchestva "Pomoshch'" v Tashkente. Tashkent: Pomoshch', 1909.

SECONDARY LITERATURE

Abdughafurov, A. *Zokirjon Furqat: hayoti wa ijodi.* Tashkent: Fan, 1977.
———. "Zokirjon Furqat haqida yangi ma"lumotlar." In *Furqat ijodiyoti.* Tashkent: Fan, 1990.

Abdullaev, Iuldash. *Ocherki po metodike obucheniia gramote v uzbekskoi shkole.* Tashkent: Uchitel', 1966.

Abduraimov, M. A. *Ocherki agrarnykh otnoshenii v Bukharskom khanstve v XVI–pervoi polovine XIX veka.* 2 vols. Tashkent: Fan, 1965–1970.

———. .*Voprosy feodal'nogo zemlevladeniia i feodal'noi renty v pis'makh Emira Khaidara.* Tashkent: Fan, 1961

Abdurazzakov, Abdulla. "Pedagogicheskoe nasledie uzbekskogo prosvetitelia Abdully Avloni." Candidate's diss., Tashkentskii gospedinstitut im. Nizami, Tashkent, 1979.

Abibov, A. *Doirahoi adabii Bukhoroi sharqî (Asri XIX wa ibtidoi asri XX).* Dushanbe: Donish, 1984.

Ahmad, Aziz. *Islamic Modernism in India and Pakistan, 1857–1964.* London: Oxford University Press, 1967.

Ahmad, Sirojiddin. "Munawwar qori." *Sharq yulduzi,* 1992, no. 5, 105–119.

Aitmambetov, D. *Dorevoliutsionnye shkoly v Kirgizii.* Frunze: Izd. AN Kirgizskoi SSR, 1961.

Akçuraoğlu Yusuf [Yusuf Akçura]. "Türkçülük." In *Türk Yılı 1928.* Ankara: Türk Ocağı, 1928.

Alekseenkov, P. *Kokandskaia avtonomiia.* Tashkent: Uzgiz, 1931.

Algar, Hamid. *Mīrza Malkum Khān: A Study in the History of Iranian Modernism.* Berkeley: University of California Press, 1973.

Aliev, Ahmad. *Mahmudkhŏja Behbudiy.* Tashkent: Yozuwchi, 1994.

Allworth, Edward. "The Beginnings of the Modern Turkestanian Theater." *Slavic Review* 23 (1964): 676–687..

———. *Central Asian Publishing and the Rise of Nationalism.* New York: NYPL, 1965.

———. *The Modern Uzbeks: From the Fourteenth Century to the Present: A Cultural History.* Stanford: Hoover Institution Press, 1990.

———, ed. *Central Asia: A Century of Russian Rule.* New York: Columbia University Press, 1967.

Altstadt, Audrey L. *The Azerbaijani Turks: Power and Identity under Russian Rule.* Stanford: Hoover Institution Press, 1992.

Amanzholova, D. A. *Kazakhskii avtonomizm i Rossiia: istoriia dvizheniia Alash.* Moscow: Rossiia Molodaia, 1994.

Aminov, A. M. *Ekonomicheskoe razvitie Srednei Azii (kolonial'noi period).* Tashkent: Uzbekistan, 1959.

Anderson, Benedict. *Imagined Communities: Reflections on the Origin and Spread of Nationalism.* 2nd ed. London: Verso, 1991.

Ansari, K. H. "Pan-Islam in the Making of the Early Indian Muslim Socialists." *Modern Asian Studies* 20 (1986): 509–537.

Appadurai, Arjun. "Number in the Colonial Imagination." In Carol Breckenridge and Peter van der Veer, eds., *Orientalism and the Postcolonial Predicament.* Philadelphia: University of Pennsylvania Press, 1993.

Ardashirov, A. F. "K voprosu o roli novometodnykh maktabov (Po materialam Andizhanskoi oblasti)." *Uchenye zapiski Andizhanskogo gospedinstituta,* 1957, no. 6, 131–171.

————. "Russko-tuzemnye shkoly v dorevoliutsionnom Andizhane." *Uchenye zapiski Andizhanskogo gospedinstituta,* no. 6 (1957): 81–130.

Ariès, Philippe. *Centuries of Childhood.* Trans. Robert Baldick. New York: Knopf, 1962.

Aristov, N. A. "Zametki ob etnicheskom sostave tiurkskikh plemen i svedeniia ob ikh chislennosti." *Zhivaia starina* 6 (1896): 277–456.

Arkhangel'skii, N. P. "Uchebnaia literatura na uzbekskom iazyke." *Nauka i prosveshchenie,* 1922, no. 2, 2nd pagination, 34–41.

Arsharuni, A., and Kh. Gabidullin. *Ocherki panislamizma i pantiurkizma v Rossii.* Moscow: Bezbozhnik, 1931.

Arutiunov, S. A. "Ethnichnost'—ob"ektivnaia real'nost'," *Etnograficheskoe obozrenie,* 1995, no. 5, 7–10.

Atay, Hüseyin. *Osmanlılarda Yüksek Din Eğitimi.* Istanbul: Dergâh, 1983.

Avsharova, M. P. *Russkaia periodicheskaia pechat' v Turkestane (1870–1917): Bibliograficheskii ukazatel' literatury.* Tashkent: Gosizdat UzSSR, 1960.

Aynī, Sadriddīn. *Bukhara inqilabi tarikhi uchun materiallar.* Moscow: SSSR Khalqlarining Markazi Nashriayti, 1922.

———— [Ayniy]. *Eski maktab.* Tashkent: Yulduzcha, 1988 (orig. 1935).

———— [Aini]. *Istoriia Mangytskikh emirov.* In *Sobranie sochinenii,* 6 vols. Moscow: 1971–1975 (orig. 1921–1923).

———— ['Aynī]. *Namūna-yi adabiyāt-i Tājīk.* Moscow: Tsentral'noe izdatel'stvo narodov SSSR, 1926.

———— [Aini]. *Pages from My Own Story.* Trans. George H. Hanna. Moscow: Foreign Languages Publishing House, 1958.

———— ['Aynī]. *Yāddāshthā.* Ed. Saʿīdī Sīrjānī. Tehran: Āgāh, 1984.

Azadaev, F. *Tashkent vo vtoroi polovine XIX veka: ocherki sotsial'no-ekonomicheskoi i politicheskoi istorii.* Tashkent: Izd. AN UzSSR, 1959.

Aziatskaia Rossiia. 2 vols. St. Petersburg: Pereselencheskoe Upravlenie, 1914.

al-Azmeh, Aziz. *Islams and Modernities.* London: Verso, 1993.

Badawi, Zaki. *The Reformers of Egypt—A Critique of Al-Afghani, ʿAbduh and Ridha.* Muslim Institute Papers, no. 2. London: Open Press, 1976.

Bakhash, Shaul. *Iran: Monarchy, Bureaucracy, and Reform under the Qajars.* London, 1978.

Bakirov, F. *Chor Turkistonda sud, shariat wa odat.* Tashkent: Fan, 1967.

Baldauf, Ingeborg. "Some Thoughts on the Making of the Uzbek Nation." *Cahiers du monde russe et soviétique* 32 (1991): 79–96.

Baron, Beth. *The Women's Awakening in Egypt: The Early Years of the Press.* New Haven: Yale University Press, 1994.

Bartol'd, V. V. *Sochineniia.* 9 vols. in 10. Moscow: Izd. Vostochnoi literatury, 1963–1977.

Bassin, Mark. "Russia between Europe and Asia: The Ideological Construction of Geographical Space." *Slavic Review* 50 (1991): 1–17.

Bauer, Henning, et al. *Die Nationalitäten des Russischen Reiches in der Volkszählung von 1897.* 2 vols. Stuttgart: Klein, 1991.

Bayat, Mangol. *The First Iranian Revolution: Shiʿism and the Constitutional Revolution of 1905–1909.* New York: Oxford University Press, 1991.

Baykara, Hüseyin. *Azerbaycanda Yenileşme Hareketi: XIX. Yüzyıl*. Ankara: Türk Kültürünü Araştırma Enstitüsü, 1966.

Baysun, Abdullah Receb. *Türkistan Millî Hareketleri*. Istanbul, 1943.

Bečka, Jiří. "Traditional Schools in the Works of Sadriddin Aynī and Other Writers of Central Asia." *Archiv Orientální* 39 (1971): 284–321; 40 (1972): 130–163.

Becker, Seymour. *Russia's Protectorates in Central Asia: Bukhara and Khiva, 1865–1924*. Cambridge, Mass.: Harvard University Press, 1968.

Beisembiev, T. K. "Dukhovenstvo v politicheskoi zhizni kokandskogo khanstva v VIII–XIX vekakh." In *Dukhovenstvo i politicheskaia zhizn' na Blizhnem i Srednem Vostoke v period feodalizma*. Moscow: Nauka, 1985.

———. "Farghana's Contacts with India in the 18th and 19th Centuries." *Journal of Asian History* 28 (1994): 124–135.

———. *"Ta'rikh-i Shakhrukhi" kak istoricheskii istochnik*. Alma-Ata: Nauka Kazakhskoi SSR, 1987.

———. "Unknown Dynasty: The Rulers of Shahrisabz in the 18th and 19th Centuries." *Journal of Central Asia* 15, no. 1 (1992): 20–22.

Beliavskii. *Materialy po Turkestanu*. N.p., n.d. [St. Petersburg, 1884].

Bendrikov, K. E. *Ocherki po istorii narodnogo obrazovaniia v Turkestane (1865–1925 gody)*. Moscow: Izd. Akademii pedagogicheskikh nauk, 1960.

Bennigsen, Alexandre, and Chantal Lemercier-Quelquejay. *Islam in the Soviet Union*. Trans. Geoffrey E. Wheeler and Hubert Evans. London: Pall Mall Press, 1967.

———. *Les mouvements nationaux chez les musulmans de Russie: le «sultan-galievisme» au Tatarstan*. Paris: Mouton, 1960.

———. *La presse et le mouvement national chez les musulmans de Russie avant 1920*. Paris: Mouton, 1964.

Bennigsen, Alexandre, and S. Enders Wimbush. *Muslim National Communism in the Soviet Union: A Revolutionary Ideology for the Colonial World*. Chicago: University of Chicago Press, 1979.

Berkes, Niyazi. *The Development of Secularism in Turkey*. Montreal: McGill University Press, 1964.

Bigiev, Muhammed Zahir. *Maveraünnährdä siyahät*. Kazan: Kitab, 1908.

Bihnām, Jamshīd. "Manzilgāhī dar rāh-i tajaddud-i Īrān: Islāmbūl." *Īrānnāma* 11 (1993): 271–282

Blank, Stephen. "The Contested Terrain: Muslim Political Participation in Soviet Turkestan, 1917–19." *Central Asian Survey* 6, no. 4 (1987): 47–73.

Bobokhonov, Aziz. *Özbek matbaasi tarikhidan*. Tashkent: Ghafur Ghulom, 1979.

Bobokhonov, A., and M. Mahsumov. *Abdulla Awloniyning pedagogik faoliyati wa ta"lim-tarbiya tŏghrisidagi fikrlari*. Tashkent: Oqituwchi, 1966.

Bobrovnikov, N. A. "Russko-tuzemnye uchilishcha, mekteby i medresy v Srednei Azii." *ZhMNP*, n.s., 45 (1913): otd. narod. obraz., 189–241; 46 (1913): 49–84.

———. "Sovremennoe polozhenie uchebnogo dela u inorodtsev vostochnoi Rossii." *ZhMNP*, n.s., 69 (1917): 51–84.

Bogdanov, A. "Antropometricheskie zametki otnositel'no turkestanskikh in-orodtsev." *Izvestiia Obshchestva liubitelei estestvoznaniia, antropologii i etnografii,* 1888, no. 5: 85–87.

Borovkov, A. K. *Uzbekskii literaturnyi iazyk v period 1905–1917 gg.* Tashkent, 1940.

Bourdieu, Pierre. "Cultural Reproduction and Social Reproduction." In Richard Brown, ed., *Knowledge, Education and Cultural Change.* London: Tavistock, 1973.

———. *Distinction: A Social Critique of the Judgement of Taste.* Trans. Richard Nice. Cambridge, Mass.: Harvard University Press, 1984 (orig. 1979).

———. *The Field of Cultural Production.* New York: Columbia University Press, 1993.

———. *Homo Academicus.* Trans. Peter Collier. Stanford: Stanford University Press, 1988 (orig. 1984).

———. *In Other Words: Essays Towards a Reflexive Sociology.* Stanford: Stanford University Press, 1990 (orig. 1987).

———. *Language and Symbolic Power.* Trans. Gino Raymond and Matthew Adamson. Cambridge: Harvard University Press, 1991.

———. *The Logic of Practice.* Trans. Richard Nice. Stanford: Stanford University Press, 1990.

———. "Systems of Education and Systems of Thought." *International Social Science Journal* 19 (1967): 338–358.

Bourdieu, Pierre, and Jean-Claude Passeron. *Reproduction in Education, Society and Culture.* Trans. Richard Nice. London: Sage, 1977 (orig. 1970).

Bowen, John R. *Muslims through Discourse: Religion and Ritual in Gayo Society.* Princeton: Princeton University Press, 1993.

Bregel, Yuri. "The Sarts in the Khanate of Khiva." *Journal of Asian History* 12 (1978): 120–151.

Bringa, Tone. *Being Muslim the Bosnian Way: Identity and Community in a Central Bosnian Village.* Princeton: Princeton University Press, 1995.

Bronnikova, O. M. "Sarty v etnicheskoi istorii Srednei Azii (k postanovke problemy)." In *Etnosy i etnicheskie protsessy: pamiati R. F. Itsa.* Moscow: Vostochnaia Literatura, 1993.

Brooks, Jeffrey. *When Russia Learned to Read: Literacy and Popular Culture, 1861–1917.* Princeton: Princeton University Press, 1985.

Brower, Daniel R., and Edward J. Lazzerini, eds. *The Russian Orient: Imperial Borderlands and Peoples, 1700–1917.* Bloomington: Indiana University Press, 1997.

Burns, Alexander. *Travels into Bukhara, together with a Narrative of a Voyage on the Indus.* 3 vols. London: John Murray, 1834.

Buttino, Marco. "Politics and Social Conflict during a Famine: Turkestan Immediately after the Revolution." In Marco Buttino, ed., *In a Collapsing Empire: Underdevelopment, Ethnic Conflicts and Nationalisms in the Soviet Union.* Milan: Fondazione Giangiacomo Feltrinelli, 1993.

———. "Study of the Economic Crisis and Depopulation in Turkestan, 1917–1920." *Central Asian Survey* 9, no. 4 (1990): 59–74.

———. "'La terra a chi la lavora': la politica coloniale russa in Turkestan tra la crisi dello Zarismo e le rivoluzioni del 1917." In Alberto Masoero and Antonello Venturi, eds., *Russica: Studi e ricerche sulla Russia contemporanea*. Milan: Franco Angeli, 1990.

———. "Turkestan 1917, la révolution des russes." *Cahiers du monde russe et soviétique* 32 (1991): 61–77.

Çakıröz, Râci, and Timur Kocaoğlu. "Türkistan'da Türk Subayları." *Türk Dünyası Tarih Dergisi*, 1987–1988.

Calhoun, Craig, ed. *Habermas and the Public Sphere*. Cambridge, Mass.: MIT Press, 1992.

Carlisle, Donald S. "The Uzbek Power Elite: Politburo and Secretariat (1938–83)." *Central Asian Survey* 5, no. 3/4 (1986): 91–132.

Carrère d'Encausse, Hélène. *Réforme et révolution chez les musulmans de l'empire russe*. 2nd ed. Paris: Presses de la Fondation nationale des sciences politiques, 1981.

Castagné, J. "Le Turkestan depuis la révolution russe." *Revue du monde musulman* 50 (1922): 28–74.

de Certeau, Michel. *The Practice of Everyday Life*. Trans. Steven F. Rendall. Berkeley: University of California Press, 1984.

Chamberlain, Michael. *Knowledge and Social Practice in Medieval Damascus, 1190–1350*. Cambridge: Cambridge University Press, 1994.

Chartier, Roger. *Cultural History: Between Practices and Representations*. Trans. Lydia G. Cochrane. Ithaca: Cornell University Press, 1988.

———. *The Cultural Uses of Print in Early Modern France*. Trans. Lydia G. Cochrane. Princeton: Princeton University Press, 1987.

———. "Culture as Appropriation: Popular Cultural Uses in Early Modern France." In Stephen L. Kaplan, ed., *Understanding Popular Culture*. Berlin: Mouton, 1984.

———. "Du lire au livre." In Roger Chartier, ed., *Pratiques de la lecture*. Marseilles: Rivages, 1985.

Chatterjee, Partha. *The Nation and Its Fragments: Colonial and Postcolonial Histories*. Princeton: Princeton University Press, 1992.

Chekhovich, O. D. "Gorodskoe samoupravlenie v Tashkente XVIII v." In *Istoriia i kul'tura narodov Srednei Azii (drevnost' i srednie veka)*. Moscow: Nauka, 1976.

"Chleny Gosudarstvennoi Dumy pervogo, vtorogo i tret'ego sozyva." Self-contained section in the back of vol. 17 of *Entsiklopedicheskii slovar' russkogo bibliograficheskogo Instituta Granat*. Moscow: Granat, n.d.

Cleveland, William L. *Islam against the West: Shakib Arslan and the Campaign for Muslim Nationalism*. Austin: University of Texas Press, 1985.

Clowes, Edith, Samuel Kassow, and James West, eds. *Between Tsar and People: Educated Society and the Quest for Public Identity in Late Imperial Russia*. Princeton: Princeton University Press, 1991.

Çokay, Mustafa. *1917 Yılı Hatıra Parçaları*. Ankara: Yaş Türkistan Neşriyatı, 1988.

——— [Mustafa Chokaev]. "Dzhadidizm." Ms., 1931. L'Archive de Moustafa Tchokai Bey, carton 7.

——— [M. Tchokaieff]. "Fifteen Years of Bolshevik Rule in Turkestan." *Journal of the Royal Central Asiatic Society* 20 (1933): 351–359.

——— [Mustafa Chokaev]. "Turkestan and the Soviet Regime." *Journal of the Royal Central Asiatic Society* 18 (1931): 403–420.

Cole, Juan R. I. *Colonialism and Revolution in the Middle East: Social and Cultural Origins of Egypt's 'Urabi Movement*. Princeton: Princeton University Press, 1992

Commins, David D. *Islamic Reform: Politics and Society in Late Ottoman Syria*. New York: Columbia University Press, 1990.

Cooper, Frederick, and Ann L. Stoler. "Tensions of Empire: Colonial Control and Visions of Rule." *American Ethnologist* 16 (1989): 609–621.

Curtis, William Eleroy. *Turkestan: "The Heart of Asia."* London: Hodder & Stoughton, 1911.

Dale, Stephen Frederic. *Indian Merchants and Eurasian Trade, 1600–1750*. Cambridge: Cambridge University Press, 1994.

Darnton, Robert. "An Enlightened Revolution?" *New York Review of Books*, 24 October 1991, 33–36.

Demidov, A.P. *Ekonomicheskii ocherk khlopkovodstva, khlopkotorgovli i khlopkovoi promyshlennosti Turkestana*. Moscow: Vysshii sovet narodnogo khoziaistva, 1922.

Denny, Frederick Mathewson. "Qur'ān Recitation: A Tradition of Oral Performance and Transmission." *Oral Tradition* 4 (1989): 5–26.

Devlet, Nadir. *Rusya Türklerinin Millî Mücadele Tarihi (1905–1917)*. Ankara: Türk Kültürünü Araştırma Enstitüsü, 1985.

DeWeese, Devin. *Islamization and Native Religion in the Golden Horde: Baba Tükles and Conversion in Historical and Epic Tradition*. University Park: Pennsylvania State University Press, 1994.

Dmitriev, G. L. "Rasprostranenie indiiskikh izdanii v Srednei Azii v kontse XIX–nachale XX vekov." *Kniga: materialy i issledovaniia*, no. 6 (1962): 239–254.

Dmitriev-Mamonov, A.I., ed. *Putevoditel' po Turkestanu i sredne-aziatskoi zheleznoi doroge*. St. Petersburg, 1903.

Dobromyslov, A. *Tashkent v proshlom i nastoiashchem*. Tashkent, 1912.

Dolimov, Ulughbek. *Ishoqkhon Ibrat*. Tashkent: Sharq, 1994.

Dudoignon, Stéphane A. "Djadidisme, mirasisme, islamisme." *Cahiers du monde russe* 37 (1996): 13–40.

———. "La question scolaire à Boukhara et au Turkestan russe, du «premier renouveau» à la soviétisation (fin du XVIIIe siècle–1937)." *Cahiers du monde russe* 37 (1996): 133–210.

Dumont, Paul. "Le revue *Türk Yurdu* et les musulmans de l'empire russe, 1911–1914." *Cahiers du monde russe et soviétique* 15 (1974): 315–331.

Dzhabbarov, I. "Ob uchinichestve v remeslennykh tsekakh Srednei Azii v kontse XIX i nachale XX v." In *Materialy vtorogo soveshchaniia arkheologov i etnografov Srednei Azii*. Moscow, 1959.

Dzhumabaev. "Nash vozhd'." In *Iash Turkestan: pamiati Mustafy Chokai-beia*. Paris: Iash Turkestan, 1949.

Edwards, David B. "Mad Mullahs and Englishmen: Discourse in the Colonial Encounter." *Comparative Studies in Society and History* 31 (1989): 649–670.

Eickelman, Dale F. "The Art of Memory: Islamic Education and Its Social Reproduction." *Comparative Studies in Society and History* 20 (1978): 485–516.

———. *Knowledge and Power in Morocco: The Education of a Twentieth-Century Notable.* Princeton: Princeton University Press, 1985.

———. "Mass Higher Education and the Religious Imagination in Contemporary Arab Societies." *American Ethnologist* 19 (1992): 643–655.

———. *Moroccan Islam: Tradition and Society in a Pilgrimage Center.* Austin: University of Texas Press, 1976.

———. "The Study of Islam in Local Contexts." *Contributions to Asian Studies,* 17 (1982): 1–16.

Eisener, Reinhard. "Bukhara v 1917 godu." *Vostok,* 1994, no. 4, 131–144; no. 5, 75–92.

Eisenstein, Elizabeth L. *The Printing Press as an Agent of Change: Communications and Cultural Transformations in Early-Modern Europe.* 2 vols. Cambridge: Cambridge University Press, 1979.

Eklof, Ben. *Russian Peasant Schools: Officialdom, Village Culture, and Popular Pedagogy, 1861–1914.* Berkeley: University of California Press, 1986.

Encyclopædia Iranica. 7 vols. to date. Costa Mesa: Mazda, 1982–.

Encyclopedia of Islam. New ed. 8 vols. to date. Leiden: E. J. Brill, 1960–.

Epifanova, L. M. *Rukopis'nye istochniki Instituta Vostokovedeniia Akademii Nauk UzSSR po istorii Srednei Azii perioda prisoedineniia k Rossii (Bukhara).* Tashkent: Nauka, 1965.

Ergashev, B. Kh. "Iz istorii obshchestvenno-politicheskoi zhizni Bukhary nachala XX veka." *Obshchestvennye nauki v Uzbekistane,* 1992, no. 2, 49–53.

Ergin, Osman. *Türkiye Maarif Tarihi.* 5 vols. Istanbul: Eser, 1977.

Fattaev, M. *Vidnye pedagogi Samarkanda.* Samarkand: Samarkand. Gos. Universitet, 1961.

Febvre, Lucien, and Henri-Jean Martin. *L'apparition du livre.* Paris: Éditions A. Michel, 1958.

Fedorov, E. *Ocherki natsional'nogo-osvoboditel'nogo dvizheniia v Srednei Azii.* Tashkent: Gosizdat Uzbekskoi SSR, 1925.

Fierman, William. *Language Planning and National Development: The Uzbek Experience.* Berlin: Mouton de Gruyter, 1991.

Fisher, Alan W. *The Crimean Tatars.* Stanford: Hoover Institution Press, 1978.

Fletcher, Joseph. "The Heydey of the Ch'ing Order in Mongolia, Sinkiang and Tibet." In John K. Fairbank, ed., *Cambridge History of China,* vol. 10. Cambridge: Cambridge University Press, 1978.

Furet, François, and Jacques Ozouf. *Reading and Writing: Literacy in France from Calvin to Jules Ferry.* Cambridge: Cambridge University Press, 1982.

Galuzo, P. G. *Turkestan—koloniia (ocherk istorii Turkestana ot zavoevaniia russkimi do revoliutsii 1917 goda).* Moscow, 1929; reprint, Oxford: Society for Central Asian Studies, 1986.

Gavrilov, M. "O remeslennykh tsekakh Srednei Azii i ikh statutakh–risolia." *Izvestiia sredne-aziatskogo Komiteta po delam muzeev i okhrany pamiatnikov stariny, iskusstva i prirody,* vyp. 3. Tashkent, 1928.

———. *Risolia sartovskikh remeslennikov: izsledovanie predanii musul'man-skikh tsekhov.* Tashkent, 1912.

Geertz, Clifford. *Islam Observed: Religious Development in Morocco and Indo-nesia.* New Haven: Yale University Press, 1968.

Geier, I. "Ishany." *Sbornik materialov dlia statistiki Syr-Dar'inskoi oblasti* 1 (1894): 62–82.

Geyer, Dietrich. *Russian Imperialism: The Interaction of Domestic and Foreign Policy, 1860–1914.* Trans. Bruce Little. New Haven: Yale University Press, 1987.

Ghanoonparvar, M. R. *In a Persian Mirror: Images of the West and Westerners in Iranian Fiction.* Austin: University of Texas Press, 1993.

Gökalp, Ziya. *Kızıl Elma.* Istanbul: Hayriye Matbaası, 1914.

———. *Türkçülüğün Esasları.* Ankara: Matbuat ve Istıhbarat Matbaası, 1923.

Gordienko, A. A. *Obrazovanie Turkestanskoi ASSR.* Moscow: Iuridicheskaia Literatura, 1968.

Gramenitskii, S. *25-letie uchebnogo dela v Turkestanskom krae.* Tashkent, 1901.

———. *Ocherk razvitiia narodnogo obrazovaniia v Turkestanskom krae.* Tash-kent, 1896.

———. *Polozhenie inorodcheskogo obrazovaniia v Syr-Dar'inskoi oblasti.* Tash-kent, 1916.

Greenleaf, Monika. *Pushkin and Romantic Fashion: Fragment, Elegy, Orient, Irony.* Stanford: Stanford University Press, 1994.

Habermas, Jürgen. *The Structural Transformation of the Public Sphere: An In-quiry into a Category of Bourgeois Society.* Trans. Thomas Burger with Fred-erick Lawrence. Cambridge, Mass.: MIT Press, 1989 (orig. 1962).

Hanioğlu, M. Şükrü. *The Young Turks in Opposition.* New York: Oxford Uni-versity Press, 1995.

Harrison, Christopher. *France and Islam in West Africa, 1860–1960.* Cam-bridge: Cambridge University Press, 1988.

Hauner, Milan. *What Is Asia to Us?: Russia's Asian Heartland Yesterday and Today.* London: Unwin Hyman, 1990.

Hayit, Baymirza. *Basmatschi: Nationaler Kampf Turkestans in den Jahren 1917 bis 1934.* Cologne: Dreisam Verlag, 1992.

———. *Türkistan Rusya ile Çin Arasında.* Trans. Abdülkadir Sadak. Ankara: Otağ, 1975.

Hofman, H. F. *Turkish Literature: A Bio-Bibliographical Survey.* 6 vols. Utrecht: Library of the University of Utrecht, 1969.

Hopkirk, Peter. *The Great Game: On Secret Service in High Asia.* London: John Murray, 1990.

Horvatich, Patricia. "Ways of Knowing Islam." *American Ethnologist* 21 (1994): 811–826.

Hourani, Albert. *Arabic Thought in the Liberal Age, 1798–1939.* London: Ox-ford University Press/Royal Institute for International Affairs, 1962.

Inoiatov, Kh. Sh. *Otvet fal'sifikatoram istorii sovetskoi Srednei Azii i Kazakh-stana.* Tashkent: Gosizdat UzSSR, 1962.

Islam i zhenshchiny Vostoka: istoriia i sovremennost'. Tashkent: Fan, 1990.

Ismoilov, Sh. "XIX asrning okhiri XX asr boshlarida Turkistondagi yangi usul maktablari." *Obshchestvennye nauki v Uzbekistane,* 1976, no. 2, 55–58.

Istoriia knigi v SSSR, 1917–1921. 3 vols. Moscow: Kniga, 1986.

Istoriia Tashkenta s drevneishikh vremen do pobedy fevral'skoi burzhuazno-demokraticheskoi revoliutsii. Tashkent: Fan, 1988.

Istoriia Uzbekistana. 3 vols. to date. Tashkent: Fan, 1993–.

Iuldashev, A. *Agrarnye otnosheniia v Turkestane (konets XIX–nachalo XX vv.).* Tashkent: Uzbekistan, 1969.

Iuzhakov, Iu. "Itogi 27-letnego upravleniia nashego Turkestanskim kraem." *Russkii vestnik,* 1891, no. 7, 49–82; no. 8, 3–51.

———. "Sarty ili tadzhiki, glavnoe osedloe naselenie Turkestanskoi oblasti." *Otechestvennye zapiski* 173 (1867): 397–432.

Ivanov, P. P. *Khoziaistvo dzhuibarskikh sheikhov: k istorii feodal'nogo zemle-vladeniia v Srednei Azii v XVI–XVII vv.* Moscow: Izd. AN SSSR, 1954.

Izmailov, A. E. *Prosveshchenie v respublikakh sovetskogo Vostoka.* Moscow: Pedagogika, 1973.

Izzut-oollah, Meer. *Travels in Central Asia in the Years 1812–13.* Trans. Captain P. D. Henderson. Calcutta: Foreign Department, 1872.

"Jadidchilik nima?" *San''at,* 1990, no. 12, 4–10.

Jalolov, A. *Inqilobiy dawr özbek adabiyoti wa Shawkat ijodi.* Tashkent: Fan, 1988.

———. *XIX asr okhiri XX asr boshlaridagi özbek adabiyoti.* Tashkent: Fan, 1991.

Jalolov, A., and H. Özganboev. *Özbek ma''rifatparwar adabiyotining taraqqi-yotida waqtli matbuotining örni.* Tashkent: Fan, 1993.

Jalolov, T. *Özbek shoiralari.* 3rd ed. Tashkent: Ghafur Ghulom, 1980.

Joffe, Muriel. "Autocracy, Capitalism and Empire: The Politics of Irrigation." *Russian Review* 54 (1995): 365–388.

Kamp, Marianne R. "The Otin and the Soviet School: The End of Traditional Education for Uzbek Girls." Paper presented to the annual meeting of the American Association for the Advancement of Slavic Studies, Boston, 1996.

Kamshad, H. *Modern Persian Prose Literature.* Cambridge: Cambridge University Press, 1966.

Kappeler, Andreas. *Rußland als Vielvolkerreich: Entstehung, Geschichte, Zerfall.* Munich: Beck, 1992.

——— et al., eds. *Muslim Communities Reemerge: Historical Perspectives on Nationality, Politics, and Opposition in the Former Soviet Union and Yugoslavia.* Durham, N.C.: Duke University Press, 1994.

Kara, İsmail. *Türkiyede İslâmcılık Düşüncesi: Metinler, Kişiler.* 2 vols. Istanbul: Risale, 1986–1987.

Karimov, Naim. *Abdulhamid Sulaymon öghli Chölpon.* Tashkent: Fan, 1991.

Karimullin, Abrar. *Tatarskaia kniga nachala XX veka.* Kazan: Tatarskoe knizhnoe izdatel'stvo, 1974.

Karmysheva, B. Kh. "Etnograficheskaia gruppa «Tiurk» v sostave uzbekov." *Sovetskaia etnografiia,* 1960, no. 1, 3–22.

————. *Ocherki etnicheskoi istorii iuzhnykh raionov Tadzhikistana i Uzbeki-stana.* Moscow: Nauka, 1976.

Kastelianskii, A. I., ed. *Formy natsional'nogo dvizheniia v sovremennykh gosu-darstvakh (Avstro-Vengriia. Rossiia. Germaniia.).* St. Petersburg: Obshchest-vennaia Pol'za, 1910.

Kasymov, U. "Iz istorii musul'manskikh kommunisticheskikh organizatsii v Tur-kestane v 1919–1920 godakh." *Trudy Tashkentskogo gosudarstvennogo universiteta,* n.s., no. 207 (1962): 3–29.

Kasymova, A. G. *Istoriia bibliotechnogo dela v Uzbekistane.* Tashkent: Oqituw-chi, 1981.

Keddie, Nikkie R. *Sayyid Jamāl al Dīn "al-Afghānī": A Political Biography.* Ber-keley: University of California Press, 1972.

————, ed. and trans. *An Islamic Response to Imperialism: Political and Reli-gious Writings of Sayyid Jamāl al-Dīn "al-Afghānī."* Berkeley: University of California Press, 1968.

Kedourie, Elie. *Afghani and ʿAbduh: An Essay on Religious Unbelief and Politi-cal Activism in Modern Islam.* New York: Humanities Press, 1966.

Kerenskii, F. M. "Medrese Turkestanskogo kraia." *ZhMNP* 284 (1892): 18–52.

Kernan, Alvin. *Samuel Johnson and the Impact of Print.* Princeton: Princeton University Press, 1987.

Kerr, Malcolm H. *Islamic Reform: The Political and Legal Theories of Mu-hammad ʿAbduh and Rashīd Ridā.* Berkeley: University of California Press, 1966.

Khalfin, N. A. *Prisoedinenie Srednei Azii k Rossii (60–90-e gody XIX v.).* Mos-cow: Nauka, 1965.

Khalid, Adeeb. "The Politics of Muslim Cultural Reform: Jadidism in Tsarist Central Asia." Ph.D. diss., University of Wisconsin-Madison, 1993.

————. "Printing, Publishing, and Reform in Tsarist Central Asia," *Interna-tional Journal of Middle East Studies* 26(1994): 187–200.

————. "Tashkent 1917: Muslim Politics in Revolutionary Turkestan." *Slavic Review* 55 (1996): 270–296.

Khan, Muhammad Anwar. *England, Russia and Central Asia (A Study in Diplo-macy).* Peshawar, 1963.

[Khanykov, N. K.] *Bokhara: Its Amír and Its People.* Trans. Clement A. de Bode. London: James Madden, 1845.

Khasanov, M. "Al'ternativa: iz istorii kokandskoi avtonomii." *Zvezda Vostoka,* 1990, no. 7, 105–120.

Khodzhaev, Faizulla. *K istorii revoliutsii v Bukhare.* Tashkent: Uzbekskoe go-sizdat, 1926.

———— [Fajzulla Xoçajïv]. *Buxara inqilabïnïn tarïxïya materjallir.* Tashkent: Öznäşr, 1930.

Kırımlı, S. Hakan. *National Movements and National Identity among the Cri-mean Tatars (1905–1916).* Leiden: E. J. Brill, 1996.

Kisliakov, N. A. *Patriarkhal'no-feodal'nye otnosheniia sredi osedlogo sel'skogo naseleniia Bukharskogo khanstva v kontse XIX—nachale XX veka.* Mos-cow: Izd. AN SSSR, 1962.

Kocharov, V. T. *Iz istorii organizatsii i razvitiia narodnogo obrazovaniia v do-revoliutsionnom Uzbekistane (1865–1917 gg.)*. Tashkent: Fan, 1966.

Kodaman, Bayram. *Abdülhamid Devri Eğitim Sistemi*. Ankara: Türk Tarih Kurumu, 1991.

Komatsu, Hisao. "The Evolution of Group Identity among Bukharan Intellectuals in 1911–1928: An Overview." *Memoirs of the Research Department of the Toyo Bunko*, no. 47 (1989): 115–144.

———. *Kakumei no Chūō Ajia: aru Jadiido no shōzō*. Tokyo: University of Tokyo Press, 1996.

———. "The Program of the Turkic Federalist Party in Turkistan (1917)." In H. B. Paksoy, ed., *Central Asia Reader: The Rediscovery of History*. Armonk, N.Y.: M. E. Sharpe, 1994.

Kovalev, P. A. *Revoliutsionnaia situatsiia 1915–1917 gg. i ee proiavleniia v Turkestane*. Tashkent: Fan, 1971.

Kramer, Martin. *Islam Assembled: The Advent of the Muslim Congresses*. New York: Columbia University Press, 1986.

Kruber, A., et al., eds. *Aziatskaia Rossiia: illiustrirovannyi geograficheskii sbornik*. 3rd ed. Moscow: I. N. Kushener, 1910.

Lambek, Michael. *Knowledge and Practice in Mayotte: Local Discourses of Islam, Sorcery and Spirit Possession*. Toronto: University of Toronto Press, 1993.

Landau, Jacob. *Pan-Turkism: From Irredentism to Cooperation*. Rev. ed. London: C. Hurst, 1995.

Lazzerini, Edward J. "From Bakhchisarai to Bukhara in 1893: Ismail Bey Gasprinskii's Journey to Central Asia." *Central Asian Survey* 3, no. 4 (1984): 77–88.

———. "*Ğadidism* at the Turn of the Twentieth Century: A View from Within." *Cahiers du monde russe et soviétique* 16 (1975): 245–277.

———. "Ismail Bey Gasprinskii and Muslim Modernism in Russia, 1878–1914." Ph.D. diss., University of Washington, 1973.

———. "Ismail Bey Gasprinskii (Gaspıralı): The Discourse of Modernism and the Russians." In Edward Allworth, ed., *Tatars of the Crimea Their Struggle for Survival*. Durham, N.C.: Duke University Press, 1988.

———. "Ismail Bey Gasprinskii's *Perevodchik/Tercüman*: A Clarion of Modernism." In H. B. Paksoy, ed., *Central Asian Monuments*. Istanbul: İsis, 1992.

———. "The Revival of Islamic Culture in Pre-Revolutionary Russia: Or, Why a Prosopography of the Tatar *Ulema*?" In Ch. Lemercier Quelquejay et al., eds., *Passé turco-tatar, présent soviétique: études offertes à Alexandre Bennigsen*. Paris: Editions EHESS, 1986.

LeDonne, John P. *The Russian Empire and the World, 1700–1917: The Geopolitics of Expansion and Containment*. New York: Oxford University Press, 1997.

Lelyveld, David. *Aligarh's First Generation: Muslim Solidarity in British India*. Princeton: Princeton University Press, 1978.

Levin, Alfred. *The Third Duma: Election and Profile*. Hamden, Conn.: Archon Books, 1973.

Lewis, Bernard. *The Muslim Discovery of Europe*. New York: Norton, 1982.

Lih, Lars T. *Bread and Authority in Russia, 1914–1921*. Berkeley: University of California Press, 1990.

Logofet, D. N. *Bukharskoe khanstvo pod russkim protektoratom*. 2 vols. St. Petersburg: V. A. Berezovskii, 1911.

Lunin, B. V. *Istoriografiia obshchestvennykh nauk v Uzbekistane. bio-bibliograficheskie ocherki*. Tashkent: Fan, 1974.

———. *Nauchnye obshchestva Turkestana i ikh progressivnaia deiatel'nost': konets XIX—nachala XX v.* Tashkent: Izd. AN UzSSR, 1962.

Lykoshin, N. S. "Chapkullukskaia volost' Khodzhentskogo uezda." *Spravochnaia knizhka Samarkandskoi oblasti* 8 (1906): 1–234.

———. *"Khoroshii ton" na Vostoke*. Petrograd, 1916.

———. "Kodeks prilichii na Vostoke." *Sbornik materialov po musulmanstvu*, vyp. 2. Tashkent, 1900.

———. "O gadanii u sredneaziatskikh tuzemtsev." *Spravochnaia knizhka Samarkandskoi oblasti* 9 (1907): 163–242.

———. *Pol zhizni v Turkestane: ocherki byta tuzemnogo naseleniia*. Petrograd, 1916.

MacKenzie, David. "Expansion in Central Asia: St. Petersburg vs. the Turkestan Generals." *Canadian Slavic Studies* 3 (1969): 286–311.

———. "Kaufman of Turkestan: An Assessment of His Administration." *Slavic Review* 26 (1967): 265–285.

———. "Turkestan's Significance to Russia (1850–1917)." *Russian Review* 33 (1974): 167–188.

Madaminov, Ahmadjon, and Said Murod, eds. "Turkistonda khalq jumhuriyati." *Fan wa Turmush*, 1990, no. 7, 6–8

Madzhlisov, A. *Agrarnye otnosheniia v vostochnoi Bukhare v XIX–nachale XX veka*. Dushanbe: Irfon, 1967.

Maev, N. "Dzhizak i Samarkand." *Materialy dlia statistiki Turkestanskogo kraia* 2 (1874): 269–287.

———. "Topograficheskii ocherk Turkestanskogo kraia." *Materialy dlia statistiki Turkestanskogo kraia* 1 (1872): 7–118.

Mahmūd al-Kāšyarī. *Compendium of the Turkic Dialects (Dīwān Luγāt at-Turk)*. Ed. and trans. Robert Dankoff. 3 vols. Cambridge, Mass.: Harvard University, 1982–1985.

Mahmudî, Wadud. "Muallim Abduqodir Shakurî (qissai hujjati)." *Sadoi Sharq*, 1990, no. 8, 3–41.

Makhmutova, A. Kh. *Stanovlenie svetskogo obrazovaniia u tatar (bor'ba vokrug shkol'nogo voprosa, 1861–1917)*. Kazan: Izd. Kazanskogo universiteta, 1982.

Mämmädli, Gulam. "Azärbayjan teatrï Orta Asiyada." In *Iskusstvo Azerbaidzhana*, vol. 3. Baku: Izd. AN Azerb. SSR, 1950.

Manz, Beatrice Forbes. "Central Asian Uprisings in the Nineteenth Century: Ferghana under the Russians." *Russian Review* 46 (1987): 261–281.

Manzhara, D. I. *Revoliutsionnoe dvizhenie v Srednei Azii 1905–1920 gg. (Vospominaniia)*. Tashkent: Sredazpartizdat, 1934.

Mardin, Şerif. *The Genesis of Young Ottoman Thought: A Study in the Modernization of Turkish Political Ideas*. Princeton: Princeton University Press, 1962.

———. *Religion and Social Change in Turkey: The Case of Bediüzzaman Said Nursi.* Albany: SUNY Press, 1989.

Masal'skii, V. I. *Turkestanskii krai.* St. Petersburg: A. F. Devrien, 1913.

McChesney, R. D. *Waqf in Central Asia: Four Hundred Years in the History of a Muslim Shrine, 1480–1889.* Princeton: Princeton University Press, 1991.

McReynolds, Louise. *The News under the Old Regime: The Development of a Mass Circulation Press.* Princeton: Princeton University Press, 1992.

Merad, Ali. *Le réformisme musulman en Algérie de 1925 à 1940: essai d'histoire religieuse et sociale.* Paris: Mouton, 1972.

Messick, Brinkley. *The Calligraphic State: Textual Domination and History in a Muslim Society.* Berkeley: University of California Press, 1993.

Metcalf, Barbara Daly. *Islamic Revival in British India: Deoband, 1860–1900.* Princeton: Princeton University Press, 1982.

———, ed. *Moral Conduct and Authority: The Place of Adab in South Asian Islam.* Berkeley: University of California Press, 1984.

Meyendorff, Baron Georges de. *Voyage d'Orenbourg à Boukhara fait en 1820.* Paris, 1826.

Mikhaleva, G. A. *Torgovye i diplomaticheskie sviazi Rossii so sredneaziatskimi khanstvami cherez Orenburg.* Tashkent: Fan, 1982.

———. *Uzbekistan v XVIII–pervoi polovine XIX veka: remeslo, torgovlia i poshliny.* Tashkent: Fan, 1991.

Milliy uyghonish wa özbek filologiyasi masalalari. Tashkent: Universitet, 1993.

Mitchell, Timothy. *Colonising Egypt.* New ed. Berkeley: University of California Press, 1991.

Mohan Lal. *Travels in the Panjab, Afghanistan, and Turkistan, to Balk, Bokhara, and Herat; and a Visit to Great Britain and Germany.* London: Wm. H. Allen, 1846.

Mŏminov, Gh. "Hamza biografiyasining bir sahifasi." In *Hamza ijodi haqida.* Tashkent: Fan, 1981.

Morris, Peter. "The Russians in Central Asia, 1870–1887." *Slavonic and East European Review* 53 (1975): 521–538.

Mukhammadzhanov, A. *Shkola i pedagogicheskaia mysl' uzbekskogo naroda XIX–nachala XX v.* Tashkent: Fan, 1978.

Mukminova, R. G. "Remeslennye korporatsii i uchinichestvo (po sredneaziatskim pis'mennym istochnikam XVI i XIX vv.)." In *Materialy po istorii Uzbekistana.* Tashkent: Fan, 1973.

Muqimov, R. "Hoji Muin kim edi?" *Muloqot,* 1994, no. 5–6, 25–28.

Nalivkin, V. P. "Chto daet sredne-aziatskaia musul'manskaia shkola v obrazovatel'nom i vospitatel'nom otnosheniiakh?" In *Turkestanskii literaturnyi sbornik v pol'zu prokazhennykh.* St. Petersburg: Turkestanskoe okruzhnoe upravlenie Rossiiskogo Obshchestva Krasnogo Kresta, 1900.

———. "Polozhenie vakufnogo dela v Turkestanskom krae do i posle ego zavoevaniia." *Ezhegodnik Ferganskoi oblasti* 3 (1904): 1–56.

———. "Shkoly u tuzemtsev Srednei Azii." *Sbornik materialov dlia statistiki Samarkandskoi oblasti, 1887–1888 gg.,* 1 (Samarqand, 1889), 294–303.

———. "Svedeniia o sostoianii medrese Samarkandskoi oblasti v 1892/93 uchebnom godu." Ms., ca. 1894. TsGARUz, f. 455, d. 1.

———. *Tuzemtsy ran'she i teper'*. Tashkent, 1913.

Nalivkin, V. P., and M. Nalivkina. *Ocherk byta zhenshchiny osedlogo tuzem-nogo naseleniia Fergany*. Kazan: Tip. Imp. universiteta, 1886.

Nalivkin, V. P., et al. "Kratkii obzor sovremennogo sostoianiia i deiatel'nosti musul'manskogo dukhovenstva, raznogo roda dukhovnykh uchrezhdenii i uchebnykh zavedenii tuzemnogo naseleniia Samarkandskoi oblasti s neko-torymi ukazaniiami na ikh istoricheskoe proshloe." In *Materialy po musul'm-nastvu*, vyp. 1. Tashkent, 1898.

Nettleton, Susanna S. "Ruler, Patron, Poet: 'Umar Khan and the Blossoming of the Khanate of Qoqan, 1800–1820." *International Journal of Turkish Studies* 2, no. 2 (1981–1982): 127–140.

Nikolaeva, V. P. "Turkkomissiia kak polnomochnyi organ TsK RKP(b)." *Voprosy istorii KPSS*, 1958, no. 2, 73–88.

Ocherki revoliutsionnogo dvizheniia v Srednei Azii: sbornik statei. Moscow: Nauchnaia assotsiatsiia Vostokovedeniia pri TsIK SSSR, 1926.

O'Fahey, R. S., and Bernd Radtke. "Neo-Sufism Reconsidered." *Der Islam* 70 (1993): 52–87.

Olufsen, O. *The Emir of Bukhara and His Country: Journey and Studies in Bukhara (With a Chapter on My Voyage on the Amu Darya to Khiva)*. London: William Heinemann, 1911.

Ostroumov, N. P. *Konstantin Petrovich fon-Kaufman, ustroitel' Turkestanskogo kraia. Lichnye vospominaniia N. Ostroumova*. Tashkent, 1899.

———. "Madrasy v Turkestanskom krae." *ZhMNP*, n.s., 7 (1907): otd. narod. obraz., 1–58.

———. "Musul'manskie maktaby i russko-tuzemnye shkoly v Turkestanskom krae." *ZhMNP*, n.s., 1 (1907): otd. narod. obraz., 113–166.

———. "Poslednie po vremeni Sheikhul'-Islam i Kazy-Kalian goroda Tashkenta, brat'ia Ai-Khodzha i Khakim-Khodzha." *Protokoly zasedanii i soob-shcheniia chlenov Turkestanskogo kruzhka liubitelei arkheologii* 20 (1914–1915): 11–14.

———. *Sarty. Etnograficheskie materialy (obshchii ocherk)*. 3rd ed. Tashkent, 1908.

———. "Svedeniia o Turkestanskoi tuzemnoi gazete." In *Trudy Syr-Dar'inskogo oblastnogo statisticheskogo komiteta v 1887–1888 gg*. Tashkent, 1888.

———. *Vvedenie v kurs islamovedeniia*. Tashkent, 1914.

Otabek oghli, Fozilbek. *Dukchi Eshon woqeasi*. Tashkent: Chŏlpon, 1992 (orig. 1927).

Özbek sovet entsiklopediyasi. 14 vols. Tashkent: Özbekiston SSR Fanlar Aka-demiyasi, 1971–1980.

Pakdaman, Homa. *Djemal-ed-Din Assad Abadi dit Afghani*. Paris: Maisonneuve et Larose, 1969.

Paksoy, H. B. *Alpamysh: Central Asian Identity under Russian Rule*. Hartford: Association for the Advancement of Central Asian Research, 1989.

Pashino, P. I. *Turkestanskii krai v 1866 godu. Putevye zametki*. St. Petersburg, 1868.

Paul, Jürgen. "Forming a Faction: The *Himāyat* System of Khwaja Ahrar." *International Journal of Middle East Studies* 23 (1991): 533–548.

Peshchereva, E. M. *Remeslennye organizatsii Srednei Azii v kontse XIX i na-chale XX v.* XXV Mezhdunarodnyi Kongress Vostokovedov: Doklady dele-gatsii SSSR, no. 148. Moscow: Izd. Vostochnoi literatury, 1960.

Piaskovskii, A. V. *Revoliutsiia 1905–1907 godov v Turkestane.* Moscow: Izd. AN SSSR, 1958.

Pierce, Richard N. *Russian Central Asia, 1867–1917: A Study in Colonial Rule.* Berkeley: University of California Press, 1960.

Politicheskie deiateli Rossii 1917 g.: biograficheskii slovar'. Moscow: Izd. "Bol'shaia Rossiiskaia Entsiklopediia," 1993.

Poujol, Catherine. "Approaches to the History of Bukharan Jews' Settlement in the Fergana Valley, 1867–1917." *Central Asian Survey* 12 (1993): 549–556.

Qayumov, Laziz. *Hamza: esse.* Tashkent: Yosh Gvardiya, 1989.

Qodiriy, Habibulla. *Otam haqida: khotiralar.* Tashkent: Adabiyot wa san"at, 1983.

Qosimov, B. "Fitrat (chizgilar)." *Sharq yulduzi,* 1992, no. 10, 170–180.

———. "Mirmuhsin Shermuhamedov (Fikri) wa uning adabiy muhiti." Can-didate's diss., Toshkent Dawlat Universiteti, 1967.

———. "Reformator pedagog, ma"rifatparwar." *Sovet maktabi,* 1967, no. 5, 76–79.

———. "Shoir khotirasini izlab." *Sharq yulduzi,* 1989, no. 10, 178–184.

———. "Sources littéraires et principaux traits distinctifs du djadidisme turkes-tanais (début du XXe siècle)." *Cahiers du monde russe* 37 (1996): 107–132.

Radzhabov, Z. *Iz istorii obshchestvenno-politicheskoi mysli tadzhikskogo na-roda vo vtoroi polovine XIX i v nachale XX vv.* Stalinabad: Tadzhik. gos. izd., 1957.

Rahim, Sh. *Ozbek maārifining otkandaki wa hāzirgi hāli.* Tashkent, 1923.

——— [Rakhimi, Sh.]. "Prosveshchenie Uzbekov." *Nauka i prosveshchenie,* 1922, no. 2, 2nd pagination, 38–44.

Rajabov, Siddiq. "Özbek pedagogik fikrining asoschisi," *Özbek tili wa adabiy-oti,* 1989, no. 5.

Rakhimov, R. R. "Traditsionnoe nachal'noe shkol'noe obuchenie detei u naro-dov Srednei Azii (konets XIX–nachalo XX v.)." In *Pamiatniki traditsionno-bytovoi kul'tury narodov Srednei Azii, Kazakhstana i Kavkaza: sbornik Mu-zeia Antropologii i etnografii.* Leningrad: Nauka, 1989.

Rakhmanov, Mamadzhan. *Uzbekskii teatr s drevneishikh vremen do 1917 goda.* Tashkent: Gafur Guliam, 1968.

Reichl, Karl. *Turkic Oral Epic Poetry: Traditions, Forms, Poetic Structure.* New York: Garland, 1992.

Rickmers, W. Rickmer. *The Duab of Turkestan: A Physiographic Sketch and Account of Some Travels.* Cambridge: The University Press, 1913.

Rizaev, Shuhrat. "Khalqdin yorliq istarman. . . . " *Guliston,* 1990, no. 8, 9–10.

Robinson, Francis. "Technology and Religious Change: Islam and the Impact of Print." *Modern Asian Studies* 27 (1993): 229–251.

Rorlich, Azade-Ayşe. *The Volga Tatars: A Profile in National Resilience.* Stan-ford: Hoover Institution Press, 1986.

Rossabi, Morris. "The 'Decline' of the Central Asian Caravan Trade." In James D. Tracy, ed., *The Rise of the Merchant Empires: Long-Distance Trade in the*

Early Modern Period, 1350–1750. Cambridge: Cambridge University Press, 1990.

Rozhkova, M. K. *Ekonomicheskie sviazi Rossii so Srednei Aziei (40–60 gody XIX veka)*. Moscow: Izd. AN SSSR, 1963.

Ruud, Charles A. *Russian Entrepreneur: Publisher Ivan Sytin of Moscow, 1851–1934*. Montreal: McGill-Queen's University Press, 1990.

Ryskulov, T. *Revoliutsiia i korennoe naselenie Turkestana*. Tashkent: Uzbekskoe gos. izd., 1925.

Safarov, G. *Kolonial'naia revoliutsiia—opyt Turkestana*. Moscow, 1921; reprint, Oxford: Society for Central Asian Studies, 1985.

Saguchi, Tōru. "The Eastern Trade of the Khoqand Khanate." *Memoirs of the Research Department of the Toyo Bunko*, no. 24 (1965): 47–114.

Said, Edward. *Orientalism*. New York: Vintage, 1978.

Said, Ziyo. *Tanlangan asarlar*. Tashkent: Ghafur Ghulom, 1974.

Salïhov, M. Büzrük. *Özbek ädäbijatïda millätcilik körünişläri (qïsqaca tarïx)*. Tashkent: Özdävnäşr, 1933.

———. *Ozbek teatr tarixi ucun materiallar*. Tashkent: Oz. SSR Davlat Naşrijati, 1935.

Sal'kov, V. P. *Andizhanskoe vozstanie v 1898 g.: sbornik statei*. Kazan: Izd. P. N. Salkovoi, 1901.

Samoilovich, A. "Dramaticheskaia literatura sartov." *Vestnik Imperatorskogo Obshchestva Vostokovedeniia*, 1916, no. 5, 72–84.

———. "Pechat' russkikh musul'man." *Mir Islama*, 1912, no. 1, 463–483.

Saray, Mehmet. *Rus İşgali Devrinde Osmanlı Devleti İle Türkistan Hanlıkları Arasındaki Siyasi Münasebetler (1775–1875)*. Istanbul: İstanbul Matbaası, 1990.

Schoeberlein-Engel, John. "Identity in Central Asia: Construction and Contention in the Conceptions of 'Özbek,' 'Tâjik,' 'Muslim,' 'Samarqandi,' and Other Groups." Ph.D. diss., Harvard University, 1994.

Schuyler, Eugene. *Turkistan: Notes of a Journey in Russian Turkistan, Khokand, Bukhara, and Kuldja*. 2 vols. New York: Scribner, 1877.

Semenov, A. A. *Ocherk ustroistva tsentral'nogo administrativnogo upravleniia Bukharskogo khanstva pozdneishego vremeni*. Dushanbe: Tadzhikskii filial AN SSSR, 1954.

Semenov, Iu. I. "Sotsiosial'no-istoricheskie organizmy, etnosy, natsii." *Etnograficheskoe obozrenie*, 1996, no. 3, 3–13.

Seydahmet, Cafer. *Gaspıralı İsmail Bey*. Istanbul, 1934.

Shahrani, M. Nazif. "Local Knowledge of Islam and Social Discourse in Afghanistan and Turkistan in the Modern Period." In Robert L. Canfield, ed., *Turko-Persia in Historical Perspective*. Cambridge: Cambridge University Press, 1991.

Sharabi, Hisham. *Arab Intellectuals and the West: The Formative Years, 1875–1914*. Baltimore: Johns Hopkins Press, 1970.

Sharafiddinov, A. "XIX asr okhiri–XX asr boshlarida Farghona oblastida madaniy hayot tarikhidan," *Obshchestvennye nauki v Uzbekistane*, 1978, no. 2, 25–28.

———. "Mustafo Chŏqaev." *Sharq yulduzi*, 1992, no. 4, 85–93.

Sharipov, Jumaniyoz. *Ozbekistonda tarjima tarikhidan: Revolyutsiyadan oldingi dawr.* Tashkent: Fan, 1965.

Shcheglova, O. P. *Katalog litografirovannykh knig na persidskom iazyke v sobranii LO IV AN SSSR.* 2 vols. Moscow: Nauka, 1975.

Shukurov, Muhammadjon. "Zindaginomai Ajzî." *Sadoi Sharq,* 1992, no. 2, 123–136.

Skrine, F. H., and E. Denison Ross. *The Heart of Asia: A History of Russian Turkestan and the Central Asian Khanates from the Earliest Times.* London: Methuen, 1899.

Slezkine, Yuri. "The USSR as a Communal Apartment, or How a Socialist State Promoted Ethnic Particularism." *Slavic Review* 53 (1994): 414–452.

Sokol, Edward D. *The Revolt of 1916 in Russian Central Asia.* Baltimore: Johns Hopkins University Press, 1954.

Sotsial'no-ekonomicheskoe i politicheskoe polozhenie Uzbekistana nakanune oktiabria. Tashkent: Fan, 1973.

Stremukhov, N. "Poezdka v Bukharu," *Russkii vestnik* 117 (1875): 630–695.

Subtelny, Maria Eva. "The Symbiosis of Turk and Tajik." In Beatrice Forbes Manz, ed., *Central Asia in Historical Perspective.* Boulder, Colo.: Westview Press, 1994.

Sukhareva, O. A. *Bukhara: XIX–nachalo XX v. (Pozdnefeodal'nyi gorod i ego naselenie).* Moscow: Nauka, 1966.

———. *Kvartal'naia obshchina pozdnefeodal'nogo goroda Bukhary (v sviazi s istoriei kvartalov).* Moscow: Nauka, 1976.

———. *Pozdnefeodal'nyi gorod. Bukhara kontsa XIX–nachalo XX v.: remeslennaia promyshlennost'.* Tashkent: Izd. AN UzSSR, 1962.

Süleyman Efendi Buharî. Şeyh. *Lûgat-i Çağatay ve Turkî-yi Osmanî.* Istanbul: Mihran Matbaası, 1298/1880–81

Sultanov, T. I. "Sredneaziatskaia i vostochno-turkestanskaia pozdnesrednevekovaia rukopis'naia kniga." In *Rukopis'naia kniga v kul'ture narodov Vostoka: ocherki.* Moscow: Nauka, 1987.

Swietochowski, Tadeusz. *Russian Azerbaijan, 1905–1920: The Shaping of National Identity in a Muslim Community.* Cambridge: Cambridge University Press, 1985.

Taymas, Abdullah Battal. *Kazan Türkleri.* 3rd ed. Ankara: Türk Kültürü Araştırma Enstitüsü, 1988.

———. *Rus Ihtılâlinden Hâtıralar.* Istanbul: Güven, 1947.

Tazhibaev, T. T. *Prosveshchenie i shkoly Kazakhstana vo vtoroi polovine XIX veka.* Alma Ata: Kazgosizdat, 1962.

Thongchai Winichakul. *Siam Mapped: A History of the Geo-Body of a Nation.* Honolulu: University of Hawaii Press, 1994.

Tillett, Lowell. *The Great Friendship: Soviet Historians on the Non-Russian Nationalities.* Chapel Hill: University of North Carolina Press, 1969.

Togan, A. Zeki Velidî. *Bugünkü Türkili (Türkistan) ve Yakın Tarihi.* 2nd ed. Istanbul: Enderun Kitabevi, 1981.

———. *Hâtıralar. Türkistan ve Diğer Müslüman Doğu Türklerinin Millî Varlık ve Kültür Mücadeleleri.* Istanbul: Hikmet Gazetecilik, 1969.

Troitskaia, A. L. "Iz proshlogo kalandarov i maddakhov v Uzbekistane." In *Domusul'manskie verovaniia i obriady v Srednei Azii*. Moscow: Nauka, 1975.

———. *Katalog arkhiva kokandskikh khanov XIX veka*. Moscow: Nauka, 1968.

Tunaya, Tarik Zafer. *İslâmcılık Cereyanı*. Istanbul: Baha, 1962.

Turdiev, Sherali. "Mahmudkhŏja Behbudiy." *Muloqot*, 1994, no. 3–4, 44–48.

Tursunov, Kh. *Vosstanie 1916 goda v Srednei Azii i Kazakhstane*. Tashkent: Gosudarstvennoe Izdatel'stvo Uzbekskoi SSR, 1962.

Tursunov, T. T. *Oktiabr'skaia revoliutsiia i uzbekskii teatr*. Tashkent: Fan, 1983.

Tynyshpaev, M. *Istoriia kazakhskogo naroda*. Ed. A. S. Takenov and B. Baigaliev. Alma Ata: Qazaq Universiteti, 1993.

Ujfalvy de Mező-Kovesd, Ch. E. de. *Expédition scientifique française en Russie, en Sibérie et dans le Turkestan*. 5 vols. Paris: Ernest Leroux, 1878–1879.

Urumbaev, Zh. A. *Ocherki istorii shkoly v Karakalpakstane (1810–1967 gg.)*. Nukus: Karakalpakistan, 1974.

———. "O novometodnykh shkolakh na territorii Karakalpakii (1907–1918 gg.)." *Trudy Karakalpakskogo gospedinstituta*, no. 2 (1964): 133–149.

Usmon, Olim. *Özbekistonda rus tilining ilk targhibotchilari*. Tashkent, 1962.

Usmonov, O., and Sh. Hamidov. *Özbek tili leksikasi tarikhidan materiallar (XIX asrning okhiri–XX asrning boshlari)*. Tashkent: Fan, 1981.

Validov, Dzh. *Ocherk istorii obrazovannosti i literatury tatar*. Moscow, 1923; reprint, Oxford: Society for Central Asian Studies, 1986.

Vámbéry, Arminius. *Travels in Central Asia, Being the Account of a Journey from Teheran across the Turkoman Desert on the Eastern Shore of the Caspian to Khiva, Bokhara, and Samarcand, Performed in the Year 1863*. London: John Murray, 1864.

Vil'danova, A. B. "O sostoianii nauki v sredneaziatskikh gorodakh XVI–pervoi poloviny XIX veka." *Obshchestvennye nauki v Uzbekistane*, 1989, no. 7, 32–36.

Wathen, W. H. "Note of a Pilgrimage Undertaken by an Úsbek and His Two Sons from Khokend or Kokan, in Tartary, through Russia, &c. to Mecca. Obtained in Conversation with the Parties" *Journal of the Asiatic Society of Bengal* 3 (1834): 379–382.

Wheeler, Geoffrey. *The Modern History of Soviet Central Asia*. London: Weidenfeld & Nicholson, 1964.

Wolff, Joseph. *Narrative of a Mission to Bokhara, in the Years 1843–1845, to Ascertain the Fate of Colonel Stoddart and Captain Conolly*. 2 vols. London: J. W. Parker, 1845.

Yamauchi, Masayuki. *The Green Crescent under the Red Star: Enver Pasha in Soviet Russia, 1919–1922*. Tokyo: Institute for the Study of Languages and Cultures of Asia and Africa, 1991.

Yavuz, M. Hakan. "The Patterns of Political Islamic Identity: Dynamics and Transnational Loyalties and Identities." *Central Asian Survey* 14 (1995): 341–372.

Zarcone, Thierry, and Fariba Zarinebaf-Shahr, eds. *Les iraniens d'Istanbul*. Paris: Institut français de recherches en Iran, 1994.

Zavadskaia, E. V. *Vasilii Vasilevich Vereshchagin.* Moscow: Iskusstvo, 1986.

el-Zein, Abdul Hamid. "Beyond Ideology and Theology: The Search for the Anthropology of Islam." *Annual Review of Anthropology* 6 (1977): 227–254.

Zenkovsky, Serge A. "*Kulturkampf* in Pre-Revolutionary Central Asia." *American Slavic and East European Review* 14 (1955): 15–42.

———. *Pan-Turkism and Islam in Russia, 1905–1920.* Cambridge: Harvard University Press, 1960.

Ziiaev, Kh. Z. *Ekonomicheskie sviazi Srednei Azii s Sibir'iu v XVI–XIX vv.* Tashkent: Fan, 1983.

Zimin, L. "Bibliografiia." *Sredniaia Aziia,* 1911, nos. 2, 3, 4, 6, 8.

Zufarov, Tŏkhtamurod. "«Milliy She"rlar Majmualari»ga doir yangi hujjatlar." *Ŏzbek tili wa adabiyoti,* 1989, no. 1, 42–52.

Zykin, V. *Vosstanie v Tashkente v 1892 g.* Tashkent, 1934.

Index

Compositor: G&S Typesetters, Inc.
Text: 10/13 Sabon
Display: Sabon
Printer: Thompson-Shore, Inc.
Binder: Thompson-Shore, Inc.